POETRY

A
CRITICAL AND
HISTORICAL
INTRODUCTION

Irving Ribner Tulane University

Harry Morris Florida State University

SCOTT · FORESMAN

&

COMPANY

Chicago Atlanta Dallas Palo Alto Fair Lawn, N.J.

W. H. AUDEN "In Memory of W. B. Yeats": Copyright 1940 by W. H. Auden.
"O what is that sound which so thrills" (Ballad): Copyright 1937 by Wystan Hugh
Auden. Reprinted from *The Collected Poetry of W. H. Auden* by permission of the
publishers, Random House, Inc., New York, and Faber and Faber, Ltd., London.
GEORGE BARKER "On the Death of Manolete": From *A Vision of Beasts and
Gods* (London: Faber and Faber, Ltd., 1954). Reprinted by permission of the pub-
lishers. ROBERT BRIDGES "Cheddar Pinks": From *New Verse* (Oxford: The
Clarendon Press, 1925). Reprinted by permission of the publishers. HART CRANE
"At Melville's Tomb," "The Bridge: To Brooklyn Bridge," "The Mermen": From
The Collected Poems of Hart Crane. Copyright 1933, © 1961 by Liveright Publish-
ing Corporation and reprinted by their permission. STEPHEN CRANE "Once I
Saw Mountains Angry": Reprinted from *The Collected Poems of Stephen Crane* by
permission of Alfred A. Knopf, Inc. Copyright 1930 by Alfred A. Knopf, Inc. E. E.
CUMMINGS "since feeling is first": Copyright 1926 by Horace Liveright, renewed
1954 by E. E. Cummings. Reprinted from *Poems 1923-1954* by E. E. Cummings
by permission of Harcourt, Brace & World, Inc. EMILY DICKINSON "After
great pain, a formal feeling comes": Copyright 1929, © 1957 by Martha Dickinson
Bianchi. Reprinted from *The Complete Poems of Emily Dickinson* by permission of
Little, Brown & Company. T. S. ELIOT "Journey of the Magi," "The Love Song
of J. Alfred Prufrock": From *Collected Poems 1909-1935* by T. S. Eliot. Copyright
1936 by Harcourt, Brace & World, Inc., and reprinted with their permission, and
with the permission of Faber and Faber, Ltd., London. ROBERT FROST "After
Apple-Picking," "A Considerable Speck (Microscopic)," "Mending Wall," "The
Road Not Taken," "Stopping by Woods on a Snowy Evening": From *Complete
Poems of Robert Frost.* Copyright 1916, 1921, 1923, 1930, 1939, 1942 by Holt,
Rinehart and Winston, Inc. Copyright renewed 1944, 1951 by Robert Frost. Reprint-
ed by permission of Holt, Rinehart and Winston, Inc. ROBERT GRAVES "In the
Wilderness": From *Poems, 1914-1926* (New York: Doubleday & Co., Inc.; London:
Cassell and Co., Ltd., 1929). Reprinted by permission of Roturman S. A. THOM-
AS HARDY "After the Last Breath," "The Oxen": From *Collected Poems.* Copy-
right 1925 by The Macmillan Company and reprinted with their permission, and
with the permission of the Trustees of the Hardy Estate, The Macmillan Co. of
Canada, Ltd., and Macmillan & Co., Ltd., London. GERARD MANLEY HOPKINS
"Felix Randal," "Ribblesdale," "Thou Art Indeed Just, Lord," "The Windhover":
From *Poems of Gerard Manley Hopkins* (London: Oxford University Press, 1948).
Reprinted by permission of the publishers. A. E. HOUSMAN "Epitaph on an
Army of Mercenaries": Copyright 1922 by Holt, Rinehart and Winston, Inc., re-
newed 1950 by Barclays Bank, Ltd. "I hoed and trenched and weeded," "On Wen-
lock Edge": Copyright © 1959 by Holt, Rinehart and Winston, Inc. Reprinted from
Complete Poems by permission of the publishers, Holt, Rinehart and Winston, Inc.,
New York, and Jonathan Cape, Ltd., London, and The Society of Authors as literary
representative of the estate of the author. ROBINSON JEFFERS "Shine, Perishing
Republic": Copyright 1925 and renewed 1953 by Robinson Jeffers. Reprinted from
The Selected Poetry of Robinson Jeffers by permission of Random House, Inc.
D. H. LAWRENCE "Cherry Robbers": From *Collected Poems.* Copyright 1929 by
Jonathan Cape and Harrison Smith, Inc., renewed 1957 by Frieda Lawrence Ravagli.
Reprinted by permission of The Viking Press, Inc. ROBERT LOWELL "For the
Union Dead": Reprinted from *The Atlantic,* Vol. 206, No. 5, November 1960, pp.
54-55, by permission of the author. ARCHIBALD MacLEISH "Starved Lovers":
From *Collected Poems 1917-1952.* Copyright 1952 by Archibald MacLeish. Reprint-
ed by permission of the Houghton Mifflin Company. MARIANNE MOORE "O To
Be a Dragon": From *O To Be a Dragon.* Copyright 1957 by Marianne Moore. Re-
printed by permission of The Viking Press, Inc. "What Are Years?": From *The
Collected Poems of Marianne Moore.* Copyright 1941 by Marianne Moore. Reprinted with the permission of The Macmillan Company. WILFRED OWEN

iv

PREFACE

In the following pages we have sought to present a comprehensive selection of poetry in English from its beginnings to the present day—a selection broad and varied enough in scope to represent the preferences and tastes of nearly all teachers and students. As its title suggests, POETRY: A CRITICAL AND HISTORICAL INTRODUCTION combines two approaches to poetry. To illustrate the historical continuity of English verse, we have organized the poems chronologically in seven sections, each introduced by a brief discussion of the background from which the poems emerged. Within each section the poems are grouped by types; for example, *The Renaissance* has the subsections "The Amatory," "The Pastoral," "The Devotional," and "The Native Survival," each with its own introductory essay. To introduce the student to the esthetic analytical approach associated with much modern criticism, we have subjected one poem in each section to close textual analysis and explication. These explications are not intended as definitive statements of the meaning and substance, but rather as illustrations of a method which individual readers may apply in their own way.

The editors of *Tulane Studies in English* have kindly permitted us to reprint some paragraphs already published in its pages. Tom H. Long, Max F. Schulz, Lamar Stephens, and Dick Taylor, Jr., have each made a contribution.

H. M. *Tallahassee, Fla.* I. R. *New Orleans, La.*

CONTENTS

THE NATIVE SURVIVAL **105**

THE STUART AGE 119

THE CLASSICAL AND COURTLY **125**

THE METAPHYSICAL **151**

THE ELEGIAC **173**

INTROSPECTION AND MEDITATION **260**

INDIVIDUALISM **284**

THE TWENTIETH CENTURY 401 VII

THE TRANSITIONAL PERIOD 407

SYMBOLISM 422

REGIONALISM **469**

Introduction

N O general definition of poetry can be fully satisfying, for poetry has meant different things in different periods of civilization, and even in a single period it has offered diverse values to different individuals. We can say, however, that poetry has been an essential and valued aspect of every civilization the world has known. It is older than prose, providing some of our earliest records of human activity; its place in religious chant and ritual relates it to the fundamental spiritual aspirations of mankind. In short, creating poetry and responding to it with pleasure and excitement are characteristic of the human spirit.

Response to some form of verbal music is common to all peoples, including the most primitive. With increased sophistication comes a demand for more sophisticated poetic expression. The pleasure of the highest kind of poetry is that to which men of the most highly developed minds and sensibilities are able to respond. To read poetry well is to be receptive to the most intricate nuances of rhythm and sound, to explore the infinite potentialities of language; and since language is a vehicle for thought, total response to poetry engages the intellect fully as much as the senses.

Poetry may or may not include rhyme or meter. Although historically it has included both, neither is essential. What is essential is rhythm, for the appeal of poetry to the senses is one element which differentiates poetry from prose. Rhythm may be important in prose also, but there it is always subservient to clear and rational statement, the primary end of prose. The prose writer's principal address is to reason, and accordingly he relies upon logic and fact. The poet aims at a total response which is at least as much emotional as rational, and for this reason he uses language which is more dense and ambiguous than can ordinarily be used in prose. The poet uses words of multiple meanings, often with deliberately contradictory connotations, for he is frequently concerned with the exploration of paradox, the reconciliation of extremes and opposites. In general, the poet relies upon the suggestive and connotative aspects of language, while the prose writer is concerned with its power to name, to specify, to denote.

The truth of poetry

Poetry, like prose, is a form of discourse whose instrument is language. Its function, like that of prose, is to communicate, and it must never allow its emotional content to obliterate its message. The poet is a thinker, and although not all great thinkers are great poets, few great poets are shoddy thinkers. Poetry communicates with economy and precision, but its precision differs from that of expository prose. Poetry is frequently concerned with the very feelings, reactions, and attitudes which the prose writer may avoid because they interfere with the directness and clarity of his statement. With metaphor and symbol the poet expresses concepts that are so far-ranging and complex that they could be encompassed in factual prose only with the greatest difficulty.

The poem does not need to communicate fact, advice, or instruction, though some poems do all these things. The truth of poetry is the truth of an experience which the reader is made to know in its totality, emotionally and rationally, with a large number of its implications simultaneously explored. The truth of a poem does not need external verification. It is implicit in the poem itself, and for this reason a poem can never be really paraphrased.

The moral value of poetry

Matthew Arnold regarded poetry as the highest kind of teacher available to humanity. He did not mean that poetry preaches explicitly about how to live the good life. To perceive the moral value of poetry is not to search for "morals." What Arnold meant, and what is true, is that poetry, through the complete experience it conveys, enables us to see human life as no other instrument can. Through poetry we come to view the world more fully and more vividly, and this acute perception makes us better people. We feel the multiple implications of all the aspects of human existence, the good and the evil, and their relations to one another. In the very process of reading poetry, we are engaged in a concentrated pursuit of truth which, while it raises us above the trivial considerations of ordinary life, may also reveal the importance and significance of the commonplace.

Long before the time of Arnold, the Roman poet Horace had argued that poetry must teach while it delights, that it is *utile et dulce*. We may observe that this principle has been adhered to, in one way or another, throughout the course of poetry in English. Some poets have emphasized one aspect and some the other, but we can say that, to the extent that it conveys a total human experience, all poetry—no matter what the author's intention—teaches while it delights.

Of course, poetry conveys things other than moral experience. It may be valuable as a means of recording man's most primitive ways of knowing and describing reality, through myth, chant, and ritual. It may explore the limits of language and extend its range. It may be used for specific sermonizing, as in Milton; for philosophy, as in Wordsworth; or for social criticism, as in Pope. But regardless of these other uses and values, poetry is the supreme conveyor of truth, and truth is moral value.

READING POETRY

The charge is often made that poetry—and, in particular, much of modern poetry—is needlessly obscure and difficult to read. In answer we must note that great art is never easy. What makes art great, after all, is the richness and complexity of the experience it captures and the multiple facets of the artist's insight into that experience. We cannot expect that grasping a complex experience can ever be a simple task. The reading of poetry we must all recognize as an act of intelligence and understanding. Truly to know even what appears to be a simple poem calls for concentrated use of these faculties, and the greater the poem, the more acute they must be.

The difficulty of poetry

In contemporary poetry there has been much of what some readers interpret as intentional obscurity, and this has led some to argue that poetry in our time is being written not for ordinary people but for a small, select body of initiates, many of whom are themselves poets. That there has been some eccentricity in modern poetry is undeniable. It is inevitable that eccentricity should occur in a time when poets, along with other artists, have sought to advance beyond earlier technical limits while reacting to an increasingly complex, ever changing world. But we must carefully differentiate between mere eccentricity and the true originality which, though sometimes misguided, lends vitality to every art form and makes possible its growth.

Perhaps the greatest period of experimentation in English poetry was that which followed the First World War, when a reaction against the forms and diction of traditional poetry resulted in an outburst of innovation and individualism. In more recent poetry, however, reëmphasis of form and structure has taken the place of unrestricted freedom of expression with its attendant obscurity. Whereas the poets of several decades ago were sometimes content merely to reproduce the confusion of the times, more recent poets have concerned themselves with interpreting this confusion and searching for a means of ordering experience. Poetry today is not the property of a small group of initiates; it has the widest reading public poetry has ever enjoyed.

When we complain about the difficulty of modern poetry as contrasted with that of earlier times, we forget how strange the prophetic books of William Blake must have seemed to readers at the end of the eighteenth century and how obscure Robert Browning's poems must have been for the Victorians. Thirty years ago T. S. Eliot was regarded as an almost impossibly difficult poet, but with some training most of us now can read his work with comparative ease. We must remind ourselves that there is little obscurity in worthwhile poetry that does not yield finally to the onslaughts of determined readers. The true artist is always in advance of his public. The reader must follow him, and to do so, he must give to the poem, as Allen Tate has written, "the fullest cooperation of his intellectual resources, all his knowledge of the world, and all the persistence and alertness that he now thinks of giving to scientific studies."

The complexity of poetry

Accusing poetry of obscurity, needless or otherwise, is one side of the coin. Refusing to acknowledge its complexity is the other. Despite overwhelming evidence of the depth and complexity of poetry, many readers are reluctant to believe that a poem is anything more than fine sentiments in attractive word combinations. When told that a poem conveys more than appears on the surface, the student frequently asks, "Are you sure?" or "Why go any deeper? This satisfies me." Yet ignoring or avoiding the depths of poetry means missing most of what poetry has to say.

Depths of meaning are not restricted to poetry. In ancient literature the Greek myths and the Old Testament are clearly concerned with higher truths as well as with some very exciting stories. Christ, in the New Testament, speaks in parables. Indeed, commentators on the Bible in the early centuries of Christianity found underlying meanings so extensive that they developed a way of reading Scripture which established four meanings for all important verses. In the Middle Ages, Dante asserted to his patron that *The Divine Comedy* employed the scriptural method, containing an allegorical statement as well as a literal narrative. The allegory itself, he explained, could be read in three different senses: the historical, the moral, and the mystical. In our own century Dylan Thomas begins one of his poems with the claim that "I, in my intricate image, stride on two levels." To those readers who say that literal statement alone satisfies them, we can only say that their enjoyment will be increased when they pursue the additional statements that are assuredly to be found in most poetry. If they still go no further than the surface meaning, we must conclude that serious reading is not for them.

From these observations the reader should understand that, while never impossibly difficult, poetry is a complex affair. If it were not, it is unlikely that it would be exalted to the status of art. If poets did not labor so arduously at their work, it is doubtful that we would turn to them, generation after generation, to fulfill our need for beauty and wisdom. Since poetry requires effort in the writing, it must be expected to demand some effort in the reading. But in terms of the rewards, the investment is small.

UNDERSTANDING POETRY

For a reader seeking the meaning of a poem, the best source of information would seem to be the poet himself. What did the poet intend? Logically, the answer to this question should solve all problems. In fact, however, when we speak of a poet's intention, we can never mean more than the evidence of his complete poem. What thoughts were in the poet's mind before he began to write, we can never know, not even if the poet should himself tell us, for no man is fully aware of his own impulses, motivations, and the multiple associations, conscious and subconscious, of whatever passes through his mind. Even when the poet has started with a very clear idea of what he wishes to create, the final product usually will bear but slight relation to this original goal, for in the act of creation the artist works out the implications of his own ideas, explores the potentialities of form, and continually reshapes the plan with which he started. Furthermore, the poet may create far more than he himself knows. For these reasons the poet's avowed aims and his estimate of his own achievement should never control the reader's reaction to the work.

On the other hand, a knowledge of the poet's intention can have value for the reader. In those rare instances where the poet has given us external evidence of his initial plan—as in Wordsworth's *Preface* to the second edition of *Lyrical Ballads,* for example—the information may be an important tool for measuring his achievement. Yet even Wordsworth's poetry is not entirely what he declared it to be in his own *Preface.* It is better, then, to consider a poet's intention not in terms of explicit statements of purpose but in terms of the poetic tradition to which his work belongs. If the finished product is a sonnet, we may frame the poet's intention in terms of the tradition of sonnet writing. In a highly didactic poem—a satire by Pope, for example—we can estimate the poet's intention in terms of the content of the work, the specific targets the poem is designed to attack, and the specific points it is designed to illustrate or expound. Beyond these limits it is dangerous to go.

Historical factors

When we talk of tradition, we are talking of history, and some knowledge of history is important to the understanding of poetry. Unfortunately, some scholars have used poetry as a taking-off place for the study of history instead of using history as a means of insight into poetry. This disastrous practice gave rise, through reaction, to a total ignoring of history by other, more recent critics. To avoid both extremes, we must decide just what historical factors are legitimate concerns of the student of poetry.

To begin with, it is important to know the status of poetry in the age in which it was written, the literary forces operating upon the poet, and the distinctive critical biases with which poetry was judged by his contemporaries. We cannot really understand the poetry of Alexander Pope without awareness of the broad assumptions of eighteenth-century neoclassicism. We must know what poetic conventions and traditions were valued so that we can see exactly how they are being used. For no poet works in a vacuum; he uses the heritage of poetry left him by his predecessors, and, except for unusual cases, he is closely in tune with the work of his contemporaries.

The social status of the poet is important. Many of the sonnets of Elizabethan writers like Daniel and Drayton are conditioned by the system of literary patronage under which they were produced, and the position of Wordsworth and his followers was influenced by the Romantic glorification of the poet as a philosopher with special powers of insight.

Sometimes political and social history is important for the student of poetry. It is difficult to comprehend fully the nineteenth-century Romantic poets without some awareness of the impact on their lives of the Industrial Revolution at home and the French Revolution across the Channel. Similarly, intellectual history can be important. The melancholy of Matthew Arnold and the struggle for faith of Alfred Tennyson need to be considered in terms of the intellectual conflicts of Victorian England, with its radical new scientific speculations and the seeming assault of the higher Biblical criticism upon the long-sanctified truths of revealed religion.

Although life histories are less helpful in some cases than in others, a poet's own biography may often be of crucial importance. Little about his life can be ignored: the collection of letters, journals, and even records of passing conversations is a constant concern of literary scholars. We need to know much about the personal relations of Pope to understand his satires; the troubled lives of Shelley and Byron, the religious faith and questioning of George Herbert and Gerard Manley Hopkins, the perils under which Robert Southwell wrote his poetry and exercised his faith—these are crucial to wholly successful reading of these men's works.

There is also the matter of our constantly changing language. Glosses have been provided to explain the obsolete and archaic terms in the medieval poems in this book, but even in many poems of the sixteenth, seventeenth, and eighteenth centuries, consciousness of former implications of still familiar words may reveal dimensions of meaning that would otherwise be lost. Not only has the English language itself undergone change, but poetic diction—the area of English which poets have considered most appropriate for their craft—has varied from generation to generation with changing attitudes and tastes. Sometimes the language of poetry has been highly artificial; at other times it has reflected the diction of ordinary speech. Modern poetry tends to reveal a greater range of styles than ever before, extending to T. S. Eliot's incorporation in his work of fragments of quotation from earlier poetry and to Ezra Pound's free use of foreign languages, including Chinese and Sanskrit.

Technical and esthetic factors

The writing of poetry is a highly technical craft, and poets may spend many years perfecting their techniques. Although it is not to be expected that the ordinary reader of poetry will comprehend fully all the complex methods by which the artist achieves his effects, some understanding of technique is essential if we are to concern ourselves with the esthetics of poetry. The following sections explain, in simplest terms, some of the devices upon which poetry depends.

The structure of poetry Meter, rhyme, and form are all parts of what we may call the structure of poetry. The smallest element of written communication is the letter; the smallest element of meaningful speech is the word; but the smallest element of poetry is, in effect, the syllable. English is an accentual language—that is, some of its syllables receive more stress, or emphasis, than others. When syllables are arranged in certain definite patterns, they make up what the prosodists—the students of metrics—call *feet*. A regularly predictable recurrence of any one kind of foot produces *meter*, and an arbitrarily established number of feet constitutes one line of verse. When the final syllable of a given line has the same sound as, or a sound similar to, that of another line, these lines *rhyme*, and related groups of rhyming lines are called *stanzas*. The combination of all syllables, feet, lines, rhymes, and stanzas makes up the overall *form* of the poem.

Meter in English poetry is described in terms borrowed from the Greek. Although books of prosody describe many types of classical feet, only six are needed to determine the scansion—the order of stressed and unstressed syllables—of any line of English verse: *iamb* (iambic foot), *trochee* (trochaic foot), *anapest* (anapestic foot), *dactyl* (dactylic foot), *spondee* (spondaic foot), and *pyrrhic* (pyrrhic foot)—all of which are described in the glossary. By far the most common is the *iamb*, or *iambus*. An iamb is a two-syllable foot, with the first syllable unstressed and the second stressed:

$$\overset{x}{\text{de}} / \overset{/}{\text{light}}$$

Since all English words of more than one syllable contain at least one stress, a knowledge of pronunciation is usually all we need to help us scan polysyllabic words. In determining which of two one-syllable words should receive the stress, we can often use normal intonation as the guide. For example, the two words might be a possessive pronoun and a noun:

my peers

Here, normal intonation would indicate that the noun should be stressed. If we had to choose between a preposition and a pronoun, however, we might hesitate:

with my

In such cases, proper stress can be determined only by examining a larger unit in which the words occur:

$$\overset{x}{\text{of}} \overset{/}{\text{bat}}/\overset{x}{\text{tle}} \overset{/}{\text{with}}/ \overset{x}{\text{my}} \overset{/}{\text{peers}}$$

From the Greek also we get the prefixes which, when attached to the word *meter*, provide the traditional names for line lengths. The most common lines in English poetry are four-foot (*tetrameter*) and five-foot (*pentameter*), though two-foot (*dimeter*), three-foot (*trimeter*), and six-foot (*hexameter*) lines are fairly common. Thus, the complete line from Tennyson's *Ulysses* is an illustration of iambic pentameter verse:

x   /   x /   x / x   /   x   /

And drunk/ delight/ of bat/tle with/ my peers

In fact, of course, metrics are more complex than these explanations suggest. Clearly, the stress on *with* in the line quoted above is not so strong as the stress on *peers*, and for precision it would be necessary to indicate this difference by some notation such as this:

/   x   /

with my peers

Another complication occurs when an overriding metrical pattern cancels the normal stress in a word. In the following line the word *promise,* normally pronounced with a stress on the first syllable, becomes the first two syllables of an anapestic foot, in which only the third syllable receives stress:

x   x /   x x   /

And forgets/ promise past

Here the scansion is determined not by the ordinary pronunciation of words but by the pattern of anapests which dominates the poem. It is almost impossible to read the line as we would if it were in a prose passage:

x   x /   / x   /

And forgets/ promise past

Rhythm, like meter, is part of the cadence of poetic language. When we talk of *rhythm* we are concerned ordinarily with units of language larger than the foot. Our natural speech consists of rhythmical units determined by natural groupings and breath pauses. In a simple sentence the rhythm will be established by such things as the subject and its modifiers, a verb cluster, the object and its modifiers, a prepositional phrase:

Calm was the day, and through the trembling air

Sweet breathing Zephyrus did softly play,

A gentle spirit, that lightly did delay

Hot Titan's beams, which then did glisten fair;

These lines tend to break in the middle, and in fact much of the rhythm of English poetry is determined by mid-line pause, which we call *caesura*. But often the rhythmical units are much more complex, as in this passage from *Epitaph on Sir Philip Sidney*, attributed to Fulke Greville:

> Silence augmenteth grief, writing increaseth rage,
>
> Staled are my thoughts, which loved and lost the wonder of our age:
>
> Yet quickened now with fire, though dead with frost ere now,
>
> Enraged I write I know not what; dead, quick, I know not how.

Since both these poems come from the Renaissance period, there is a strong tendency in them to observe the end of a syntactical unit at the end of a line; but in periods where the run-on line becomes more common, rhythm becomes looser and more flowing. For an example of considerable variation and freedom in rhythm, the reader might examine the dramatic monologues of Tennyson (see pp. 332-339) or a more modern dramatic monologue, such as T. S. Eliot's *Love Song of J. Alfred Prufrock,* in which this passage occurs:

> No! I am not Prince Hamlet, nor was meant to be;
>
> Am an attendant lord, one that will do
>
> To swell a progress, start a scene or two,
>
> Advise the prince; no doubt, an easy tool,
>
> Deferential, glad to be of use,
>
> Politic, cautious, and meticulous;
>
> Full of high sentence, but a bit obtuse;
>
> At times, indeed, almost ridiculous—
>
> Almost, at times, the Fool.

Rhyme is obtained when in two stressed syllables beginning with different consonants the vowels and the consonants which follow the vowels have the same sound: af-*fect*, col-*lect*. Compared to the Romance languages, from which English has borrowed many of its rhymed verse forms, English is not rich in rhyme. As a result, English poets have relied frequently on a variety of substitutes for this basic rhyme. The first of these may be called *slant rhyme*, or rhyme in which the final consonant sounds are identical but the vowel sounds only approximate the same pronunciation: re-*fract*, in-*spect*; *moon, gown; full, lull*. When the consonant that precedes the vowel sound is identical in both rhyme words, we have a condition described as *consonance: moon, moan; despise, dispose.*

Another substitute for basic rhyme is *half rhyme,* which is even further from perfect rhyme identity than *slant rhyme.* In *half rhyme* the vowel sounds may be more disparate than in *slant rhyme: rake, hook;* im*pure,* a*fire; tooth,* be*neath.* When the final consonant sounds differ but the vowel sounds are the same, we get a half rhyme more correctly termed *assonance: make, spate; height, file; feet, beak.* At some times the poet may employ what we call *identical rhyme,* which is merely to reproduce the syllable exactly, sound for sound: motor*cade,* ar*cade; fight, fight.*

When the rhyming syllables which end the line are stressed, we have *masculine rhyme:* pre*sent,* in*tent; pole,* con*sole.* But when the rhyming syllables are followed by identical unstressed syllables, we have *feminine rhyme: moth*er, *broth*er; un*load*ed, cor*rod*ed. *Feminine rhyme* may occur when two identical unstressed syllables follow the rhyming pair: *with*ering, *slith*ering. This is sometimes called *triple rhyme.*

Poets who work in the nonrhyming forms such as *blank verse* and *free verse* occasionally employ rhyme for special effects, but in order to meet the demands of these forms, they may not let the rhyme occur at line-endings. In such cases they may use *internal rhyme,* or rhyme which takes place at points other than at the ends of lines:

> And all is *seared* with trade, *bleared, smeared* with toil.
> And ice, mast *high,* came floating *by.*

Internal rhyme need not take place within a single line:

> Man comes and tills the field and *lies* beneath,
> And after many a summer *dies* the swan.

Poets working in rhymed forms may also use internal rhyme for additional sound correspondences.

Stanzas are the groups of lines into which a poem is divided. Stanzas appear in unrhymed verse, as with the *tercets,* or three-line stanzas, in the later work of Wallace Stevens; but more often stanza forms have developed from certain rhyme schemes. A *quatrain* is a four-line stanza; quatrains have been rhymed in every combination possible: *aabb, abba, abab, aaaa.* Poets have experimented with stanzaic forms since very early in the history of language, and they have invented as many types as ingenuity could provide; from the two-line *couplet* to the fourteen-line *sonnet* and beyond, there is a stanzaic form for almost any number of lines. Some of these forms have found more favor than others and have been given identifying names which appear in the glossary.

Form goes beyond the individual stanzas to the overall structure of a poem. *Interlocking rhyme* may take place across the stanzas of a single poem, such as in *terza rima* (*aba, bcb, cdc,* etc.). *The Pearl,* by an anonymous contemporary of Chaucer, achieves a unique interlocking effect through refrain, repetition, and individual or phrase word linkages. The sequence of seven holy sonnets by Donne, called *La Corona,* not only links one to another by repeating in the first line of a new sonnet the last line of the preceding one, but also employs an *enveloping structure* by having the very last line in the entire sequence repeat the first line of the first sonnet. Marlowe's *The Passionate Shepherd to His Love* is an example of slightly looser envelopment, and Ralegh's *The Nymph's Reply to the Shepherd* is looser still (see p. 83).

Organic form, a major concern of modern poets, represents the theory that each poem has its own overall structure which is right for that poem and for no other. It is based on the concept that the use of the proper words, images, symbols, and all other devices that make up the total poem will seek out their own inevitable structure. Perhaps the idea can be illustrated by Michelangelo's answer to one who asked him how he had produced one of his magnificent statues. He said, in effect, that the figure was already there, locked in the stone; all he had to do was chip away the refuse.

The vocabulary of poetry The poet must always use the precise word, for economy of language is essential to all poetry. Words have specific *denotations*—that is, they refer to specific objects or concepts—and no two words in the English language have exactly the same meaning; but, more important for the poet, words also have *connotations*—they suggest areas of meaning and association in addition to what they specifically denote—and these connotations, if overlooked or ignored, can destroy the poet's most sought-after effects. Thus the individual word has a significance in poetry that it seldom, if ever, has in prose.

Diction involves the selection of words and the order in which they are put down on the page. It includes *idiom* and *syntax. Poetic idiom* has undergone repeated changes throughout the history of literature. Each age seems to react against the fashions of the one preceding. When diction has been simple and unadorned, the succeeding age has reacted often with a shift to the complex and ornate; when the fashion is high seriousness and abstruse language, the new age turns to casual expression and common speech. Shakespeare's seventy-sixth sonnet records just such a change in fashion:

> Why is my verse so barren of new pride,
> So far from variation or quick change?
> Why with the time do I not glance aside
> To new-found methods and to compounds strange?

We do not know exactly to what new methods Shakespeare was referring, but it is not at all improbable that he was glancing at the new complexities ("compounds strange") of John Donne. Donne's metaphysical conceits would be the product of a change from what Shakespeare himself called in his seventy-ninth sonnet "gentle grace" to what Samuel Johnson was to describe as ideas "yoked by violence together." On the other side, Spenser, who was a contemporary of Shakespeare, found his unique poetic idiom by courting archaisms:

> Thomalin, why sitten we so,
> As were overwent with woe,
> Upon so fair a morrow?
>
> The joyous time now nigheth fast,
> That shall alegge this bitter blast,
> And slake the winter's sorrow.

> ("March Eclogue," *Shepheardes Calender*)

The same point may be made about the poetry which was being written exactly two hundred years later. Wordsworth, who was reacting against the *style* of his immediate predecessors, wrote in the *Preface* to *Lyrical Ballads* that

> There will also be found in these volumes little of what is usually called poetic diction; as much pains has been taken to avoid it as is ordinarily taken to produce it; this has been done for the reason already alleged, to bring my language near to the language of men. . . . but it has necessarily cut me off from a large portion of phrases and figures of speech which from father to son have long been regarded as the common inheritance of Poets.

This meant that Wordsworth was repudiating most of what we call *rhetoric,* all the devices of language that the poets from Quintillian to Samuel Johnson had employed as the very heart of their poetry. But in *The Rime of the Ancient Mariner,* Samuel Taylor Coleridge, Wordsworth's partner in *Lyrical Ballads,* felt compelled, like Spenser, to revert to archaic diction: "Eftsoons his hand dropt he." Furthermore, Coleridge's poem gives as good an example of wide employment of the figures of rhetoric as any that may be found in the period.

Poetic syntax is also intricately tied up with rhetoric. The varieties of language inversion, repetition, and elaborate structure are too numerous to record, and, as with poetic idiom, poetic syntax has undergone many changes—frequently veering far away from the word order of ordinary speech or prose, sometimes closely approaching these familiar forms. Both idiom and syntax can act as barriers to understanding, but careful reading will overcome the difficulties presented by the diction of a particular period or a particular poet.

The rhetoric of poetry The poet wants to create in the mind's eye of his reader pictures that give concreteness, a three-dimensional quality, to his poem. He achieves this end through devices such as the image and the symbol.

Imagery refers to patterns of language which evoke sensory responses in the mind of the reader. The simplest imagery may merely create specific pictures of color and beauty, but imagery may appeal to senses other than the visual, and in its broadest sense the term comes to include all figurative language. A simple way of providing imagery may be in a simple listing, as in this anonymous Renaissance lyric:

> When Saturn did live, there lived no poor;
> The king and the beggar with roots did dine,
> With lily, germander, and sops-in-wine,
> With sweet-briar
> And bon-fire
> And strawberry wine
> And columbine.

Sometimes, to present a concrete vision of evil, images of ugliness, rather than beauty, may be used to establish a background appropriate to the theme. These passages from *Measure for Measure* present unpleasant pictures, supporting the idea that Vienna is immoral, degenerate, and foul:

> Our natures do pursue—
> Like rats that ravin down their proper bane,—
> A thirsty evil, and when we drink we die.

> . . . I have seen corruption boil and bubble
> Till it o'er-run the stew.

Although the images from *Measure for Measure* go beyond those of the preceding lyric in making a conceptual statement, they remain relatively simple. Far more often, imagery is complex, presenting pictures not only to feed the senses but also to support involved or intricate thought progression, as in Shakespeare's sixty-fourth sonnet:

> When I have seen by Time's fell hand defaced
> The rich-proud cost of outworn buried age,
> When sometime lofty towers I see down-razed,
> And brass eternal slave to mortal rage;

> When I have seen the hungry ocean gain
> Advantage on the kingdom of the shore. . . .

By his verbal picture of time in the cruel act of destruction—of towers crumbling and the land itself eroding with the onslaughts of the sea—the poet creates an acute awareness of the nature of the chief theme of the poem:

> Ruin hath taught me thus to ruminate,
> That Time will come and take my love away.

Symbols carry meaning beyond simple denotation. They are of several kinds. We all recognize a rectangular piece of cloth with red and white stripes and fifty stars on a blue field as a symbol for the United States, a cross as a symbol of the Christian religion, a Star of David as a symbol of the Jewish faith. These are time-honored symbols, so widely accepted that they need never be explained to people of our Western culture. And there are other symbols that are understood almost as readily even though they are seldom given much thought. These are archetypal, rooted deep in the human consciousness. Water, for example, is easily accepted as a symbol for purification because of its cleansing qualities; in other contexts it is just as readily accepted as a symbol of destructive force, since for centuries men who have gone to sea have died in raging storms. Lear's raving on the heath in *King Lear* carries something of both these symbolic meanings:

> Blow, winds, and crack your cheeks! rage! blow!
> You cataracts and hurricanoes spout.

The drenching that Lear himself undergoes may symbolize the purgational, cleansing aspects of his suffering, but the cataracts and hurricanoes are also indicative of the destruction that his realm is undergoing at the hands of his evil daughters.

Frequently a symbol in a poem can be identified and explained only by the context in which it appears. This is true of private symbols, devised or invented by the poet and not part of common thought. If the poet is inept in making clear the nature of his symbol, we feel that the poem is obscure and confusing; if he communicates his meaning successfully, we feel that the poem has been enriched by his use of new visual dimensions to express abstract truth.

Both the unclear and the clear private symbol can be illustrated in these lines from *The Second Coming* by Yeats:

> Turning and turning in the widening gyre
> The falcon cannot hear the falconer;
> Things fall apart; the center cannot hold;
> Mere anarchy is loosed upon the world.

Without consulting Yeats' book *The Vision*, in which he explains his philosophy of world history, we gather that the gyre is a symbol for the way that institutions, nations, empires, and eras of humanity fall apart, as the superstructure collapses in ruins when it becomes too great for the base to support it. The gyre, a climbing, ever widening spiral, is an appropriate symbol for the process of dissolution, but we might not understand it if Yeats had not incorporated it in the image of the falcon, soaring up, out, and away until it passes beyond the falconer's guiding influence. The falcon is then no longer a controlled agent but a destructive force that preys uncontrolled on things of value (the farmer's hens, for instance). Anarchy in the barnyard is symbolic of chaos in the world; the macrocosm (the larger thing) is seen in the microcosm (the smaller).

But Yeats' symbol of the gyre is meant to stand for more than just a general symbol of dissolution. In *The Vision* we learn that a gyre is also Yeats' pictorial representation of something the poet calls the *Magnus Annus* or Great Year, that a great year runs for approximately two thousand calendar years, and that the cycles of history—the great movements that dominate mankind—can be expected to last for about two millennia before they give way to a supplanting force. All this we cannot possibly know about Yeats' gyres unless we read *The Vision*, and it has been debated whether a poet has the right to expect such devotion of his readers. In the case of a poet as great as Yeats, the answer should probably be that such labors are worth while, because the writer is philosopher as well as poet, and his philosophy, as a distinctive kind of mysticism expressed in esthetic form, has been an important commentary on human experience.

Metaphor and *simile* are the most important of the rhetorical devices of imagery—the figures of speech, as they are commonly called. (Strictly speaking, both these devices, and some related ones as well, are covered by the generic term *metaphor*, but here we shall treat *metaphor* only in its more limited sense.) Simile and metaphor are both used for purposes of comparison and analogy. As most of us learned as far back as grade school, a *simile* is almost always introduced by the conjunction *as* or the preposition *like;* comparison is made by stressing similitude. In the following illustration from *Once by the Pacific*, Robert Frost uses a simile to create a picture that would be extremely difficult to delineate through simple description; he presents a second picture to make the first picture clear:

> The clouds were low and hairy in the skies,
> Like locks blown forward in the gleam of eyes.

The *metaphor* insists that one thing *is* another, not merely like it; comparison is made by identification. The word *yoke* in Milton's sonnet *On His Blindness* denotes the collar worn by beasts of burden, by which the animal's master directs its pulling and hauling:

> Who best
> Bear his mild yoke, they serve him best.

The metaphor of the yoke stands for God's relation to man, his mastership over the human animal, whose sole purpose for being is to serve God in the best way possible. If man or animal does not pull on the yoke counter to the directions of the master but wears it easily and follows commandment, the intentions of the master are most happily accomplished. With this simple metaphor, Milton thus captures something of the complex relationship between God and man.

Other figures of speech include *synecdoche* and *metonymy*. Both are actually symbols, but of a special kind. *Synecdoche* is the device which makes a part stand for the whole. When Ralegh in *A Description of Love* writes of "lusty bloods in fresh array," that component of the human body which is only liquid flowing through veins and arteries is made to stand for the whole person—not his physical being only but also his emotional state. *Metonymy* is the use of an object closely associated with something to represent the thing itself. Robert Herrick's *His Litany to the Holy Spirit* uses *house* for all the inhabitants and *world* for the population of the whole earth:

> When the house doth sigh and weep,
> And the world is drowned in sleep.

Sometimes, as in the case of *world* in the above illustration, the figurative device is so familiar that we overlook its rhetorical nature.

The tone of poetry Tone is that aspect of poetry which reflects the attitudes and feelings of the poet. A speaker's tone is conveyed by sound—timbre, pitch, and pace—supplemented by expressions—smiles, raised eyebrows, frowns, clenched teeth. The poet, depending on the written word, must resort to other methods. Almost everything in a poem contributes to its tone; it would be impossible here to examine all the ways in which such elements as rhyme, rhythm, diction, imagery, connotation, and the other components of verse convey the attitude of the poet. Several devices which the writer uses to indicate his attitude may, however, be looked at profitably.

The device most widely used as a vehicle for tone in poetry is *irony*. Irony is achieved in many ways: through satire, cynicism, scorn, ridicule, debasement, and abuse. It is also achieved through understatement and exaggeration, but these modes of expression have uses more important than merely to convey irony, and they must be treated separately. The purpose of irony is usually to express disapproval, which may be leveled at anything under the sun—not people only, but things also; not the concrete exclusively, but abstractions as well. Irony may be gentle and pleasant as in E. A. Robinson's *Mr. Flood's Party:*

> "The bird is on the wing, the poet says,
> And you and I have said it here before.
> Drink to the bird." He raised up to the light
> The jug that he had gone so far to fill,
> And answered huskily: "Well, Mr. Flood,
> Since you propose it, I believe I will."

Here the poet presents a portrait of a drunkard and the way he rationalizes his drinking, but the treatment is gentle, for Robinson himself found life terribly demanding and excuse enough for anyone to try to ease its rigors. But irony may also be severe, intended to scourge folly and reform vanity. Samuel Johnson's advice in *One-and-Twenty* is ironic in that it prescribes a course of life exactly opposite to that which it would be wise to follow:

> Call the Betsies, Kates, and Jennys
> All the names that banish care;
> Lavish of your grandsire's guineas,
> Show the spirit of an heir.
>
> . . . .
>
> Wealth, my lad, was made to wander,
> Let it wander as it will;
> Call the jockey, call the pander,
> Bid them come, and take their fill.

Understatement, a popular mode of expression today, avoids the open and direct expression of powerful emotion. In a poem like *Bells for John Whiteside's Daughter,* John Crowe Ransom uses understatement in dealing with the death of someone beloved:

> But now go the bells, and we are ready;
> In one house we are sternly stopped
> To say we are vexed at her brown study,
> Lying so primly propped.

The language is admirably controlled to deliver a report of one of life's most trying experiences in terms which will allow all concerned to escape with emotions carefully under lock and key. Instead of a picture of wailing and lamentation, we get people "sternly stopped," halted in their daily pursuits and gathered together in a single house by "this fell sergeant, death," as Shakespeare put it in equally cold language, who "is strict in his arrest." Instead of grieving, the mourners are "vexed," and the dead little girl is not described realistically but as one in a "brown study" and "primly propped."

The opposite of *understatement* is, of course, *exaggeration*, or *hyperbole*, a mode of expression not very popular in twentieth-century poetry but one for which there was always a place in the literary conventions of earlier periods. The entire code of Courtly Love, which stretches from early medieval poetry up to that of the eighteenth century, has as central to its very existence both the braggart claims of what the lover will do for his beloved and the extremity of anguish he will suffer if his lady does not pity him. Andrew Marvell, for instance, in one of the greatest passages of hyperbole in English poetry, describes how he would love his "coy mistress":

> My vegetable love should grow
> Vaster than empires, and more slow,
> An hundred years should go to praise
> Thine eyes, and on thy forehead gaze;
> Two hundred to adore each breast,
> But thirty thousand to the rest;

The exaggeration is shocking in its magnitude and, with its images of time and space, very appropriate to a poem whose theme is the corroding effects of time.

Overstatement is not peculiar to love poetry. The Romantics, especially the second wave, found it convenient for other purposes. Shelley's *The Indian Serenade* is often cited as an extreme example:

> Oh, lift me from the grass!
> I die, I faint, I fail!

It can be used with more moderation, as in Keats' sonnet on *King Lear*, which finds the act of reading Shakespeare's play similar to undergoing torment in flames:

> But, when I am consumed in the fire,
> Give me new phoenix wings to fly at my desire.

And of course, exaggeration is always appropriate to a poem of praise for a lovely woman, as in Marvell's poem and in Byron's line "She walks in beauty, like the night."

All poetry is in one sense dramatic, but there is a special *dramatic tone*, achieved through the suggestion of deep personal emotion—either the poet's own or that of a character through whom he is speaking. Donne's *Canonization* is explosive in its opening line:

> For God's sake hold your tongue and let me love.

Herbert argues with his God:

> I struck the board, and cried, No more;
> I will abroad!

But Tennyson's drama is subdued, contemplative, gentle:

> for my purpose holds
> To sail beyond the sunset, and the baths
> Of all the western stars, until I die.
> It may be that the gulfs will wash us down:
> It may be we shall touch the Happy Isles,
> And see the great Achilles, whom we knew.

A tone which sometimes creeps into poetry and which today is almost universally disapproved of is *sentimentality.* There is little need to point out the mawkish emotionalism of *Going Down Hill on a Bicycle* by H. C. Beeching:

> Swifter and yet more swift,
> Till the heart with a mighty lift
> Makes the lungs laugh, the throat cry:—
> "O bird, see; see, bird, I fly."
> . . . .
> Alas, that the longest hill
> Must end in a vale; but still,
> Who climbs with toil, wheresoe'er,
> Shall find wings waiting there.

The sound of poetry In the old books on rhetoric a surprising number of chapters were devoted to sound. In general, the devices of sound are based on repetition. In one device, *anaphora,* an arbitrary number of lines begin with the same word:

> Tell fortune of her blindness;
> Tell nature of decay;
> Tell friendship of unkindness;
> Tell justice of delay.

For the most part, poets since the Renaissance have contented themselves with relatively few of the rhetorical sound devices. Most important of these are assonance, consonance, alliteration, onomatopoeia, repetition, and refrain.

Assonance and *consonance* were explained earlier in connection with rhyme. *Alliteration* is the repetition of identical consonantal sounds:

> I caught this *m*orning *m*orning's *m*inion, king*d*om
> of *d*aylight's *d*auphin, *d*apple-*d*awn-*d*rawn Falcon. . . .

There are two sets of alliteration in this line from Hopkins' *Windhover,* the *m*'s and the *d*'s. Purists who insist that alliteration is restricted to the initial letters of words might reject the *d* in *kingdom* and the *d* in *drawn,* since the first is in the middle of the word and the second is affected by the *r* which follows it and constitutes an integral part of the initial sound; but both may be called alliteration, since they contribute to the sound effect.

Onomatopoeia is a selection of language in which sound and sense are allied: pronunciation of the words produces sounds which imitate what the words stand for. Individual examples, such as *purr, buzz, roar,* and *tintinnabulation,* are plentiful, many such words having been invented simply because they are onomatopoetic. The creation of several lines of suggestive sound is no easy task, however:

> Listen! you hear the grating roar
> Of pebbles which the waves draw back, and fling
> At their return, up the high strand.
>
> Begin, and cease, and then again begin
> With tremulous cadence slow, and bring
> The eternal note of sadness in.

Not only do words like *Listen* and *grating* and *roar* capture the hiss of water, the thunder of the breakers, and the friction of the pebbles, but the rhythm of the lines, the rush and pause of phrasing and caesura, punctuation and vowel sound produce the action of the waves, their ebb and flow.

Repetition and *refrain* may be treated together and are indeed sometimes indistinguishable. A clear case of pure repetition, not serving in any way as refrain, is the ending of Robert Frost's *Stopping by Woods on a Snowy Evening.* Here the device is used to express the distance and tedium the driver faces:

> The woods are lovely, dark and deep.
> But I have promises to keep,
> And miles to go before I sleep,
> And miles to go before I sleep.

Refrain serves the function more of music than of meaning. Frequently a refrain may be made up of nothing more than an expletive or wail—"That was so fair to see O"—or a group of nonsense syllables—"Hey nonny, nonny," "With a down, derrie, derrie, derrie, down, down." This is not to say that refrain may not have an important syntactic and communicative function, for frequently it does.

Repetition and refrain may undergo from slight to considerable variation as they recur throughout a poem. When each new appearance adds some measure of meaning to what was known before, the device is called *incremental repetition*. See the line third from the end in each of the stanzas of Spenser's *Prothalamion* (p. 74).

THE EXPLICATION OF POETRY

By the explication of poetry we mean the exposure of as many aspects as possible of a poem's meaning, achieved through intensive reading. Different explicators will often arrive at differing interpretations, and this divergence is neither "wrong" nor surprising, for the potential meanings of any work of art are manifold. Only if two readings of a poem are absolutely exclusive is one of them likely to be wrong. Explication is not paraphrase, because a poem always contains more than can be paraphrased literally; but paraphrase is one of the many tools which the reader may use. Explication must also involve a consideration of the form of the poem and an intensive analysis of diction, meter, imagery—all the techniques that the poet has available to him.

The art of explication has developed considerably during the past half century, largely through the efforts of such well-known "new critics" as Cleanth Brooks and Allen Tate, and today many methods are applied to the analysis of poetry. No one method can ever fully explicate a poem—indeed, it is doubtful that any poem can ever be fully explicated—but every method can contribute something, and the reader of poetry must feel free to use any device whatsoever that will yield insight into a poem's meaning.

A poem consists of words, but its network of images may carry meaning beyond the literal statement of those words. The earliest "new critics" worked through direct textual analysis, considering only the implications of the words and images of the poem they were studying. They deliberately ignored all considerations outside the language of the poem itself—such matters as the author's life, his other poems, the period in which he wrote, with its distinctive attitudes and biases. This approach was partly a reaction against the nineteenth-century belletristic response to poetry, which had often neglected direct analysis of the poem itself in order to concentrate on the external factors. In its own way, each of these extremes in critical method is inadequate.

In the explications in this book, the methods of direct textual analysis, as developed by the "new critics," have been combined with a consideration of whatever external, historical factors have bearing on the poem. The test of any critical method is the understanding and enlightenment it produces; the critic who ignores any means of understanding is not fully exercising his function. The historical introductions to the sections and subsections which follow are designed to provide the background information necessary for fuller understanding of the poetic milieu; the explications of individual poems attempt to use this background in conjunction with close textual examination.

These analyses all start with the premise that the poem communicates to us through all our senses as well as through our minds, that its form is organic to its meaning and can never be separated from it, and that our understanding of this form is of first importance. The explications recognize also that the poem is the sum of all its instruments—meter, rhythm, diction, tone, and symbol—and that these must be studied closely. When we have considered all these elements, we still do not have the fullest possible understanding of the poem until we know its author, his life story, and the historical and intellectual circumstances from which the poem originated. A poem is not only a timeless personal expression in a self-contained, definable form; it is also a historical phenomenon.

The poems in this book are presented in an order which reflects the convictions with which the work was undertaken. Because of the absolute relevance to criticism of a sense of the historical continuity of poetry in English, they have been divided into seven large chronological sections, each representing a distinctive historical epoch. Within each section, the poems have been further divided into the types characteristic of each period. This does not mean that these types represent all the poetry written in any period or that these types were not written in other periods as well; for example, a subsection of narrative poetry on medieval and classical themes appears in the section on Victorian poetry because such poetry was very common in the Victorian era, but there was probably no age in English poetry when at least some such poems were not being written.

An attempt has been made to keep the work of individual poets together, but when necessary the poems of a single author have been divided among several of the subsections within a given age. Thus the advantages of both a chronological arrangement and an arrangement by type have been achieved. The characteristic types of English poetry are given emphasis within the framework of historical continuity.

The Middle Ages

I

WHEN the Anglo-Saxons came to Britain from northern Europe in the fifth century A.D., they brought with them a crude poetic tradition which was to take root and develop in the country to which the invaders bequeathed their language. Little Anglo-Saxon poetry was ever written down, but we have extant in the Anglo-Saxon language—called Old English—the heroic epic *Beowulf,* which extols the exploits of a legendary folk hero and mingles with its pagan themes some elements of the Christianity which was to shape the literature of medieval England; other poems and fragments which sing the praises of heroes and celebrate great battles, like those of Maldon and Brunanburh; moving elegiac poems such as *The Wife's Lament, The Wanderer,* and *The Seafarer,* which express a high degree of personal emotion; and a rich store of religious verse, including short hymns as well as long poetic retellings of Bible stories.

Of these earliest English poems, no examples are included here, for though the language in which they are written is the parent of our own English, it is so different as to make very difficult reading for most modern students. We must note, however, a continuity of tradition between these Old English poems and those of the twelfth and thirteenth centuries with which we begin. Anglo-Saxon poetry depended for its effect not upon rhyme or upon the metrical systems which we know, but upon alliteration—the repetition of a common sound throughout the line—and upon a system of recurring beats foreign to our own system of scansion, which is based upon accented and unaccented syllables. The tradition of alliterative verse was slow in dying. Its strong survival is apparent in the later medieval verse with which we will be concerned, and up to our own day it continues as an important device of English poetry.

There were both religious and secular poets in the Old English period. Monasteries were everywhere, and the monks in these centers of learning spent much of their time in writing—a skill known to very few. It is not surprising, then, that monks should be among our earliest English poets and that it should be their work which most often achieved written form. But there was also the minstrel—the scop or gleeman—who traveled from castle to castle with his songs and recitations. In a primitive, illiterate society, the minstrel served as a sort of living history book and newspaper, singing out the legends of the past and creating new songs to record contemporary events.

These two groups of poets remained active in the Middle English period, which may be dated roughly from the Norman invasion in 1066 to the end of the fifteenth century. Learned monks continued to write didactic religious poetry, as well as some more personal lyrics of great beauty and intensity; and wandering minstrels continued to sing their songs of heroic adventure, while turning also to songs of love, which in Middle English poetry becomes an important theme. With the approach of the fourteenth

century, the monk and the minstrel were joined by a new breed of poet—
the learned courtier, who wrote his verses for the amusement of a court
which, largely through French influence, had begun to attain a high degree
of sophistication. Although religious poetry has survived in far greater
quantity, the Middle English period was rich in secular poetry, too. Among
the courtier poets belongs the greatest single writer of medieval England,
Geoffrey Chaucer.

To understand the poetry of the Middle Ages, we must remember the
circumscribed world in which man lived, with its rigid social stratification
and with a universal church dominating virtually every aspect of human
life. To the man and woman of the Middle Ages, the unquestioned reality
of heaven renders unimportant the things of the present world; the most
influential philosophy is one of scorn for the pleasures of this world in
anticipation of the joys of heaven, a doctrine taught most notably in a
widely influential book, the *De Contemptu Mundi* of Pope Innocent III.
This scorn for the world is a constant theme of medieval poetry, warning
man against the pleasures on which he might be tempted to set his values
and reminding him always of the inevitable death and decay which await
him. The constant absorption with death marks almost every aspect of
medieval art.

Religious themes in medieval poetry Religion dominates every phase of
medieval society. There is some continuity between medieval English
life and that of the pagan civilization of ancient Rome, but even when
pagan themes are taken over—as in the many medieval treatments of the
Trojan War—these are colored with Christian mysticism and given a
didactic overlay. The teaching function of poetry is always stressed in the
Middle Ages, and what it must teach is a religious view of life, strict and
circumscribed, centered in a few familiar themes.

But while theological doctrine worked to restrict the range of imaginative expression, there was a native genius, an English brilliance with
words, which produced shining instances of poetry that displayed vigor,
beauty, charm, and lyricism. The simple joys of living, which men at no
period of civilization have ever ceased to feel, come through in spite of all,
and we have the happy celebration of the coming of springtime, as in *Sumer Is Icumen In*, perhaps the earliest nature poem in a language which has
produced more nature poetry than any other. Medieval poetry is rich in
lyrics which express the ordinary feelings of humanity. By the end of the
fourteenth century it has produced also such sustained masterpieces as
The Pearl, Gawain and the Green Knight, and *Piers Plowman*, as well as
The Canterbury Tales of Geoffrey Chaucer.

Because of problems of space, the poems which follow have been limited
to shorter lyrics, divided into religious and secular groups. Religious lyrics

are devoted almost always to episodes in the lives of the Holy Family, with special reference to the Virgin and Christ; the infancy of the Child and the Crucifixion are dealt with over and over again. In the religious poetry of the Middle Ages we do not find the kind of spiritual questioning which marks that of later periods. The Christian premises are universally accepted.

Courtly Love and secular poetry Secular poetry of lyric intensity is most often concerned with love and tends to reflect certain conventional attitudes developed first by the minstrels, or troubadours, of southern France. In this region of Europe had developed an elaborate set of conventions governing relations between men and women of the nobility, the system we call Courtly Love. From France it spread to England, and since almost all medieval love poetry is based upon the assumptions of this love code, some knowledge of it is essential. Marriage in the feudal society of the Middle Ages included little of what we today call romance, for it was essentially a financial and family arrangement in which the woman was little more than the property of her husband. Romantic affection came to be expressed outside of marriage among the upper classes —we must remember that Courtly Love had little to do with the lives of ordinary, humble people—according to a formula in which the lady was placed upon a pedestal and worshiped by a lover who entered her service just as the feudal vassal entered the service of his lord. The lover was obliged to obey any demands his lady might make of him, and in return for his service he could hope only for some favor or attention to be bestowed by his beloved out of pity for his suffering. His devotion must be eternal, and it must be proof against all misadventures. While such singleness of purpose may not always have won the lover a lady, it frequently produced very fine poetry, marked by recurring themes: the suffering of the lover, the cruelty of the lady, the lover's fear that he may lose her to another.

Medieval verse differs from that of later ages in that it represents, even in its greatest specimens, an oral rather than a written tradition. Chaucer's *Canterbury Tales* were designed to be read aloud to an audience at court, and the lyrics with which we are most immediately concerned were sung to musical accompaniment. These lyrics consequently have come down to us in various versions, since individual singers felt free to alter the lines of poems they had learned from others. Eventually some of them came to be written down, often by monks in monasteries. Only a few of these poems have survived to the present day, and only in recent times have they reached print.

FOR FURTHER READING:

Bennett, H. S. *Chaucer and the Fifteenth Century*. Oxford, 1947.

Chambers, E. K. *English Literature at the Close of the Middle Ages*. Oxford, 1945.

Holzknecht, Karl J. *Literary Patronage in the Middle Ages*. Philadelphia, 1923.

Kennedy, C. W. *The Earliest English Poetry*. Oxford, 1943.

Renwick, W. L., and Orton, Harold. *The Beginnings of English Literature to Skelton, 1509*. London, 1940.

Salzman, L. F. *English Life in the Middle Ages*. Oxford, 1926.

I

THE MIDDLE AGES

THE RELIGIOUS LYRIC

O F the five following examples of the religious lyric, two deal with episodes in the lives of Christ and the Virgin and three with the theme of *contemptus mundi*—scorn for worldly pleasures. *The Falcon* and *I Syng of a Mayden* are highly original, unlike the large body of religious poems which somewhat slavishly follow accounts of the four Gospels. The deposition from the Cross, retold in *The Falcon,* is expressed in terms of medieval chivalry, but the mysticism frequently accompanying early religious verse, based for the most part on the imagery of *The Revelation of St. John,* is in evidence also. *I Syng of a Mayden* reaches high lyric excellence, lofted by exquisite simplicity of diction and by repetition, as distinct from refrain, that is altered slightly in each of the three middle stanzas.

Wen the Turuf is Thi Tuur is a fine example of a didactic lyric which seeks to teach by terrifying imagery the disdain for worldly pursuits that the Middle Ages believed to be so necessary for the salvation of the soul. *A Winter Song* not only emphasizes the decay of worldly beauty but also the uncertainty of existence itself. Although the imagery, through reference to vegetal nature, does not carry the stark horror of bodily decomposition in the grave, the fear of hell and the realization that life may be cut off tomorrow by disease or accident provide the exhortation through grisly warning which is so characteristic of these medieval poems.

What these five poems share with the best of medieval lyric verse is their freedom from baroque diction and their songlike quality. Although not intricate, their meter is not so regular or simple as to synchronize with the metronome. They are full of pictures, with sharp clear outlines and much color. Sometimes they are tender, at other times severe, but always they are devoted to the greater glory of God and the salvation of His people.

FOR FURTHER READING:

Brown, Carleton. *English Lyrics of the XIIIth Century.* Oxford, 1932.
Brown, Carleton. *Religious Lyrics of the XIVth Century.* Oxford, 1924.
Brown, Carleton. *Religious Lyrics of the XVth Century.* Oxford, 1939.
Chambers, E. K., and Sidgwick, F. *Early English Lyrics.* London, 1907.
Greene, Richard L. *The Early English Carols.* Oxford, 1935.
Patterson, F. A. *The Middle English Penitential Lyric.* New York, 1911.

ANONYMOUS

WEN THE TURUF IS THI TUUR

Wen the turuf is thi tuur,
& thi put is thi bour,
Thi wel & thi wite throte
ssulen wormes to note.
Wat helpit the thenne
al the worilde wnne?

WEN THE TURUF IS THI TUUR This poem is taken from a thirteenth-century manuscript collection, probably compiled by a religious order. To know this is crucial to understanding the poem, for it is cast in terms of a particularly medieval view of life. In six short lines the poet uses simple concrete imagery to express that philosophy of contempt for the things of the world to which so much of medieval literature is devoted. According to this philosophy, only the joys of heaven are permanent. All earthly bliss is fleeting and insignificant, and undue pleasure in life will lead only to a corresponding loss of happiness after death.

Because of the many changes in the language which have taken place since the poem was written, it may present an initial, though slight, linguistic problem for the modern student. With very little trouble, however, we can ascertain that the word *tuur* is our modern "tower," that *bour* is "bower," *wel* is "skin," *ssulen* is "shall," *to note* is "to enjoy," and *wnne* is "bliss." A loose modern rendering of the poem would then read:

When the turf is thy tower,
And thy pit is thy bower,
Thy skin and thy white throat
Shall worms enjoy.
What will help thee then
All the world's bliss?

Similarly, the metrical scheme of the poem is a medieval rather than a modern one, being based primarily upon alliteration in the Old English manner. The lines cannot be scanned by modern metrical practices. Each line carries only two stresses, these falling upon the alliterated syllables in the first, second, third, and sixth lines of the poem. In the fourth and fifth lines there are still only two stresses per line, though alliteration is ignored.

We may experience the richness of the poem by a study of its imagery. The poem is constructed upon a small group of contrasting images, each pair reflecting, on the one hand, the decay of the human body after death and, on the other, physical delights of life. Thus in the first line, the *turf,* which will be the ultimate home of the body, is contrasted with *tower,* a symbol of man's lofty estates reaching toward the clouds. The alliteration serves to emphasize and underscore the closeness of the two concepts: man must exchange his lofty *tower* for the lowly *turf.*

The alliteration is repeated in the juxtaposition of *put* and *bour* in the following line, for the *p* and *b* differ only in the voicing of the latter. Here the *pit* is used to evoke all the horrors of the grave, and it is contrasted with *bower,* a word to evoke the joys of love and dalliance, those very pleasures against which the poem is directed. The word *bower* leads naturally to the figure of the fair beloved, which is contrasted to the grim reality of the worm who will be the only lover in the *pit.* The symbolic use of *tower* to represent perhaps the closest that man may come to heaven in this world is opposed to the symbol of the *pit,* which literally stands for the grave but symbolically suggests hell and incidentally reminds the reader that hell is where he will end if he fails to provide for the salvation of his soul.

The intellectual content of the poem is made to hinge upon the Middle English word *note,* which we translate as "enjoy." Its central position emphasizes the contrast of the two controlling ideas: the body that man thinks he enjoys in this life will rot in the grave after death, to be enjoyed only by *wormes.* The syntax is inverted so that *note* falls with emphasis at the end of the line. Perhaps also involved in the poet's use of *wormes* is a reference to Satan and his attendant devils, who are frequently called worms in medieval literature.

The basic idea of the poem is thus a harrowing one. The poet displays restraint, however, by his use of simple diction. He merely denotes his objects, leaving his reader to visualize the fuller picture which comes from the assemblage of these objects.

ADAM LAY I-BOWNDYN

> Adam lay i-bowndyn,
>> bowndyn in a bond,
> Fowre thowsand wynter
>> thowt he not to long;
> And al was for an appil,
>> an appil that he tok,
> As clerkes fyndyn wretyn
>> in here book.
> Ne hadde the appil take ben,
>> the appil taken ben,
> Ne hadde never our lady
>> a ben hevene quen.

Blyssid be the tyme
that appil take was!
Therfore we mown syngyn
Deo gracias.

i-bowndyn bound / *thowt* thought / *here* their / *mown* must

THE FALCON

Lully, lulley, lully, lulley!
The fawcon hath born my make away!

He bare hym up, he bare hym down,
He bare hym into an orchard brown.

Yn that orchard there was an halle
That was hangid with purpill and pall.

And yn that hall there was a bede,
Hit was hangid with gold so rede.

And yn that bed there lythe a knyght,
His woundis bledyng day and nyght.

By that bedeside kneleth a may,
And she wepeth both nyght and day.

And by that bedeside there stondith a ston,
'Corpus Christi' wretyn theron.

Lully, lulley, lully, lulley!
The fawcon hath born my make away!

make mate / *pall* funereal black / *lythe* lieth / *may* maid / *wretyn* written

I SYNG OF A MAYDEN

I syng of a mayden
that is makeles;
Kyng of alle kynges
to here sone che ches.

He cam also stylle
ther his moder was,

As dew in Aprylle
that fallyt on the gras.

He cam also stylle
to his moderes bowr,
As dew in Aprille
that fallyt on the flour.

He cam also stylle
ther his moder lay,
As dew in Aprille
that fallyt on the spray.

Moder & maydyn
was never none but che;
Wel may swych a lady
Godes moder be.

makeles matchless / *che* she / *ches* chose / *also* as / *fallyt* falls / *swych* such

A WINTER SONG

Wynter wakeneth al my care,
nou this leues waxeth bare;
ofte y sike & mourne sare
    when hit cometh in my thoht
    of this worldes ioie hou hit geth al to noht.

Noh hit is & nou hit nys,
also hit ner nere ywys,
that moni mon seith soth hit ys:
    'al goth bote godes wille,
    alle we shule deye thah vs like ylle.'

al that grein me graueth grene
nou hit faleweth al by-dene—
ihesu, help that hit be sene
    ant shild vs from helle,
    for y not whider y shal ne hou longe her duelle.

sike sigh / *sare* sorely / *ioie* joy / *geth* goes / *nys* is not / *also* as though /
ner nere never had been / *ywys* I know / *moni* many / *seith* says / *soth* truth /
goth passes / *alle we shale* that we must / *than vs like ylle* that us pleases
ill / *grein* grain, seed / *graueth* bury / *grene* possessing vitality / *faleweth*
fades / *by-dene* straightway / *ant* and / *shild* shield / *not* know not / *whider*
whither / *duelle* dwell

I

THE MIDDLE AGES

THE SECULAR LYRIC

SECULAR lyrics are unknown in English before the middle of the thirteenth century, and just where they came from has long been debated by scholars. Some have held that they stem from English translations of the love songs of the French troubadours; others, that they grew out of the so-called Goliardic verses, often irreligious and sometimes obscene, which were written in Latin and sung by university students. There may be truth in both suppositions, but we must note that there probably has been no period in human history when there was not some kind of folk dancing, and it is likely that the music which accompanied the dance expressed itself in song. What is certain about these lyrics is that, whatever their origins, they were all intended to be sung and that those few which have come down to us are distinctively English in character.

While they carry on the conventions of the French code of Courtly Love, the English love songs are much less conventional and stylized than their Continental counterparts. They tend to be more personal, more intimate, and more filled with genuine feeling than the French. The lover of *Alysoun* is still at the mercy of the mistress to whom he is enthralled, but there is more than artificial emotion in his praise for her physical charms, and there is a moving poignancy in his fear that some rival may steal her from him:

> *Icham for wowyng al forwake,*
> *wery so water in wore;*
> *lest eny reue me my make.*

Medieval English love poetry often achieves realism by dwelling upon the physical aspects of love, sometimes in a manner we would consider crude. Although the lady was at times worshiped with real spiritual intensity, more generally the poet's sincerest adoration was reserved for what he regarded as the highest type of love, his devotion to the Virgin Mary. Earthly love in the medieval scale of values was usually of a lesser order, transitory and evanescent. It could not be denied, however, and thus we have a body of love poetry which, though less of it survives, is as much a part of medieval England as its religious verse.

Chaucer's *Ballade* is a fine illustration of the gallantry and grace with which the medieval lover was able to extol his lady's beauty. It shows, probably through the French influence, a considerable advance in sophistication and gentility from the brutal early medieval view of life conveyed in the imagery of *Wen the Turuf is Thi Tuur*. Chaucer's poem is highly stylized and conventional; it says what a medieval lover was expected to say. In this it differs from *Sumer Is Icumen In,* more fully treated below, which is an outpouring of genuine feeling at the return of spring, capturing in its cadence the very notes of the cuckoo's song. The emotion is free and universal, even though the poetic diction and syntax are entirely medieval in their rigidity. This poem is a kind of love song also, for springtime was traditionally associated with the rites of love; flowering meadows, cool grasses, and shady groves were an invitation to dalliance. It is not at all improbable that part of the exuberance of *Sumer Is Icumen In* comes from the poet's anticipation that with the emerging sun the shepherdesses will again be bringing their flocks to the fields.

It must not be thought that love was the only subject of the secular lyric. Although generally of poor quality, a number of poems have survived which comment on political events, and there were songs to accompany drinking and conviviality. Song, in short, was a part of medieval life. Living could be enjoyed by ordinary people even as the churchmen proclaimed most loudly that all earthly pleasure must be scorned in preparation for the other world.

FOR FURTHER READING:

Chaytor, H. J. *The Troubadours and England.* London, 1923.
Lewis, C. S. *The Allegory of Love.* Oxford, 1936.

ANONYMOUS

SUMER IS ICUMEN IN

Sumer is icumen in,
Lhude sing cuccu!
Groweth sed and bloweth med
and springth the wde nu.
Sing cuccu!

Awe bleteth after lomb,
lhouth after calue cu;
Bulluc sterteth, bucke uerteth;
Murie sing cuccu!
Cuccu, cuccu,
Wel singes thu cuccu.
ne swik thu nauer nu!

Sing cuccu nu, Sing cuccu!
Sing cuccu, Sing cuccu nu!

icumen come / *Lhude* Loud / *sed* seed / *med* meadow / *wde* wood / *nu* anew / *Awe* Ewe / *lhouth* loweth / *calue* calf / *cu* cow / *uerteth* breaks wind / *swik* cease / *nauer* never / *nu* now

SUMER IS ICUMEN IN This lyric, also known as *The Cuckoo Song,* delights us by its spirit and melody. Refrain, a device that the limited rhetoric of the Middle Ages often employed in its religious poems—perhaps in imitation of the antiphonal and liturgical repetition which were a part of religious services—is here brilliantly employed. The poet is bursting with joy at the expansiveness of life found in summer, especially after the rigors of a harsh winter. The cuckoo bird is a happy choice for the poet to invoke, for it is the nature of the bird to imitate the sounds it hears in the fields. As the sights and sounds of nature are extolled—the growing grass, the blossoming meadows, the bleating ewe, and the lowing cow—the poet asks the bird in effect to mimic *the spirit* of these things he describes. The refrain—"Sing cuccu"—is incremental, mounting in its number of appearances, until finally the poet asks that the bird never stop singing at all. The poem then concludes with the cuckoo song alone.

A simple joy in living is expressed in the poem, quite alien to the scorn for temporal things which marks so much of medieval verse. The poem is, nevertheless, distinctly a part of its age, for it reveals a characteristically medieval poetic diction and sense of form which link it to *Wen the Turuf is Thi Tuur* as surely as it differs from that poem in feeling and tone. *Sumer Is Icumen In* shows its medievalism in a rigidity of structure. It is comprised of simple parallels, omitted connectives, and a stiff, unyielding, and unfluid syntax. These lend the poem an impersonal quality which is very characteristic of medieval art. We do not know the names of the sculptors who decorated the medieval cathedrals and we do not know the name of the man who wrote these lines. The anonymity of art and the rigid conventionality of its form are appropriate to a world in which to seek fame was regarded as sinful and in which individual self-expression had not yet come to be conceived of as a function of art.

The poem is based on a single terminal rhyme, but it depends for additional music upon internal rhyme and assonance. It might be regarded as composed of two quatrains which start the first and second stanzaic divisions. All the rest belongs to the province of refrain and its increment. The quatrains rhyme *abcb,* but the rhyme is based on the same vowel sound as that which concludes all lines of the refrain, the vowel *u.* Internal rhyme is achieved in the third line of each of the first two stanzas, where *groweth* rhymes with *bloweth,* *sed* with *med,* and *sterteth* with *uerteth.* But this is less than half the story of the melody in this poem. Only two lines in all fourteen fail to include words with some variation of the very *u* sound which is used also for rhyme, and these words are not the rhyme words themselves.

Song is the chief purpose of this poem; song is the metaphor upon which it is based; and song is what we get.

ALYSOUN

Bytuene Mersh & Aueril,
when spray biginneth to springe,
the lutel foul hath hire wyl
on hyre lud to synge.
Ich libbe in louelonginge
for semlokest of alle thynge;
He may me blisse bringe,
icham in hire baundoun.
An hendy hap ichabbe yhent,
ichot from heuene it is me sent—
from alle wymmen mi loue is lent,
& lyht on Alysoun.

On heu hire her is fayr ynoh,
hire browe broune, hire eye blake,
With lossum chere he on me loh;
with middel smal & wel ymake.
Bote he me wolle to hire take
forte buen hire owen make,
Longe to lyuen ichulle forsake
& feye fallen adoun.
An hendy hap, etc.

Nihtes when y wende & wake—
for-thi myn wonges waxeth won—
leuedi, al for thine sake,
longinge is ylent me on.
In world nis non so wyter mon
that al hire bounte telle con;
Hire swyre is whittore then the swon,
& feyrest may in toune.
An hendy, etc.

Icham for wowyng al forwake,
wery so water in wore;
lest eny reue me my make.
ychabbe y-yirned yore.
Betere is tholien whyle sore
then mournen euermore;
geynest vnder gore,
Herkne to my roun.
An hendy, etc.

lud song / *libbe* live / *semlokest* comeliest / *He* She / *icham* I am / *baundoun* power / *hendy hap* happy chance / *ichabbe* I have / *yhent* received / *ichot* I believe / *lent* taken away / *lyht* lights / *On* In / *heu* hue / *hire her* her hair / *ynoh* enough / *lossom chere* lovely face / *loh* looks / *middel* waist / *Bote* Unless / *wolle* will / *forte buen* for to be / *make* sweetheart / *ichulle* I shall / *wende* turn / *wonges* cheeks / *won* pale / *leuedi* lady / *ylent* lighted on / *non so wyter mon* no man so cunning / *swyre* neck / *wowyng* wooing / *forwake* wearied with waking / *so* as / *wore* sea beach / *reue* take away / *y-yirned* yearned / *yore* for a long time / *tholien* to endure / *geynest* most beautiful / *gore* clothing / *roun* song

THE MAID OF THE MOOR

Maiden in the mor lay,
        In the mor lay,
Seuenyst fulle, seuenist fulle,
Maiden in the mor lay,
        In the mor lay,
Seuenistes fulle ant a day.

Welle was hire mete;
        Wat was hire mete?
        The primerole ant the,—
        The primerole ant the,—
Welle was hire mete;
Wat was hire mete?
        The primerole ant the violet.

Well was hire dryng;
        Wat was hire dryng?
The chelde water of the welle-spring.

Welle was hire bour;
        Wat was hire bour?
The rede rose an te lilie flour.

Seuenyst A week / *mete* food / *primerole* primrose / *drying* drink / *chelde* cold / *bour* bower

THE IRISH DANCER

Icham of Irlaunde,
Ant of the holy londe
Of Irlaunde
Gode sire, pray ich thee,
For of saynte charité,
Come ant daunce wyt me,
In Irlaunde.

GEOFFREY CHAUCER

BALLADE

Hyd, Absolon, thy gilte tresses clere;
Ester, ley thou thy meknesse al adoun;
Hyd, Jonathas, al thy frendly manere;
Penalopee, and Marcia Catoun,
Mak of your wyfhod no comparisoun;
Hyde ye your beautes, Isoude and Eleyne;
My lady cometh, that al this may disteyne.

Thy faire body, lat hit nat appere,
Lavyne; and thou, Lucresse of Rome toun,
And Polixene, that boghten love so dere,
And Cleopatre, with al thy passioun,
Hyde ye your trouthe of love and your renoun;
And thou, Tisbe, that hast for love swich peyne:
My lady cometh, that al this may disteyne.

Herro, Dido, Laudomia, alle yfere
And Phyllis, hanging for thy Demophoun,

GEOFFREY CHAUCER (1340?-1400) was born in London, the son of a wine merchant. After service in various military campaigns and on diplomatic missions abroad, during one of which he is said to have met Petrarch, he lived at court, spending the best years of his career under the patronage of John of Gaunt and his son, King Henry IV. He was buried in Westminster Abbey, in what was to become the Poets' Corner.

And Canace, espyed by thy chere,
Ysiphile, betraysed with Jasoun,
Maketh of your trouthe neyther boost ne soun;
Nor Ypermistre or Adriane, ye tweyne;
My lady cometh, that al this may disteyne.

Hyd Cover / *disteyne* bedim / *yfere* together / *soun* vaunt

The
Renaissance **II**

THE English Renaissance, which for historical convenience we may date from the accession of King Henry VII in 1485 to the death of Queen Elizabeth in 1603, was a period of great expansion and achievement in poetry. This age of the Tudor monarchs is not only one of literary Titans—Shakespeare, Spenser, and Sidney—but also one in which poetry as an art form is perhaps more solidly a part of the general social fabric than it ever had been before or ever has been since. The medieval distinction between the active and the contemplative life, the soldier and the scholar, gives way to a belief in the universal man, and some of the greatest poetry of the age is written by soldier-statesmen like Sir Philip Sidney and Sir Walter Ralegh. Poems in praise of Queen Elizabeth I, who herself wrote poetry, reflect the attempts of courtiers to win royal favor, and the eager reception of poetry at court fostered its development throughout Elizabethan society.

In the court of Elizabeth's father, King Henry VIII, who was also a poet, there had sprung up a group of "courtly makers," chief among whom were Sir Thomas Wyatt and Henry Howard, Earl of Surrey. These men traveled to Italy and brought back the new poetic forms which had revitalized Continental poetry. The growth of humanism, with the high premium set upon accomplishment in the Greek and Latin tongues, led also to the spread of ancient poetic forms and a vogue of classical imitation. It is not only in form that Renaissance poets show their affinity to the classics, for they came to stress as well the classical ideal—derived from the *Ars Poetica* of the Roman poet Horace—that the function of poetry was to teach and to delight simultaneously. This credo is repeated again and again in the literary criticism of the age; poetry's didactic content touched on every aspect of life, from the duty of the courtier to his prince to the principles of farming, as in Thomas Tusser.

The Tudor poets The earliest Tudor poets, such as Stephen Hawes and Alexander Barclay, still carry on the traditions of medieval poetry, writing long moral allegories in established verse forms, octosyllabic and iambic pentameter couplets and the rhyme royal which had been used by Chaucer. Barclay, however, shows his affinity to the Renaissance by his introduction into English of the pastoral poetry which had become a favorite medium of Continental humanist poets. John Skelton is more of a transitional figure; he reveals much of the coarseness and asceticism of the medieval mentality and in his *Bowge of Court* presents a medieval satire based upon the conventional dream allegory, but he also displays an eagerness to experiment which makes him the first original poet of the Renaissance.

With Wyatt, Surrey, and Thomas, Lord Vaux, we have a new kind of poetry which, following the lead of French and Italian models, develops forms unknown before in English verse and expresses attitudes quite foreign to the Middle Ages. In the middle years of the sixteenth century these poets have many imitators, and their contribution becomes solidified, so that no poet can again write like Hawes, Barclay, or even Skelton. In 1579 Edmund Spenser's *Shepheardes Calender* ushered in the greatest flowering of poetry that England had ever known, for Spenser could give freshness and vitality to a greater number of poetic media than any poet had ever successfully attempted before—or perhaps since—and his achievement set the standards which other poets sought to equal.

With Spenser, the professional man of letters became a particular phenomenon of the English Renaissance. Such men were of several types. Young writers like Robert Greene, Thomas Nashe, and George Peele came down to London from the great universities of Oxford and Cambridge, eager to earn their living by their pens instead of following their fellow graduates into the ministry. Most of these young men took to the writing of plays, for the flourishing popular drama offered the writer of talent the best means of earning a livelihood. Still others, like Spenser and Samuel Daniel, wrote nondramatic poetry under a system of noble patronage. Spenser spent his most fruitful years in the service of the Earl of Leicester; Daniel acted as tutor first in the household of the Countess of Pembroke and later in that of the Countess of Cumberland.

Many of the patrons, including Essex, Sidney, and Ralegh, wrote poetry themselves. For a noble author to publish his own writings, however, was considered unseemly and immodest. A pervading ideal was the Italian notion of *sprezzatura*—a careless disdain for one's own accomplishments. To publish, moreover, was to exhibit oneself to the mob in a manner unthinkable to any Elizabethan aristocrat. On the other hand, he might circulate his verses in manuscript among his friends, and this was widely done. It was the fashion among Elizabethan gentlemen to keep commonplace books, notebooks in which they recorded whatever items of moral precept or of wit struck their fancies. Into these compilations the privately circulated poems began inevitably to find their way, and certain commonplace books themselves began at last to fall into the hands of printers, who issued them to the public as poetic miscellanies. Thus, in 1557, Richard Tottel printed his *Miscellany,* the first important collection of Tudor poetry. Others went under such eye-catching titles as *A Handful of Pleasant Delights, A Gorgeous Gallery of Gallant Inventions, Britton's Bower of Delight, England's Helicon,* and *The Paradise of Dainty Devices.* Poems were printed also in sonnet cycles, in individual collections of verse by poets who had become popular, and in prose narratives like Sidney's *Arcadia,* where they interrupted frequently the flow of episode. As lyrics in the popular songbooks and as snatches of song in the great dramas of the age, they also reached a wide audience.

The very existence of the printing press helped to create the difference between medieval and Renaissance poetry, for it meant the difference between an oral and a written tradition. Thanks to printing, poetry in the sixteenth century found a wider public than it ever could have known before; and this led to an expansion of poetic forms, for there were numberless tastes to be satisfied.

Themes of Renaissance poetry To understand Renaissance poetry, we must have some knowledge of the ideas upon which much of it is based. Most significant, perhaps, was the Neoplatonic attitude toward love which we call Petrarchism. This idealized conception of man's relation to woman has its origins in Renaissance Italy, where the idea of beauty came to be worshiped as a more meaningful object for devotion than the physical woman in whom it was embodied. The Italian scholar Francesco Petrarch, in his sonnet sequences to Laura living and to Laura dead, celebrated this ideal of beauty in terms which came to be highly conventionalized, establishing the stock subject matter for sonneteers in France and England who followed the Italian models. Since the idea rather than the reality was worshiped, the love object was unattainable, and the role of the lover had to be one of hopeless suffering. As in the literature of medieval chivalry, the lover was the servant of his lady. In his sonnets he detailed his sufferings and her cruelty; he begged in vain for her pity, prayed for sleep as a release from torment, and boasted of his power to make the beloved one live forever through his verse. In the voluminous sonnet sequences of the English Renaissance these stock sentiments were played upon in an infinite variety of ways.

Another common theme of Renaissance poetry is that of friendship between man and man. Usually, as in Shakespeare's sonnets, friendship is regarded as a nobler emotion than love between man and woman. In the Renaissance, friendship was looked on as a relationship which could exist only between equals, one in which each friend gave all of himself and asked nothing in return. No such relationship could exist between man and woman, partly because woman was considered inferior to man, partly because the man-woman relationship could never be an unselfish one— man expected heirs to carry on his name, and woman expected protection and security. Renaissance poetry often reflects a code of manners which is particularly a part of the age. It is described most notably in Baldassare Castiglione's *Courtier,* which, as translated by Sir Thomas Hoby, became one of the favorite books of Elizabethan gentlemen.

The English Reformation—marked by the break with Roman Catholicism and the establishment of the Anglican Church, then by the Puritan rebellion against Anglicanism—is reflected also in the poetry of the age. When it touches upon religion, most of Elizabethan poetry is in the Anglican tradition, but the voice of the Catholic martyr is heard in Robert South-well, and there is a strong Puritan element in Spenser. Religious issues in the Renaissance were inseparably bound to political ones, and strong re-flections of Reformation conflict are apparent in the political and social poetry with which the Tudor age abounds. The Reformation spirit dom-inates the verse satires which John Skelton at the beginning of the century directed against his archenemy, Cardinal Wolsey. Specific Reformation conflicts are found in some of the allegory in Spenser's *Shepheardes Cal-ender,* one of the most influential single productions of the age, and Reformation issues persist in the poetry of John Marston and George Wither. The Puritan influence, of course, reaches its most profound expres-sion in the work of John Milton, after the Renaissance.

In the sixteenth century, paradoxically, Puritans were engaged in con-stant attack upon poetry as an art form. They objected to its supposed immorality, argued that Plato had banned poets from his Republic because their work led man into error and away from the path of virtue, and in general held that the reading and writing of poetry were not conducive to Christian salvation. Among the most significant of the Puritan attacks was Stephen Gosson's *School of Abuse* (1579). The poets themselves were quick to defend their craft; their counterarguments produced the first considerable body of literary criticism in the English language. Sir Philip Sidney's *Defence of Poesie,* perhaps the most important critical treatise of the age, defended the creation of poetry as a greater activity than the writing of either history or philosophy, for its end was always the incul-cation of virtue, and toward this end it could embody the precepts of the philosopher in moving examples, without being limited by the historian's need to be faithful to the facts of the past. The growth of this new art of literary criticism led to an awareness in the poet of his own craft and a concern with its purposes and techniques—something quite absent from the poetry of the Middle Ages.

It must not be thought that the poems which follow represent the only kinds of poetry written in the English Renaissance. There was, for in-stance, a prolific and vigorous tradition of narrative poetry; we give no examples, chiefly because the extant specimens are all too lengthy to be reprinted in their entirety and because we believe that to cut any of them could only convey distorted impressions. For these reasons, the most sig-nificant poetic work of the entire era, Edmund Spenser's *Faerie Queene,* is not represented. Among other important examples of narrative poetry are such love poems as Shakespeare's *Venus and Adonis* and Marlowe's *Hero and Leander,* both based on the example of the Roman poet Ovid. There was also a tradition of verse history, carried on in such lengthy works as Samuel Daniel's *Civil Wars,* Drayton's *Barons' Wars,* and William Warner's *Albion's England,* to say nothing of *A Mirror for Magistrates,* a collection of tragic verse tales drawn from history which was perhaps the most widely read poetic work of the entire Tudor age.

FOR FURTHER READING:

Berdan, J. M. *Early Tudor Poetry.* New York, 1920.

Bush, Douglas. *Mythology and the Renaissance Tradition in English Poetry.* Minneapolis, 1932.

Craig, Hardin. *The Enchanted Glass: The Elizabethan Mind in Literature.* New York, 1936.

Ing, Catherine. *Elizabethan Lyrics.* London, 1951.

Lewis, C. S. *English Literature in the Sixteenth Century, Including Drama.* Oxford, 1954.

Rosenberg, Eleanor. *Leicester, Patron of Letters.* New York, 1956.

Smith, Hallett. *Elizabethan Poetry.* Cambridge, Mass., 1952.

Tuve, Rosemond. *Elizabethan and Metaphysical Imagery.* Chicago, 1945.

Zocca, L. R. *Elizabethan Narrative Poetry.* New Brunswick, N.J., 1950.

II

THE RENAISSANCE

THE AMATORY

IF we compare the medieval *Sumer Is Icumen In* with *Description of Spring,* written in the first half of the sixteenth century by Henry Howard, Earl of Surrey, we find some indication of how poetry has progressed. Although the medieval poet may have celebrated the return of springtime in anticipation of the love and courtship which accompany it, this fact is not stated directly in the verse. In Surrey's poem the connection is made, and it is all in the final five words, "and yet my sorrow springs." Here the pose of the melancholy lover, which is so much a part of Renaissance love poetry, becomes the excuse for the entire poem: the beauty and joy of springtime are called upon to emphasize that sadness. The celebration of spring was a traditional motif of poetry, as in *Sumer Is Icumen In,* but Surrey has imposed upon this traditional motif a new poetic form and a new point of view.

Renaissance love poems are not confined to any specific form. The quatrain and the six-line stanza were very popular, but the Petrarchan commonplaces of the age appeared in almost every other measure, including rhymed couplets in tetrameter or pentameter (*Phyllida and Corydon* and *The Shepherd's Wife's Song*), tercets (*Forget Not Yet*), rhyme royal (*They Flee from Me*), octaves (*Love in My Bosom Like a Bee*), and elaborate but controlled longer stanzaic forms (*Prothalamion*). The variations of these forms and others are too numerous to describe. Surrey's poem is a sonnet, and the sonnet, as the traditional and most common form of love poetry in the sixteenth century, must be considered in some detail.

The sonnet in English poetry The sonnet was introduced to England by Sir Thomas Wyatt, probably in the 1530's after his return from Italy. The form he brought back was that which had been used by the Italian poet Petrarch; it is known as the Italian or Petrarchan sonnet. While all sonnets (except some very rare experimental forms) confine themselves to fourteen lines of iambic pentameter, the Italian form is distinguished by its division into an ordinary *octave*—the first eight lines—and a concluding *sestet*—the last six lines. The division sets it apart from the English form, which was introduced by Henry Howard, Earl of Surrey, in some fifteen sonnets printed in Tottel's *Miscellany* in 1557 and which was brought to perfection by William Shakespeare in the 1590's. In the English form a theme is developed in the first twelve lines, divided into three quatrains, and a precise summation or epigrammatic close is provided by the final couplet. Form and content are also allied in the Italian form, with the last six lines frequently providing a resolution of the problem posed in the first eight.

The octave of the Italian sonnet rhymed *abbaabba.* The sestet, as the form was written in Italy, offered several variations based upon two or three new rhymes such as *cdecde, cdcdcd,* or *cddece;* the only bar to the poet's ingenuity was that the last two lines could not be a couplet. Wyatt broke this rule, frequently using a couplet to end his sonnets, and this became common practice in the Petrarchan sonnets written in English (see *Whoso List to Hunt*).

It may have been a desire for greater ease and fluidity of expression which led Wyatt's younger friend Surrey to develop what has become known as the English sonnet, for this form is better suited to the English language with its relative scarcity of rhyming sounds. The suggestion for the new form may have come from Wyatt's use of the final couplet. As the English sonnet developed, it usually consisted of three quatrains, rhyming *abab cdcd efef,* followed by a sharp break and then the epigrammatic couplet *gg.* Sometimes the first twelve lines were rhymed in a continuing series, *abababababab,* but the final couplet *cc* had to follow (see *Description of Spring*). The English sonnet was marked usually by the continuous development of a proposition in the first twelve lines and its resolution in the concluding couplet.

Although Wyatt did his great work in a foreign literary form, there is much in his poetry that carries on the native English tradition. Most marked in this respect are his directness of expression and his willingness to rely upon bare, stark imagery. His meters are often rough, approximating the rhythms of ordinary speech in a manner which links him also to the seventeenth-century metaphysical poets and which has done much to increase his popularity in our own time. He has little of the metrical smoothness of Sidney or Spenser.

Following the deaths of Wyatt and Surrey, not many sonnets were written until the final two decades of the sixteenth century, when there was a great rebirth of interest in the form. When they reappeared, sonnets were printed in loosely joined cycles, telling a story usually of a Petrarchan lover's experiences in the courtship of his lady. Of this sort were the first two sequences of the 1580's, Thomas Watson's *Passionate Century of Love* and Sir Philip Sidney's *Astrophel and Stella.* Sidney's sonnets, supposedly celebrating a frustrating love affair with Penelope Devereux, daughter of the Earl of Essex, were the inspiration for many other cycles in the Elizabethan period, in which poets recorded their successive raptures and sorrows and extolled the beauty of various scornful ladies—usually given such exotic names as Stella, Diana, or Idea—who remained, in true Petrarchan fashion, unmoved by the poets' lyrical pleas. For the most part the ladies so celebrated were noble patronesses, and since the emotion of the sonnets usually had little basis in fact, the sonnet cycles tended to become highly stylized and artificial. By 1600 the vogue had virtually exhausted itself; few cycles were written in the seventeenth century.

Among the more important Elizabethan sonneteers are Constable, Drayton, and Daniel. Shakespeare and Spenser are two giants who must be considered separately. The first 126 of Shakespeare's sonnet sequence —154 sonnets in all—are addressed to a young man, whose identity scholars have argued about for generations. These poems celebrate the Renaissance ideal of male friendship discussed earlier (p. 44). The next twenty-six sonnets—numbers 127 to 152—are concerned with Shakespeare's relation to the "Dark Lady," a second figure whom no scholar has as yet satisfactorily unmasked. The remaining two are inferior poems, not associated with the story of these persons or with the equally mysterious "Rival Poet," who also figures in the sequence story.

Edmund Spenser must be mentioned for his divergence from the conventions of the sonnet sequence, with respect to form as well as content. Although marriage is never the goal of the ordinary Petrarchan lover, Spenser clearly wrote his poems to Elizabeth Boyle, the girl who was later to become his wife. He celebrates their courtship in his sonnets and concludes them with his marriage hymn, *Epithalamion*. Spenser's innovation in form made the three quatrains of the English sonnet an interlocking sequence, much in the manner of the nine-line stanza he invented for his *Faerie Queene*. His sonnets rhyme *abab bcbc cdcd ee*. Whereas the English or Shakespearian sonnet has become the most common sonnet form among later English poets, the Spenserian sonnet, with its demanding pattern of quadruple rhyme, has been very little used.

FOR FURTHER READING:

Hubler, Edward. *The Sense of Shakespeare's Sonnets*. Princeton, 1952.

John, L. C. *The Elizabethan Sonnet Sequences*. New York, 1938.

Knights, L. C. "Shakespeare's Sonnets," *Explorations*. New York, 1947.

Lever, J. W. *The Elizabethan Love Sonnet*. London, 1956.

Lewis, C. S. *The Allegory of Love*. Oxford, 1936.

Myrick, K. O. *Sir Philip Sidney As a Literary Craftsman*. Cambridge, Mass., 1935.

Pearson, L. E. *Elizabethan Love Conventions*. Berkeley, Calif., 1933.

Renwick, W. L. *Edmund Spenser, an Essay in Renaissance Poetry*. London, 1925.

SIR THOMAS WYATT

WHOSO LIST TO HUNT

Whoso list to hunt, I know where is an hind,
But as for me—alas, I may no more.
The vain travail hath wearied me so sore,
I am of them that farthest cometh behind.
Yet may I, by no means, my wearied mind
Draw from the deer; but as she fleeth afore
Fainting I follow. I leave off therefore,
Since in a net I seek to hold the wind.
Who list her hunt, I put him out of doubt,
As well as I, may spend his time in vain.
And graven with diamonds in letters plain
There is written, her fair neck round about:
Noli me tangere, for Caesar's I am,
And wild for to hold, though I seem tame.

THEY FLEE FROM ME

They flee from me that sometime did me seek,
With naked foot stalking in my chamber.
I have seen them gentle, tame, and meek,
That now are wild, and do not remember
That some time they put themselves in danger
To take bread at my hand; and now they range,
Busily seeking with a continual change.

Thanked be fortune, it hath been otherwise
Twenty times better; but once, in speciall,
In thin array, after a pleasant guise,
When her loose gown from her shoulders did fall,
And she me caught in her arms long and small,
Therewith all sweetly did me kiss,
And softly said, Dear heart, how like you this?

It was no dream; I lay broad waking.
But all is turned, thorough my gentleness,

SIR THOMAS WYATT (1503?-1542) spent most of his life in the service of Henry VIII. During those periods in which he enjoyed the royal favor, he carried out missions abroad which brought him into close contact with the cultural ferment of the Italian Renaissance. A tradition has persisted that he was the lover of Anne Boleyn.

Into a strange fashion of forsaking;
And I have leave to go of her goodness,
And she also to use newfangleness.
But since that I so kindely am served,
I fain would know what she hath deserved.

HENRY HOWARD, EARL OF SURREY

DESCRIPTION OF SPRING

The soote season that bud and bloom forth brings
With green hath clad the hill and eke the vale,
The nightingale with feathers new she sings,
The turtle to her make hath told her tale.
Summer is come, for every spray now springs,
The hart hath hung his old head on the pale,
The buck in brake his winter coat he flings,
The fishes float with new repairèd scale,
The adder all her slough away she slings,
The swift swallow pursueth the flyès smale,
The busy bee her honey now she mings,—
Winter is worn, that was the flowers' bale:
And thus I see, among these pleasant things
Each care decays—and yet my sorrow springs.

ANONYMOUS

O WESTERN WIND

O western wind, when wilt thou blow,
That the small rain down can rain?
Christ, that my love were in my arms
And I in my bed again!

HENRY HOWARD, EARL OF SURREY (1517?-1547), was one of the most brilliant young courtiers of the age, but his haughtiness antagonized Henry VIII, and he was executed for treason at the age of thirty. Surrey was the friend and literary associate of Sir Thomas Wyatt.

QUEEN ELIZABETH I

WHEN I WAS FAIR AND YOUNG

When I was fair and young, and favor gracèd me,
    Of many was I sought, their mistress for to be;
But I did scorn them all, and answered them therefore,
      Go, go, go, seek some otherwhere,
        Importune me no more!

How many weeping eyes I made to pine with woe,
    How many sighing hearts, I have no skill to show;
Yet I the prouder grew, and answered them therefore,
      Go, go, go, seek some otherwhere,
        Importune me no more!

Then spake fair Venus' son, that proud victorious boy,
    And said: Fine Dame, since that you be so coy,
I will so pluck your plumes that you shall say no more,
      Go, go, go, seek some otherwhere,
        Importune me no more!

When he had spake these words, such change grew in my breast
    That neither night nor day since that, I could take any rest.
Then lo! I did repent that I had said before,
      Go, go, go, seek some otherwhere,
        Importune me no more!

BARNABE GOOGE

OUT OF SIGHT, OUT OF MIND

The oftener seen, the more I lust,
The more I lust, the more I smart,
The more I smart, the more I trust,
The more I trust, the heavier heart,

QUEEN ELIZABETH I (1533-1603) ruled England during a period of tumult and excitement in politics, commerce, religion, and literature. She was accomplished in languages and apparently could write poetry with some skill.
BARNABE GOOGE (1540-1594) had a considerable contemporary reputation as a translator of classical works.

The heavy heart breeds mine unrest,
Thy absence, therefore, like I best.

The rarer seen, the less in mind,
The less in mind, the lesser pain,
The lesser pain, less grief I find,
The lesser grief, the greater gain,
The greater gain, the merrier I,
Therefore I wish thy sight to fly.

The further off, the more I joy,
The more I joy, the happier life,
The happier life, less hurts annoy,
The lesser hurts, pleasure most rife,
Such pleasures rife shall I obtain
When distance doth depart us twain.

GEORGE TURBERVILLE

TO HIS FRIEND

I wot full well that beauty cannot last;
No rose that springs but lightly doth decay,
And feature like a lily leaf doth waste,
Or as the cowslip in the midst of May;
I know that tract of time doth conquer all,
And beauty's buds like fading flowers do fall.

That famous dame, fair Helen, lost her hue
When withered age with wrinkles changed her cheeks,
Her lovely looks did loathsomeness ensue
That was the *A per se* of all the Greeks.
And sundry mo that were as fair as she,
Yet Helen was as fresh as fresh might be.

No force for that, I price your beauty light
If so I find you steadfast in good will.
Though few there are that do in age delight,

GEORGE TURBERVILLE (1540?-1610?) translated both classical and contemporary works and described Russia in verse after a visit there in the service of the queen's ambassador.

I was your friend, and so do purpose still;
No change of looks shall breed my change of love,
Nor beauty's want my first good will remove.

GEORGE GASCOIGNE

INSCRIPTION IN A GARDEN

If any flower that there is grown,
Or any herb, may ease your pain,
Take, and accompt it as your own,
But recompense the like again:
For some and some is honest play,
And so my wife taught me to say.

If here to walk you take delight,
Why, come and welcome, when you will;
If I bid you sup here this night,
Bid me another time, and still
Think some and some is honest play,
For so my wife taught me to say.

Thus if you sup or dine with me,
If you walk here or sit at ease,
If you desire the thing you see,
And have the same, your mind to please,
Think some and some is honest play,
And so my wife taught me to say.

GASCOIGNE'S LULLABY

Sing lullaby, as women do,
Wherewith they bring their babes to rest,
And lullaby can I sing too
As womanly as can the best.
With lullaby they still the child,
And if I be not much beguiled,

GEORGE GASCOIGNE (1525?-1577) served in Parliament and with the
army in the Low Countries. In addition to poetry, he produced pioneering works in
prose comedy and blank verse tragedy and satire, frequently adapting Italian originals.

Full many wanton babes have I
Which must be stilled with lullaby.

First, lullaby my youthful years,
It is now time to go to bed,
For crooked age and hoary hairs
Have won the haven within my head;
With lullaby, then, youth be still,
With lullaby, content thy will,
Since courage quails and comes behind,
Go sleep, and so beguile thy mind.

Next, lullaby my gazing eyes,
Which wonted were to glance apace;
For every glass may now suffice
To show the furrows in my face.
With lullaby, then, wink awhile,
With lullaby, your looks beguile,
Let no fair face nor beauty bright
Entice you eft with vain delight.

And lullaby, my wanton will,
Let reason's rule now reign thy thought,
Since all too late I find by skill
How dear I have thy fancies bought;
With lullaby, now take thine ease,
With lullaby, thy doubts appease;
For trust to this, if thou be still,
My body shall obey thy will.

Eke, lullaby my loving boy,
My little Robin, take thy rest;
Since age is cold and nothing coy,
Keep close thy coin, for so is best;
With lullaby, be thou content,
With lullaby, thy lusts relent,
Let others pay which have mo pence,
Thou art too poor for such expense.

Thus lullaby, my youth, mine eyes,
My will, my ware, and all that was!
I can no mo delays devise,
But welcome pain, let pleasure pass;

With lullaby, now take your leave,
With lullaby, your dreams deceive,
And when you rise with waking eye,
Remember Gascoigne's lullaby.

EDWARD DE VERE, EARL OF OXFORD

WHAT CUNNING CAN EXPRESS?

What cunning can express
The favor of her face,
To whom in this distress
I do appeal for grace?
    A thousand Cupids fly
    About her gentle eye:

From whence each throws a dart
That kindleth soft sweet fire
Within my sighing heart,
Possessed by desire.
    No sweeter life I try
    Than in her love to die.

The lily in the field
That glories in his white,
For pureness now must yield
And render up his right.
    Heaven pictured in her face
    Doth promise joy and grace.

Fair Cynthia's silver light
That beats on running streams
Compares not with her white,
Whose hairs are all sunbeams.
    Her virtues so do shine
    As day unto mine eyne.

With this there is a red
Exceeds the damask rose,

EDWARD DE VERE, 17th Earl of Oxford (1550-1604), had a reputation as a foppish and dissolute courtier, although he was one of Queen Elizabeth's favorites. He was a generous patron of poets as well as a poet himself.

Which in her cheeks is spread,
Whence every favour grows.
    In sky there is no star
    That she surmounts not far.

When Phoebus from the bed
Of Thetis doth arise,
The morning blushing red
In fair carnation wise,
    He shows it in her face
    As queen of every grace.

This pleasant lily-white,
This taint of roseate red,
This Cynthia's silver light,
This sweet fair Dea spread,
    These sun-beams in mine eye,
    These beauties make me die.

SIR PHILIP SIDNEY

WITH HOW SAD STEPS, O MOON, THOU CLIMB'ST THE SKIES

With how sad steps, O moon, thou climb'st the skies!
  How silently, and with how wan a face!
  What! may it be that even in heav'nly place
  That busy archer his sharp arrows tries?
Sure, if that long-with-love-acquainted eyes
  Can judge of love, thou feel'st a lover's case;
  I read it in thy looks; thy languished grace
  To me, that feel the like, thy state decries.
Then, ev'n of fellowship, O moon, tell me,
  Is constant love deemed there but want of wit?
  Are beauties there as proud as here they be?
Do they above love to be loved, and yet
  Those lovers scorn whom that love doth possess?
  Do they call virtue there ungratefulness?

SIR PHILIP SIDNEY (1554-1586), nephew of Queen Elizabeth's favorite, the Earl of Leicester, and son of her lord deputy of Ireland, distinguished himself as a courtier, diplomat, and soldier as well as a writer. Until his death at the Battle of Zutphen in Holland, he was the most brilliant figure in Elizabeth's court.

COME SLEEP! O SLEEP, THE CERTAIN
KNOT OF PEACE

Come sleep! O sleep, the certain knot of peace,
  The baiting place of wit, the balm of woe,
  The poor man's wealth, the prisoner's release,
  Th' indifferent judge between the high and low;
With shield of proof shield me from out the prease
  Of those fierce darts despair at me doth throw;
  O make in me those civil wars to cease;
  I will good tribute pay, if thou do so.
Take thou of me smooth pillows, sweetest bed,
  A chamber deaf to noise and blind to light,
  A rosy garland and a weary head;
And if these things, as being thine by right,
  Move not thy heavy grace, thou shalt in me,
  Livelier than elsewhere, Stella's image see.

SIR WALTER RALEGH

A DESCRIPTION OF LOVE

Now what is love? I pray thee, tell.
It is that fountain and that well
Where pleasure and repentance dwell.
It is perhaps that saucing bell
That tolls all into heaven or hell:
And this is love, as I hear tell.

Yet what is love? I pray thee say.
It is a work on holy-day;
It is December matched with May;
When lusty bloods, in fresh array,
Hear ten months after of the play:
And this is love, as I hear say.

Yet what is love? I pray thee sain.
It is a sunshine mixed with rain;

SIR WALTER RALEGH (1552?-1618) rose from modest beginnings to become poet, courtier, scholar, explorer, and statesman. Under Queen Elizabeth he was
soon one of the most influential men in England, especially during his reign as her
favorite from 1582 to 1592. When James I succeeded Elizabeth in 1603, Ralegh was
put in the Tower. He remained there, except for a brief period of freedom toward the
end, for fifteen years and was finally beheaded.

It is a tooth-ache, or like pain;
It is a game where none doth gain;
The lass saith no, and would full fain:
And this is love, as I hear sain.

Yet what is love? I pray thee say.
It is a yea, it is a nay,
A pretty kind of sporting fray;
It is a thing will soon away;
Then take the vantage while you may:
And this is love, as I hear say.

Yet what is love, I pray thee show.
A thing that creeps, it cannot go;
A prize that passeth to and fro;
A thing for one, a thing for mo;
And he that proves must find it so:
And this is love, sweet friend, I trow.

AS YOU CAME FROM THE HOLY
LAND OF WALSINGHAM

As you came from the holy land
  Of Walsingham,
Met you not with my true love,
  By the way as you came?
How should I know your true love,
  That have met many a one,
As I came from the holy land,
  That have come, that have gone?

She is neither white nor brown,
  But as the heavens fair;
There is none hath her form so divine,
  On the earth, in the air.
Such a one did I meet, good sir,
  With angel-like face,
Who like a nymph, like a queen did appear
  In her gait, in her grace.

She hath left me here alone,
  All alone unknown,
Who sometime loved me as her life,

And callëd me her own.
What is the cause she hath left thee alone,
 And a new way doth take,
That sometime did thee love as herself,
 And her joy did thee make?

I have loved her all my youth,
 But now am old as you see;
Love likes not the falling fruit,
 Nor the withered tree.
For love is a careless child,
 And forgets promise past;
He is blind, he is deaf, when he list,
 And in faith never fast.

His desire is fickle found,
 And a trustless joy;
He is won with a world of despair,
 And is lost with a toy.
Such is the love of women-kind,
 Or the word, love, abused,
Under which many childish desires
 And conceits are excused.

But love, it is a durable fire
 In the mind ever burning,
Never sick, never dead, never cold,
 From itself never turning.

THOMAS LODGE

ROSALIND'S MADRIGAL

Love in my bosom like a bee
 Doth suck his sweet;
Now with his wings he plays with me,
 Now with his feet.

THOMAS LODGE (1558?-1625) led a crowded life, even for Elizabethan times. Son of the lord mayor of London, this "university wit" studied law, turned to literature, made an expedition to South America, became a convert to Roman Catholicism, and ended his career as a physician. He wrote songs, sonnets, plays, pamphlets, and prose romances, including *Rosalynde*, the source of Shakespeare's *As You Like It*.

Within mine eyes he makes his nest,
His bed amidst my tender breast,
My kisses are his daily feast,
And yet he robs me of my rest—
  Ah, wanton, will ye?

And if I sleep, then percheth he
  With pretty flight,
And makes his pillow of my knee
  The livelong night.
Strike I my lute, he tunes the string,
He music plays if so I sing,
He lends me every lovely thing,
Yet cruel he my heart doth sting—
  Whist, wanton, still ye!

Else I with roses every day
  Will ship ye hence,
And bind you, when you long to play,
  For your offence.
I'll shut mine eyes to keep you in,
I'll make you fast it for your sin,
I'll count your power not worth a pin;
Alas! what hereby shall I win
  If he gainsay me?

HENRY LOK

WORDS MAY WELL WANT

Words may well want, both ink and paper fail,
  Wits may grow dull, and will may weary grow,
  And world's affairs may make my pen more slow,
  But yet my heart and courage shall not quail.
Though cares and troubles do my peace assail
  And drive me to delay thy praise awhile,
  Yet all the world shall not from thoughts exile
  Thy mercies, Lord, by which my plaints prevail.

HENRY LOK (1553?-1608?) wrote very little other than religious verse, nearly all of it in the sonnet form.

And though the world with face should grateful smile
And me her peddler's pack of pleasures show,
No hearty love on her I would bestow,
Because I know she seeks me to beguile;
    Ne will defile my happy peace of mind
    For all the solace I in earth may find.

HENRY CONSTABLE

MINE EYE WITH ALL THE DEADLY SINS

Mine eye with all the deadly sins is fraught.
    First *proud,* sith is presumed to look so high;
    A watchman being made, stood gazing by,
And *idle,* took no heed till I was caught;
And *envious* bears envy that my thought
    Should in his absence be to her so nigh;
    To kill my heart, mine eye let in her eye,
And so consent gave to a *murder* wrought;
    And *covetous,* it never would remove
From her fair hair, gold so doth please his sight;
Unchaste, a bawd between my heart and love;
A *glutton* eye, with tears drunk every night:
    These sins procurëd have a goddess' ire,
    Wherefore my heart is damned in love's sweet fire.

FAIR GRACE OF GRACES

Fair grace of graces, muse of muses all,
    Thou paradise, thou only heaven I know,
    What influence hath bred my hateful woe,
That I from thee and them am forced to fall?
Thou fall'n from me, from thee I never shall;
    Although my fortunes thou hast brought so low,
    Yet shall my faith and service with thee go,
For live I do on heaven and thee to call.
Banished all grace, no graces with me dwell;

HENRY CONSTABLE (1562-1613) became a convert to Roman Catholicism in his youth and spent most of his life abroad. In 1599 he was papal envoy to Edinburgh. Later, while visiting London, he was imprisoned for a time in the Tower.

Compelled to muse, my muses from me fly;
Excluded heaven, what can remain but hell?
Exiled from paradise, in hate I lie
Cursing my stars; albeit I find it true,
I lost all these when I lost love and you.

SAMUEL DANIEL

THOU CANST NOT DIE

Thou canst not die whilst any zeal abound
In feeling hearts that can conceive these lines;
Though thou, a Laura, hast no Petrarch found,
In base attire yet clearly beauty shines.
And I, though born within a colder clime,
Do feel mine inward heat as great (I know it);
He never had more faith, although more rhyme;
I love as well, though he could better show it.
But I may add one feather to thy fame,
To help her flight throughout the fairest isle,
And if my pen could more enlarge thy name,
Then shouldst thou live in an immortal style.
For though that Laura better limnéd be,
Suffice, thou shalt be loved as well as she.

MICHAEL DRAYTON

TRUCE, GENTLE LOVE

Truce, gentle love, a parley now I crave;
Methinks 'tis long since first these wars begun,
Nor thou, nor I, the better yet can have;
Bad is the match where neither party won.
I offer free conditions of fair peace,

SAMUEL DANIEL (1562-1619) served as a tutor in noble households and wrote voluminously in both prose and verse. His poetry ranged from sonnets to epics and from masques to tragedies.
MICHAEL DRAYTON (1563-1631) has been called the most representative of Elizabethan poets because in his extremely long career he mirrored all the changing literary fashions of the sixteenth and early seventeenth centuries.

My heart for hostage that it shall remain;
Discharge our forces, here let malice cease,
So for my pledge thou give me pledge again;
Or if no thing but death will serve thy turn,
Still thirsting for subversion of my state,
Do what thou canst, raze, massacre, and burn,
Let the world see the utmost of thy hate;
    I send defiance, since if overthrown,
    Thou vanquishing, the conquest is mine own.

SIR JOHN DAVIES

THE HARDNESS OF HER HEART

The hardness of her heart and truth of mine
When the all-seeing eyes of heaven did see,
They straight concluded that by power divine
To other forms our hearts should turnèd be.
Then hers, as hard as flint, a flint became,
And mine, as true as steel, to steel was turned;
And then between our hearts sprang forth the flame
Of kindest love, which unextinguished burned.
And long the sacred lamp of mutual love
Incessantly did burn in glory bright,
Until my folly did her fury move
To recompense my service with despite;
And to put out with snuffers of her pride
The lamp of love which else had never died.

JOHN LYLY

CUPID AND CAMPASPE

Cupid and my Campaspe played
At cards for kisses; Cupid paid.

SIR JOHN DAVIES (1569-1626), after a long and distinguished career as a jurist, was named lord chief justice but died before taking office. He excelled at writing eloquent philosophical poetry.

JOHN LYLY (1554?-1606) achieved fame for the polish and sophistication of his court comedies and prose romances—particularly *Euphues*—but never won the post of master of revels which he sought throughout his career.

He stakes his quiver, bow, and arrows,
His mother's doves and team of sparrows;
Loses them too; then down he throws
The coral of his lip, the rose
Growing on's cheek (but none knows how);
With these the crystal of his brow,
And then the dimple of his chin;
All these did my Campaspe win.
At last he set her both his eyes;
She won, and Cupid blind did rise.
O Love, has she done this to thee?
What shall, alas! become of me?

CUPID AND CAMPASPE A song from John Lyly's play *Alexander and Campaspe,* this lyric is sung by the artist-lover Apelles. The poem's dramatic origin may in part explain its artificial tone; the lyric is not an expression of any real emotion on the part of the poet but is rather a *jeu d'esprit* in which the poet displays his wit and virtuosity for the sophisticated court audience.

As a love song the poem uses the conventional motifs of Renaissance Petrarchism: the beauty of the lady, her cruelty to the lover, and his fear that her torments will cause his death. The ideas themselves are part of an elaborate love code that bears little relation to any real interplay between sixteenth-century lovers.

In a straightforward but imaginative way, the poet creates an elaborate conceit of the manner in which Cupid was made blind. This narrative element is made to embody the themes of the lady's beauty, the lover's torment, and his fears: the three conventions of Courtly Love and the chief business of the poem. Our knowledge that the story was often so used by Renaissance poets adds to our sense of the poem's artificiality and our awareness of the poet's virtuosity. To read the poem outside of the context of other accounts of Cupid's blinding is to slight an important dimension.

The first couplet, which suggests that Cupid might desire Campaspe's kisses, is subtle praise of the lady's charms; and in the simple statement "Cupid paid," we have the first sign of her cruelty, though it is implicitly rather than explicitly expressed. The game of love itself has close similarities to a game of cards; both involve a gamble and both are painful to the loser. In lines 3 and 4 this aspect of the poem is developed further. Here we see Cupid, led on by his desire for Campaspe's kisses, losing all his possessions and those of his mother, Venus, as well. With the fifth line the poet reverts to his theme of the lady's beauty, upon which he now elaborates, though the theme of her cruelty is continued as an undertone. From the lovely child Cupid the cruel Campaspe wins all the attributes of physical beauty: "the coral of his lip," "the rose / Growing on's cheek," "the crystal of his brow," "the dimple of his chin." With these exaggerated compliments the poet completes his praise of the lady's beauty.

In the next couplet the theme of the lady's cruelty reaches its climax at the same time that the account of Cupid's blinding is brought to a close:

> At last he set her both his eyes;
> She won, and Cupid blind did rise.

Now the poet has only to state the final couplet to which the others have led inevitably:

> O Love, has she done this to thee?
> What shall, alas! become of me?

If the god of love himself can be so completely ruined by Campaspe's beauty, what can a mere mortal expect?

Part of the success of this poem can be accounted for in the poet's felicitous blending of the lightly treated manner of Cupid's blinding with the serious plight of any hopelessly enamored lover. First the lover loses his *own* material possessions, either through bestowing them upon his beloved or by failing to care for them because of his complete absorption with the lady. If the woman is cruel and demanding, the lover will give to her even those things which do not belong to him. When there is nothing more of material value to give, he begins to divest himself of his own personality, which is accompanied by a corresponding loss of well-being and, literally, of physical beauty. Finally, when he has lost the lady completely, he becomes *blind* to anything of worth, even to love itself.

Structurally, the poem depends for its effect upon the neatness, precision, and economy with which the three themes are combined and executed. To these ends the simple and fast-moving tetrameter couplets, the succession of strong monosyllabic verbs ("Cupid paid," "He stakes," "She won," etc.), and the alliteration on the hard *c* throughout the entire poem all contribute. By focusing on the Cupid story for the first twelve lines, the poet achieves his greatest economy; yet by indirection, he has told his more important story with the addition of only the final two lines.

GEORGE PEELE

WHAT THING IS LOVE

> What thing is love? for, well I wot, love is a thing.
> It is a prick, it is a sting,

GEORGE PEELE (1558?-1597?) wrote poems and plays, enlivening the latter with charming lyrics. He was notorious for his dissolute living.

It is a pretty, pretty thing;
It is a fire, it is a coal,
Whose flame creeps in at ev'ry hole;
And as my wit doth best devise,
Love's dwelling is in ladies' eyes,
From whence do glance loves' piercing darts
That make such holes into our hearts;
And all the world herein accord
Love is a great and mighty lord;
And when he list to mount so high,
With Venus he in heaven doth lie,
And evermore hath been a god
Since Mars and she played even and odd.

WHENAS THE RYE

Whenas the rye reach to the chin,
And chopcherry, chopcherry ripe within,
Strawberries swimming in the cream,
And schoolboys playing in the stream;
Then oh, then oh, then oh, my true love said,
Till that time come again,
She could not live a maid.

WILLIAM SHAKESPEARE

SHALL I COMPARE THEE TO A SUMMER'S DAY?

Shall I compare thee to a summer's day?
Thou art more lovely and more temperate:
Rough winds do shake the darling buds of May,
And summer's lease hath all too short a date:
Sometime too hot the eye of heaven shines,
And often is his gold complexion dimm'd;
And every fair from fair sometime declines,

WILLIAM SHAKESPEARE (1564-1616), England's greatest dramatist, was born in Stratford-on-Avon in Warwickshire and educated at the village grammar school. After an early marriage and possibly a short career as a country schoolmaster, he arrived in London sometime before 1592 and devoted himself to the theater until around 1610, when he returned to Stratford in semiretirement. During his early years in London he sought the patronage of the Earl of Southampton, to whom he dedicated two long narrative poems and to whom the sonnets probably were written.

By chance or nature's changing course untrimm'd;
But thy eternal summer shall not face,
Nor lose possession of that fair thou owest;
Nor shall Death brag thou wander'st in his shade,
When in eternal lines to time thou grow'st:
   So long as men can breathe or eyes can see,
   So long lives this and this gives life to thee.

WHEN, IN DISGRACE WITH FORTUNE AND MEN'S EYES

When, in disgrace with fortune and men's eyes,
I all alone beweep my outcast state,
And trouble deaf heaven with my bootless cries,
And look upon myself, and curse my fate,
Wishing me like to one more rich in hope,
Featured like him, like him with friends possess'd,
Desiring this man's art and that man's scope,
With what I most enjoy contented least;
Yet in these thoughts myself almost despising,
Haply I think on thee, and then my state,
Like to the lark at break of day arising
From sullen earth, sings hymns at heaven's gate;
   For thy sweet love remember'd such wealth brings
   That then I scorn to change my state with kings.

WHEN TO THE SESSIONS OF SWEET SILENT THOUGHT

When to the sessions of sweet silent thought
I summon up remembrance of things past,
I sigh the lack of many a thing I sought,
And with old woes' new wail my dear time's waste:
Then can I drown an eye, unused to flow,
For precious friends hid in death's dateless night,
And weep afresh love's long since canceled woe,
And moan the expense of many a vanish'd sight:
Then can I grieve at grievances foregone,
And heavily from woe to woe tell o'er
The sad account of fore-bemoanèd moan,
Which I new pay as if not paid before.
   But if the while I think on thee, dear friend,
   All losses are restored and sorrows end.

NOT MARBLE, NOR THE GILDED MONUMENTS

Not marble, nor the gilded monuments
Of princes, shall outlive this powerful rhyme;
But you shall shine more bright in these contents
Than unswept stone, besmear'd with sluttish time.
When wasteful war shall statues overturn,
And broils root out the work of masonry,
Nor Mars his sword nor war's quick fire shall burn
The living record of your memory.
'Gainst death and all-oblivious enmity
Shall you pace forth; your praise shall still find room
Even in the eyes of all posterity
That wear this world out to the ending doom.
    So, till the judgment that yourself arise,
    You live in this, and dwell in lovers' eyes.

TIRED WITH ALL THESE, FOR RESTFUL DEATH I CRY

Tired with all these, for restful death I cry,
As, to behold desert a beggar born,
And needy nothing trimm'd in jollity,
And purest faith unhappily forsworn,
And gilded honor shamefully misplaced,
And maiden virtue rudely strumpeted,
And right perfection wrongfully disgraced,
And strength by limping sway disablèd,
And art made tongue-tied by authority,
And folly, doctor-like, controlling skill,
And simple truth miscall'd simplicity,
And captive good attending captain ill;
    Tired with all these, from these would I be gone,
    Save that, to die, I leave my love alone.

THAT TIME OF YEAR THOU MAYST IN ME BEHOLD

That time of year thou mayst in me behold
When yellow leaves, or none, or few, do hang
Upon those boughs which shake against the cold,
Bare ruin'd choirs, where late the sweet birds sang.
In me thou see'st the twilight of such day
As after sunset fadeth in the west;

Which by and by black night doth take away,
Death's second self, that seals up all in rest.
In me thou see'st the glowing of such fire,
That on the ashes of his youth doth lie,
As the death-bed whereon it must expire,
Consumed with that which it was nourish'd by.
    This thou perceivest, which makes thy love more strong,
    To love that well which thou must leave ere long.

HOW LIKE A WINTER HATH MY ABSENCE BEEN

How like a winter hath my absence been
From thee, the pleasure of the fleeting year:
What freezings have I felt, what dark days seen!
What old December's bareness every where!
And yet this time removed was summer's time,
The teeming autumn, big with rich increase,
Bearing the wanton burthen of the prime,
Like widowed wombs after their lord's decease:
Yet this abundant issue seem'd to me
But hope of orphans and unfather'd fruit;
For summer and his pleasures wait on thee,
And, thou away, the very birds are mute;
    Or, if they sing, 'tis with so dull a cheer
    That leaves look pale, dreading the winter's near.

LET ME NOT TO THE MARRIAGE OF TRUE MINDS

Let me not to the marriage of true minds
Admit impediments. Love is not love
Which alters when it alteration finds,
Or bends with the remover to remove:
O, no; it is an ever-fixèd mark,
That looks on tempests and is never shaken;
It is the star to every wandering bark,
Whose worth's unknown, although his height be taken.
Love's not Time's fool, though rosy lips and cheeks
Within his bending sickle's compass come;
Love alters not with his brief hours and weeks,
But bears it out even to the edge of doom.
    If this be error, and upon me proved,
    I never writ, nor no man ever loved.

THE EXPENSE OF SPIRIT IN A WASTE OF SHAME

The expense of spirit in a waste of shame
Is lust in action; and till action, lust
Is perjured, murderous, bloody, full of blame,
Savage, extreme, rude, cruel, not to trust;
Enjoy'd no sooner but despisèd straight;
Past reason hunted; and no sooner had,
Past reason hated, as a swallowed bait,
On purpose laid to make the taker mad:
Mad in pursuit, and in possession so;
Had, having, and in quest to have, extreme;
A bliss in proof, and proved, a very woe;
Before a joy proposed; behind, a dream.
  All this the world well knows; yet none knows well
  To shun the heaven that leads men to this hell.

MY MISTRESS' EYES ARE NOTHING LIKE THE SUN

My mistress' eyes are nothing like the sun;
Coral is far more red than her lips' red:
If snow be white, why then her breasts are dun;
If hairs be wires, black wires grow on her head.
I have seen roses damask'd, red and white,
But no such roses see I in her cheeks;
And in some perfumes is there more delight
Than in the breath that from my mistress reeks.

I love to hear her speak, yet well I know
That music hath a far more pleasing sound:
I grant I never saw a goddess go,
My mistress, when she walks, treads on the ground:
  And yet, by heaven, I think my love as rare
  As any she belied with false compare.

POOR SOUL, THE CENTER OF MY SINFUL EARTH

Poor soul, the center of my sinful earth,
[Thrall to] these rebel powers that thee array,
Why dost thou pine within and suffer dearth,
Painting thy outward walls so costly gay?
Why so large cost, having so short a lease,
Dost thou upon thy fading mansion spend?

Shall worms, inheritors of this excess,
Eat up thy charge? is this thy body's end?
Then, soul, live thou upon thy servant's loss,
And let that pine to aggravate thy store;
Buy terms divine in selling hours of dross;
Within be fed, without be rich no more:
   So shalt thou feed on Death, that feeds on men,
   And Death once dead, there's no more dying then.

COME AWAY, COME AWAY, DEATH

Come away, come away, Death!
   And in sad cypress let me be laid;
Fly away, fly away, breath;
   I am slain by a fair cruel maid.
My shroud of white, stuck all with yew,
      O, prepare it!
My part of death, no one so true
      Did share it.

Not a flower, not a flower sweet,
   On my black coffin let there be strown;
Not a friend, not a friend greet
   My poor corpse, where my bones shall be thrown:
A thousand thousand sighs to save,
      Lay me, O where
Sad true lover never find my grave,
      To weep there!

EDMUND SPENSER

MOST GLORIOUS LORD OF LIFE

Most glorious Lord of life, that on this day
Didst make thy triumph over death and sin,
And having harrowed hell, didst bring away
Captivity thence captive, us to win:

EDMUND SPENSER (1552?-1599) served the powerful Earl of Leicester and enjoyed the friendship of Sir Philip Sidney, but, except for a secretaryship to the lord deputy of Ireland, he was unable to secure advancement in public life. He married Elizabeth Boyle, the lady of his sonnets, in 1594.

This joyous day, dear Lord, with joy begin,
And grant that we, for whom thou diddest die,
Being with thy dear blood clean washed from sin,
May live for ever in felicity:
And that thy love we weighing worthily,
May likewise love thee for the same again;
And for thy sake, that all like dear didst buy,
With love may one another entertain.
So let us love, dear love, like as we ought:
Love is the lesson which the Lord us taught.

ONE DAY I WROTE HER NAME UPON THE STRAND

One day I wrote her name upon the strand,
But came the waves and washèd it away:
Again I wrote it with a second hand,
But came the tide, and made my pains his prey.
Vain man, said she, that dost in vain essay
A mortal thing so to immortalize;
For I myself shall like to this decay,
And eke my name be wipèd out likewise.
Not so, (quod I) let baser things devise,
To die in dust, but you shall live by fame;
My verse your virtues rare shall eternize,
And in the heavens write your glorious name:
Where, whenas death shall all the world subdue,
Our love shall live, and later life renew.

FAIR IS MY LOVE

Fair is my love, when her fair golden hairs
With the loose wind ye waving chance to mark;
Fair, when the rose in her red cheeks appears,
Or in her eyes the fire of love does spark:
Fair, when her breast, like a rich laden bark,
With precious merchandise, she forth doth lay:
Fair, when that cloud of pride, which oft doth dark
Her goodly light, with smiles she drives away.
But fairest she, when so she doth display
The gate with pearls and rubies richly dight,
Through which her words so wise do make their way,
To bear the message of her gentle spright.
The rest be works of Nature's wonderment,
But this the work of heart's astonishment.

PROTHALAMION

Calm was the day, and through the trembling air
Sweet, breathing Zephyrus did softly play
A gentle spirit, that lightly did delay
Hot Titan's beams, which then did glister fair;
When I (whom sullen care,
Through discontent of my long fruitless stay
In Prince's Court, and expectation vain
Of idle hopes, which still do fly away,
Like empty shadows, did afflict my brain)
Walked forth to ease my pain
Along the shore of silver streaming Thames;
Whose rutty bank, the which his river hems,
Was painted all with variable flowers,
And all the meads adorned with dainty gems
Fit to deck maidens' bowers,
And crown their paramours,
Against the bridal day, which is not long:
   Sweet Thames! run softly, till I end my song.

There, in a meadow, by the river's side,
A flock of nymphs I chancèd to espy,
All lovely daughters of the flood thereby,
With goodly greenish locks, all loose untied,
As each had been a bride;
And each one had a little wicker basket,
Made of the twigs, entrailèd curiously,
In which they gathered flowers to fill their flasket,
And with fine fingers cropt full feateously
The tender stalks on high.
Of every sort, which in that meadow grew,
They gathered some; the violet, pallid blue,
The little daisy, that at evening closes,
The virgin lily, and the primrose true,
With store of vermeil roses,
To deck their bridegrooms' posies
Against the bridal day, which was not long:
   Sweet Thames! run softly, till I end my song.

With that I saw two swans of goodly hue
Come softly swimming down along the lea;
Two fairer birds I yet did never see;

The snow which doth the top of Pindus strew,
Did never whiter show;
Nor Jove himself, when he a swan would be
For love of Leda, whiter did appear;
Yet Leda was (they say) as white as he,
Yet not so white as these, nor nothing near;
So purely white they were,
That even the gentle stream, the which them bare,
Seemed foul to them, and bade his billows spare
To wet their silken feathers, lest they might
Soil their fair plumes with water not so fair,
And mar their beauties bright,
That shone as heaven's light,
Against their bridal day, which was not long:
  Sweet Thames! run softly, till I end my song.

Eftsoons the Nymphs, which now had flowers their fill,
Ran all in haste to see that silver brood,
As they came floating on the crystal flood;
Whom when they saw, they stood amazèd still,
Their wondering eyes to fill;
Them seemed they never saw a sight so fair,
Of fowls, so lovely, that they sure did deem
Them heavenly born, or to be that same pair
Which through the sky draw Venus' silver team;
For sure they did not seem
To be begot of any earthly seed,
But rather angels, or of angels' breed;
Yet were they bred of summer's heat, they say,
In sweetest season, when each flower and weed
The earth did fresh array;
So fresh they seemed as day,
Even as their bridal day, which was not long:
  Sweet Thames: run softly, till I end my song.

Then forth they all out of their baskets drew
Great store of flowers, the honour of the field,
That to sense did fragrant odours yield,
All which upon those goodly birds they threw
And all the waves did strew,
That like old Peneus' waters they did seem,
When down along by pleasant Tempe's shore,
Scattered with flowers, through Thessaly they stream.

That they appear, through lilies' plenteous store,
Like a bride's chamber floor.
Two of those Nymphs, meanwhile, two garlands bound
Of freshest flowers which in that mead they found,
The which presenting all in trim array,
Their snowy foreheads therewithal they crowned,
Whilst one did sing this lay,
Prepared against that day,
Against their bridal day, which was not long:
   Sweet Thames! run softly, till I end my song.

"Ye gentle birds! the world's fair ornament,
And heaven's glory, whom this happy hour
Doth lead unto your lovers' blissful bower,
Joy may you have, and gentle heart's content
Of your love's couplement;
And let fair Venus, that is queen of love,
With her heart-quelling son upon you smile,
Whose smile, they say, hath virtue to remove
All Love's dislike, and friendship's faulty guile
For ever to assoil.
Let endless Peace your steadfast hearts accord,
And blessèd Plenty wait upon your board;
And let your bed with pleasures chaste abound,
That fruitful issue may to you afford,
Which may your foes confound,
And make your joys redound
Upon your bridal day, which is not long:
   Sweet Thames! run softly, till I end my song."

So ended she; and all the rest around
To her redoubled that her undersong,
Which said their bridal day should not be long:
And gentle Echo from the neighbour ground
Their accents did resound.
So forth those joyous birds did pass along,
Adown the lea, that to them murmured low,
As he would speak, but that he lacked a tongue,
Yet did by signs his glad affection show,
Making his stream run slow.
And all the fowl which in his flood did dwell
'Gan flock about these twain, that did excel
The rest, so far as Cynthia doth shend

The lesser stars. So they, enrangèd well,
Did on those two attend,
And their best service lend
Against their wedding day, which was not long:
   Sweet Thames! run softly, till I end my song.

At length they all to merry London came,
To merry London, my most kindly nurse,
That to me gave this life's first native source,
Though from another place I take my name,
An house of ancient fame:
There when they came, whereas those bricky towers
The which on Thames' broad agèd back do ride,
Where now the studious lawyers have their bowers
There whilom wont the Templar knights to bide,
Till they decayed through pride:
Next whereunto there stands a stately place,
Where oft I gainèd gifts and goodly grace
Of that great Lord, which therein wont to dwell,
Whose want too well now feels my friendless case;
But ah! here fits not well
Old woes, but joys, to tell
Against the bridal day, which is not long:
   Sweet Thames! run softly, till I end my song.

Yet therein now doth lodge a noble peer,
Great England's glory, and the world's wide wonder,
Whose dreadful name late through all Spain did thunder,
And Hercules' two pillars standing near
Did make to quake and fear:
Fair branch of Honour, flower of Chivalry!
That fillest England with thy triumph's fame,
Joy have thou of thy noble victory,
And endless happiness of thine own name
That promiseth the same;
That through thy prowess, and victorious arms,
Thy country may be freed from foreign harms;
And great Eliza's glorious name may ring
Through all the world, filled with thy wide alarms,
Which some brave muse may sing
To ages following
Upon the bridal day, which is not long:
   Sweet Thames! run softly, till I end my song.

From those high towers this noble Lord issuing,
Like radiant Hesper, when his golden hair
In th' ocean billows he hath bathèd fair,
Descended to the river's open viewing,
With a great train ensuing.
Above the rest were goodly to be seen
Two gentle knights of lovely face and feature,
Beseeming well the bower of any queen,
With gifts of wit, and ornaments of nature,
Fit for so goodly stature,
That like the twins of Jove they seemed in sight,
Which deck the baldrick of the heavens bright;
They two, forth pacing to the river's side,
Received those two fair brides, their love's delight;
Which, at th' appointed tide,
Each one did make his bride
Against their bridal day, which is not long:
   Sweet Thames! run softly, till I end my song.

II
THE RENAISSANCE

THE PASTORAL

EXCEPT for a few isolated instances, English pastoral verse appeared first in the translations of Mantuan (an Italian imitator of Virgil's *Eclogues*) by Alexander Barclay in 1515. From that time until late in the century, only Barnabe Googe and George Turberville seriously experimented with the type. But with Spenser's *Shepheardes Calender* (1579) and Sidney's prose *Arcadia* (printed in 1590), so liberally provided with verses, pastoralism became the most widespread literary movement of the times.

As a convention, pastoralism makes of the bucolic life an ideal existence, unfettered by the tribulations of court and city, unmarred by the pursuit of glory and temptations of vice. Implicit is the notion that civilization is a corrupting force upon man; the simple shepherd's life is viewed as a means through which one may escape its debilitating forces and regain a state of innocence approximating that of a mythical "golden age." The appeal of the simple life, the lazy pace, was particularly attractive to the England of the Renaissance, for though the age was marked by progress, vigor, and expansiveness, the nation—reigned over by an aging queen without heirs and threatened by the formidable power of Spain—faced a multitude of problems.

Pastoralism had its beginnings in the Greek of Theocritus, Bion, and Moschus. Virgil brought the Latin development to its peak, and the Italians, who began to experiment with the pastoral in the Middle Ages, brought the tradition to a culmination in the sixteenth century. The English poets borrowed from all their Continental predecessors. When the tradition remained pure, it expressed itself in shepherds' singing contests, in elegies for dead friends, in praise of country lasses and country love. But in the verse of London poets like Christopher Marlowe, playing shepherd becomes an elaborate pretense; sophisticated men attempt to seduce sophisticated ladies, and the simple gifts that the foolish Giles in *Phillada Flouts Me* gives to the difficult girl are replaced by golden buckles, amber studs, and other valuable objects which no ordinary shepherd could possess.

The pastoral did more than sing of romance—whether simple or sophisticated. Because of the seeming innocence of the shepherd's diction and his boorish country thought, the form was a natural allegorical cover-up for points of view that might be dangerous to the author because of their political, theological, or moral implications. Frequently the surface pastoral is a vehicle for discussion of the burning issues of the day. Under the guise of Colin or Rowland, Meliboeus or Daphnis, the poets expressed their dismay at the behavior of the clergy or the privy council. At the safe distance of an imaginary copse in mythical Arcadia, they condemned the values of the court and the vices of the city. Although most often these intellectual concepts are submerged in the longer poems that can more easily carry their burden, such as Spenser's *Colin Clout's Come Home Again,* the short pastoral may also deal with universal concerns. Marlowe's *Passionate Shepherd to His Love* and Ralegh's *Nymph's Reply to the Shepherd* treat respectively the *carpe diem* theme of the evanescence of life and the need to live fully while there is time and the inevitable response that "fancy's spring" is "sorrow's fall."

FOR FURTHER READING:

Empson, William. *Some Versions of Pastoral.* London, 1935.
Greg, W. W. *Pastoral Poetry and Pastoral Drama.* London, 1906.
Harrison, T. P. *The Pastoral Elegy.* Austin, 1939.

ROBERT GREENE

THE SHEPHERD'S WIFE'S SONG

Ah, what is love? It is a pretty thing,
As sweet unto a shepherd as a king;
       And sweeter too:
For kings have cares that wait upon a crown,
And cares can make the sweetest love to frown.
       Ah then, ah then,
If country loves such sweet desires do gain,
What lady would not love a shepherd swain?

His flocks once folded, he comes home at night,
As merry as a king in his delight;
       And merrier too:
For kings bethink them what the state require,
Where shepherds careless carol by the fire.

ROBERT GREENE (1560?-1592), "university wit" and vagabond author, made a reputation in London as a writer of plays, prose romances, and journalistic pamphlets purporting to expose the underworld. He led a dissolute life and died penniless.

Ah then, ah then,
If country loves such sweet desires do gain,
What lady would not love a shepherd swain?

He kisseth first, then sits as blithe to eat
His cream and curds as doth the king his meat;
            And blither too:
For kings have often fears when they do sup,
Where shepherds dread no poison in their cup.
            Ah then, ah then,
If country loves such sweet desires do gain,
What lady would not love a shepherd swain?

To bed he goes, as wanton then, I ween,
As is a king in dalliance with a queen;
            More wanton too:
For kings have many griefs affects to move,
Where shepherds have no greater grief than love.
            Ah then, ah then,
If country loves such sweet desires do gain,
What lady would not love a shepherd swain?

Upon his couch of straw he sleeps as sound,
As doth the king upon his bed of down;
            More sounder too:
For cares cause kings full oft their sleep to spill,
Where weary shepherds lie and snort their fill.
            Ah then, ah then,
If country loves such sweet desires do gain,
What lady would not love a shepherd swain?

Thus with his wife he spends the year, as blithe
As does the king at every tide or sithe;
            And blither too:
For kings have wars and broils to take in hand
Where shepherds laugh and love upon the land.
            Ah then, ah then,
If country loves such sweet desires do gain,
What lady would not love a shepherd swain?

THE SHEPHERD'S WIFE'S SONG Much of the appeal of Greene's poem is in the music which comes from its varied line lengths, its repetition, and its refrain. Each stanza is composed of three iambic pentameter couplets, alternated with single short lines of iambic dimeter. The first short line in each stanza invariably takes one word from the initial couplet, alters it to the comparative form, and adds the adverb *too*:

> As sweet unto a shepherd as a king;
> And sweeter too:

The second short line—"Ah then, ah then"—unchanged throughout the poem, serves as a refrain and introduces the final couplet:

> If country loves such sweet desires do gain,
> What lady would not love a shepherd swain?

This couplet is repeated in each of the following stanzas. So much repetition would seem excessive if it were not for Greene's skillful handling, particularly his use of variations in line length.

The theme is based on a pastoral commonplace. The simple shepherd may delight in the joys of love as well as—in fact, better than—any king. In large measure the appeal of all pastoral poetry is rooted in this concept, which is called *otium*—the belief that the good life can be lived only in the simplest societies. It includes not only physical joys but also mental serenity. In Greene's poem it is the loss of this mental serenity on almost every score which reduces the king to a condition less desirable than that of the shepherd.

In each of the first four stanzas, a new state of mental anguish is introduced, and these states progress in intensity from stanza to stanza. The last two stanzas stress physical anguish. Cares give way to thoughts, thoughts to fears, and fears to griefs. All give way to severer physical penalties, loss of sleep, and finally "wars and broils." Such progression is important in a poem if anticlimax is to be avoided. But the mounting woes of kingship do not make this light and charming poem less of a *jeu d'esprit,* for opposed always to the monarch's problems are the shepherd's joys. Each stanza relaxes first into the soft refrain which is almost like a sigh and then into the repetitive final couplet which explains the shepherd's wife's contentment:

> Ah then, ah then,
> If country loves such sweet desires do gain,
> What lady would not love a shepherd swain

The Shepherd's Wife's Song belongs to a large group of poems which begin with the question, "Ah, what is love?" See, for instance, the poem by Ralegh (p. 58) and that by Peele (p. 66), and for a comic answer to the question, turn to *Phillada Flouts Me* (p. 89). Greene's somewhat more serious resolution is the real concern of his poem, and it is appropriate that while internal stanzas deal with other matters such as caroling, eating, and sleeping, the first and last stanzas, as well as a pivot-ally placed central stanza, are squarely concerned with the subject at hand—love.

The poem then has an enveloping structure. It opens and closes on the same note. But, the reader may say, we have established that there is a progression—how can the poem move forward from first to last and yet go also in a circle? The answer is, of course, that only the king's cares mount; the shepherd's joys remain constant and undiminished; together the two movements create a pleasing counterpoint.

CHRISTOPHER MARLOWE

THE PASSIONATE SHEPHERD TO HIS LOVE

Come live with me and be my Love,
And we will all the pleasures prove
That hills and valleys, dales and fields,
Or woods or steepy mountain yields.

And we will sit upon the rocks,
And see the shepherds feed their flocks
By shallow rivers, to whose falls
Melodious birds sing madrigals.

And I will make thee beds of roses
And a thousand fragrant posies,
A cap of flowers, and a kirtle
Embroidered all with leaves of myrtle;

A gown made of the finest wool,
Which from our pretty lambs we pull;
Fair-linéd slippers for the cold,
With buckles of purest gold;

A belt of straw and ivy buds,
With coral clasps and amber studs—
And if these pleasures may thee move,
Come live with me and be my Love.

CHRISTOPHER MARLOWE (1564-1593), son of a Canterbury shoemaker, attended Cambridge and became the greatest English dramatist before Shakespeare. Much mystery surrounds his brief career, but there is evidence that he may have been involved in the political intrigues of the times—perhaps as a government spy—and that his death in a tavern brawl could have been an assassination.

The shepherd swains shall dance and sing
For thy delight each May morning—
If these delights thy mind may move,
Then live with me and be my Love.

SIR WALTER RALEGH

THE NYMPH'S REPLY TO THE SHEPHERD

If all the world and love were young,
And truth in every shepherd's tongue,
These pretty pleasures might me move,
To live with thee and be thy love.

Time drives flocks from field to fold,
When rivers rage, and rocks grow cold;
And Philomel becometh dumb;
The rest complains of cares to come.

The flowers do fade, and wanton fields
To wayward Winter reckoning yields;
A honey tongue, a heart of gall,
Is fancy's spring, but sorrow's fall.

Thy gowns, thy shoes, thy bed of roses,
Thy cap, thy kirtle, and thy posies,
Soon break, soon wither, soon forgotten,
In folly ripe, in reason rotten.

Thy belt of straw and ivy buds,
Thy coral clasps and amber studs,
All these in me no means can move,
To come to thee and be thy love.

But could youth last, and love still breed,
Had joys no date, nor age no need,
Then these delights my mind might move,
To live with thee and be thy love.

NICHOLAS BRETON

PHYLLIDA AND CORYDON

In the merry month of May,
In a morn by break of day,
Forth I walked by the wood-side,
Whenas May was in his pride:
There I spiëd all alone,
Phyllida and Corydon.
Much ado there was, God wot!
He would love and she would not.
She said, Never man was true;
He said, None was false to you.
He said, he had loved her long;
She said, Love should have no wrong.
Corydon would kiss her then;
She said, maids must kiss no men,
Till they did for good and all;
Then she made the shepherd call
All the heavens to witness truth:
Never loved a truer youth.
Thus, with many a pretty oath,
Yea and nay, and faith and troth,
Such as silly shepherds use
When they will not love abuse,
Love which had been long deluded,
Was with kisses sweet concluded;
And Phyllida, with garlands gay,
Was made the Lady of the May.

WILLIAM SHAKESPEARE

WHEN DAISIES PIED

When daisies pied and violets blue
And lady-smocks all silver-white

NICHOLAS BRETON (1545?-1626?) produced a variety of writings in both poetry and prose. He is best remembered for his pastoral verse and other lyrics.

And cuckoo buds of yellow hue
   Do paint the meadows with delight,
The cuckoo then on every tree,
Mocks married men; for thus sings he,
     "Cuckoo!
Cuckoo, cuckoo!" Oh word of fear,
Unpleasing to a married ear!

When shepherds pipe on oaten straws,
   And merry larks are ploughmen's clocks,
When turtles tread, and rooks, and daws,
   And maidens bleach their summer smocks,
The cuckoo then, on every tree,
Mocks married men; for thus sings he,
     "Cuckoo!
Cuckoo, cuckoo!" Oh word of fear,
Unpleasing to a married ear!

IT WAS A LOVER AND HIS LASS

It was a lover and his lass,
   With a hey, and a ho, and a hey nonino,
That o'er the green corn-field did pass,
   In the spring time, the only pretty ring time,
When birds do sing, hey ding a ding, ding;
Sweet lovers love the spring.

Between the acres of the rye,
   With a hey, and a ho, and a hey nonino,
These pretty country folks would lie,
   In the spring time, etc.

This carol they began that hour,
   With a hey, and a ho, and a hey nonino,
How that a life was but a flower
   In the spring time, etc.

And, therefore, take the present time
   With a hey, and a ho, and a hey nonino,
For love is crowned with the prime
   In the spring time, etc.

HENRY CONSTABLE

DAMELUS' SONG TO HIS DIAPHENIA

Diaphenia, like the daffadowndilly,
White as the sun, fair as the lily,
 Heighho, how I do love thee!
I do love thee as my lambs
Are beloved of their dams:
How blest were I if thou wouldst prove me!

Diaphenia, like the spreading roses,
That in thy sweets all sweets encloses,
 Fair sweet, how I do love thee!
I do love thee as each flower
Loves the sun's live-giving power;
 For dead, thy breath to life might move me.

Diaphenia, like to all things blessed,
When all thy praises are expressed,
 Dear joy, how I do love thee!
As the birds do love the Spring,
Or the bees their careful king:
 Then in requite, sweet virgin, love me!

RICHARD BARNFIELD

PHILOMEL

As it fell upon a day
In the merry month of May,
Sitting in a pleasant shade
Which a grove of myrtles made,
Beasts did leap and birds did sing,
Trees did grow and plants did spring;
Everything did banish moan
Save the Nightingale alone;

RICHARD BARNFIELD (1574-1627), still another writer of pastorals, odes, and sonnets, had the distinction of producing poems that were long thought to be the work of Shakespeare.

She, poor bird, as all forlorn,
Lean'd her breast against a thorn,
And there sung the dolefull'st ditty,
That to hear it was great pity.
Fie, fie, fie! now would she cry;
Teru, teru! by-and-by.
That to hear her so complain
Scarce I could from tears refrain;
For her griefs so lively shown
Made me think upon mine own.
Ah, thought I, thou mourn'st in vain,
None takes pity on thy pain.
Senseless trees, they cannot hear thee;
Ruthless beasts, they will not cheer thee;
King Pandion he is dead,
All thy friends are lapp'd in lead;
All thy fellow birds do sing,
Careless of thy sorrowing;
Whilst as fickle fortune smiled,
Thou and I were both beguiled.
Every one that flatters thee
Is no friend in misery:
Words are easy, like the wind,
Faithful friends are hard to find;
Every man will be thy friend
Whilst thou hast wherewith to spend,
But if store of crowns be scant,
No man will supply thy want.
If that one be prodigal,
Bountiful they will him call;
And with such-like flattering
Pity but he were a king.
If he be addict to vice,
Quickly him they will entice;
If to women he be bent,
They have at commandëment;
But if fortune once do frown,
Then farewell his great renown;
They that fawned on him before
Use his company no more.
He that is thy friend indeed
He will help thee in thy need:
If thou sorrow, he will weep;

If thou wake, he cannot sleep;
Thus of every grief, in heart,
He with thee doth bear a part.
These are certain signs to know
Faithful friend from flatt'ring foe.

ANONYMOUS

PHILLADA FLOUTS ME

O what a plague is love!
How shall I bear it?
She will inconstant prove,
I greatly fear it.
She so torments my mind
That my strength faileth,
And wavers with the wind
As a ship saileth.
Please her the best I may,
She loves still to gainsay;
Alack and well-a-day!
    Phillada flouts me.

At the fair yesterday
She did pass by me;
She looked another way
And would not spy me:
I wooed her for to dine,
But could not get her;
Will had her to the wine—
He might entreat her.
With Daniel she did dance,
On me she looked askance:
O thrice unhappy chance!
    Phillada flouts me.

Fair maid, be not so coy,
Do not disdain me!
I am my mother's joy:
Sweet, entertain me!
She'll give me, when she dies,

All that is fitting:
Her poultry and her bees,
And her goose sitting,
A pair of mattress beds,
And a bag full of shreds;
And yet, for all this guedes,
   Phillada flouts me!

She hath a clout of mine
Wrought with blue coventry,
Which she keeps for a sign
Of my fidelity.
But i' faith, if she flinch
She shall not wear it;
To Tib, my t'other wench,
I mean to bear it.
And yet it grieves my heart
So soon from her to part:
Death strikes me with his dart!
   Phillada flouts me.

Thou shalt eat crudded cream
All the year lasting,
And drink the crystal stream
Pleasant in tasting;
Whig and whey whilst thou lust,
And bramble-berries,
Pie-lid and pastey-crust,
Pears, plums, and cherries.
Thy raiment shall be thin,
Made of a weevil's skin—
Yet all's not worth a pin!
   Phillada flouts me.

In the last month of May
I made her posies;
I heard her often say
That she loved roses.
Cowslips and gillyflowers
And the white lily
I brought to deck the bowers
For my sweet Philly.
But she did all disdain,

And threw them back again;
Therefore 'tis flat and plain
  Phillada flouts me.

Fair maiden, have a care,
And in time take me;
I can have those as fair,
If you forsake me.
For Doll the dairy-maid
Laughed at me lately,
And wanton Winifred
Favours me greatly.
One throws milk on my clothes,
T' other plays with my nose;
What wanting signs are those?
  Phillada flouts me.

I cannot work nor sleep
At all in season:
Love wounds my heart so deep
Without all reason.
I 'gin to pine away
In my love's shadow,
Like as a fat beast may,
Penned in a meadow.
I shall be dead, I fear,
Within this thousand year:
And all for that my dear
  Phillada flouts me.

II

THE RENAISSANCE

THE DEVOTIONAL

I N an age of political and social expansion, with the growth of a variety of secular interests fostered by the impact upon English thought of French and Italian humanism, it is not surprising to find a considerable lessening in the bulk of devotional poetry. Poetry had been an ideal medium for expression of the earlier relationship of man to God, but prose appeared to be better for the expression of the new questioning spirit. It has been estimated that two fifths of all the prose written from the beginning of the English Reformation under Henry VIII to the death of Elizabeth was on religious matters, most of it devoted to the claims and counterclaims of opposing religious factions. There was some poetry in this vein as well, including the May, July, and September eclogues of Spenser's *Shepheardes Calender* and some parts of *The Faerie Queene*, but the amount was relatively small.

Still, many writers, in moments of awesome fear or guilty awareness of their sinful condition or out of simple, genuine love for God, turn to the solace of their faith and give us, in the briefer lyric forms, profoundly moving expressions of religious passion. These three emotions, then—fear, guilt, serenity—may figure in any system of classifying the religious verse of the age. Thomas Nashe's *In Plague Time* gives stark recognition to the slender thread by which life hung in an age when plagues devastated the land with horrifying frequency. Robert Southwell's *Upon the Image of Death* belongs to a type that is one with Nashe's; both reveal a fascination with physical decay which Renaissance poetry carried on from the Middle Ages and which becomes even more prominent in the seventeenth-century poems of John Donne.

Feelings of guilt lead to longings for virtue. The sinner seeks to mend his ways in order to escape eternal damnation. John Skelton's *Upon a Dead Man's Head,* Lord Vaux' *I Loathe That I Did Love,* and Sir Philip Sidney's *Leave Me, O Love* deal with the contemplations of once amorous courtiers as they realize that they have placed their love of woman before their love of God.

In the verse wherein the poet affirms that, for him, death holds no terror, we find secure belief that the soul is destined for heaven, where it will be much better off than the body ever can be among the vicissitudes of this world. Ralegh's *Passionate Man's Pilgrimage,* composed, according to tradition, in the Tower of London before the poet's reprieve from execution in 1603, illustrates the calm that the poet has reached through contemplation of his arrival in paradise. Southwell's *I Die Alive* expresses the fervent faith of a Jesuit priest who has been hunted down, tried, and tortured and now awaits death by hanging with joyful anticipation. It is not surprising to find such faith expressed by the author of *The Burning Babe,* a piece that goes back almost to medieval ways of thought in its devout and unsophisticated adoration.

FOR FURTHER READING:

Campbell, L. B. *Divine Poetry and Drama in Sixteenth-Century England.* Berkeley, Calif., 1959.

Devlin, Christopher. *The Life of Robert Southwell, Poet and Martyr.* New York, 1956.

Guiney, L. I. *Recusant Poets.* New York, 1938.

JOHN SKELTON

UPON A DEAD MAN'S HEAD

Sent to him from an honourable gentlewoman for a token, he devised this ghostly meditation in English covenable, in sentence commendable, lamentable, lacrimable, profitable for a soul.

> Your ugly token
> My mind hath broken
> From wordly lust:
> For I have discust
> We are but dust
> And die we must.
>   It is general
> To be mortal:
> I have well espied
> No man may him hide
> From Death hollow-eyed,
> With sinews witherèd,
> With bonès shiverèd,
> With his worm-eaten maw,

JOHN SKELTON (1460?-1529) served as tutor to Prince Henry, the future Henry VIII. He became rector of Diss in Norfolk but maintained his connections at court. He was noted as a bitter satirist and in his last years made Cardinal Wolsey the particular object of his attacks.

And his ghastly jaw
Gasping aside,
Naked of hide,
Neither flesh nor fell.
    Then, by my counsell,
Look that ye spell
Well this gospell:
For whereso we dwell
Death will us quell,
And with us mell.
    For all our pampered paunches
There may no fraunchis,
Nor worldly bliss,
Redeem us from this:
Our days be dated
To be check-mated
With draughtès of death
Stopping our breath:
Our eyen sinking,
Our bodies stinking,
Our gummès grinning,
Our soulès brinning.
To whom, then, shall we sue,
For to have rescue,
But to sweet Jesu
On us then for to rue?
    O goodly Child
Of Mary mild,
Then be our shield!
That we be not exiled
To the dyn dale
Of bootless bale,
Nor to the lake
Of fiendès blake.
    But grant us grace
To see thy Face,
And to purchase
Thine heavenly place,
And thy palace
Full of solace
Above the sky
That is so high,
Eternally

To behold and see
The Trinitie!
　　　Amen.
Myrres vous y.

THOMAS, LORD VAUX

I LOATHE THAT I DID LOVE

I loathe that I did love;
In youth that I thought sweet,
As time requires for my behove,
Me thinks they are not meet.

My lusts they do me leave,
My fancies all be fled,
And tract of time begins to weave
Gray hairs upon my head.

For age, with stealing steps,
Hath clawed me with his crutch;
And lusty life away she leaps
As there had been none such.

My muse doth not delight
Me as she did before,
My hand and pen are not in plight
As they have been of yore.

For reason me denies
This youthly idle rhyme,
And day by day to me she cries,
Leave off these toys in time!

The wrinkles in my brow,
The furrows in my face,
Say limping age will hedge him now
Where youth must give him place.

The harbinger of death,
To me I see him ride;
The cough, the cold, the gasping breath,
Doth bid me to provide

A pickaxe and a spade,

THOMAS, LORD VAUX (1510-1556) was one of the "courtly makers" of Henry VIII's reign. Most of his work is lost, but it is clear that among contemporaries he ranked only slightly below Wyatt and Surrey.

And eke a shrouding sheet;
A house of clay for to be made
For such a guest most meet.
   Me thinks I hear the clerk
That knolls the careful knell,
And bids me leave my woeful work
Ere nature me compel.
   My keepers knit the knot
That youth did laugh to scorn;
Of me that clean shall be forgot
As I had not been born.
   Thus must I youth give up,
Whose badge I long did wear;
To them I yield the wanton cup
That better may it bear.
   Lo, here the barëd skull
By whose bald sign I know
That stooping age away shall pull
Which youthful years did sow.
   For beauty, with her band,
These crooked cares hath wrought,
And shippëd me into the land
From whence I first was brought.
   And ye that bide behind,
Have ye none other trust;
As ye of clay were cast by kind,
So shall ye waste to dust.

SIR PHILIP SIDNEY

LEAVE ME, O LOVE, WHICH REACHEST BUT TO DUST

Leave me, O love, which reachest but to dust,
And thou, my mind, aspire to higher things;
Grow rich in that which never taketh rust,
Whatever fades but fading pleasure brings.
Draw in thy beams, and humble all thy might
To that sweet yoke where lasting freedoms be;
Which breaks the clouds and opens forth the light,
That doth both shine and give us sight to see.
O take fast hold; let that light be thy guide

In this small course which birth draws out to death,
And think how evil becometh him to slide,
Who seeketh heav'n, and comes of heav'nly breath.
  Then farewell, world; thy uttermost I see;
  Eternal Love, maintain thy life in me.

ROBERT SOUTHWELL

UPON THE IMAGE OF DEATH

Before my face the picture hangs
  That daily should put me in mind
Of those cold names and bitter pangs
  That shortly I am like to find;
But yet, alas, full little I
  Do think hereon that I must die.
I often look upon a face
  Most ugly, grisly, bare, and thin;
I often view the hollow place
  Where eyes and nose had sometimes been;
I see the bones across that lie,
  Yet little think that I must die.
I read the label underneath,
  That telleth me whereto I must;
I see the sentence eke that saith
  Remember, man, that thou are dust!
But yet, alas, but seldom I
  Do think indeed that I must die.
Continually at my bed's head
  A hearse doth hang, which doth me tell
That I ere morning may be dead,
  Though now I feel myself full well;
But yet, alas, for all this, I
  Have little mind that I must die.
The gown which I do use to wear,
  The knife wherewith I cut my meat,
And eke that old and ancient chair

ROBERT SOUTHWELL (1561?-1595) was educated abroad and became a Jesuit priest. Sent back to England at his own request, he administered to English Catholics in defiance of the law. He was finally arrested, imprisoned for three years, and then executed.

Which is my only usual seat,—
All those do tell me I must die,
And yet my life amend not I.
My ancestors are turned to clay,
    And many of my mates are gone;
My youngers daily drop away,
    And can I think to 'scape alone?
No, no, I know that I must die,
    And yet my life amend not I.
Not Solomon for all his wit,
    Nor Samson, though he were so strong,
No king nor person ever yet
    Could 'scape but death laid him along;
Wherefore I know that I must die,
    And yet my life amend not I.
Though all the East did quake to hear
    Of Alexander's dreadful name,
And all the West did likewise fear
    To hear of Julius Caesar's fame,
Yet both by death in dust now lie;
    Who then can 'scape but he must die?
If none can 'scape death's dreadful dart,
    If rich and poor his beck obey,
If strong, if wise, if all do smart,
    Then I to 'scape shall have no way.
Oh, grant me grace, O God, that I
    My life may mend, sith I must die.

THE BURNING BABE

As I in hoary winter's night stood shivering in the snow,
Surprised I was with sudden heat which made my heart to glow;
And lifting up a fearful eye to view what fire was near,
A pretty babe all burning bright did in the air appear,
Who, scorchèd with exceeding heat such floods of tears did shed,
As though His floods should quench His flames with what His tears were
        fed:
"Alas!" quoth He, "but newly born in fiery heats I fry,
Yet none approach to warm their hearts or feel my fire but I!
My faultless breast the furnace is, the fuel wounding thorns;
Love is the fire and sighs the smoke, the ashes shame and scorns;
The fuel Justice layeth on, and Mercy blows the coals;
The metal in this furnace wrought are men's defilèd souls;

For which, as now on fire I am, to work them to their good,
So will I melt into a bath, to wash them in my blood:"
With this He vanished out of sight, and swiftly shrunk away,
And straight I called unto mind that it was Christmas-day.

I DIE ALIVE

O life! what lets thee from a quick decease?
O death! what draws thee from a present prey?
My feast is done, my soul would be at ease,
My grace is said, O death! come take away.

I live, but such a life as ever dies;
I die, but such a death as never ends;
My death to end my dying life denies,
And life my living death no wit amends.

Thus still I die, yet still I do revive;
My living death by dying life is fed;
Grace more than nature keeps my heart alive,
Whose idle hopes and vain desires are dead.

Not where I breath, but where I love, I live;
Not where I love, but where I am, I die;
The life I wish, must future glory give,
The deaths I feel in present dangers lie.

I DIE ALIVE Southwell's poem might be said almost to come from the tomb, for it is written by a man himself at the point of death. Imprisoned for treason and soon to be executed for practicing his faith in violation of the law, Southwell writes as one confident of salvation. He achieves an intensity of religious feeling which may be found also in Ralegh's *Passionate Man's Pilgrimage* (p. 102) and Donne's *Hymn to God, My God in My Sickness* (p. 164). It is not often that men who are about to die have the ability and the inclination to write poetry in their extremity; the real imminence of death, which gives this poem its emotional power, also makes it one of the most remarkable in literature.

I Die Alive is built upon the most fundamental of all antitheses—life and death—and is concerned with the paradox expressed in the title. To emphasize the antithesis, it employs a formal and balanced rhetoric common in Elizabethan verse. One might suppose that this artificiality would interfere with the naturalness and intensity of the emotional expression; but instead of inhibiting the emotion, the rhetoric in *I Die Alive* is the device by which we experience more readily the anguish of the poet.

Although the metrical regularity of the poem is quickly apparent, an otherwise almost unbroken cadence is disturbed at the outset by the two sets of double spondees (see glossary) in the first two lines: "O life! what lets" (hinders) and "O death! what draws." Some prosodists might insist that these are iambics (and it should be observed here that scansion not infrequently can be debated), but such a reading disregards the poet's intention. These four opening syllables carry a great deal of the poem's emotion. First we are moved by the conjunction of the lamenting *O* with the word *life,* ordinarily a word associated with joy. Then our pity is developed by the paradoxical request that life be taken quickly away. The long soul-fed plea for death which follows is designed to put us in the same state of suffering as the poet. Continued life is tedious, and this seeming endlessness of a weary existence is echoed in the near-perfect iambic measure of the rest of the poem. Only at one place is the regularity of the meter noticeably broken: "Grace more than nature" in the third quatrain. The trochaic foot here is used to emphasize the important word *grace,* the only benediction the poet craves. He will not commit suicide and thus remove himself from a state of grace and lose the paradise he seeks. Grace is the one spark which is capable of starting him out of his deep despair, and the unique quality of this power is appropriately mirrored in the shift of meter.

The word *grace* is used with another common meaning in the last line of the first quatrain—as the prayer said at a meal. The feast image is crucial to the poem. Allegorically the feast is life, and Southwell's life is really over. It remains only for death, the servant, to "take away" (clear away the dishes)—i.e., to come and put the actual seal upon his now living death. In some religious practices grace is said after the meal instead of, or as well as, before it. Southwell has made his final act of contrition, and he stands in a state of grace. He is prepared for death to take away. We may also take the feast as associated with the sacrament of Communion. The very act of feasting here places the communicant in a state of grace, and thus grace follows the feast.

Southwell achieves his greatest tension (see glossary) in this poem through the paradox implied in the feast image. He wishes the banquet to end. All the joy, the festivity, the life which we associate normally with feasting is denied. Instead, through the mystical sacrament of Communion, especially in the sense of *last* supper, Southwell looks forward to dining with Christ in Heaven (compare George Herbert's *Love,* p. 169). But this tension, inherent in the single symbol, is extended by use of the feast image in other places as well. In the second line of the poem, through the carrion image of "present prey," Southwell seems to be inviting death to join him in a grisly dinner, at which, we might say with Hamlet, he is "not where he eats, but where he is eaten."

That death will be the only one left at the close of the meal is suggested through the end of the fourth line: "O death! come take away." By splitting the two appeals to death with the life-feast image, Southwell draws the two contrasting feasts brilliantly into relation with one another. But neither of these feasts is over, though the poet has cried, "My feast is done." In the third stanza we are reminded that his "living death by dying life is fed," the antitheses here being neatly stressed. And as he has to deny that his "feast is done," so also he must modify the claim that his "grace is said." Since living death continues, the attempt to remain in a state of grace must be the never ceasing labor of the poet, for there are great *dangers* that, through lapsing into despair, he will go from a state of grace to one of reprobation and thus lose his salvation-feast.

Finally, it must be pointed out that the paradox of the title, *I Die Alive*, carried out so well in the imagery of the poem, is furthered also by the rhymes. Almost every line ending sustains the tension fostered by antithesis through the use of loosely alternating words which may be associated with life or death. Separating these into two categories, in the first we might list the life words *ease, amends, revive, fed, alive, give;* in the second are the death words *decease, prey, take away, dies, ends, denies, dead, die, lie*. This deliberate paralleling of opposites accounts for all sixteen endings, although *give* in the first group and *lie* in the second admittedly are weak.

THOMAS NASHE

IN PLAGUE TIME

Adieu, farewell earth's bliss,
This world uncertain is;
Fond are life's lustful joys,
Death proves them all but toys,
None from his darts can fly.
I am sick, I must die.
     Lord, have mercy on us!

Rich men, trust not in wealth,
Gold cannot buy you health;
Physic himself must fade,

THOMAS NASHE (1567-1601), as one of the most brilliant satirists of his age, won great reputation for the prose pamphlets he directed against his enemies. One of the "university wits," he is best remembered today for his racy picaresque romance *The Unfortunate Traveller*.

All things to end are made.
The plague full swift goes by;
I am sick, I must die.
      Lord, have mercy on us!

Beauty is but a flower
Which wrinkles will devour:
Brightness falls from the air,
Queens have died young and fair,
Dust hath closed Helen's eye.
I am sick, I must die.
      Lord, have mercy on us!

Strength stoops unto the grave,
Worms feed on Hector brave,
Swords may not fight with fate.
Earth still holds ope her gate;
Come! come! the bells do cry.
I am sick, I must die.
      Lord, have mercy on us!

Wit with his wantonness
Tasteth death's bitterness;
Hell's executioner
Hath no ears for to hear
What vain art can reply.
I am sick, I must die.
      Lord, have mercy on us!

Haste, therefore, each degree,
To welcome destiny.
Heaven is our heritage,
Earth but a player's stage;
Mount we unto the sky.
I am sick, I must die.
      Lord, have mercy on us!

SIR WALTER RALEGH

THE PASSIONATE MAN'S PILGRIMAGE

Give me my scallop-shell of quiet,
My staff of faith to walk upon,

My scrip of joy, immortal diet,
My bottle of salvation,
My gown of glory, hope's true gage;
And thus I'll take my pilgrimage.

Blood must be my body's balmer;
No other balm will there be given;
Whilst my soul, like a quiet palmer,
Travelleth towards the land of heaven,
Over the silver mountains,
Where spring the nectar fountains.
There will I kiss
The bowl of bliss;
And drink mine everlasting fill
Upon every milken hill.
My soul will be a-dry before;
But, after, it will thirst no more.

Then by that happy blissful day
More peaceful pilgrims I shall see,
That have cast off their rags of clay,
And walk apparelled fresh like me.
I'll take them first,
To quench their thirst
And taste of nectar suckets,
At those clear wells
Where sweetness swells,
Drawn up by saints in crystal buckets.

And when our bottles and all we
Are filled with immortality,
Then the blessed paths we'll travel,
Strewed with rubies thick as gravel;
Ceilings of diamonds, sapphire floors,
High walls of coral, and pearly bowers.

From thence to heaven's bribeless hall,
Where no corrupted voices brawl;
No conscience molten into gold;
Nor forged accuser bought or sold;
No cause deferred, no vain-spent journey,
For there Christ is the king's attorney,
Who pleads for all, without degrees,

And he hath angels but no fees.
And when the grand twelve million jury
Of our sins, with direful fury,
Against our souls black verdicts give,
Christ pleads his death; and then we live.

Be Thou my speaker, taintless pleader!
Unblotted lawyer! true proceeder!
Thou giv'st salvation, even for alms,
Not with a bribèd lawyer's palms.
And this is mine enternal plea
To Him that made heaven and earth and sea:
That, since my flesh must die so soon,
And want a head to dine next noon,
Just at the stroke, when my veins start and spread,
Set on my soul an everlasting head!
Then am I ready, like a palmer fit,
To tread those blest paths; which before I writ.

Of death and judgment, heaven and hell,
Who oft doth think, must needs die well.

II

THE RENAISSANCE

THE NATIVE SURVIVAL

W HILE the English Renaissance is a period of new directions in poetry, with bold experimentation in metrical forms and assiduous
adaptation of poetic modes made popular in France and Italy, it also carries a poetic heritage from medieval England. This is a heritage generally
unmarked by the sophisticated artistry of the Continental Renaissance.
Native English prosody survives in the widely popular "Poulter's Measure"
stanza of alternating seven- and six-foot lines, itself a development from
the "fourteener," the origin of the ballad stanza as well. Poetry in these
measures is usually crude, but it could also achieve aesthetic excellence.

The most important of the native survivals in the sixteenth century is
the ballad. This is a form of popular narrative poetry which has always
been a part of oral tradition, passing by word of mouth from singer to
singer and from generation to generation. Its origins are obscure, but
there is at least one example dating from the thirteenth century, and we
know that it had fully emerged by the end of the Middle English period.
Ballads continued to be written in great quantities throughout the sixteenth
and seventeenth centuries, with the Elizabethan as probably the greatest
age of original English balladry.

Although there is great diversity among surviving English ballads, all
share certain characteristics which make the form distinctive. The ballad
is, to begin with, a narrative poem comprised of simple stanzas, the most
common variety being the four-line quatrain rhyming *abcb,* with alternating four- and three-stress lines. This is illustrated in *Sir Patrick Spens,
The Wife of Usher's Well,* and *The Daemon Lover.* There are simple
variations of this basic form in *The Twa Corbies* and *Kemp Owyne,*
where a recurring refrain is added to some of the stanzas and where there
is considerable embellishment by means of internal rhyme. Another common ballad form is the question-and-answer stanzaic arrangement of
Edward, Edward and *The Three Ravens.* In the latter we find also the
"Downe a downe" kind of refrain, which recurs in every stanza and which
may have been sung by the original audience gathered about the minstrel.

The ballad story usually involves a single striking episode, the events
being conveyed by bare suggestion rather than direct statement. Each stanza is usually a brief scene presented without comment—often in the form
of unintroduced dialogue—with incremental repetition (see glossary) as
a primary means of emphasis. With no transition between stanzas, a high
degree of narrative and poetic economy is achieved. The ballad method is
essentially dramatic rather than expository.

Since the ballad is of folk origin and survives through folk transmission, its subject matter tends to consist of things most likely to interest simple people. Murder is a common theme, particularly unnatural murder as in *Edward, Edward* and in *The Twa Corbies,* where it is combined with another common theme, marital infidelity. There are many ballads on the tragedies of betrayal and unrequited love. Shipwrecks are a common subject also, as in *Sir Patrick Spens* and *The Wife of Usher's Well;* and in the latter, as in *The Daemon Lover,* we have concern with the supernatural and the simple pathos of the mother mourning for her sons, often repeated in ballad literature. In an age when the law stood frequently for oppression, there were many ballads on outlaw heroes—there are more extant ballads about Robin Hood than about any other single subject—and this interest has survived in modern balladry in the celebrations in verse of Jesse James and Billy the Kid. Border feuds, folk heroes, historic battles—all are grist for the ballad maker, and we must not neglect what is perhaps best illustrated in *Kemp Owyne*: the folk lore motifs which have been enshrined in the fairy tales of every land.

Because they are folk literature, recited by illiterate people—though often written by highly sophisticated artists—and carried on through oral transmission, ballads are of unstable form. The best of them exist in hundreds of versions. They are reshaped by various tellers, altered to conform to changing social conditions and changing locales. It is not unusual even today to hear an uneducated American mountain woman sing a ballad which can be traced back to a fifteenth-century Scottish original but which through subtle transformation has become a story of the American Civil War or of a murder in nineteenth-century Tennessee.

FOR FURTHER READING:

Child, F. J. *The English and Scottish Popular Ballads.* Boston, 1883-1898.
Gerould, G. H. *The Ballad of Tradition.* Oxford, 1932.
Graves, R. *The English Ballad.* London, 1927.

ANONYMOUS

EDWARD, EDWARD

"Why dois your brand sae drap wi bluid,
Edward, Edward?

Why dois your brand sae drap wi bluid,
   And why sae sad gang yee O?"
"O I hae killed my hauke sae guid,

         Mither, mither,

O I hae killed my hauke sae guid,
   And I had nae mair bot hee O."

"Your haukis bluid was nevir sae reid,

         Edward, Edward,

Your haukis bluid was nevir sae reid,
    My deir son I tell thee O."
"O I hae killed my reid-roan steid,

         Mither, mither,

O I hae killed my reid-roan steid,
    That erst was sae fair and frie O."

"Your steid was auld, and ye hae gat mair,

         Edward, Edward,

Your steid was auld, and ye hae gat mair,
    Sum other dule ye drie O."
"Oh I hae killed my fadir deir,

         Mither, mither,

O I hae killed my fadir deir,
    Alas, and wae is mee O!"

"And whatten penance wul ye drie for that,

         Edward, Edward,

And whatten penance wul ye drie for that?
    My deir son, now tell me O."
"Ile set my feit in yonder boat,

         Mither, mither,

Ile set my feit in yonder boat,
    And Ile fare ovir the sea O."

"And what wul ye doe wi your towirs and your ha,

         Edward, Edward?

And what wul ye doe wi your towirs and your ha,
   That were sae fair to see O?"
"Ile let thame stand tul they doun fa,

         Mither, mither,

"Ile let thame stand tul they doun fa,
    For here nevir mair maun I bee O."

"And what wul ye leive to your bairns and your wife,
                              Edward, Edward?
And what wul ye leive to your bairns and your wife,
       Whan ye gang ovir the sea O?"
"The warldis room, late them beg thrae life,
                              Mither, mither,
The warldis room, late them beg thrae life,
       For thame nevir mair wul I see O."

"And what wul ye leive to your ain mither deir,
                              Edward, Edward?
And what wul ye leive to your ain mither deir?
       My deir son, now tell me O."
"The curse of hell frae me sall ye beir,
                              Mither, mither,
"The curse of hell frae me sall ye beir,
       Sic counseils ye gave to me O."

THE TWA CORBIES

As I was walking all alane,
I heard twa corbies making a mane;
The tane unto the t' other say,
"Where sall we gang and dine to-day?"

"In behint yon auld fail dyke,
I wot there lies a new-slain knight;
And naebody kens that he lies there,
But his hawk, his hound, and lady fair.

"His hound is to the hunting gane,
His hawk to fetch the wild-fowl hame,
His lady's ta'en another mate,
So we may mak our dinner sweet.

"Ye'll sit on his white hause-bane,
And I'll pike out his bonny blue een;
Wi'ae lock o' his gowden hair
We'll theek our nest when it grows bare.

"Mony a one for him makes mane,
But nane sall ken where he is gane;
O'er his white banes, when they are bare,
The wind sall blaw for evermair."

THE THREE RAVENS

There were three ravens sat on a tree,
   Downe a downe, hay downe, hay downe
There were three ravens sat on a tree,
    With a downe
There were three ravens sat on a tree,
They were as blacke as they might be.
    With a downe derrie, derrie, derrie, downe, downe.

The one of them said to his mate,
"Where shall we our breakfast take?"

"Downe in yonder greene field,
There lies a knight slain under his shield;

"His hounds they lie downe at his feete,
So well they can their master keepe;

"His haukes they flie so eagerly,
There's no fowle dare him come nigh."

Downe there comes a fallow doe,
As great with yong as she might goe.

She lift up his bloudy hed,
And kist his wounds that were so red.

She got him up upon her backe,
And carried him to earthen lake.

She buried him before the prime,
She was dead herselfe ere even-song time.

God send every gentleman,
Such haukes, such hounds, and such a leman.

THE WIFE OF USHER'S WELL

   There lived a wife at Usher's Well,
     And a wealthy wife was she;
   She had three stout and stalwart sons,
     And sent them o'er the sea.

They hadna been a week from her,
 A week but barely ane,
Whan word came to the carlin wife
 That her three sons were gane.

They hadna been a week from her,
 A week but barely three,
Whan word came to the carlin wife
 That her sons she'd never see.

"I wish the wind may never cease,
 Nor fashes in the flood,
Till my three sons come hame to me,
 In earthly flesh and blood."

It fell about the Martinmass,
 When nights are lang and mirk,
The carlin wife's three sons came home,
 And their hats were o' the birk.

It neither grew in syke nor ditch,
 Nor yet in ony sheugh;
But at the gates o' Paradise,
 That birk grew fair eneugh.

"Blow up the fire, my maidens,
 Bring water from the well;
For a' my house shall feast this night,
 Since my three sons are well."

And she has made to them a bed,
 She's made it large and wide,
And she's taen her mantle her about,
 Sat down at the bed-side.

Up then crew the red, red cock,
 And up and crew the gray;
The eldest to the youngest said,
 " 'Tis time we were away."

The cock he hadna crawd but once,
 And clapp'd his wings at a',
When the youngest to the eldest said,
 "Brother, we must awa."

"The cock doth craw, the day doth daw,
 The channerin worm doth chide;
Gin we be mist out o' our place,
 A sair pain we maun bide.

"Fare ye weel, my mother dear!
 Fareweel to barn and byre!
And fare ye weel, the bonny lass
 That kindles my mother's fire!"

KEMP OWYNE

Her mother died when she was young,
 Which gave her cause to make great moan;
Her father married the warst woman
 That ever lived in Christendom.

She served her with foot and hand,
 In every thing that she could dee,
Till once, in an unlucky time,
 She threw her in ower Craigy's sea.

Says, "Lie you there, dove Isabel,
 And all my sorrows lie with thee;
Till Kemp Owyne come over the sea,
 And borrow you with kisses three:
Let all the warld do what they will,
 Oh borrowed shall you never be."

Her breath grew strang, her hair grew lang,
 And twisted thrice about the tree,
And all the people, far and near,
 Thought that a savage beast was she.

These news did come to Kemp Owyne,
 Where he lived, far beyond the sea;
He hasted him to Craigy's sea,
 And on the savage beast looked he.

Her breath was strang, her hair was lang,
 And twisted was about the tree,
And with a swing she came about:
 "Come to Craigy's sea, and kiss with me.

"Here is a royal belt," she cried,
   "That I have found in the green sea;
And while your body it is on,
   Drawn shall your blood never be;
But if you touch me, tail or fin,
   I vow my belt your death shall be."

He stepped in, gave her a kiss,
   The royal belt he brought him wi';
Her breath was strang, her hair was lang,
   And twisted twice about the tree,
And with a swing she came about:
   "Come to Craigy's sea, and kiss with me.

"Here is a royal ring," she said,
   "That I have found in the green sea;
And while your finger it is on,
   Drawn shall your blood never be;
But if you touch me, tail or fin,
   I swear my ring your death shall be."

He stepped in, gave her a kiss,
   The royal ring he brought him wi';
Her breath was strang, her hair was lang,
   And twisted ance about the tree,
And with a swing she came about:
   "Come to Craigy's sea, and kiss with me.

"Here is a royal brand," she said,
   "That I have found in the green sea;
And while your body it is on,
   Drawn shall your blood never be;
But if you touch me, tail or fin,
   I swear my brand your death shall be."

He stepped in, gave her a kiss,
   The royal brand he brought him wi';
Her breath was sweet, her hair grew short,
   And twisted nane about the tree,
And smilingly she came about,
   As fair a woman as fair could be.

KEMP OWYNE This ballad is of interest because it combines the celebration of a legendary hero with an ancient tale that appears in various

forms in almost every European language. Kemp Owyne was a warrior hero of ancient Wales, known also as Ewein (or Owain) ap Urien, the king of Reged. His exploits are sung by the Welsh bards Taliesin and Llywarch-Hen, and he is referred to in the Welsh historical triads. In this ballad he appears as the hero of a "Loathly Lady" story, a folk motif which Chaucer adapted in his *Wife of Bath's Tale* and which appears in variant forms in such fairy lore as *Sleeping Beauty* and *Beauty and the Beast*. In more recent poetry it appears in William Morris' *Lady of the Land.* It is the legend of the beautiful and virtuous young girl transformed by enchantment into a monster and then rescued by the lover who is undaunted by the horror of her transformation. In telling his story the anonymous author of *Kemp Owyne* captures the magical quality of the fairy tale.

In the opening stanza the author immediately establishes the familiar folk situation of the wicked stepmother (as in the Cinderella story). The plight of the overworked daughter is presented with utmost economy. Tight structure is achieved—and the transformation of the girl made explicit—by reference to *foot* and *hand* in the second stanza, to *tail* and *fin* in later stanzas. The reverse order (*foot* before *hand,* rather than *hand* before *foot*) is preserved in *tail* before *fin,* making the deliberate parallel clear. The second quatrain culminates in the enchantment. There is no need for the poet to explain why Isabel is thrown into Craigy's sea (presumably a lake or pond familiar to the people of the region where the ballad originated), for it is in the nature of folklore stepmothers to do such things.

The third stanza takes on a new rhyme scheme and structure as the terms of the enchantment are made clear. It is axiomatic in folklore that for every enchantment there must be a release. Isabel can be *borrowed* (rescued) only by three kisses from the great hero Kemp Owyne. To emphasize this important point, the author adds two additional lines to his traditional ballad stanza. *Isabel* is probably meant to rhyme with *will,* and the rhyme scheme becomes *abbbab.* This six-line stanza recurs exactly at the point where the terms of the enchantment are met. The rhyme scheme of the third stanza is not retained, however, and this alteration may possibly indicate the corruption that many poems suffer in the process of oral transmission.

The fourth stanza tells of Isabel's transformation and in the last two lines bluntly states the monstrous nature of the change. The movement of Kemp Owyne from the mysterious distant land to the place where Isabel awaits him is accomplished in another terse stanza. In the usual manner of the ballad, it begins where he is and ends where she is. A sixth stanza, employing repetition, describes her and presents to the hero his unpleasant task. The rest of the poem details Isabel's release from enchantment.

Here again the author uses a familiar folklore motif, the talisman or magical object with which the hero must be bribed to perform his task. Since three kisses are called for, there must be three talismans: the belt, the ring, and the brand (sword), all of which have magical power to preserve the hero's life. In folk legendry there is always an injunction which the hero must observe before he can win the talisman; here he must not touch her "tail or fin," and in the repetition of this refrain throughout the poem, we are reminded of the heroine's hideous transformation and of the consequent difficulty of the champion's task.

Many ballads are highly realistic, but *Kemp Owyne* maintains a magical, fairy-tale quality. To create this feeling of the strange and unnatural, the author relies upon repetition of certain lines. For example, the iteration before each of the kisses of "With a swing she came about" creates the feeling of the ritual dance frequently attendant upon supernatural gatherings. With each such movement, there is a new talisman, a new kiss, and Isabel's hair is twisted around the tree one ring the less. With each action of the poem a sense of inevitability mounts. We never doubt that the hero will be successful, and in the final stanza, when the last condition has been fulfilled, the menace of the swinging motion with which Isabel comes about is altered to a smiling gesture, though association with the former *swing* is retained through the *-ing* syllable. Narrative economy is preserved to the end; the ballad has nothing to say of the future, closing abruptly once Isabel has become "As fair a woman as fair could be."

SIR PATRICK SPENS

The king sits in Dunfermline toune,
　　Drinking the blude-red wine:
"O whar will I get a guid sailor,
　　To sail this schip of mine?"

Up and spak an eldern knicht,
　　Sat at the kings richt kne:
"Sir Patrick Spens is the best sailor
　　That sails upon the sea."

The king has written a braid letter,
　　And signd it wi' his hand,
And sent it to Sir Patrick Spens,
　　Was walking on the sand.

The first line that Sir Patrick red,
　　A loud lauch lauched he:

The next line that Sir Patrick red,
    The teir blinded his ee.

"O wha is this has don this deid,
    This ill deid don to me,
To send me out this time o' the yeir,
    To sail upon the se!

"Mak hast, mak haste, my mirry men all,
    Our guid schip sails the morne":
"O say na sae, my master deir,
    For I feir a deadlie storme.

"Late late yestreen I saw the new moone,
    Wi' the auld moone in hir arme;
And I feir, I feir, my deir master,
    That we will come to harme."

O our Scots nobles wer richt laith
    To weet their cork-heild schoone;
But lang owre a' the play wer playd,
    Thair hats they swam aboone.

O lang, lang may their ladies sit,
    Wi' thair fans into their hand,
Or eir they see Sir Patrick Spens
    Cum sailing to the land.

O lang, lang may the ladies stand
    Wi' their gold kems in their hair,
Waiting for thair ain deir lords,
    For they'll se them na mair.

Haf owre, haf owre to Aberdour,
    It's fiftie fadom deip,
And thair lies guid Sir Patrick Spens,
    Wi' the Scots lords at his feit.

THE DAEMON LOVER

"O where have you been, my long, long love,
    This long seven years and mair?"
"O I'm come to seek my former vows
    Ye granted me before."

"O hold your tongue of your former vows,
    For they will breed sad strife;
O hold your tongue of your former vows,
    For I am become a wife."

He turned him right and round about,
    And the tear blinded his ee:
"I wad never hae trodden on Irish ground,
    If it had not been for thee.

"I might hae had a king's daughter,
    Far, far beyond the sea;
I might have had a king's daughter,
    Had it not been for love o thee."

"If ye might have had a king's daughter,
    Yersel ye had to blame;
Ye might have taken the king's daughter,
    For ye kend that I was nane.

"If I was to leave my husband dear,
    And my two babes also,
O what have you to take me to,
    If with you I should go?"

"I hae seven ships upon the sea—
    The eighth brought me to land—
With four-and-twenty bold mariners,
    And music on every hand."

She has taken up her two little babes,
    Kissd them baith cheek and chin:
"O fair ye weel, my ain two babes,
    For I'll never see you again."

She set her foot upon the ship,
    No mariners could she behold;
But the sails were o the taffetie,
    And the masts of the beaten gold.

She had not saild a league, a league,
    A league but barely three,
When dismal grew his countenance,
    And drumlie grew his ee.

They had not saild a league, league,
    A league but barely three,
Until she espied his cloven foot,
    And she wept right bitterlie.

"O hold your tongue of your weeping," says he,
    "Of your weeping now let me be;
I will shew you how the lilies grow
    On the banks of Italy."

"O what hills are yon, yon pleasant hills,
    That the sun shines sweetly on?"
"O yon are the hills of heaven," he said,
    "Where you will never win."

"O whaten a mountain is yon," she said,
    "All so dreary wi frost and snow?"
"O yon is the mountain of hell," he cried,
    "Where you and I will go."

He strack the tap-mast wi his hand,
    The fore-mast wi his knee,
And he brake that gallant ship in twain,
    And sank her in the sea.

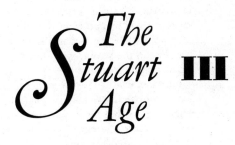

The
*S*tuart
Age **III**

WHEN Queen Elizabeth, last of the Tudor monarchs, died in 1603 and the young James VI of Scotland succeeded her as James I of England, first of the Stuart line, there were great changes in English politics; but these did not markedly affect the course of poetry. When we compare Stuart with Elizabethan verse, we are struck more by a sense of continuity and development than we are by any sudden change or reorientation. We must not forget that such "Elizabethan" poets as Chapman, Ralegh, Drayton, and Daniel lived well into the Stuart period, and that Shakespeare's greatest achievements are the plays he wrote after James' accession to the throne. Those poets who were unwilling to limit themselves to the theater still wrote under a system of noble patronage which differed from the Elizabethan only in that the new king's avowed cultivation of the arts, coupled with the rapid rise of his favorites under a more personal system of government, increased the number of patrons; and the greater expenditures of a lavish, fun-loving court led to rewards of patronage more generous than they ever had been under the more parsimonious Queen Elizabeth. This was the age of the court masque (an elaborate entertainment featuring spectacle, music, and dance), which could bring handsome fees to a poet like Ben Jonson and enable him to associate with great nobles like the Earl of Pembroke in spite of his own lowly origins. The poet in the seventeenth century acquired a greater respectability and social mobility than he had ever before enjoyed.

Courtiers who cultivated poetry as an elegant accomplishment continued to flourish in the court of James I. Under Charles I they became quite numerous, writing their "Cavalier" lyrics against the background of civil war. This war, the outstanding fact of seventeenth-century English history, grew out of religious conflicts, and these conflicts are powerfully reflected in the poetry of the times. The seventeenth century is a great age of religious poetry—Anglican, Catholic, and Puritan; to the other classes of Stuart poets must be added the very important group represented by John Donne, George Herbert, Robert Herrick, and Henry King—learned clergyman poets. Many in this group, including Donne and King, enjoyed high position in the Anglican Church.

The Spenserian tradition, with its emphasis upon elaboration and ornament and its constant quest for the smooth, mellifluous line, is carried on into the Stuart age. Although we tend to think of Daniel and Drayton as Elizabethans, Daniel lived until 1619 and Drayton continued to write until 1631, both carrying on the influence of Spenser. But with the exception of John Milton, who represents its final development, the Spenserian tradition did not produce the age's most notable poetry. The poems of Giles and Phineas Fletcher, perhaps Spenser's most assiduous seventeenth-century imitators, have been all but forgotten today. And although the peculiar quality which Spenser gave to the English pastoral is captured in the eclogues of George Wither and William Browne of Tavistock—we must not forget that the pastoral tradition continued to grow and flourish in the seventeenth century—it is not their contribution which most surely characterizes the poetry of the age.

The classical and the metaphysical poets The poets who give to Stuart poetry its distinctive modes are those who write in reaction to the Spenserian tradition. These include the classical poets, whose greatest figure is Ben Jonson, and those poets we have come to call metaphysical—poets interested in the play of wit and intellect, of startling comparisons and rare metaphors, among whom the outstanding figure is John Donne. Both Donne and Jonson began their poetic careers during the reign of Queen Elizabeth and represent the development of modes of expression already present in the Tudor age.

The lines of cleavage which separate the types of poetry in the Stuart era are far from exact. Classical and metaphysical poems have much in common, and many poems—such as those of Thomas Carew and Andrew Marvell—draw fully upon both traditions. Elegiac verse in the seventeenth century develops directly from that of the sixteenth, where it had been brought to great polish by Edmund Spenser. Perhaps the finest funeral elegy in the English language is John Milton's *Lycidas,* closely modeled upon Spenserian examples which were themselves developed out of the classical tradition of Theocritus, Bion, Moschus, and Virgil; but we must note also that other elegies show affinities to the metaphysical as well as the classical.

The Petrarchan commonplaces of Elizabethan love poetry continue into the Stuart era, but even more marked is the anti-Petrarchism (already noticeable in Tudor verse) which develops more strongly in reaction to it. John Donne, in particular, exaggerates the Petrarchan commonplaces so that they are rendered absurd and, turning his back on these conventions, composes love poetry based upon the reality of physical passion. Anti-Petrarchism appears also in the work of Cavalier poets like Thomas Carew and Sir John Suckling, who assumed a pose of scorn for the lover's woes and of careless indifference to the lady's charms.

This questioning of old conventions and exposing of their limitations may be related to the critical and scientific spirit which becomes so marked in the age of James I. There is more independence of mind in the search for truth, less willingness than ever before to accept without question the old views of man's position in the universe. There is a new skepticism that challenges the notion of a harmonious, ordered universe which Elizabethans had carried on from the Middle Ages, and there is, in men like Sir Francis Bacon (1561-1626), a willingness to follow knowledge no matter where it may lead. The questioning of traditional values in the seventeenth century generates a profound pessimism reflected in a constant concern with melancholy, with the physical realities of death and decay, and with the notion that the physical earth is in its final phase, approaching dissolution. These motifs appear very markedly in the poetry of John Donne. While there is an almost universal belief in Christianity, the poems of George Herbert show the conflict between skepticism and faith.

The age's scientific spirit appears in a concern with paradox and the exploration of ambiguities. Paradoxes, the insistence that seeming opposites are not opposites at all, are a favorite prose exercise, and they are at the heart also of metaphysical poetry. The seventeenth century comes to value a poetry based not upon Spenserian ornament, decoration, and elaborate detail but upon the intellectual exploration of paradoxical propositions. It has been pointed out that whereas the wit of Elizabethan poetry had depended largely upon sophisticated wordplay, wit in the time of James I (the Jacobean age) is intellectual rather than verbal, pursuing the implications of ideas and depending upon the agility of the poet's mind. It is, finally, more imaginative than Elizabethan wit, for it allows for greater flights of the fancy; its principal instrument is the conceit, or extended metaphor, which comes to replace the double entendre (words of ambiguous meaning), adding rich imagery to the frequently pictureless pun. This is as true of the classical Jonson as it is of the metaphysical Donne.

Satire in the Stuart age The intellectual and critical interests of the time helped also to foster the growth of poetic satire, which comes to loom larger and larger. At the end of the seventeenth century satire is the favorite medium of John Dryden, and by the early eighteenth century it has become the dominant mode. The Renaissance had carried on the medieval type of satire, reflected in the social criticism of the fourteenth-century *Piers Plowman* and in the writings of such Tudor poets as John Skelton and George Gascoigne. It had also produced formal verse satire in imitation of the ancient Roman models. Horace, the best known of the classical satirists, was read in the English schools and was imitated by Sir Thomas Wyatt at the beginning of the Tudor period. The Horatian satire tends to be an urbane account of personal experience in which the poet comments on human follies. Such satires continued to be written in the seventeenth century, but more common were those that imitated Juvenal and Persius—direct castigations of evil, harsh and bitter in tone. These served as models for Thomas Lodge, whose *A Fig for Momus* was published in 1595. Lodge was followed by John Marston, Everard Guilpin, and Joseph Hall. John Donne's satires, not printed until 1633, were probably written before the end of the sixteenth century. Indeed, recent scholarship has come to regard Donne as a pioneer in this as in other seventeenth-century literary movements.

Formal verse satire (see Donne's *Satire III, p.* 139) came to be written in the iambic pentameter couplet, with each two consecutive lines rhyming, and a large part of the history of seventeenth-century prosody is that of the gradual emergence of the heroic couplet, with its marked stop at the end of every second line, as a dominant verse form. At the beginning of the Stuart period two kinds of such couplets are written: some poets use them loosely, employing enjambment (see glossary) and running the sense of the verse from couplet into couplet without grammatical pause; others use the closed couplet. At the end of the century the closed heroic couplet has developed, in poems like *Absalom and Achitophel,* as John Dryden's favorite instrument, although he varies it with triple rhymes. In the eighteenth century Alexander Pope is able to use it with such mastery that it has no real rivals in his age's prosody.

Stuart poetry in general is marked by great metrical richness and variety. The common stanzas of Tudor verse are carried over and developed with new variations. In his attempt to capture the cadences of actual speech and to avoid the smoothness of the Spenserians, John Donne introduces a roughness into his stanzaic patterns, shocking his reader into attention rather than soothing him with melody. Donne also excels in his management of the verse paragraph, with rhyme and meter used to emphasize rather than hinder the normal flow of almost colloquial poetic statement. George Herbert is a great experimenter, rarely using the same verse form twice and creating unusual "shaped" poems in the forms of altars and angel wings. Metrics and stanzaic arrangement were fields in which Stuart poets could display their wit and ingenuity. Among the most skillful prosodists of the seventeenth century is John Milton. In *Lycidas* and the choruses to *Samson Agonistes* he broke new ground in his use of varying line lengths. In *Paradise Lost* and *Paradise Regained* he gave to English blank verse a new tonal quality and showed that it was capable of effects never before achieved.

FOR FURTHER READING:

Allen, Don Cameron. *Image and Meaning.* Baltimore, 1960.

Bush, Douglas. *English Literature in the Earlier 17th Century, 1600-1660.* London, 1945.

Grierson, H. J. C. *Cross Currents in English Literature of the XVIIth Century.* London, 1929.

Mahood, M. M. *Poetry and Humanism.* London, 1950.

Nicolson, Marjorie. *The Breaking of the Circle: Studies in the Effect of the New Science upon Seventeenth Century Poetry.* Evanston, Ill., 1950.

Sharp, R. L. *From Donne to Dryden*. Chapel Hill, 1940.

Tuve, Rosemond. *Elizabethan and Metaphysical Imagery*. Chicago, 1947.

Willey, Basil. *The Seventeenth Century Background*. London, 1934.

Wilson, F. P. *Elizabethan and Jacobean*. London, 1945.

THE STUART AGE

THE CLASSICAL AND COURTLY

T HE most powerful critical voice in English letters at the beginning of the seventeenth century was Ben Jonson, who in his critical writings, in his pronouncements to the followers who crowded about him in London taverns, and in his own example, proclaimed the virtues of the classical ideal. In classical poetry he found a simplicity and a neatness congenial to his tastes; he found also a succinctness and a precision which he extolled in contrast to the effusions of Petrarchan love poetry. He wrote many epigrams, following the example of the Roman poet Martial. Jonson himself showed no real interest in love poetry; when he was forced to write fashionable lyrics for his plays and masques, he turned to his own classical learning for inspiration. *Song: To Celia,* which he wrote for his play *Volpone,* is adapted from Catullus; *Still To Be Neat* is a loose rendition of Horace; other imitations come from Tibullus, Propertius, and the Greek Anacreon. Jonson was the first English poet to imitate the Greek Pindaric ode; he was followed later in the seventeenth century by Abraham Cowley, and at the end of the eighteenth century by Thomas Gray, who could imitate the Greek with more learning than either of his predecessors.

The practice of loosely rendering in English equivalents the love lyrics of the Roman poets became very fashionable in the seventeenth century, not only with Jonson but also with his followers. Among these "sons of Ben," as they came to be known, Robert Herrick was perhaps the most important. Not only were Latin originals translated, but also new variations were written on the familiar classical themes. Names of ladies were borrowed from the Roman poets—Chloe, Julie, Lesbia, and Corinna—and of all Roman themes, the poets came to play their own changes most frequently upon the Horatian *carpe diem*: let us love while we may, for beauty perishes, and there are no joys beyond the grave. This pagan motif, so contrary to the Christian celebration of chastity that runs through Renaissance Petrarchism and to the Christian hopes of afterlife, is repeated over and over again, often by devout clergymen in academic exercises. We find it most notably in Herrick's *To the Virgins, to Make Much of Time* and *Corinna's Going a-Maying,* and in Andrew Marvell's *To His Coy Mistress,* considered by many to be the greatest *carpe diem* poem in the language. All these poems repeat the themes of Roman love poetry while they imitate the forms, just as John Donne captures the form and spirit of the satires of Persius and Juvenal.

For the most part the classical imitators were content to render the long and short syllables (quantitative measures) of Latin poetry in the stressed and unstressed (qualitative) measures native to the English language. Some, like Thomas Campion, tried to write quantitative verse in English, but this movement was not widespread, and even Campion's most successful classical lyrics are those he wrote in English meters. Jonson himself preferred simple verse patterns, his favorite being the decasyllabic (ten-syllable) couplet, which he used more often than any other form. Jonson seems to have scorned sonnets, although he did write a few. He censured Drayton for his Alexandrines (lines of six iambic feet) and Donne for the unevenness of his accent.

Classical poetry is marked by precision, wit, and economy of style—the feeling that one unnecessary word will destroy the poem. It represents condensation and refinement of emotion rather than profuse elaboration. Classical poems are elegant and sophisticated, and they come to reflect, as in those of Sir John Suckling, the attitudes of the court. They range from the highly intellectual, metaphysical complexity of Carew's *Ask Me No More* to the simple and precise imagery of Herrick's *Upon Julia's Clothes*. And while they are controlled and spare, they are no less sincere in their emotional intensity.

FOR FURTHER READING:

Johnston, George Burke. *Ben Jonson, Poet.* New York, 1945.
McEuen, Kathryn A. *Classical Influence upon the Tribe of Ben.* Cedar Rapids, Iowa, 1939.
Schelling, Felix E. "Ben Jonson and the Classical School," *Shakespeare and Demi-Science.* Philadelphia, 1927.
Walton, Geoffrey. *Metaphysical to Augustan.* London, 1955. See especially chapters 1, 2, and 6.

BEN JONSON

TO JOHN DONNE

Who shall doubt, Donne, where I a poet be,
When I dare send my *Epigrams* to thee?

BEN JONSON (1573?-1637) was born in London, son of a minister and step-son of a bricklayer. He studied at Westminster School under the great antiquary William Camden. After military service in the Low Countries, he returned to London and achieved success as a writer of plays and masques. In 1616 he was appointed official court poet by James I. His sharp tongue and his biting satires involved him in numerous feuds, but many of the greatest writers of the day were his devoted admirers.

That so alone canst judge, so alone dost make;
 And, in thy censures, evenly dost take
As free simplicity to disavow
 As thou hast best authority t ' allow.
Read all I send; and if I find but one
 Marked by thy hand, and with the better stone,
My title's sealed. Those that for claps do write,
 Let pui'nes', porters', players' praise delight,
And till they burst their backs, like asses load;
 A man should seek great glory, and not broad.

ON LUCY, COUNTESS OF BEDFORD

This morning, timely rapt with holy fire,
 I thought to form unto my zealous muse
What kind of creature I could most desire,
 To honor, serve, and love; as poets use.
I meant to make her fair, and free, and wise,
 Of greatest blood, and yet more good than great;
I meant the day-star should not brighter rise,
 Nor lend like influence from his lucent seat;
I meant she should be courteous, facile, sweet,
 Hating that solemn vice of greatness, pride;
I meant each softest virtue, there should meet,
 Fit in that softer bosom to reside.
Only a learnéd, and a manly soule
 I purposed her; that should, with even powers,
The rock, the spindle, and the shears control
 Of destiny, and spin her own free hours.
Such when I meant to feign, and wished to see,
 My muse bade, Bedford write, and that was she.

HERE SHE WAS WONT TO GO

Here she was wont to go, and here! and here!
Just where those daisies, pinks, and violets grow;
The world may find the spring by following her,
For other print her airy steps ne'er left;
Her treading would not bend a blade of grass!
Or shake the downy blow-ball from his stalk!
But like the soft west-wind she shot along,
And where she went the flowers took thickest root,
As she had sowed 'em with her odorous foot.

STILL TO BE NEAT

Still to be neat, still to be dressed
As you were going to a feast;
Still to be powdered, still perfumed:
Lady, it is to be presumed,
Though art's hid causes are not found,
All is not sweet, all is not sound.

Give me a look, give me a face
That makes simplicity a grace;
Robes loosely flowing, hair as free:
Such sweet neglect more taketh me
Than all th' adulteries of art;
They strike mine eyes, but not my heart.

THOUGH I AM YOUNG

Though I am young, and cannot tell,
   Either that death or love is well,
Yet I have heard they both bear darts,
   And both do aim at human hearts.
And then again I have been told
   Love wounds with heat, as death with cold;
So that I fear they do but bring
   Extremes to touch, and mean one thing.

As in a ruin we it call
   One thing to be blowne up, or fall;
Or to our end, like way may have
   By a flash of lightning, or a wave;
So love's inflamèd shaft or brand
   May kill as soon as death's cold hand;
Except love's fires the virtue have
   To fright the frost out of the grave.

SONG: TO CELIA

Come, my Celia, let us prove
While we may, the sports of love;
Time will not be ours for ever:

He at length our good will sever.
Spend not then his gifts in vain:
Suns that set, may rise again;
But if once we lose this light,
'Tis with us perpetual night.
Why should we defer our joys?
Fame and rumour are but toys.
Cannot we delude the eyes
Of a few poor household spies?
Or his easier ears beguile,
So removèd by our wile?
'Tis no sin love's fruits to steal,
But the sweet theft to reveal:
To be taken, to be seen,
These have crimes accounted been.

OH, THAT JOY SO SOON SHOULD WASTE

Oh, that joy so soon should waste!
  Or so sweet a bliss
  As a kiss
Might not forever last!
So sugared, so melting, so soft, so delicious!
  The dew that lies on roses
When morn herself discloses,
  Is not so precious.
Oh, rather than I would it smother,
Were I to taste such another,
  It should be my wishing
  That I might die kissing.

BUZ, QUOTH THE BLUE FLY

  Buz, quoth the blue fly,
    Hum, quoth the bee;
  Buz and hum they cry,
    And so do we.
  In his ear, in his nose,
    Thus, do you see?
  He eat the dormouse,
    Else it was he.

THOMAS CAMPION

MY SWEETEST LESBIA

My sweetest Lesbia, let us live and love;
And though the sager sort our deeds reprove,
Let us not weigh them. Heaven's great lamps do dive
Into their west, and straight again revive;
But, soon as once set is our little light,
Then must we sleep one ever-during night.

If all would lead their lives in love like me,
Then bloody swords and armour should not be;
No drum nor trumpet peaceful sleeps should move,
Unless alarm came from the camp of love.
But fools do live and waste their little light,
And seek with pain their ever-during night.

When timely death my life and fortune ends,
Let not my hearse be vexed with mourning friends;
But let all lovers, rich in triumph, come
And with sweet pastimes grace my happy tomb.
And, Lesbia, close up thou my little light,
And crown with love my ever-during night.

WHEN TO HER LUTE CORINNA SINGS

When to her lute Corinna sings,
Her voice revives the leaden strings,
And doth in highest notes appear
As any challenged echo clear;
But when she doth of mourning speak,
Ev'n with her sighs the strings do break.

And as her lute doth live or die,
Led by her passion, so must I:
For when of pleasure she doth sing,
My thoughts enjoy a sudden spring,
But if she doth of sorrow speak,
Ev'n from my heart the strings do break.

THOMAS CAMPION (1567-1620) wrote court masques and charming lyrics, some of which he set to music. He was the author of the tract against rhyme which prompted Daniel's *Defence of Rhyme*.

WHEN THOU MUST HOME

When thou must home to shades of underground,
And there arrived, a new admired guest,
The beauteous spirits do engirt thee round,
White Iope, blithe Helen and the rest,
To hear the stories of thy finished love
From that smooth tongue, whose music hell can move:

Then wilt thou speak of banqueting delights,
Of masques and revels which sweet youth did make,
Of tourneys and great challenges of knights,
And all these triumphs for thy beauty's sake.
When thou hast told these honours done to thee,
Then tell, O tell, how thou didst murder me.

THOU ART NOT FAIR

Thou art not fair for all thy red and white,
For all those rosy ornaments in thee;
Thou art not sweet, though made of mere delight,
Nor fair nor sweet, unless you pity me.
I will not soothe thy fancies; thou shalt prove
That beauty is no beauty without love.

Yet love not me, nor seek thou to allure
My thoughts with beauty, were it more divine;
Thy smiles and kisses I cannot endure,
I'll not be wrapped up in those arms of thine.
Now show it, if thou be a woman right,—
Embrace, and kiss, and love me in despite.

ROBERT HERRICK

TO THE VIRGINS, TO MAKE MUCH OF TIME

Gather ye rosebuds while ye may,
Old Time is still a-flying:

ROBERT HERRICK (1591-1674), son of a London goldsmith, was a fervent disciple of Ben Jonson. Although he spent most of his career as the vicar of a country parish, Jonson's classical paganism exerted a lasting influence on his love songs and pastoral lyrics.

And this same flower that smiles today,
    Tomorrow will be dying.

The glorious lamp of heaven, the sun,
    The higher he's a-getting
The sooner will his race be run,
    And nearer he's to setting.

That age is best which is the first,
    When youth and blood are warmer;
But being spent, the worse, and worst
    Times will succeed the former.

Then be not coy, but use your time;
    And while ye may, go marry:
For having lost but once your prime,
    You may for ever tarry.

CORINNA'S GOING A-MAYING

Get up, get up for shame! The blooming morn
Upon her wings presents the god unshorn.
    See how Aurora throws her fair
    Fresh-quilted colours through the air:
    Get up, sweet slug-a-bed, and see
    The dew bespangled herb and tree!
Each flower has wept and bowed toward the east
Above an hour since: yet you not dressed;
    Nay! not so much as out of bed?
    When all the birds have matins said
    And sung their thankful hymns, 'tis sin,
    Nay, profanation, to keep in,
Whenas a thousand virgins on this day
Spring sooner than the lark, to fetch in May.

Rise and put on your foliage, and be seen
To come forth, like the spring-time, fresh and green,
    And sweet as Flora. Take no care
    For jewels for your gown or hair:
    Fear not; the leaves will strew
    Gems in abundance upon you:
Besides, the childhood of the day has kept,
Against you come, some orient pearls unwept.

Come and receive them while the light
Hangs on the dew-locks of the night:
And Titan on the eastern hill
Retires himself, or else stands still
Till you come forth! Wash, dress, be brief in praying:
Few beads are best when once we go a-Maying.

Come, my Corinna, come; and coming, mark
How each field turns a street, each street a park
Made green and trimmed with trees! see how
Devotion gives each house a bough
Or branch! each porch, each door, ere this,
An ark, a tabernacle is,
Made up of white-thorn, neatly interwove;
As if here were those cooler shades of love.
Can such delights be in the street
And open fields, and we not see't?
Come, we'll abroad; and let's obey
The proclamation made for May,
And sin no more, as we have done, by staying;
But, my Corinna, come, let's go a-Maying.

There's not a budding boy or girl this day
But is got up, and gone to bring in May.
A deal of youth ere this is come
Back, and with white-thorn laden home.
Some have despatched their cakes and cream,
Before that we have left to dream:
And some that have wept and wooed, and plighted troth,
And chose their priest, ere we can cast off sloth:
Many a green-gown has been given,
Many a kiss, both odd and even:
Many a glance too has been sent
From out the eye, love's firmament:
Many a jest told of the keys betraying
This night, and locks picked, yet we're not a-Maying!

Come, let us go while we are in our prime,
And take the harmless folly of the time!
We shall grow old apace, and die
Before we know our liberty.
Our life is short, and our days run
As fast away as does the sun.

And, as a vapour or a drop of rain,
Once lost, can ne'er be found again,
 So when or you or I are made
 A fable, song, or fleeting shade,
 All love, all liking, all delight
 Lies drowned with us in endless night.
Then, while time serves, and we are but decaying,
Come, my Corinna, come, let's go a-Maying.

TO HIS MISTRESS

You say I love not, 'cause I do not play
Still with your curls, and kiss the time away.
You blame me too because I can't devise
Some sport to please those babies in your eyes;
By love's religion, I must here confess it,
The most I love when I the least express it.
Some griefs find tongues; full casks are ever found
To give, if any, yet but little sound.
Deep waters noiseless are; and this we know,
That chiding streams betray small depths below.
So when love speechless is, she doth express
A depth in love, and that depth bottomless.
Now since my love is tongueless, know me such
Who speak but little 'cause I love so much.

UPON JULIA'S CLOTHES

Whenas in silks my Julia goes,
Then, then, methinks, how sweetly flows
The liquefaction of her clothes.

Next, when I cast mine eyes, and see
That brave vibration, each way free,
O how that glittering taketh me!

CHERRY-RIPE

Cherry-ripe, ripe, ripe, I cry,
Full and fair ones; come and buy!
If so be you ask me where
They do grow, I answer: There,
Where my Julia's lips do smile;

There's the land, or cherry-isle,
Whose plantations fully show
All the year where cherries grow.

EDMUND WALLER

ON A GIRDLE

That which her slender waist confined,
Shall now my joyful temples bind;
No monarch but would give his crown,
His arms might do what this has done.

It was my heaven's extremest sphere,
The pale which held that lovely deer,
My joy, my grief, my hope, my love,
Did all within this circle move!

A narrow compass! and yet there
Dwelt all that's good, and all that's fair!
Give me but what this ribband bound,
Take all the rest the sun goes round!

GO, LOVELY ROSE

Go, lovely Rose—
Tell her that wastes her time and me,
That now she knows,
When I resemble her to thee,
How sweet and fair she seems to be.

Tell her that's young,
And suns to have her graces spied,
That hadst thou sprung
In deserts where no men abide,
Thou must have uncommended died.

EDMUND WALLER (1606-1687), one of the most admired poets of his time, at first opposed King Charles but later deserted the Puritan cause and joined the Royalists in exile. He was eventually pardoned by Cromwell. After the Restoration he returned to Parliament, where he had first served before he was twenty.

Small is the worth
Of beauty from the light retired:
Bid her come forth,
Suffer herself to be desired,
And not blush so to be admired.

Then die—that she
The common fate of all things rare
May read in thee;
How small a part of time they share
That are so wondrous sweet and fair!

ANDREW MARVELL

TO HIS COY MISTRESS

Had we but world enough, and time,
This coyness, Lady, were no crime.
We would sit down and think which way
To walk and pass our long love's day.
Thou by the Indian Ganges' side
Shouldst rubies find: I by the tide
Of Humber would complain. I would
Love you ten years before the Flood,
And you should, if you please, refuse
Till the conversion of the Jews.

My vegetable love should grow
Vaster than empires, and more slow;
An hundred years should go to praise
Thine eyes and on thy forehead gaze;
Two hundred to adore each breast,
But thirty thousand to the rest;
An age at least to every part,
And the last age should show your heart.
For, Lady, you deserve this state,
Nor would I love at lower rate.

ANDREW MARVELL (1621-1678), a minister's son, worked as a tutor, assisted John Milton during Cromwell's rule, and served in Parliament after the Restoration. His bold political writings received more attention in his own time than the distinguished lyrics for which he has been remembered.

But at my back I always hear
Time's wingèd chariot hurrying near;
And yonder all before us lie
Deserts of vast eternity.
Thy beauty shall no more be found,
Nor, in thy marble vault, shall sound
My echoing song; then worms shall try
That long preserved virginity;
And your quaint honor turn to dust,
And into ashes all my lust:
The grave's a fine and private place,
But none, I think, do there embrace.

Now therefore, while the youthful hue
Sits on thy skin like morning dew,
And while thy willing soul transpires
At every pore with instant fires,
Now let us sport us while we may,
And now, like amorous birds of prey,
Rather at once our time devour
Than languish in his slow-chapped power.
Let us roll all our strength and all
Our sweetness up into one ball,
And tear our pleasures with rough strife
Thorough the iron gates of life:
Thus, though we cannot make our sun
Stand still, yet we will make him run.

THE GARDEN

How vainly men themselves amaze,
To win the palm, the oak, or bays,
And their incessant labors see
Crowned from some single herb or tree
Whose short and narrow-vergèd shade
Does prudently their toils upbraid,
While all the flowers and trees do close
To weave the garlands of repose!

Fair Quiet, have I found thee here,
And Innocence, thy sister dear?
Mistaken long, I sought you then
In busy companies of men.

Your sacred plants, if here below,
Only among the plants will grow;
Society is all but rude
To this delicious solitude.

No white nor red was ever seen
So amorous as this lovely green.
Fond lovers, cruel as their flame,
Cut in these trees their mistress' name.
Little, alas! they know or heed,
How far these beauties hers exceed!
Fair trees! wheres'e'r your barks I wound
No name shall but your own be found.

When we have run our passion's heat,
Love hither makes his best retreat.
The gods, that mortal beauty chase,
Still in a tree did end their race;
Apollo hunted Daphne so,
Only that she might laurel grow;
And Pan did after Syrinx speed,
Not as a nymph, but for a reed.

What wondrous life is this I lead!
Ripe apples drop about my head;
The luscious clusters of the vine
Upon my mouth do crush their wine;
The nectarine, and curious peach,
Into my hands themselves do reach;
Stumbling on melons, as I pass,
Insnared with flowers, I fall on grass.

Meanwhile the mind, from pleasure less,
Withdraws into its happiness;—
The mind, that ocean where each kind
Does straight its own resemblance find;
Yet it creates, transcending these,
Far other worlds, and other seas,
Annihilating all that's made
To a green thought in a green shade.

Here at the fountain's sliding foot,
Or at some fruit-tree's mossy root,

Casting the body's vest aside,
My soul into the boughs does glide:
There, like a bird, it sits and sings,
Then whets and combs its silver wings,
And, till prepared for longer flight,
Waves in its plumes the various light.

Such was that happy garden-state,
While man there walked without a mate
After a place so pure and sweet,
What other help could yet be meet!
But 'twas beyond a mortal's share
To wander solitary there:
Two paradises 'twere in one,
To live in paradise alone.

How well the skilful gardener drew
Of flowers, and herbs, this dial new;
Where, from above, the milder sun
Does through a fragrant zodiac run,
And, as it works, the industrious bee
Computes its time as well as we!
How could such sweet and wholesome hours
Be reckoned but with herbs and flowers?

JOHN DONNE

SATIRE III

Kind pity chokes my spleen; brave scorn forbids
Those tears to issue which swell my eyelids;
I must not laugh, nor weep sins and be wise;
Can railing then cure these worn maladies?
Is not our mistress, fair religïon,
As worthy of all our souls' devotïon

JOHN DONNE (1572-1631) was born in London, the son of a prosperous Catholic ironmonger. In 1596 he served under the Earl of Essex in his expedition against Cádiz and the following year in that against the Azores. His secret marriage in 1601 to Anne More, daughter of the powerful Sir George More, ended his political career. Having joined the Anglican Church, Donne took holy orders in 1615 and rose to be dean of St. Paul's in London, where he won wide recognition with his sermons and religious writings.

As virtue was in the first blinded age?
Are not heaven's joys as valiant to assuage
Lusts as earth's honor was to them? Alas,
As we do them in means, shall they surpass
Us in the end? and shall thy father's spirit
Meet blind philosophers in heaven, whose merit
Of strict life may be imputed faith, and hear
Thee, whom he taught so easy ways and near
To follow, damned? Oh, if thou dar'st, fear this;
This fear great courage and high valor is.
Dar'st thou aid mutinous Dutch, and dar'st thou lay
Thee in ships, wooden sepulchers, a prey
To leaders' rage, to storms, to shot, to dearth?
Dar'st thou dive seas, and dungeons of the earth?
Hast thou courageous fire to thaw the ice
Of frozen North discoveries? and thrice
Colder than salamanders, like divine
Children in th' oven, fires of Spain and the Line,
Whose countries limbecs to our bodies be,
Canst thou for gain bear? and must every he
Which cries not, Goddess, to thy mistress, draw
Or eat thy poisonous words? Courage of straw!
O desperate coward, wilt thou seem bold and
To thy foes and His, who made thee to stand
Sentinel in his world's garrison, thus yield,
And for forbidden wars leave th' appointed field?
Know thy foes: the foul devil, whom thou
Strivest to please, for hate, not love, would allow
Thee fain his whole realm to be quit; and as
The world's all parts wither away and pass,
So the world's self, thy other loved foe, is
In her decrepit wane, and thou, loving this,
Dost love a withered and worn strumpet; last,
Flesh, itself death, and joys which flesh can taste
Thou lovest, and thy fair goodly soul, which doth
Give this flesh power to taste joy, thou dost loathe.
Seek true religion. Oh, where? Mirreus,
Thinking her unhoused here and fled from us,
Seeks her at Rome; there, because he doth know
That she was there a thousand years ago;
He loves her rags so, as we here obey
The statecloth where the prince sat yesterday.
Crantz to such brave loves will not be enthralled,

But loves her only, who at Geneva is called
Religion, plain, simple, sullen, young,
Contemptuous, yet unhandsome; as among
Lecherous humors, there is one that judges
No wenches wholesome, but coarse country drudges.
Graius stays still at home here, and because
Some preachers, vile ambitious bawds, and laws,
Still new like fashions, bid him think that she
Which dwells with us is only perfect, he
Embraceth her whom his godfathers will
Tender to him, being tender; as wards still
Take such wives as their guardians offer, or
Pay values. Careless Phrygius doth abhor
All, because all cannot be good; as one,
Knowing some women whores, dares marry none.
Gracchus loves all as one, and thinks that so
As women do in divers countries go
In divers habits, yet are still one kind,
So doth, so is religion; and this blind-
Ness to much light breeds; but unmovèd, thou
Of force must one, and forced but one allow,
And the right; ask thy father which is she,
Let him ask his; though truth and falsehood be
Near twins, yet truth a little elder is;
Be busy to seek her; believe me this,
He's not of none, nor worst, that seeks the best.
To adore, or scorn an image, or protest,
May all be bad. Doubt wisely; in strange way
To stand inquiring right, is not to stray;
To sleep, or run wrong, is. On a huge hill,
Cragged and steep, Truth stands, and he that will
Reach her, about must and about must go,
And what the hill's suddenness resists, win so.
Yet strive so that before age, death's twilight,
Thy soul rest, for none can work in that night.
To will implies delay, therefore now do
Hard deeds, the body's pains; hard knowledge too
The mind's endeavors reach, and mysteries
Are like the sun, dazzling, yet plain to all eyes.
Keep the truth which thou hast found; men do not stand
In so ill case, that God hath with his hand
Signed kings blank charters to kill whom they hate;
Nor are they vicars, but hangmen, to fate.

Fool and wretch, wilt thou let thy soul be tied
To man's laws, by which she shall not be tried
At the last day? Will it then boot thee
To say a Philip or a Gregory,
A Harry or a Martin, taught thee this?
Is not this excuse for mere contraries
Equally strong? Cannot both sides say so?
That thou mayest rightly obey power, her bounds know;
Those past, her nature and name is changed; to be
Then humble to her is idolatry.
As streams are, power is; those blest flowers that dwell
At the rough stream's calm head, thrive and do well,
But having left their roots, and themselves given
To the stream's tyrannous rage, alas, are driven
Through mills and rocks and woods, and at last, almost
Consumed in going, in the sea are lost.
So perish souls, which more choose men's unjust
Power from God claimed, than God himself to trust.

WILLIAM CARTWRIGHT

TO CHLOE

Chloe, why wish you that your years
    Would backwards run till they meet mine,
That perfect likeness, which endears
    Things unto things, might us combine?
Our ages so in date agree
That twins do differ more than we.

There are two births: the one when light
    First strikes the new awakened sense;
The other when two souls unite,
    And we must count our life from thence.
When you loved me and I loved you,
Then both of us were born anew.

WILLIAM CARTWRIGHT (1611-1743), as one of the "sons of Ben," wrote three plays which were greatly admired by his contemporaries. He was also a celebrated preacher.

Love then to us did new souls give,
  And in those souls did plant new powers;
Since when another life we live,
  The breath we breathe is his, not ours;
Love makes those young whom age doth chill,
And whom he finds young, keeps young still.

Love, like that angel that shall call
  Our bodies from the silent grave,
Unto one age doth raise us all,
  None too much, none too little have;
Nay, that the difference may be none,
He makes two not alike, but one.

And now since you and I are such,
  Tell me what's yours and what is mine?
Our eyes, our ears, our taste, smell, touch,
  Do, like our souls, in one combine;
So by this, I as well may be
Too old for you, as you for me.

SIR JOHN SUCKLING

WHY SO PALE AND WAN?

Why so pale and wan, fond lover?
  Prithee, why so pale?
Will, when looking well can't move her,
  Looking ill prevail?
  Prithee, why so pale?

Why so dull and mute, young sinner?
  Prithee, why so mute?
Will, when speaking well can't win her,

SIR JOHN SUCKLING (1609-1642), the son of a courtier, took part in military campaigns on the Continent and in Scotland. Loyal to King Charles, he was forced to flee to France, where he died by his own hand.

Saying nothing do't?
Prithee, why so mute?

Quit, quit for shame! This will not move;
This cannot take her.
If of herself she will not love,
Nothing can make her:
The devil take her!

THE CONSTANT LOVER

Out upon it, I have loved
Three whole days together!
And am like to love three more,
If it prove fair weather.

Time shall moult away his wings
Ere he shall discover
In the whole wide world again
Such a constant lover.

But the spite on't is, no praise
Is due at all to me:
Love with me had made no stays,
Had it any been but she.

Had it any been but she,
And that very face,
There had been at least ere this
A dozen dozen in her place.

A SONG TO A LUTE

Hast thou seen the down in the air,
When wanton blasts have tossed it?
Or the ship on the sea,
When ruder waves have crossed it?
Hast thou marked the crocodile's weeping
Or the fox's sleeping?
Or hast viewed the peacock in his pride,
Or the dove by his bride,
When he courts for his lechery?
O, so fickle, O, so vain, O, so false, so false is she!

THOMAS CAREW

SONG: ASK ME NO MORE

Ask me no more where Jove bestows,
When June is past, the fading rose;
For in your beauty's orient deep
These flowers, as in their causes, sleep.

Ask me no more whither doth stray
The golden atoms of the day;
For in pure love heaven did prepare
Those powders to enrich your hair.

Ask me no more whither doth haste
The nightingale when May is past;
For in your sweet dividing throat
She winters and keeps warm her note.

Ask me no more where those stars light
That downwards fall in dead of night;
For in your eyes they sit, and there
Fixèd become as in their sphere.

Ask me no more if east or west
The Phoenix builds her spicy nest;
For unto you at last she flies,
And in your fragrant bosom dies.

SONG: ASK ME NO MORE This poem is an excellent illustration of the way in which classical and metaphysical traditions were united in the poetry of the seventeenth century. It shows also how the old Petrarchan symbols were altered and given new significance. On first reading, the poem appears to be merely conventional in its praise of a lady; after close analysis we find a more serious probing into the meaning of love and beauty, although exaggerated flattery remains a dominant purpose. Carew's method is to treat the double theme which is met so frequently in metaphysical poetry: primary is the consideration of death and decay; secondary, and dependent on the first, is the plight of the lover in a world in which all beauty, including that of his beloved, is short-lived.

THOMAS CAREW (1595?-1639?) spent his life in service to the nobility and the court. He is regarded as the earliest of the Cavalier poets, who turned the dull and even distasteful incidents of court life into delicate and colorful poetry.

These are ancient problems. The medieval mind, as we have seen, had met them with scorn for worldly delights (*de contemptu mundi*) and devotion to the permanent joys of afterlife. Renaissance and later classicism responded with a theme drawn from Horace (*carpe diem*): celebrate the immediate pleasures of life while they still may be enjoyed, for there is no avoiding the inevitability of death. Metaphysical poets like Donne had seen an intimate relationship between death and love, the one acting as a constant reminder of the other.

Carew joins the classical and the metaphysical in such a way that he gives to the *carpe diem* convention a new significance. *Ask Me No More* becomes a celebration of the joys of love by an affirmation of their permanence in spite of their seeming decay. The entire poem explores the paradox of life and death, treating it as a threefold conception: natural beauty must die each winter in order to be reborn each spring; the lover must die in his old personality in order to be reborn into the new union with his beloved; and man must die a mortal death in order to be born into life eternal. Each stanza of the poem plays a variation on the love-death theme, which grows more and more intense until it culminates in the figure of the phoenix, traditional symbol of the process of death and rebirth. The phoenix stands at once for the eternal rebirth of nature and for the death and Resurrection of Christ, the passionate mystery which promises the mortal death of all men and the resurrection and salvation of the good.

In the first stanza the lady is linked to nature; the fading rose reminds us that the lady, like the flower, is a part of nature which must inevitably die. The rose is a common symbol in *carpe diem* poetry, representing the fleeting nature of youth and beauty as well as woman's sexuality. The first couplet raises the melancholy prospect of the decay both of beauty and of love and implies the ultimate end of both in death's finality. The second couplet reverses expectation; instead of becoming the final resting place of all beauty—all life—the lady, with her "beauty's orient deep," is transformed into a well of loveliness, a sepulcher comparable to the seed from which the new rose springs, the bed from which the new love swells, the tomb from which the living Christ rises. It is through his selection of "orient deep" that Carew expresses the multiple meaning of this stanza. The specific reference is to the eastern ocean from which the sun rises. There before sunrise the lady's beauty sleeps with the flowers; both are brought to bloom by the ascending sun. There after sunset the flowers and the lady's beauty sleep once more, inevitably to rise again. The lady's beauty is a part of the eternal awakening of nature itself. The word *orient* is a magnificent stroke, engendering all the exotic associations of the East: spice, fragrance, mystery.

The comparison of the lady's beauty to the sun leads naturally to the next stanza, which amplifies the theme of the first. Again the poet evokes a familiar Petrarchan symbol in his praise of the lady's golden hair, glorified by the rays of the sun. "Golden atoms" are the motes in a sunbeam. In actual practice, ladies of the seventeenth century dusted their hair with gold-colored powder. Retaining theological overtones, the poem asserts that it is the "pure love" of "heaven" which prepares the powders.

In the third stanza the theme of the lady's union with nature is resumed, for her "sweet dividing throat" (that is, her throat from which issues trilling song) is the winter abode of the nightingale. The use again of a seasonal phenomenon reinforces the theme of rebirth. Played paradoxically against this theme is the suggestion that since the lady herself is the place to which all beauty goes in the winter, she has, therefore, the freshness of spring all year round.

In the fourth stanza the poet elaborates his conceit by drawing once again upon a poetic convention that by the seventeenth century had become commonplace: reference to the nine heavenly spheres of medieval astronomical theory, in which the fixed stars belonged to the eighth sphere. While the immortality of the lady's beauty is emphasized through this new use of an ancient symbol, the lady herself is brought closer to heaven through the simple device of bringing one of the higher reaches of heaven closer to her. The entire plane of love is being raised to a sanctity which the poet hopes will convince the lady that their union was ordained in heaven.

Everything, then, has been leading inevitably to the final stanza, in which the central symbol is the phoenix. This magical bird lives for five hundred years and then builds a perfumed nest in which its body bursts into flames; out of the ashes is born the new phoenix. Traditionally a symbol for Christ as well as for reviving nature, the phoenix, dying in the lady's bosom, reiterates in the final stanza, in more spiritual terms, the threefold action of the poem: all nature and all beauty die and are reborn again in the poet's lady; the lover himself dies into new life in the lady's bosom; and the love made on earth is hallowed in heaven through the figure of Christ Himself. But the poet has not moved away from the idea of the sexual act in purely physical terms, for the verb *to die* in the Renaissance is a common reference to the consummation of sexual union, and the phoenix being born again after having "died" refers to the possible children that may be born from the lovers' act. The *carpe diem* theme, in part, traditionally exhorted the beloved to give to the world a copy of her beauty in the form of lovely children. The request was phrased in terms of the lady's duty to posterity.

Appropriately, the degree of mystery increases from stanza to stanza. The dying rose is perhaps a less mysterious phenomenon than the motes in a sunbeam, which in turn are more frequently seen than the migration of nightingales. The falling star is a lesser mystery than the fabled phoenix.

In addition, it may be observed that the first four stanzas deal with natural history; the final mystery, that of the self-resurrecting bird, is supernatural, mystical, and exotic.

As a song, probably designed to be sung, the poem is divided into five stanzas, interesting in their varied iambic tetrameter and identical word order. The poet relies upon an imaginary question in the first two lines of each stanza and supplies the reason for his answer in the last two. The imperative "Ask me no more" begins each quatrain, and the conjunction *For* begins every third line. The rhyme scheme supports this pattern, for instead of using the more familiar quatrain in which the lines rhyme alternately, Carew employs a pair of couplets for each stanza.

RICHARD LOVELACE

TO ALTHEA, FROM PRISON

When Love with unconfinèd wings
  Hovers within my gates,
And my divine Althea brings
  To whisper at the grates;
When I lie tangled in her hair
  And fettered to her eye,
The birds that wanton in the air
  Know no such liberty.

When flowing cups run swiftly round
  With no allaying Thames,
Our careless heads with roses bound,
  Our hearts with loyal flames;
When thirsty grief in wine we steep,
  When healths and draughts go free,
Fishes that tipple in the deep
  Know no such liberty.

When, like committed linnets, I
  With shriller throat shall sing
The sweetness, mercy, majesty,
  And glories of my king;

RICHARD LOVELACE (1618-1658) lost both his fortune and his freedom in the service of the king. It was during two terms of imprisonment that the handsome young Royalist wrote and edited his romantic lyrics. He died in poverty.

When I shall voice aloud how good
　　He is, how great should be,
Enlargèd winds, that curl the flood,
　　Know no such liberty.

Stone walls do not a prison make,
　　Nor iron bars a cage;
Minds innocent and quiet take
　　That for an hermitage;
If I have freedom in my love
　　And in my soul am free,
Angels alone, that soar above,
　　Enjoy such liberty.

TO LUCASTA, GOING TO THE WARS

Tell me not, Sweet, I am unkind,
　　That from the nunnery
Of thy chaste breast and quiet mind
　　To war and arms I fly.

True, a new mistress now I chase,
　　The first foe in the field;
And with a stronger faith embrace
　　A sword, a horse, a shield.

Yet this inconstancy is such
　　As thou too shalt adore;
I could not love thee, Dear, so much,
　　Loved I not honor more.

ORLANDO GIBBONS

THE SILVER SWAN

The silver swan, who living had no note,
When death approached, unlocked her silent throat;
Leaning her breast against the reedy shore,

ORLANDO GIBBONS (1583-1625), musician and composer, is best remembered for his church music. He was organist of the Chapel Royal and of Westminster Abbey.

Thus sung her first and last, and sung no more.
Farewell, all joys; O death, come close mine eyes;
More geese than swans now live, more fools than wise.

ROBERT JONES

THINK'ST THOU, KATE

Think'st thou, Kate, to put me down
With a no or with a frown?
Since love holds my heart in bands,
I must do as love commands.

Love commands the hands to dare
When the tongue of speech is spare;
Chiefest lesson in love's school,
Put it in adventure, fool.

Fools are they that fainting flinch
For a squeak, a scratch, a pinch.
Women's words have double sense,
Stand away, a simple fence.

If thy mistress swears she'll cry,
Fear her not; she'll swear and lie.
Such sweet oaths no sorrow bring
Till the prick of conscience sting.

ROBERT JONES was famous in the early seventeeth century as a performer
on the lute. He composed songs and sets of madrigals.

THE STUART AGE

THE METAPHYSICAL

THE metaphysical poets of the seventeenth century are not a homogeneous group, nor do they represent so complete a break from their Elizabethan forebears as is sometimes supposed; what poets like John Donne, George Herbert, Richard Crashaw, and Henry Vaughan all have in common is their rejection of those elements in Elizabethan poetry which had become stylized and conventional and their need to come to terms with experience in their own way. All were pious men and all wrote religious poetry, but most of the metaphysical poets wrote secular love poetry as well. The poetry of each of these men bears the stamp of his personality, but John Donne is the outstanding figure in the group, and many of his attitudes characterize the work of the poets associated with him.

Following a suggestion in Dryden, Samuel Johnson gave currency to the term *metaphysical* in an essay on Abraham Cowley, whom he linked with John Donne and John Cleveland. Johnson used the term as one of censure, complaining that in metaphysical poems "the most heterogeneous ideas are yoked by violence together." But Johnson, in spite of his hostility, perceived the essence of what he was deriding: the ability of this kind of poetry to show new relationships by joining seemingly disparate images. Johnson saw that the metaphysical poets depended not upon the sensuous effect of sound so much as upon intricacy of thought, that they tried to generate excitement by display of mind. Donne and his followers used an original poetic diction to convey an intensity of feeling greater than could be conveyed in the old conventional poetic terms. Their chief poetic device was the conceit, an elaborate intellectual figure of speech, developed in its implications, extended in its scope, with extraordinary flights of the imagination. Donne was, in effect, returning to the practice of Sir Thomas Wyatt, who may be the true father of metaphysical poetry, with Walter Ralegh and George Chapman as important transitional figures linking Wyatt to Donne.

Donne himself was fond of paradox, the resolution of opposites, and his conceits often are explorations of intellectual propositions in seeming contradiction. For his imagery he does not rely, like most Elizabethan poets, upon mythology and nature, but upon law, scholastic philosophy, the new scientific learning of his own day, and the commonplace details of ordinary life. Such unusual imagery gives to his poetry and to that of his imitators a vivid sense of freshness. The element of surprise in metaphysical poetry is helped also by a dramatic quality. Particularly in Donne and Herbert there is usually a kind of argument with an imaginary hearer of the poem. In their religious poetry all the metaphysicals—and Herbert especially—speak directly to God in familiar terms and attain a mystical quality of direct personal relation to the Deity. In this they have much in common with Robert Southwell.

Like the poetry of Jonson and his followers, metaphysical poetry sets a value upon wit. In Donne this wit is often associated with dark and grisly imagery, for he is not afraid to face directly the physical reality of death and decay. There is in metaphysical poetry a medieval quality of grotesqueness and a fondness for medieval poetic symbols. In love poetry the metaphysicals, like the classicists, reject Petrarchism. They write about physical passion, achieving a depth of feeling rarely attained in Elizabethan love poetry, just as in religious poetry they reach an intensity of spiritual passion which few Elizabethans other than Southwell approached.

John Donne rebelled against the metrical regularity of Spenserian poetry. He made his lines deliberately harsh and rugged out of the same desire to startle his reader that conditions his unusual imagery and out of an accompanying urge to adapt poetry to the cadences of colloquial speech, free of the poetic ornamentation which may impede meaning for the sake of sound. But the roughness of Donne's lines should not be allowed to obscure the fact that he is a master prosodist. He breaks and distorts his meter skillfully to give emphasis to the shocks and contradictions in his intellectual argument, and this kind of metrical dexterity marks the poetry of his followers as well.

We have no evidence of direct relation between Donne and George Herbert, although it is likely that Herbert read Donne's poems in manuscript. The affinity between them is in the dazzling simplicity Herbert is able to attain in his approaches to God and in the extraordinary inner complexity he achieves in his lyrics, while rejecting the conventions of Renaissance poetic diction. In Richard Crashaw there is a mystical quality and a fondness for the elaborate conceit which links him to Herbert and Donne. Henry Vaughan, after a religious conversion, wrote highly mystical poetry celebrating his personal union with God. Thomas Traherne was a mystic like Vaughan, whom he imitated; his poems were not discovered until 1910. Both Vaughan and Traherne were Neoplatonists obsessed with childhood in a manner which looks forward to Wordsworth.

The metaphysical and the classical poets may have more in common than that which separates them, and the lines of distinction are very difficult to draw. Poets like Marvell and Carew may be placed in either school, for they draw fully upon both. There are few poets of the seventeenth century who are not touched by the metaphysical spirit; even John Milton felt its influences. Many poets of our own time have been deeply impressed by the metaphysicals in general and by Donne in particular.

FOR FURTHER READING:

Bennett, Joan. *Four Metaphysical Poets: Donne, Herbert, Vaughan, Crashaw.* London, 1934.

Garner, Ross. *Henry Vaughan: Experience and the Tradition.* Chicago, 1959.

Hunt, James Clay. *Donne's Poetry: Essays in Literary Analysis.* New Haven, 1954.

Leishman, J. B. *The Metaphysical Poets: Donne, Herbert, Vaughan, Traherne.* New York, 1934.

Martz, Louis. *The Poetry of Meditation.* New Haven, 1954.

Tuve, Rosemond. *A Reading of George Herbert.* Chicago, 1952.

Warren, Austin. *Richard Crashaw, a Study in Baroque Sensibility.* Baton Rouge, 1939.

White, Helen C. *The Metaphysical Poets.* New York, 1936.

Williamson, George. *The Donne Tradition.* Cambridge, Mass., 1930.

JOHN DONNE

LOVE'S ALCHEMY

Some that have deeper digged love's mine than I,
Say where his centric happiness doth lie;
      I have loved, and got, and told,
But should I love, get, tell, till I were old,
I should not find that hidden mystery;
      Oh, 'tis imposture all.
And as no chemic yet th' elixir got,
      But glorifies his pregnant pot,
      If by the way to him befall
Some odoriferous thing, or medicinal,
      So lovers dream a rich and long delight,
But get a winter-seeming summer's night.

Our ease, our thrift, our honor, and our day,
Shall we for this vain bubble's shadow pay?
      Ends love in this, that my man
Can be as happy as I can, if he can
Endure the short scorn of a bridegroom's play?
      That loving wretch that swears
'Tis not the bodies marry, but the minds,

Which he in her angelic finds,
Would swear as justly that he hears,
In that day's rude hoarse minstrelsy, the spheres.
Hope not for mind in women; at their best,
Sweetness and wit, they are but mummy possessed.

THE INDIFFERENT

I can love both fair and brown;
Her whom abundance melts, and her whom want betrays;
Her who loves loneness best, and her who masks and plays;
Her whom the country formed, and whom the town;
Her who believes, and her who tries;
Her who still weeps with spongy eyes,
And her who is dry cork and never cries.
I can love her, and her, and you, and you;
I can love any, so she be not true.

Will no other vice content you?
Will it not serve your turn to do as did your mothers?
Or have you all old vices spent and now would find out others?
Or doth a fear that men are true torment you?
O we are not, be not you so;
Let me—and do you—twenty know;
Rob me, but bind me not, and let me go.
Must I, who came to travel thorough you,
Grow your fixed subject, because you are true?

Venus heard me sigh this song;
And by love's sweetest part, variety, she swore,
She heard not this till now; it should be so no more.
She went, examined, and returned ere long,
And said, "Alas! some two or three
Poor heretics in love there be,
Which think to stablish dangerous constancy.
But I have told them, 'Since you will be true,
You shall be true to them, who're false to you.' "

SONG

Go and catch a falling star,
Get with child a mandrake root,
Tell me where all past years are,

Or who cleft the devil's foot;
Teach me to hear mermaids singing,
Or to keep off envy's stinging,
      And find
      What wind
Serves to advance an honest mind.

If thou be'st born to strange sights,
      Things invisible go see,
Ride ten thousand days and nights
      Till Age snow white hairs on thee;
Thou, when thou return'st, wilt tell me
All strange wonders that befell thee,
      And swear
      No where
Lives a woman true and fair.

If thou find'st one, let me know;
      Such a pilgrimage were sweet.
Yet do not; I would not go,
      Though at next door we might meet.
Though she were true when you met her,
And last till you write your letter,
      Yet she
      Will be
False, ere I come, to two or three.

THE FUNERAL

Whoever comes to shroud me, do not harm
      Nor question much
That subtle wreath of hair about mine arm;
The mystery, the sign you must not touch,
      For 'tis my outward soul,
Viceroy to that which, unto heav'n being gone,
      Will leave this to control
And keep these limbs, her provinces, from dissolution.

For if the sinewy thread my brain lets fall
      Through every part
Can tie those parts, and make me one of all;
Those hairs, which upward grew, and strength and art
      Have from a better brain,

Can better do't: except she meant that I
　　　By this should know my pain,
As prisoners then are manacled, when they're condemned to die.

Whate'er she meant by't, bury it with me,
　　　For since I am
Love's martyr, it might breed idolatry
If into other hands these reliques came.
　　　As 'twas humility
To afford to it all that a soul can do,
　　　So 'tis some bravery
That, since you would have none of me, I bury some of you.

THE RELIC

　　　When my grave is broke up again
　　　Some second guest to entertain,
　　　(For graves have learn'd that womanhead
　　　To be to more than one a bed)
　　　　　And he that digs it, spies
A bracelet of bright hair about the bone,
　　　　　Will he not let us alone,
And think that there a loving couple lies,
Who thought that this device might be some way
To make their souls, at the last busy day,
Meet at this grave, and make a little stay?

　　　If this fall in a time, or land,
　　　Where mis-devotion doth command,
　　　Then he that digs us up will bring
　　　Us to the Bishop and the King,
　　　　　To make us Relics; then
Thou shalt be a Mary Magdalen, and I
　　　　　A something else thereby;
All women shall adore us, and some men;
And since at such time, miracles are sought,
I would have that age by this paper taught
What miracles we harmless lovers wrought.

　　　First, we loved well and faithfully,
　　　Yet knew not what we loved, nor why,
　　　Difference of sex no more we knew
　　　Than our Guardian Angels do;

Coming and going, we
Perchance might kiss, but not between those meals;
Our hands n'er touched the seals
Which nature, injured by late law, sets free:
These miracles we did; but now alas,
All measure, and all language, I should pass
Should I tell what a miracle she was.

THE ANNIVERSARY

All kings, and all their favorites,
All glory of honors, beauties, wits,
The sun itself, which makes times, as they pass,
Is elder by a year, now, than it was
When thou and I first one another saw:
All other things to their destruction draw,
Only our love hath no decay;
This, no tomorrow hath, nor yesterday,
Running it never runs from us away,
But truly keeps his first, last, everlasting day.

Two graves must hide thine and my corse,
If one might, death were no divorce.
Alas! as well as other princes, we
(Who prince enough in one another be)
Must leave at last in death, these eyes, and ears,
Oft fed with true oaths, and with sweet salt tears;
But souls where nothing dwells but love
(All other thoughts being inmates) then shall prove
This, or a love increasèd there above,
When bodies to their graves, souls from their graves remove.

And then we shall be throughly blest,
But we no more than all the rest;
Here upon earth, we are kings, and none but we
Can be such kings, nor of such subjects be.
Who is so safe as we? where none can do
Treason to us, except one of us two.
True and false fears let us refrain,
Let us love nobly, and live, and add again
Years and years unto years, till we attain
To write threescore: this is the second of our reign.

THE SUN RISING

Busy old fool, unruly Sun,
      Why dost thou thus,
Through windows, and through curtains, call on us?
Must to thy motions lovers' seasons run?
      Saucy pedantic wretch, go chide
      Late school-boys and sour prentices,
   Go tell court-huntsmen that the king will ride,
   Call country ants to harvest offices;
Love, all alike, no season knows nor clime,
Nor hours, days, months, which are the rags of time.

      Thy beams, so reverend and strong
      Why shouldst thou think?
I could eclipse and cloud them with a wink,
But that I would not lose her sight so long.
      If her eyes have not blinded thine,
      Look, and tomorrow late tell me,
   Whether both th'Indias of spice and mine
   Be where thou left'st them, or lie here with me.
Ask for those kings whom thou saw'st yesterday,
And thou shalt hear, "All here in one bed lay."

      She's all states, and all princes I;
      Nothing else is;
Princes do but play us; compared to this,
All honour's mimic, all wealth alchemy.
      Thou, Sun, art half as happy as we,
      In that the world's contracted thus;
   Thine age asks ease, and since thy duties be
   To warm the world, that's done in warming us.
Shine here to us, and thou art everywhere;
This bed thy center is, these walls thy sphere.

THE CANONIZATION

For God's sake hold your tongue, and let me love;
      Or chide my palsy, or my gout;
My five gray hairs, or ruined fortune flout;
   With wealth your state, your mind with arts improve;
         Take you a course, get you a place,
         Observe his honour, or his grace;

Or the king's real, or his stamped face
   Contemplate; what you will, approve,
   So you will let me love.

Alas! alas! who's injured by my love?
    What merchants' ships have my sighs drowned?
Who says my tears have overflowed his ground?
    When did my colds a forward spring remove?
      When did the heats which my veins fill
      Add one more to the plaguy bill?
Soldiers find wars, and lawyers find out still
   Litigious men, which quarrels move,
   Though she and I do love.

Call us what you will, we are made such by love;
   Call her one, me another fly,
We're tapers too, and at our own cost die,
    And we in us find th'eagle and the dove.
      The phoenix riddle hath more wit
      By us; we two being one, are it;
So, to one neutral thing both sexes fit.
   We die and rise the same, and prove
   Mysterious by this love.

We can die by it, if not live by love,
   And if unfit for tombs and hearse
Our legend be, it will be fit for verse;
    And if no piece of chronicle we prove,
      We'll build in sonnets pretty rooms;
      As well a well-wrought urn becomes
The greatest ashes, as half-acre tombs,
   And by these hymns all shall approve
   Us canonized for love;

And thus invoke us, "You, whom reverend love
   Made one another's hermitage;
You, to whom love was peace, that now is rage;
    Who did the whole world's soul contract, and drove
      Into the glasses of your eyes—
      So made such mirrors, and such spies,
That they did all to you epitomize—
   Countries, towns, courts beg from above
   A pattern of your love!"

A VALEDICTION FORBIDDING MOURNING

As virtuous men pass mildly away,
And whisper to their souls to go,
Whilst some of their sad friends do say,
The breath goes now, and some say, No:

So let us melt, and make no noise,
No tear-floods, nor sigh-tempests move;
'Twere profanation of our joys
To tell the laity our love.

Moving of th' earth brings harms and fears,
Men reckon what it did, and meant;
But trepidation of the spheres,
Though greater far, is innocent.

Dull sublunary lovers' love
—Whose soul is sense—cannot admit
Absence, because it doth remove
Those things which elemented it.

But we by a love so much refined
That ourselves know not what it is,
Inter-assurèd of the mind,
Care less eyes, lips and hands to miss.

Our two souls therefore, which are one,
Though I must go, endure not yet
A breach, but an expansion,
Like gold to airy thinness beat.

If they be two, they are two so
As stiff twin compasses are two;
Thy soul, the fixed foot, makes no show
To move, but doth, if th' other do.

And though it in the centre sit,
Yet, when the other far doth roam,
It leans and hearkens after it,
And grows erect, as that comes home.

Such wilt thou be to me, who must,
Like th' other foot, obliquely run;

Thy firmness makes my circle just,
And makes me end where I begun.

A VALEDICTION OF WEEPING

Let me pour forth
My tears before thy face whilst I stay here,
For thy face coins them, and thy stamp they bear,
And by this mintage they are something worth,
For thus they be
Pregnant of thee;
Fruits of much grief they are, emblems of more—
When a tear falls, that thou fallst which it bore,
So thou and I are nothing then, when on a diverse shore.

On a round ball
A workman that hath copies by, can lay
An Europe, Afric, and an Asïa,
And quickly make that which was nothing, all;
So doth each tear
Which thee doth wear,
A globe, yea world, by that impression grow,
Till thy tears mixed with mine do overflow
This world; by waters sent from thee, my heaven dissolvèd so.

O more than moon,
Draw not up seas to drown me in thy sphere;
Weep me not dead, in thine arms, but forbear
To teach the sea what it may do too soon;
Let not the wind
Example find,
To do me more harm than it purposeth;
Since thou and I sigh one another's breath,
Whoe'er sighs most is cruellest, and hastes the other's death.

A VALEDICTION OF WEEPING When Dr. Samuel Johnson chose to discuss the extravagances of metaphysical poetry, he selected for special opprobrium the entire second stanza of *A Valediction of Weeping*. With wry humor Johnson indicates the difficulties that are met frequently in the more extreme conceits of the metaphysicals: "The tears of the lovers are always of great poetical account; but Donne has extended them into worlds. If the lines are not easily understood, they may be read again."

Perhaps no other poem is so well qualified to illustrate both the nature of metaphysical poetry and its abuses. But whereas Johnson had only disdain for such poems, modern poets and modern critics have found in them much to admire; while we are aware of the strained quality of the extended metaphor, we are impressed also by the intellectual vigor of the mind that was able to pursue these ramifications of a tear-world analogy. We do not readily accept Johnson's belief that the metaphysical poets "were not successful in representing or moving the affections." Instead, the twentieth-century poet T. S. Eliot, who felt at the beginning of his career that English poetry was suffering a "dissociation of sensibility," turned to poets like Donne and tried in his own verse to reunite intellect and feeling by imitating the practice of the metaphysicals.

A Valediction of Weeping is composed of three stanzas of great irregularity. Not only are the line lengths varied but the meter is rough and the rhymes imperfect. Each stanza opens with a two-foot line followed by three lines in pentameter. The fifth and sixth lines comprise an iambic dimeter couplet. The final tercet is composed of two pentameter lines and a heptameter or fourteener. In two cases lines of unequal length are made to rhyme: line 1 in dimeter with line 4 in pentameter; line 9 in heptameter with lines 7 and 8 in pentameter. Ben Jonson once said that "Donne, for not keeping of accent, deserved hanging." He may have had in mind lines such as:

For thy face coins them, and thy stamp they bear.

Holding a place in the stanza that calls for a pentameter line, this line is completely irregular.

Donne is also free with rhyme. Although we take into account the differences between Elizabethan pronunciation and our own, combinations such as *forth, worth; here, bear; tear, wear; sphere, forbear* are only half rhymes. In the second stanza, *lay* and *Asïa* cannot be said to rhyme at all; and in the third stanza the syllable *-eth* of *purposeth*—either a very weakly stressed or unstressed syllable—is made to rhyme with the strongly accented *breath* and *death*. These irregularities are not unique; Donne proceeds along similar lines in almost all his poems.

Donne's handling of the metaphysical conceit is perhaps better shown in this poem than in any other. The entire poem is constructed around the image of a tear. In the poet's teeming imagination the relationships which that tear conjures up are extravagant. First, each tear is like a coin. The speaker's beloved is the mint which creates them, for the sight of her and his realization that they are about to part (the poem is a valediction—a farewell) bring them forth. The poet has observed that any small globule of glass, crystal, or water (thus the tear) reflects the image of a person who stares into it. In this manner the beloved, who stares into her weeping lover's eyes, imprints her face upon his tears and her "stamp they bear." Because it is her precious image which adorns the "coin," they have special value ("are something worth").

The idea that the tear carries a replica of the lady then suggests to Donne the metaphor of conception. The tear is shaped like the womb and is "pregnant" with his lady's image. The birth metaphor is pursued, and the tears themselves are seen as newborn objects, conceived in the womb of his grief; they are "Fruits of much grief." But they are "emblems of more," and we may here note Donne's fondness for punning on names, for the lady to whom the poem is addressed is Anne More, his wife. The coin metaphor has given rise to the sister image of the medallion or emblem. But *emblem* is used in a double sense of (1) a portent of sorrow to come and (2) a medal struck to commemorate their parting. The tear changes from medallion to omen of grief when it drops from the lover's eye to the floor and loses its spherical shape, thereby dashing the beloved to the ground and shattering her reflection.

The poet now brilliantly merges the metaphoric with the actual in a daring image. Just as they will become "nothing" by being separated (they love each other so much that they cease to exist when apart), so also she becomes nothing when her image is destroyed in the fallen tear (and if she is destroyed, then so is he who cannot live without her). But the tear image proves to have more appropriateness than merely to suggest separation and destruction. Apparently the poet's journey involves travel by water. They will stand on opposite ("diverse") shores when he completes the outward leg of his journey; and they are on opposite sides of the body of water (only a tear) which has fallen between them. In the first stanza alone the tear conceit is developed until it stands variously for *coin, womb, medallion, portent,* and *sea,* but still the poet is not done.

The extended metaphor of the second stanza is developed around a reconstruction of the entire cosmos. Workmen can reproduce on any round ball an image of the world; a tear is spherical, and since the lady is the poet's "everything," his "world," and since her image is reflected in the tear, that tear becomes his "globe, yea world." In both cases a universe ("all," "globe," "world") is created out of nothing("Round ball," "tear"). Donne has used as a pivotal word in the second stanza the *nothing* of the final line of the first stanza. There is an implied allusion to Genesis, in which the world is created out of the darkness and the void. But then the lady adds her tears to the poet's and drowns his world. The reference here is to the Biblical Flood.

So far as the universe is concerned, Donne has now created land and sea; it remains for him to establish the skies. This he does in the last line by stating that any world with his lady in it is also his heaven, and thus the full cosmos is made. But this heaven is flooded equally with the poet's world, and a third reference to Genesis is probably made at this point. Medieval thought held that the Garden of Eden, though empty after the fall of man, continued to exist until the flood. At that time it was washed away. In Dante's *Divine Comedy* Eden floats all the way from the eastern end of the Mediterranean to what would now be our South Pole, where it comes to rest on the top of Mount Purgatory. Donne implies that so long as he and his beloved are together they are in paradise, but when she is taken from him—that is, when her tears destroy his, thus ruining her own reflection therein—his "heaven" is "dissolvèd."

The third stanza follows a course natural to the images developed in the second. Since the movement of tides is known to be affected by the moon, Donne identifies his lady, who is causing floods, with the moon. He asks her to stop her tears in fear that she may be showing the real sea, which he soon must cross, the way to destroy him. Storms are whipped up by high winds, which the poet equates with his beloved's sighs. He asks her to stop sighing as well. With wind and water quieted, his journey will be safer; with sighs and tears abated, their parting will be more serene. The poet, who wept first, ceases first; and having caused his lady to weep, he urges her to stop also. This he does by referring to an old wives' tale which held that each sigh extracted a drop of blood from the heart. Since the two are so closely united, they draw one another's breath: when she sighs, a drop of blood comes from his heart; when he sighs, it comes from hers. They must stop their lamentation or they will be the death of one another—

> Whoe'er sighs most is cruellest, and hastes the other's death.

HYMN TO GOD MY GOD, IN MY SICKNESS

> Since I am coming to that holy room,
>   Where, with thy choir of saints for evermore,
> I shall be made thy music; as I come
>   I tune the instrument here at the door,
>   And what I must do then, think here before.
>
> Whilst my physicians by their love are grown
>   Cosmographers, and I their map, who lie
> Flat on this bed, that by them may be shown
>   That this is my south-west discovery,
>   *Per fretum febris,* by these straits to die,

I joy, that in these straits, I see my west;
    For, though their currents yield return to none,
What shall my west hurt me? As west and east
    In all flat maps (and I am one) are one,
    So death doth touch the Resurrection.

Is the Pacific sea my home? Or are
    The eastern riches? Is Jerusalem?
Anyan, and Magellan, and Gibraltar,
    All straits, and none but straits, are ways to them,
    Whether where Japhet dwelt, or Cham, or Sem.

We think that Paradise and Calvary,
    Christ's cross, and Adam's tree, stood in one place;
Look, Lord, and find both Adams met in me;
    As the first Adam's sweat surrounds my face,
    May the last Adam's blood my soul embrace.

So, in his purple wrapped, receive me Lord;
    By these, his thorns give me his other crown;
And as to others' souls I preached thy word,
    Be this my text, my sermon to mine own,
    Therefore that he may raise, the Lord throws down.

THIS IS MY PLAY'S LAST SCENE

This is my play's last scene; here heavens appoint
My pilgrimage's last mile; and my race,
Idly yet quickly run, hath this last pace;
My span's last inch, my minutes' latest point;
And gluttonous death will instantly unjoint
My body and my soul, and I shall sleep a space;
But my'ever-waking part shall see that face
Whose fear already shakes my every joint.
Then as my soul to'heaven, her first seat, takes flight,
And earth-born body in the earth shall dwell,
So fall my sins, that all may have their right,
To where they'are bred, and would press me,—to hell.
Impute me righteous, thus purged of evil,
For thus I leave the world, the flesh, the devil.

HENRY KING

SONNET

Tell me no more how fair she is,
　　I have no mind to hear
The story of that distant bliss
　　I never shall come near;
By sad experience I have found
That her perfection is my wound.

And tell me not how fond I am
　　To tempt a daring fate,
From whence no triumph ever came
　　But to repent too late;
There is some hope ere long I may
In silence dote myself away.

I ask no pity, Love, from thee,
　　Nor will thy justice blame,
So that thou wilt not envy me
　　The glory of my flame,
Which crowns my heart whene'er it dies,
In that it falls her sacrifice.

GEORGE HERBERT

THE PULLEY

When God at first made man,
Having a glass of blessings standing by—
Let us (said He) pour on him all we can;

HENRY KING (1592-1669) became Anglican Bishop of London, in which capacity he ordained John Donne. Bishop of Chichester at the time of the Civil War, he was removed by the Puritans but was returned to his see after the Restoration.
GEORGE HERBERT (1593-1633), a member of one of the most distinguished and powerful noble families in England, gave up the post of university orator at Cambridge, became an Anglican priest, and in 1630 retired to a small rectory, where he spent the rest of his life. None of his poems were published during his lifetime.

Let the world's riches, which dispersèd lie,
 Contract into a span.

 So strength first made a way;
Then beauty flow'd, then wisdom, honour, pleasure:
When almost all was out, God made a stay,
Perceiving that, alone, of all His treasure,
 Rest in the bottom lay.

 For if I should (said He)
Bestow this jewel also on My creature,
He would adore My gifts instead of Me,
And rest in Nature, not the God of Nature:
 So both should losers be.

 Yet let him keep the rest,
But keep them with repining restlessness;
Let him be rich and weary, that at least,
If goodness lead him not, yet weariness
 May toss him to My breast.

CONSCIENCE

 Peace, prattler, do not lour!
Not a fair look but thou dost call it foul.
Not a sweet dish but thou dost call it sour.
 Music to thee doth howl.
 By list'ning to thy chatting fears,
 I have both lost mine eyes and ears.

 Prattler, no more, I say!
My thoughts must work, but like a noiseless sphere;
Harmonious peace must rock them all the day,
 No room for prattlers there.
 If thou persistest, I will tell thee
 That I have physic to expel thee.

 And the receipt shall be
My Savior's blood. Whenever at his board
I do but taste it, straight it cleanseth me
 And leaves thee not a word;
 No, not a tooth or nail to scratch,
 And at my actions carp or catch.

Yet if thou talkest still,
Besides my physic know there's some for thee;
Some wood and nails to make a staff or bill
For those that trouble me.
The bloody cross of my dear Lord
Is both my physic and my sword.

THE COLLAR

I struck the board, and cried, "No more;
I will abroad!
What! shall I ever sigh and pine?
My lines and life are free; free as the road,
Loose as the wind, as large as store.
Shall I be still in suit?
Have I no harvest but a thorn
To let me blood, and not restore
What I have lost with cordial fruit?
Sure there was wine
Before my sighs did dry it; there was corn
Before my tears did drown it;
Is the year only lost to me?
Have I no bays to crown it,
No flowers, no garlands gay? all blasted,
All wasted?
Not so, my heart; but there is fruit,
And thou hast hands.
Recover all thy sigh-blown age
On double pleasures; leave thy cold dispute
Of what is fit and not; forsake thy cage,
Thy rope of sands
Which petty thoughts have made; and made to thee
Good cable, to enforce and draw,
And be thy law,
While thou didst wink and wouldst not see.
Away! take heed;
I will abroad.
Call in thy death's-head there, tie up thy fears:
He that forbears
To suit and serve his need
Deserves his load."
But as I raved, and grew more fierce and wild
At every word,

Methought I heard one calling, "Child";
And I replied, "My Lord."

LOVE

Love bade me welcome; yet my soul drew back,
 Guilty of dust and sin.
But quick-eyed Love, observing me grow slack
 From my first entrance in,
Drew nearer to me, sweetly questioning
 If I lacked anything.

"A guest," I answered, "worthy to be here":
 Love said, "You shall be he."
"I, the unkind, ungrateful? Ah, my dear,
 I cannot look on Thee."
Love took my hand, and smiling did reply,
 "Who made the eyes but I?"

"Truth, Lord; but I have marred them; let my shame
 Go where it doth deserve."
"And know you not," says Lord, "who bore the blame?"
 "My dear, then I will serve."
"You must sit down," says Love, "and taste my meat."
 So I did sit and eat.

RICHARD CRASHAW

A SONG

Lord, when the sense of thy sweet grace
Sends up my soul to seek thy face,
Thy blessed eyes breed such desire
I die in love's delicious fire.
 O love, I am thy sacrifice.
Be still triumphant, blessed eyes;
Still shine on me, fair suns! that I
Still may behold, though still I die,

RICHARD CRASHAW (1612?-1649), the son of a London clergyman of
strong Puritan leanings, was converted to Roman Catholicism and went to Paris and
later to Rome, where he became secretary to the governor, Cardinal Palotta. In 1649
he was appointed canon at the shrine of Loretto.

Though still I die, I live again,
Still longing so to be still slain;
So gainful is such loss of breath,
I die even in desire of death.
    Still live in me this loving strife
Of living death and dying life;
For while thou sweetly slayest me,
Dead to myself, I live in thee.

HENRY VAUGHAN

AND DO THEY SO?

Romans viii. 19
Etenim res creatæ exerto capite observantes expectant
revelationem Filiorum Dei.

And do they so? Have they a sense
    of aught but influence?
Can they their heads lift, and expect,
    And groan too? Why th' elect
Can do no more; my volumes said
    They were all dull, and dead;
They judged them senseless, and their state
    Wholly inanimate.
    Go, go, seal up thy looks,
      And burn thy books.

I would I were a stone, or tree,
    Or flower, by pedigree,
Or some poor highway herb, or spring
    To flow, or bird to sing!
Then should I, tied to one sure state,
    All day expect my date;
But I am sadly loose, and stray
    A giddy blast each way;
    O let me not thus range,
      Thou canst not change!

HENRY VAUGHAN (1622-1695), the son of a Welsh squire, first studied law and then medicine. In 1658 he inherited his father's small estate and spent the rest of his days as a country doctor in rural Wales.

Sometimes I sit with thee and tarry
    An hour or so, then vary;
Thy other creatures in this scene
    Thee only aim and mean;
Some rise to seek thee, and with heads
    Erect, peep from their beds;
Others, whose birth is in the tomb,
    And cannot quit the womb,
      Sigh there, and groan for thee,
        Their liberty.

O let me not do less! shall they
    Watch, while I sleep or play?
Shall I thy mercies still abuse
    With fancies, friends, or news?
O brook it not! thy blood is mine,
    And my soul should be thine;
O brook it not! why wilt thou stop,
After whole showers, one drop?
Sure, thou wilt joy to see
    Thy sheep with thee.

THOMAS TRAHERNE

INSATIABLENESS

This busy, vast, inquiring soul
    Brooks no control,
    No limits will endure,
    Nor any rest; it will all see,
Not time alone, but ev'n eternity.
    What is it? Endless, sure.

'Tis mean ambition to desire
    A single world;
    To many I aspire,
    Though one upon another hurled;
Nor will they all, if they be all confined,
    Delight my mind.

THOMAS TRAHERNE (1637?-1674), after taking a B.A. in 1656 from Brasenose College, Oxford, entered the ministry and served as rector of Credenhill, near Hereford, until 1667, when he went to London as chaplain to the lord keeper of the seals. This post he kept until his death.

This busy, vast, inquiring soul
　　　Brooks no control;
　　'Tis very curious too.
　　Each one of all those worlds must be
Enriched with infinite variety
　　　And worth, or 'twill not do.

　　'Tis nor delight nor perfect pleasure
　　　To have a purse
　　That hath a bottom in its treasure,
Since I must thence endless expense disburse.
Sure there's a God, for else there's no delight,
　　　One infinite.

III
THE STUART AGE

THE ELEGIAC

T HE elegy in English poetry is a difficult mode to define; yet elegies have been written throughout English literary history. Among the very greatest of the early poems must be named the elegiac *Deor's Lament*, the funereal *The Pearl*, and Chaucer's compassionate *Book of the Duchess.* In the seventeenth century the genre reached perhaps its widest use; many books of the age, like Henry King's *Poems, Elegies, Paradoxes, and Sonnets* (1657), carried some form of the word *elegy* in their titles.

Elegiac in Greek and Latin poetry referred at first only to a metrical arrangement—couplets of alternating dactylic hexameter and pentameter —and any poem employing it was called an elegy. Because of its distinctive quality, elegiac meter became a common vehicle for mournful poetry, but while the term *elegy* in modern English usage applies solely to a lament for the dead, in earlier times there was no restriction as to subject matter. The eighteenth-century poet William Shenstone, in an introduction to his volume entitled *Elegies,* maintained that the type allowed of "any kind of subject treated so as to diffuse a pleasing melancholy." Somewhat later, Coleridge echoed Shenstone on the matter of subject and added, "Elegy is the form of poetry natural to the reflective mind." Perhaps the easiest solution to the problem of definition is to go to Dr. Johnson's dictionary, where an elegy is called simply "a mournful song."

J. C. Bailey, who is one of the few critics ever to attempt a comprehensive definition of the form and who has made a thorough survey of the poetry itself, says that though any subject may be treated in an elegy, "Love, Grief, and Death are its three notes." He says also that "The more passionate the grief is, the less obvious should be the metrical system"; and in English the elegy does indeed employ various meters and various verse forms, since its special quality is found not in its metrics but in its spirit.

The funeral elegy is rooted firmly in the pastoral tradition, going back to Theocritus, Bion, and Moschus. This form was one of Spenser's favorites; his lament for Dido in the November eclogue of *The Shepheardes Calender* and his commemoration of Sir Philip Sidney in *Astrophel* are in the tradition that starts with the Greeks and finds perhaps its most perfect expression in John Milton. *Lycidas,* in which Milton immortalized his dead classmate Edward King, becomes also, in the manner common to the pastoral, an attack upon the clerical abuses of the day. Seventeenth-century elegiac poetry draws upon the classical and metaphysical as well as the pastoral tradition. Ben Jonson and Robert Herrick had a particular fondness for funeral epitaphs; Herrick wrote them even for persons still alive, and Jonson composed some of his most perfectly controlled classical poems on the death of his first son, on that of the child actor Salomon Pavy, and on Elizabeth, L. H., who, though she has never been satisfactorily identified, will live forever in Jonson's lines. The classical precision of William Browne's epitaph for the Countess of Pembroke has made it one of the memorable poems of its type.

Forms used traditionally for other themes were used for elegiac purposes also. One of Milton's finest achievements was the sonnet *On His Deceased Wife*, and poets like Edward Herbert, Lord Cherbury, wrote elegiac poetry using the devices of the metaphysicals. That the funeral lament and the epitaph are so common in the seventeenth century may afford another instance of the peculiar fascination with death which conditions almost every aspect of this age's art.

FOR FURTHER READING:

Bailey, J. C., ed. "Introduction," *English Elegies.* London, 1900.
Norlin, George. "The Conventions of the Pastoral Elegy," *American Journal of Philology,* XXXII (1911), 294-312.
Fisher, J. "Shenstone, Gray, and the Moral Elegy," *Modern Philology,* XXXIV (1937), 273-294.
Wallerstein, Ruth C. *Studies in Seventeenth-Century Poetic.* Madison, Wis., 1950.

BEN JONSON

ON MY FIRST SON

Farewell, thou child of my right hand, and joy;
    My sin was too much hope of thee, loved boy.
Seven years thou wert lent to me, and I thee pay,
    Exacted by thy fate, on the just day.
Oh, could I lose all father now! for why
    Will man lament the state he should envy?
To have so soon 'scaped world's and flesh's rage,
    And, if no other misery, yet age!
Rest in soft peace, and asked, say, here doth lie
    Ben Jonson his best piece of poetry.
For whose sake henceforth all his vows be such,
    As what he loves may never like too much.

AN EPITAPH ON SALOMON PAVY, A CHILD OF QUEEN ELIZABETH'S CHAPEL

Weep with me, all you that read
    This little story;
And know, for whom a tear you shed
    Death's self is sorry.
'Twas a child that so did thrive
    In grace and feature,
As heaven and nature seemed to strive
    Which owned the creature.
Years he numbered scarce thirteen
    When fates turned cruel,
Yet three filled zodiacs had he been
    The stage's jewel:
And did act (what now we moan)
    Old men so duly,
As, sooth, the Parcae thought him one,
    He played so truly.
So, by error, to his fate
    They all consented;
But, viewing him since, alas, too late!
    They have repented;
And have sought, to give new birth,
    In baths to steep him;
But, being so much too good for earth,
    Heaven vows to keep him.

EPITAPH ON ELIZABETH, L. H.

Wouldst thou hear what man can say
    In a little? Reader, stay.
Underneath this stone doth lie
    As much beauty as could die;
Which in life did harbor give
    To more virtue than doth live.
If at all she had a fault,
    Leave it buried in this vault.
One name was Elizabeth,
    Th' other let it sleep with death;
Fitter, where it died to tell,
    Than that it lived at all. Farewell.

JOHN MILTON

ON HIS DECEASED WIFE

Methought I saw my late espousèd saint
Brought to me like Alcestis' from the grave,
Whom Jove's great son to her glad husband gave,
Rescued from death by force though pale and faint.
Mine as whom washed from spot of child-bed taint,
Purification in the old law did save,
And such, as yet once more I trust to have
Full sight of her in Heaven without restraint,
Came vested all in white, pure as her mind.
Her face was veiled, yet to my fancied sight
Love, sweetness, goodness, in her person shined,
So clear, as in no face with more delight.
But O, as to embrace me she inclined,
I waked, she fled, and day brought back my night.

ON HIS DECEASED WIFE In Milton's poem we note at once that
though the basic rhyme scheme of the Petrarchan or Italian sonnet is retained, the break between octave (*abbaabba*) and sestet (*cdcdcd*), cus-
tomary in English Petrarchan sonnets, is ignored. In place of the old question-and-answer, or problem-and-resolution, relation between octave and
sestet, which had given to the Petrarchan sonnet its tone of clever epigram and its note of finality, with the implication that a truth has been
stated and therefore nothing further may be said, Milton creates a steadily
increasing and developing effect for the full fourteen lines, as the details
of his sorrow are made gradually more and more clear. The final line of
the sestet comes not as the resolution of some artificial problem in the octave but as the final and culminating revelation of a deep and abiding grief.
It is this Miltonic use of the form which Wordsworth (see pp. 68-70) was
later to imitate when the sonnet had its great revival in the nineteenth
century.

JOHN MILTON (1608-1674) was born in London, the son of a prosperous
scrivener of strong Puritan leanings who had been disowned by his own stanchly
Roman Catholic parents. Young Milton was educated first by a private tutor, then
at St. Paul's School in London and at Christ's College, Cambridge, where he took
a B.A. in 1629 and an M.A. in 1632. After a six-year period of study and travel
he settled in London and soon became involved in the developing Civil War, eventually being appointed Latin secretary to Cromwell's Council of State. In 1652,
while in the service of the government, he went totally blind. His life was spared
after the Restoration through the influence of powerful friends; he lived in London
for the rest of his days in relative poverty and obscurity.

Milton's modification of the Elizabethan sonnet form is not arbitrary but an essential part of his poem, for this sonnet is no mere expression of commonplace Petrarchan love sentiment, as most Elizabethan sonnets were. Milton's sonnet is a vehicle for profound emotion intimately associated with the poet's life; it affords another instance in which some knowledge of the poem's external circumstances is essential to full understanding. In 1656, some two years after he had lost his eyesight, John Milton married Katherine Woodcock. In October of 1657 she bore a child, but in February of 1658 she died, and a few weeks later the child died as well. This poem is an expression of Milton's poignant sorrow over the loss of a wife he had never seen.

We must be familiar also with the classical legends that provide the basis of the poem. In a dream Milton sees the restitution of his dead wife in terms of the restoration of Alcestis to her husband. To King Admetus, the Fates (upon the suit of Apollo) had granted deliverance from death if his father, mother, or wife would consent to die in his place. When his time came to die, his wife, Alcestis, offered herself as his substitute. The great hero Hercules journeyed to Hades and brought Alcestis back to her husband. The story is told in the *Alcestis* of Euripides; it is a traditional myth of loving sacrifice rewarded by the gods.

Milton sees the death of his wife through the sufferings of childbirth as her sacrifice so that he may live (through offspring), a motif stressed also by Euripides, but there is no joyful restitution of the dead bride in Milton's poem, only the powerful awareness of his loss and of the eternal darkness which surrounds him. To make this final point, which reverses the traditional import of the Alcestis legend, Milton calls again upon Euripides, who had related this legend to another classical myth of rescue from death—that of Orpheus and Eurydice. This myth, which from his constant use of it seems to have been Milton's favorite among ancient legends, ends not with joyful reunion but with sorrow and loss as Eurydice is haled shrieking back to Hades.

The first line of the poem sets the dream mood of the whole, for the blind Milton in actual life could never have seen his wife. She appears to him as a saint, newly welcomed in heaven, dressed in the white which is the traditional symbol of purity and of the redeemed souls in heaven, as described by St. John (Revelations 8:13-14). Milton then compares her to Alcestis, who is heavily veiled when Hercules brings her to Admetus in Euripides' play.

In the fifth and sixth lines Milton emphasizes the purity of his wife and stresses the sacrificial nature of her death in childbirth. He does this by reference to Old Testament law (Leviticus, Chapter 12), which regarded a woman as unclean after childbirth until she had been purified by a ritual sacrifice. The poet then expresses his belief that he will see her in heaven in all her purity. Here there seems to be a slight rest in the movement of the poem, but the tenth line carries it on with renewed vigor, gaining momentum until the poignant last two lines are reached. As the figure seeks to embrace the poet, he awakens, and now the Orpheus story is invoked, for while the poet strives to see the figure of love before him, his dream vision departs, just as Eurydice had gone back to Hades when Orpheus had turned to look upon her. Daytime, the end of his dream, brings back only the eternal night of his blindness, just as the loss of Eurydice, in some versions of the myth, had led to the silencing forever of the music of Orpheus.

The final line employs verbal ambiguity which adds to the scope and complexity of the poem. The "night" which returns to the poet is not only his blindness but also the darkness of the soul brought on by the loss of his wife, and this is related to the blighting of Orpheus' soul, the destruction of his music.

The poem is similarly enriched by the implications of the word *restraint,* which as the final word of the octave receives a particular poetic emphasis. To have the sight of his wife without restraint is to know her free from the encumbrances of mortal life—his blindness for one, with all its implications, both physical and spiritual, but also those restrictions upon sexual union which we know from Milton's theological writings he regarded as resulting from the fall of man from paradise. In heaven they will experience the kind of total union of mind and spirit envisaged in Renaissance Neoplatonism, and a union of body as well, for Milton believed in the resurrection of the body after death and in the physical mating of heavenly spirits free from the shame which must accompany physical union on earth. "Night," which is a traditional metaphor for death (see Shakespeare, *That Time of Year* p. 69), is a state of being which the poet desires implicitly for himself and indirectly looks forward to.

There is in this poem the kind of elegiac reconciliation more fully expressed in *Lycidas.* Much of this effect centers in the forceful "I waked," for ordinarily man wakes to life, whereas Milton wakes to blindness and death. For Milton, literal death will bring the most perfect kind of life; he will know in reality what he now can experience only in a dream.

LYCIDAS

In this Monody the Author bewails a learned Friend, unfortunately drowned in his passage from Chester on the Irish Seas, 1637; and by occasion, foretells the ruin of our corrupted Clergy, then in their height.

> Yet once more, O ye laurels, and once more,
> Ye myrtles brown, with ivy never sear,

I come to pluck your berries harsh and crude,
And with forced fingers rude
Shatter your leaves before the mellowing year.
Bitter constraint and sad occasion dear
Compels me to disturb your season due;
For Lycidas is dead, dead ere his prime,
Young Lycidas, and hath not left his peer.
Who would not sing for Lycidas? He knew
Himself to sing, and build the lofty rime.
He must not float upon his watery bier
Unwept, and welter to the parching wind,
Without the need of some melodious tear.

    Begin, then, Sisters of the sacred well,
That from beneath the seat of Jove doth spring;
Begin, and somewhat loudly sweep the string.
Hence with denial vain and coy excuse;
So may some gentle muse
With lucky words favor my destined urn,
And as he passes turn
And bid fair peace be to my sable shroud!

    For we were nursed upon the selfsame hill,
Fed the same flock, by fountain, shade, and rill;
Together both, ere the high lawns appeared
Under the opening eyelids of the Morn,
We drove afield, and both together heard
What time the gray-fly winds her sultry horn,
Battening our flocks with the fresh dews of night,
Oft till the star that rose at evening, bright,
Toward heaven's descent had sloped his westering wheel.
Meanwhile the rural ditties were not mute,
Tempered to the oaten flute;
Rough Satyrs danced, and Fauns with cloven heel
From the glad sound would not be absent long;
And old Damoetas loved to hear our song.

    But, oh! the heavy change, now thou art gone,
Now thou art gone, and never must return!
Thee, Shepherd, thee the woods and desert caves,
With wild thyme and the gadding vine o'ergrown,
And all their echoes, mourn.
The willows, and the hazel copses green,
Shall now no more be seen,
Fanning their joyous leaves to thy soft layes.
As killing as the canker to the rose,

Or taint-worm to the weanling herds that graze,
Or frost to flowers, that their gay wardrobe wear,
When first the white-thorn blows—
Such, Lycidas, thy loss to shepherd's ear.
    Where were ye, Nymphs, when the remorseless deep,
Closed o'er the head of your loved Lycidas?
For neither were ye playing on the steep
Where your old bards, the famous Druids, lie,
Nor on the shaggy top of Mona high,
Nor yet where Deva spreads her wizard stream.
Aye me! I fondly dream
"Had ye been there"—for what could that have done?
What could the Muse herself that Orpheus bore,
The Muse herself, for her enchanting son,
Whom universal nature did lament,
When, by the rout that made the hideous roar,
His gory visage down the stream was sent,
Down the swift Hebrus to the Lesbian shore?
    Alas! what boots it with uncessant care
To tend the homely, slighted, shepherd's trade,
And strictly meditate the thankless Muse?
Were it not better done as others use,
To sport with Amaryllis in the shade,
Or with the tangles of Neaera's hair?
Fame is the spur that the clear spirit doth raise
(That last infirmity of noble mind)
To scorn delights, and live laborious days;
But the fair guerdon when we hope to find,
And think to burst out into sudden blaze,
Comes the blind Fury with the abhorrèd shears,
And slits the thin-spun life. "But not the praise,"
Phoebus replied, and touched my trembling ears;
"Fame is no plant that grows on mortal soil,
Nor in the glistering foil
Set off to the world, nor in broad rumor lies,
But lives and spreads aloft by those pure eyes
And perfect witness of all-judging Jove;
As he pronounces lastly on each deed,
Of so much fame in heaven expect thy meed."
    O fountain Arethuse, and thou honored flood,
Smooth-sliding Mincius, crowned with vocal reeds,
That strain I heard was of a higher mood.
But now my oat proceeds,

And listens to the Herald of the Sea
That came in Neptune's plea.
He asked the waves, and asked the felon winds,
What hard mishap hath doomed this gentle swain!
And questioned every gust of rugged wings
That blows from off each beakèd promontory.
They knew not of his story;
And sage Hippotades their answer brings,
That not a blast was from his dungeon strayed;
The air was calm, and on the level brine
Sleek Panope with all her sisters played.
It was that fatal and perfidious bark,
Built in the eclipse, and rigged with curses dark,
That sunk so low that sacred head of thine.
   Next, Camus, reverend sire, went footing slow,
His mantle hairy, and his bonnet sedge,
Inwrought with figures dim, and on the edge
Like to that sanguine flower inscribed with woe.
"Ah! who hath reft," quoth he, "my dearest pledge?"
Last came, and last did go,
The Pilot of the Galilean Lake;
Two massy keys he bore of metals twain
(The golden opes, the iron shuts amain).
He shook his mitered locks, and stern bespake:
"How well could I have spared for thee, young swain,
Enow of such as, for their bellies' sake,
Creep, and intrude, and climb into the fold!
Of other care they little reckoning make
Than how to scramble at the shearers' feast,
And shove away the worthy bidden guest.
Blind mouths! that scarce themselves know how to hold
A sheep-hook, or have learned aught else the least
That to the faithful herdman's art belongs!
What recks it them? What need they? They are sped;
And, when they list, their lean and flashy songs
Grate on their scrannel pipes of wretched straw;
The hungry sheep look up, and are not fed,
But, swoln with wind and the rank mist they draw,
Rot inwardly, and foul contagion spread;
Besides what the grim wolf with privy paw
Daily devours apace, and nothing said.
But that two-handed engine at the door
Stands ready to smite once, and smite no more."

Return, Alpheus; the dread voice is past
That shrunk thy streams; return, Sicilian Muse,
And call the vales, and bid them hither cast
Their bells and flowerets of a thousand hues.
Ye valleys low, where the mild whispers use
Of shades, and wanton winds, and gushing brooks,
On whose fresh lap the swart star sparely looks,
Throw hither all your quaint enameled eyes,
That on the green turf suck the honeyed showers,
And purple all the ground with vernal flowers.
Bring the rathe primrose that forsaken dies,
The tufted crow-toe, and pale jessamine,
The white pink, and the pansy freaked with jet,
The glowing violet,
The musk-rose, and the well-attired woodbine,
With cowslips wan that hang the pensive head,
And every flower that sad embroidery wears;
Bid amaranthus all his beauty shed,
And daffodillies fill their cups with tears,
To strew the laureate hearse where Lycid lies.
For so, to interpose a little ease,
Let our frail thoughts dally with false surmise.
Aye me! Whilst thee the shores, and sounding seas
Wash far away, where'er thy bones are hurled,
Whether beyond the stormy Hebrides,
Where thou perhaps under the whelming tide
Visit'st the bottom of the monstrous world;
Or whether thou, to our moist vows denied,
Sleep'st by the fable of Bellerus old,
Where the great Vision of the guarded mount
Looks toward Namancos and Bayona's hold.
Look homeward, Angel, now, and melt with ruth;
And, O ye dolphins, waft the hapless youth.
   Weep no more, woeful shepherds, weep no more,
For Lycidas, your sorrow, is not dead,
Sunk though he be beneath the watery floor;
So sinks the day-star in the ocean bed,
And yet anon repairs his drooping head,
And tricks his beams, and with new-spangled ore
Flames in the forehead of the morning sky.
So Lycidas sunk low, but mounted high,
Through the dear might of Him that walked the waves,
Where, other groves and other streams along,

With nectar pure his oozy locks he laves,
And hears the unexpressive nuptial song,
In the blest kingdoms meek of joy and love.
There entertain him all the Saints above,
In solemn troops, and sweet societies,
That sing, and singing in their glory move,
And wipe the tears forever from his eyes.
Now, Lycidas, the shepherds weep no more;
Henceforth thou art the Genius of the shore,
In thy large recompense, and shalt be good
To all that wander in that perilous flood.

   Thus sang the uncouth swain to the oaks and rills,
While the still morn went out with sandals gray;
He touched the tender stops of various quills,
With eager thought warbling his Doric lay.
And now the sun had stretched out all the hills,
And now was dropt into the western bay.
At last he rose, and twitched his mantle blue;
Tomorrow to fresh woods and pastures new.

EDWARD HERBERT, LORD CHERBURY

ELEGY OVER A TOMB

Must I then see, alas, eternal night
    Sitting upon those fairest eyes,
And closing all those beams, which once did rise
    So radiant and bright
That light and heat in them to us did prove
    Knowledge and love?

Oh, if you did delight no more to stay
    Upon this low and earthly stage,
But rather chose an endless heritage,
    Tell us at least, we pray,
Where all the beauties that those ashes owed
    Are now bestowed.

EDWARD HERBERT, LORD CHERBURY (1583-1648), elder brother of the poet George Herbert, tried to remain neutral during the Civil War but threw in with the anti-Royalists when the Parliamentary army besieged his castle. He died soon after, in disgrace with his Royalist associates.

Doth the sun now his light with yours renew?
  Have waves the curling of your hair?
Did you restore unto the sky and air
  The red, and white, and blue?
Have you vouchsafed to flowers since your death
  That sweetest breath?

Had not heav'n's lights else in their houses slept,
  Or to some private life retired?
Must not the sky and air have else conspired,
  And in their regions wept?
Must not each flower else the earth could breed,
  Have been a weed?

But thus enriched may we not yield some cause
  Why they themselves lament no more?
That must have changed the course they held before,
  And broke their proper laws,
Had not your beauties giv'n this second birth
  To heaven and earth.

Tell us, for oracles must still ascend
  For those that crave them at your tomb,
Tell us where are those beauties now become,
  And what they now intend;
Tell us, alas, that cannot tell our grief,
  Or hope relief.

WILLIAM BROWNE OF TAVISTOCK

ON THE COUNTESS DOWAGER OF PEMBROKE

Underneath this sable hearse
Lies the subject of all verse: ·
Sidney's sister, Pembroke's mother.
Death, ere thou has slain another
Fair and learn'd and good as she,
Time shall throw a dart at thee.

WILLIAM BROWNE OF TAVISTOCK (1591-1643) was born at Tavistock in Devonshire, and the pastoral beauties of Devonshire inspired most of his poems.

Marble piles let no man raise
To her name, for after-days
Some kind woman, born as she,
Reading this, like Niobe
Shall turn marble, and become
Both her mourner and her tomb.

THOMAS RANDOLPH

ON THE DEATH OF A NIGHTINGALE

Go, solitary wood, and henceforth be
Acquainted with no other harmony
Than the pies' chattering, or the shrieking note
Of boding owls, and fatal raven's throat.
Thy sweetest chanter's dead, that warbled forth
Lays that might tempests calm, and still the north,
And call down angels from their glorious sphere
To hear her songs, and learn new anthems there.
That soul is fled and to Elysium gone;
Thou a poor desert left; go then and run,
Beg there to stand a grove, and if she please
To sing again beneath thy shadowy trees,
The souls of happy lovers crowned with blisses
Shall flock about thee, and keep time with kisses.

THOMAS RANDOLPH (1605-1635), a fellow of Trinity College, Cambridge, and one of the "sons of Ben," achieved fame as a poet and playwright during his brief career.

The
Restoration
and the
Eighteenth
Century

IV

T HERE may be some value in considering the course of English poetry from the emergence of John Dryden after the Restoration in 1660 to the beginnings of the Romantic movement at the end of the eighteenth century as a single epoch. Although this long period is far from homogeneous, being marked by changing tastes and competing poetic modes, it does represent more than anything else a dominance of the classical values that we have seen developing in the seventeenth century with Jonson and his following. The most commonly written metrical form is the heroic couplet, and the most valued poetry is satiric and didactic. The entire period is dominated by the critical principles and the poetic example of John Dryden, who raised verse satire to a new level of effectiveness, changing its focus at times from the general vices of mankind to the sins of individual men, so that it could be used as an incisive weapon of invective. His greatest disciple in the early eighteenth century is Alexander Pope. In the middle years of the century, Roman formal verse satire serves as a model for another arbiter of English letters, Samuel Johnson, perhaps the last great defender in his time of the classical ideal.

The rise of neoclassicism The period beginning with the restoration of Charles II has been called the Augustan Age. The return of the king was likened to that of Augustus Caesar, which reëstablished monarchy in ancient Rome after the defeat of the Republicans; and it was remembered that, under Augustus, Rome had had its greatest flowering of letters. This identification of England with the high point of Roman culture went hand in hand with the reverence for the classics that developed with such force in the seventeenth century. The age of Dryden and his followers was neoclassical. Without slavishly imitating Roman authors, poets strove for a poetic ideal which they believed only Roman literature had fully attained. The clarity and precision of Latin literature and its avoidance of sentimentality were congenial also because of the scientific spirit of the age, with its confidence that man could resolve his problems and its corollary tendency to reduce these human problems to the simplest possible terms. There could be no metaphysical tensions in the Age of Reason; there was room only for the expression of "truth," which the age in its complacency believed science could make clear and apparent. The emphasis was not upon intellectual conflict but upon the common agreement at which all men by the power of reason could arrive. The dominant drive of thinking men after the Restoration was for clarity and order.

The growth of scientific inquiry was marked by the founding of the Royal Society by Charles II and by the consequent growth of scientific knowledge, particularly in mathematics and astronomy, culminating in Newtonian physics. Accordingly, there was great cosmic optimism, the belief that men were living in the best of all possible worlds and that science could demonstrate the truth of revealed religion—for the members of the Royal Society were all religious men. This profound faith in the rational powers of man led to a concern in poetry with the direct rational statement, expressed in the most precise and elegant of terms. The members of the Royal Society included distinguished men of letters who voiced the need for "mathematical plainness" in language rather than for ornate, complex diction. Augustan writers do not deny the imaginative and emotional aspects of poetry, but there is the strong belief that these must be controlled by reason and judgment.

These forces were at work at the end of the seventeenth century and, in combination, were to banish metaphysical poetry to ridicule and obscurity and extend classicism to the point where the inevitable reaction against it set in. Among these forces also was the growth of literary criticism, for the Augustan becomes the first age in English literature consciously to prescribe, evaluate, and censure its own poetic activity. Although there had been some important writers of criticism, like Sir Philip Sidney in the sixteenth century with his *Defence of Poesie* and Ben Jonson in the seventeenth with his *Timber, or Discoveries* and his prefaces to poems and plays, John Dryden is the first great critic in the English language. The doctrines he proclaimed were influenced by French and Italian neoclassicists as well as by the classical critics themselves.

Classical influences Among the most important influences upon neoclassical literary theory in England was the rhetorical tradition of Cicero and Quintillian. These men had been concerned with oratory (and poetry had long been taught as a branch of oratory in the schools), with the artful embellishment of speech so as to make it more effective in convincing an audience. We must note that eighteenth-century poetry is essentially rhetorical. It is usually addressed to an audience which it appears to be trying to influence rationally. It seeks its effect not through flights of imagination but through statements of universal truths, expressed with clarity enhanced by linguistic elegance. Such a conception of poetry made it possible for Samuel Johnson to regard the seventeenth-century metaphysical poets as fit subjects for ridicule.

Another great influence was the creed which Horace had expressed in his *Ars Poetica*: the function of poetry was to teach while delighting; and although delight might be the immediate consideration, the end of poetry was always moral and didactic. Such a critical faith supported the growth of satire, which we have seen as a developing influence in the seventeenth century; for formal verse satire in the hands of Horace and Juvenal had been the most effective weapon developed by the Roman poets for the exposure of social evils and the statement of moral truth. In the eighteenth century the satiric spirit affects virtually every form of poetry from the epic to the pastoral. We have in Alexander Pope the highest evolution of elegant, precise poetry, exploring all the potentialities of the heroic couplet while never exceeding its rigid limits, exposing human vice and folly, and stating what the author considered to be profound moral truth. This is the Augustan poetic ideal, and it is the culmination of a movement that developed steadily from Jonson through Dryden.

This was the ideal, but like most ideals it was one very rarely attained. The respect for literal statement created many long, dull poems on the commonplaces of ordinary life, and concern with the moral function of art led to lengthy rehearsals of tedious platitudes in poorly managed couplets. The eighteenth century is extraordinary for the amount of bad poetry it produced by now-forgotten hacks and poetasters. We must remember also that, like all critical ideals, the classical produced its re-action even while it was most dominant; many poets turned to earlier English writers rather than to the ancients for inspiration. John Milton, who was scorned by the classical critics, nevertheless had many imitators; and the Spenserian stanza reappeared—though sometimes, as in William Shenstone's lengthy *Schoolmistress,* it was used for satiric purposes entirely alien to all Spenser stood for.

Poetic genres An important part of the classical heritage of the eighteenth century, coming largely through Dryden, was a concern with poetic genres. When an eighteenth-century poet sat down to write, it was to compose not a poem, but an epic, a satire, an ode, a pastoral, or one of the numerous subgenres which developed out of these. Each genre came to have its "rules," to which the poet was expected scrupulously to conform. Of the classical poetic genres, the epic continued to be the most respected, and an extraordinary number were written, but not by the more talented poets of the period. These preferred the mock-heroic poem, of which Pope's *Rape of the Lock* is the supreme example. Applied to an insignificant subject, the external characteristics of the epic created a superb instrument of social satire. The mock-heroic technique could be used also, as Pope used it in his lengthy *Dunciad,* for personal ridicule.

This tendency to burlesque the very poetic genres which were most respected is a characteristic of the age. It appears also in John Gay's *The Shepherd's Week,* where the pastoral is made to deal with the inanities of country bumpkins; it has been suggested, however, that Gay in these comic poems may have come closer to the true pastoral spirit of Theocritus than did any of the more serious practitioners of pastoral poetry in his time. Few today would bother to read the eclogues of Thomas Tickell or Ambrose Philips. Pope's first important efforts were serious pastorals, but the interests of the Augustan Age were never really in rural life, and skillful as Pope's eclogues are, they reveal the essential artificiality of a poetic exercise. More congenial to eighteenth-century tastes was the unique variation of the pastoral called the "town eclogue," in which the conventional devices of pastoral poetry were applied to city people in a London setting. Of this means of social satire John Gay was a master also; his poem *The Toilet* shows the form at its best.

True feeling for nature appears not in the stylized confines of the pastoral tradition but in lengthy philosophical poems such as *The Seasons,* which James Thomson composed in blank verse. It sometimes appears also in descriptive or topographical poems, such as Pope's *Windsor Forest,* which were often written by eighteenth-century poets hoping for patronage by the great lords whose parks and estates they glorified.

Decline and fall It is possible to view eighteenth-century poetry as the triumph of Jonsonian traditions over those of Donne, but we must remember also that it is an age of antithesis, of conflict between the classical ideal and an ideal of freedom of expression which slowly rises in opposition to it. If there is a classical emphasis upon the rational component of man, there is also a concern with "sensibility," the emotional aspects of human life. In the eighteenth century a new value is placed upon emotion and sensation and upon the altruistic feelings of love and charity. These foster the concern with expression of the human personality that issues into Romanticism. At the beginning of the eighteenth century the classical force is dominant, with its emphasis upon wit and controlled art; but as the century progresses, the opposing forces grow stronger and stronger until in the latter half of the century Johnson is the last champion of a dying classical ideal. We are ready then for the melancholy of Thomas Gray, for William Blake and Robert Burns, and the beginning of the Romantic era.

FOR FURTHER READING:

Arthos, John. *The Language of Natural Description in Eighteenth Century Poetry.* Ann Arbor, Mich., 1949.

Aubin, R. A. *Topographical Poetry in Eighteenth Century England.* New York, 1936.

Bond, Richmond P. *English Burlesque Poetry, 1700-1750.* Cambridge, Mass., 1932.

Bredvold, Louis. *The Intellectual Milieu of John Dryden.* Ann Arbor, Mich., 1934.

Dobrée, Bonamy. *English Literature in the Early Eighteenth Century.* New York, 1959.

Havens, R. D. *The Influence of Milton on English Poetry.* New York, 1960.

Sutherland, James R. *A Preface to Eighteenth Century Poetry.* Oxford, 1948.

Tillotson, Geoffrey. "Eighteenth Century Poetic Diction," *Essays in Criticism and Research.* London, 1942.

Wasserman, E. R. *Elizabethan Poetry in the Eighteenth Century.* Urbana, Ill., 1947.

IV

THE RESTORATION AND THE EIGHTEENTH CENTURY

THE SATIRIC AND DIDACTIC

O F the many means that Augustan poets used to teach while delighting, satire was the most important and the most common. There are few poetic genres, in fact, which the spirit of satire did not touch in some way. It was a spirit congenial to an age which in its celebration of nature could envision attitudes and ways of life as universally "correct." In its code of values, the Augustan Age tends to be rigid and static, and from its perspective of a fixed standard of correctness it censures all who fail to conform. The satirists depend upon an audience which accepts such a standard without question.

The eighteenth century cherished the notion of human perfectibility in the best of all possible worlds—a world ruled by scientific laws which human reason was capable of discovering. Satire is congenial to such an intellectual milieu because it is essentially an optimistic form of literature. It always envisages an ideal capable of attainment; and no matter how bitterly it may attack specific deviations, it does so always with the purpose of destroying them so that the ideal may be realized. If the satirist assumes at times a pose of cruelty and of uncharitable scorn for ordinary human weakness, as Swift often does, it is because to do otherwise is to make possible the error he is eager to destroy, to render more distant the ideal he seeks to attain. It is impossible to have a literature of social correction which does not embody a hope for the improvement of mankind. Even when they direct invective against specific individuals, the Augustan satirists are always aware of a high moral purpose.

Eighteenth-century satire is a realistic art form, for its basic ingredient is the poet's observation of actual experience. In a poem like *Description of the Morning,* Jonathan Swift evokes all the sights and smells of an awakening London. The foibles of Betty the maid, of the lazy apprentice, and of his lordship who must avoid his creditors are made believable by the background—a living, real city—against which they are drawn. Swift, whose greatest achievements were in prose, does not have the metrical dexterity or the poetic range of some of his contemporaries, but he is the peer of the best of them in his ability to evoke reality.

The favorite classical satirist of the seventeenth-century poets had been Juvenal; but the eighteenth century preferred the more urbane, discursive style of Horace, who served as a model for Pope, the greatest satirist of his time. The *Moral Essay* addressed to the Earl of Burlington is a perfect imitation of Horatian satire. Pope is the author also of perhaps the finest mock-heroic poem in the English language, *The Rape of the Lock*. Here a feud over the theft of a ringlet of hair is treated in the style of heroic poetry, with long passages which parody the *Iliad* of Homer; at the same time the larger moral objective is realized as general human vanity and pretense are rendered absurd.

Just as Pope uses the epic as a point of departure for ridicule, John Gay uses the pastoral in his "town eclogue" *The Toilet,* where he censures with broad comedy the affectations of aged beauty. There was little in the life of the eighteenth century which escaped the satirist's wit. In poets like Gay, the comic spirit is so strong that it sometimes tends to obscure the seriousness of the author's purpose, but Gay is as morally dedicated as Pope, though he may not always be so pretentious about it. We must note, finally, that the greatest writers of Augustan satire are all city men, Pope and Gay living most of their lives in the thick of London literary society, and Swift yearning for it always from his "exile" in Ireland.

FOR FURTHER READING:

Brower, Reuben A. *Alexander Pope: The Poetry of Allusion.* New York, 1959.

Clifford, J. L. *Eighteenth-Century English Literature.* New York, 1959.

Jack, Ian. *Augustan Satire.* New York, 1952.

Tillotson, Geoffrey. *On the Poetry of Pope.* New York, 1938.

———. *Pope and Human Nature.* New York, 1958.

Warren, Austin. "Alexander Pope," *Rage for Order.* Chicago, 1948.

Watkins, W. B. C. *Perilous Balance.* Princeton, 1939.

JONATHAN SWIFT

A SATIRICAL ELEGY ON THE
DEATH OF A LATE FAMOUS GENERAL, 1722[1]

His Grace! impossible! what dead!
Of old age too, and in his bed!

1 The Duke of Marlborough

JONATHAN SWIFT (1667-1745), born in Ireland of English parents, achieved great influence in England as a writer of political pamphlets and rose in the Church of England to the position of dean of St. Patrick's Cathedral in Dublin. After 1713, however, his hopes for political preferment were crushed, and his last years were spent in a melancholy which deepened into madness. Swift's famous *Gulliver's Travels* appeared in 1726.

And could that Mighty Warrior fall?
And so inglorious, after all!
Well, since he's gone, no matter how,
The last loud trump must wake him now:
And, trust me, as the noise grows stronger,
He'd wish to sleep a little longer.
And could he be indeed so old
As by the news-papers we're told?
Threescore, I think, is pretty high;
'Twas time in conscience he should die.
This world he cumbered long enough;
He burnt his candle to the snuff;
And that's the reason, some folks think,
He left behind so great a stink.

Behold his funeral appears,
Nor widow's sighs, nor orphan's tears,
Wont at such times each heart to pierce,
Attend the progress of his hearse.
But what of that, his friends may say,
He had those honors in his day.
True to his profit and his pride,
He made them weep before he died.

   Come hither, all ye empty things,
Ye bubbles raised by breath of Kings;
Who float upon the tide of state,
Come hither, and behold your fate.
Let pride be taught by this rebuke,
How very mean a thing's a Duke;
From all his ill-got honors flung,
Turned to that dirt from whence he sprung.

A DESCRIPTION OF THE MORNING

Now hardly here and there an hackney-coach
Appearing, showed the ruddy morn's approach.
Now Betty from her master's bed had flown,
And softly stole to discompose her own.
The slipshod prentice from his master's door,
Had pared the dirt, and sprinkled round the floor.
Now Moll had whirled her mop with dext'rous airs,
Prepared to scrub the entry and the stairs.

The youth with broomy stumps began to trace
The kennel-edge, where wheels had worn the place.
The smallcoal-man was heard with cadence deep,
'Till drowned in shriller notes of chimney-sweep,
Duns at his lordship's gate began to meet,
And brickdust Moll had screamed through half the street.
The turnkey now his flock returning sees,
Duly let out at nights to steal for fees.
The watchful bailiffs take their silent stands,
And school-boys lag with satchels in their hands.

THE FURNITURE OF A WOMAN'S MIND

A set of phrases learnt by rote;
A passion for a scarlet-coat;
When at a play to laugh, or cry,
Yet cannot tell the reason why:
Never to hold her tongue a minute;
While all she prates has nothing in it.
Whole hours can with a coxcomb sit,
And take his nonsense all for wit:
Her learning mounts to read a song,
But, half the words pronouncing wrong;
Has ev'ry repartee in store,
She spoke ten thousand times before.
Can ready compliments supply
On all occasions, cut and dry.
Such hatred to a parson's gown,
The sight will put her in a swown.
For conversation well endued;
She calls it witty to be rude;
And, placing raillery in railing,
Will tell aloud your greatest failing;
Nor makes a scruple to expose
Your bandy leg, or crooked nose.
Can, at her morning tea, run o'er
The scandal of the day before.
Improving hourly in her skill,
To cheat and wrangle at quadrille.

In choosing lace a critick nice,
Knows to a groat the lowest price;

Can in her female clubs dispute
What lining best the silk will suit;
What colors each complexion match:
And where with art to place a patch.

If chance a mouse creeps in her sight,
Can finely counterfeit a fright;
So, sweetly screams if it comes near her,
She ravishes all hearts to hear her.
Can dext'rously her husband tease,
By taking fits whene'er she please:
By frequent practice learns the trick
At proper seasons to be sick;
Thinks nothing gives one airs so pretty;
At once creating love and pity.
If Molly happens to be careless,
And but neglects to warm her hair-lace,
She gets a cold as sure as death;
And vows she scarce can fetch her breath.
Admires how modest women can
Be so robustious like a man.

In party, furious to her power;
A bitter Whig, or Tory sour;
Her arguments directly tend
Against the side she would defend:
Will prove herself a Tory plain,
From principles the Whigs maintain;
And, to defend the Whiggish cause,
Her topics from the Tories draws.

O yes! If any man can find
More virtues in a woman's mind,
Let them be sent to Mrs. Harding;[1]
She'll pay the charges to a farthing:
Take notice, she has my commission
To add them in the next edition;
They may out-sell a better thing;
So, holla boys; God save the King.

1 Wife of Swift's printer, who maintained her husband's shop after his death.

ALEXANDER POPE

MORAL ESSAY FOUR: OF THE USE OF RICHES
To Richard Boyle, Earl of Burlington

'Tis strange, the miser should his cares employ
To gain those riches he can ne'er enjoy:
Is it less strange, the prodigal should waste
His wealth, to purchase what he ne'er can taste?
Not for himself he sees, or hears, or eats;
Artists must choose his pictures, music, meats:
He buys for Topham, drawings and designs,
For Pembroke, statues, dirty gods, and coins;
Rare monkish manuscripts for Hearne alone,
And books for Mead, and butterflies for Sloane.[1]
Think we all these are for himself! no more
Than his fine wife, alas! or finer whore.
  For what has Virro painted, built, and planted?
Only to show, how many tastes he wanted.
What brought Sir Visto's ill got wealth to waste?
Some Daemon whispered, "Visto! have a taste."
Heaven visits with a taste the wealthy fool,
And needs no rod but Ripley[2] with a rule.
See! sportive fate, to punish awkward pride,
Bids Bubo build, and sends him such a guide:
A standing sermon, at each year's expense,
That never coxcomb reached magnificence!
  You show us, Rome was glorious, not profuse,
And pompous buildings once were things of use.
Yet shall (my Lord) your just, your noble rules
Fill half the land with imitating fools;
Who random drawings from your sheets shall take,
And of one beauty many blunders make;
Load some vain church with old theatric state,
Turn arcs of triumph to a garden gate;
Reverse your ornaments, and hang them all

1 For Topham, Pembroke, and Hearne, see analysis, page 204. Richard Mead (1673-1754) and Sir Hans Sloane (1660-1753) were two eminent contemporary physicians, renowned for their collections of books and butterflies respectively.
2 Thomas Ripley (d. 1758), an architect and builder, was the protégé of Sir Robert Walpole, whose country house he built.

ALEXANDER POPE (1688-1744), most famous poet of his age, was born in London, the son of a successful linen draper. His Catholic persuasion prevented him from attending a university, but he was well educated by private tutors. After an active life in literary London, he retired in 1719 to his estate at Twickenham.

On some patched dog-hole eked with ends of wall;
Then clap four slices of pilaster on't,
That, laced with bits of rustic, makes a front.
    Oft have you hinted to your brother peer,
A certain truth, which many buy too dear:
Something there is more needful than expense,
And something previous ev'n to taste—'tis sense:
Good sense, which only is the gift of heaven,
And though no science, fairly worth the seven:
A light, which in yourself you must perceive;
Jones and Le Nôtre have it not to give.[3]
    To build, to plant, whatever you intend,
To rear the column, or the arch to bend,
To swell the terrace, or to sink the grot;
In all, let nature never be forgot.
But treat the goddess like a modest fair,
Nor over-dress, nor leave her wholly bare;
Let not each beauty every where be spied,
Where half the skill is decently to hide.
He gains all points, who pleasingly confounds,
Surprises, varies, and conceals the bounds.
    Consult the genius of the place in all;
That tells the waters or to rise, or fall;
Or helps th' ambitious hill the heavens to scale,
Or scoops in circling theatres the vale;
Calls in the country, catches op'ning glades,
Joins willing woods, and varies shades from shades;
Now breaks, or now directs, th' intending lines;
Paints as you plant, and, as you work, designs.
    Still follow sense, of every art the soul,
Parts answering parts shall slide into a whole,
Spontaneous beauties all around advance,
Start even from difficulty, strike from chance;
Nature shall join you; time shall make it grow
A work to wonder at—perhaps a STOWE.[4]
    Without it, proud Versailles!—thy glory falls;
And Nero's terraces desert their walls:
The vast parterres a thousand hands shall make,
Lo! COBHAM[5] comes, and floats them with a lake:

3 Inigo Jones (1573-1652), the celebrated seventeenth-century architect who designed
the settings for Ben Jonson's masques, and Andre Le Nôtre (1613-1700), who laid
out the gardens at Versailles and Fontainebleau in France.
4 The famous country house and gardens of Lord Viscount Cobham in Buckingham-
shire.
5 Sir Richard Temple, Viscount Cobham (1675-1749), a Whig politician and soldier.

Or cut wide views through mountains to the plain,
You'll wish your hill or sheltered seat again.
Even in an ornament its place remark,
Nor in an hermitage set Dr. Clarke.[6]
Behold Villario's[7] ten years' toil complete;
His quincunx darkens, his espaliers meet;
The wood supports the plain, the parts unite,
And strength of shade contends with strength of light;
A waving glow the bloomy beds display,
Blushing in bright diversities of day,
With silver-quivering rills meandered o'er—
Enjoy them, you! Villario can no more:
Tired of the scene parterres and fountains yield,
He finds at last he better likes a field.

   Through his young woods how pleased Sabinus[8] strayed,
Or sat delighted in the thickening shade,
With annual joy the reddening shoots to greet,
Or see the stretching branches long to meet!
His son's fine taste an opener vista loves,
Foe to the dryads of his father's groves;
One boundless green, or flourished carpet views,
With all the mournful family of yews:
The thriving plants, ignoble broomsticks made,
Now sweep those alleys they were born to shade.

   At Timon's villa let us pass a day,
Where all cry out, "What sums are thrown away!"
So proud, so grand: of that stupendous air,
Soft and agreeable come never there.
Greatness, with Timon, dwells in such a draught
As brings all Brobdignag[9] before your thought.
To compass this, his building is a town,
His pond an ocean, his parterre a down:
Who but must laugh, the master when he sees,
A puny insect, shivering at a breeze!
Lo, what huge heaps of littleness around!
The whole, a laboured quarry above ground.
Two cupids squirt before: a lake behind
Improves the keenness of the northern wind.
His gardens next your admiration call,

6 Samuel Clarke (1675-1729), a distinguished English philosopher whose bust was
placed in the Hermitage by Queen Caroline. Pope disliked Clarke intensely.
7 An unidentified landscape artist, probably a synthetic figure.
8 Another synthetic figure. It has been suggested that he is meant to be the son of Benjamin Styles of Moor Park, whom Pope may have intended to caricature as Virro.
9 The land of giants in *Gulliver's Travels,* by Jonathan Swift.

On every side you look, behold the wall!
No pleasing intricacies intervene,
No artful wildness to perplex the scene;
Grove nods at grove, each alley has a brother,
And half the platform just reflects the other.
The suffering eye inverted nature sees,
Trees cut to statues, statues thick as trees;
With here a fountain, never to be played;
And there a summer-house, that knows no shade;
Here Amphitrite sails through myrtle bowers;
There gladiators fight, or die in flowers;
Unwatered see the drooping sea-horse mourn,
And swallows roost in Nilus' dusty urn.

My lord advances with majestic mien,
Smit with the mighty pleasure, to be seen:
But soft—by regular approach—not yet—
First through the length of yon hot terrace sweat;
And when up ten steep slopes you've dragged your thighs,
Just at his study-door he'll bless your eyes.

His study! with what authors is it stor'd?
In books, not authors, curious is my lord;
To all their dated backs he turns you round,
These Aldus printed, those Du Suëil[10] has bound.
Lo, some are vellom, and the rest as good
For all his lordship knows, but they are wood.
For Locke or Milton[11] 'tis in vain to look,
These shelves admit not any modern book.

And now the chapel's silver bell you hear,
That summons you to all the pride of prayer:
Light quirks of music, broken and uneven,
Make the soul dance upon a jig to heaven.
On painted ceilings you devoutly stare,
Where sprawl the saints of Verrio or Laguerre,[12]
On gilded clouds in fair expansion lie,
And bring all paradise before your eye.
To rest, the cushion and soft dean invite,
Who never mentions Hell to ears polite.

But hark! the chiming clocks to dinner call;
A hundred footsteps scrape the marble hall:

10 Aldus Manutius (1450-1515), a Venetian printer of the Renaissance, and Abbé Du Suëil, a Parisian bookbinder of Pope's time.
11 John Locke (1632-1704), the eminent Restoration philosopher, and John Milton (1608-1674), the poet.
12 Antonio Verrio (1639-1707) and Louis Laguerre (1663-1721) had painted walls and ceilings in various eighteenth-century houses.

The rich buffet well-colored serpents grace,
And gaping Tritons spew to wash your face.
Is this a dinner? this a genial room?
No, 'tis a temple, and a hecatomb.
A solemn sacrifice, performed in state,
You drink by measure, and to minutes eat.
So quick retires each flying course, you'd swear
Sancho's dread doctor and his wand[13] were there.
Between each act the trembling salvers ring,
From soup to sweet wine, and God bless the king.
In plenty starving, tantalized in state,
And complaisantly helped to all I hate,
Treated, caressed, and tired, I take my leave,
Sick of his civil pride from morn to eve;
I curse such lavish cost, and little skill,
And swear no day was ever passed so ill.

Yet hence the poor are clothed, the hungry fed;
Health to himself, and to his infants bread
The laborer bears: What his hard heart denies,
His charitable vanity supplies.

Another age shall see the golden ear
Imbrown the slope, and nod on the parterre,
Deep harvests bury all his pride has plann'd,
And laughing Ceres[14] re-assume the land.

Who then shall grace, or who improve the Soil?
Who plants like BATHURST,[15] or who builds like BOYLE.
'Tis use alone that sanctifies expense,
And splendor borrows all her rays from sense.

His father's acres who enjoys in peace,
Or makes his neighbors glad, if he increase:
Whose cheerful tenants bless their yearly toil,
Yet to their lord owe more than to the soil;
Whose ample lawns are not ashamed to feed
The milky heifer, and deserving steed;
Whose rising forests, not for pride or show,
But future buildings, future navies, grow:
Let his plantations stretch from down to down,
First shade a country, and then raise a town.

You too proceed! make falling arts your care,
Erect new wonders, and the old repair;

13 Sancho Panza, the servant of Cervantes' Don Quixote.
14 The Greek goddess of the harvest.
15 Allen Bathurst, Baron Bathurst (1685-1775), a Tory member of Parliament for Cirencester with whom Pope had close connections.

Jones and Palladio[16] to themselves restore,
And be whate'er Vitruvius was before:[17]
Till kings call forth th' ideas of your mind,
(Proud to accomplish what such hands designed)
Bid harbors open, public ways extend,
Bid temples, worthier of the God, ascend;
Bid the broad arch the dang'rous flood contain,
The mole projected break the roaring main;
Back to his bounds their subject sea command,
And roll obedient rivers through the land;
These honors, peace to happy Britain brings,
These are imperial works, and worthy kings.

MORAL ESSAY FOUR: OF THE USE OF RICHES Pope's *Moral Essay* (or *Ethic Epistle*, as he originally named it) to Richard Boyle, Earl of Burlington (1695-1753), is a perfect example of the Augustan imitation of the Horatian satire, an urbane and sophisticated vehicle for social commentary. It is cast in the form of a letter to an eminent amateur architect who had helped Pope in the planning and building of his own villa and who had been influential in restoring a Roman style in eighteenth-century architecture. The tone throughout is deliberately Roman, that of one sophisticated aristocrat to another, of Horace to his Maecenas; the poet maintains a familiar epistolary style in the Horatian manner while he makes his general moral statements and illustrates them by ridiculing the offenses against his precepts committed by various individuals.

There is nothing striking or original in the poem's moral content. It is a statement of principles which the Augustan Age could accept without much dissent. The poet's art lies not in his philosophical acumen but in his ability to endow the commonplace with freshness by a striking originality in poetic diction and to create satiric portraits so closely based upon his own observations as to give to old moral injunctions a new illumination in terms of specific example. Perhaps the philosophical pretensions of Pope's satires are their weakest element, but the satirical portraits justify the place of the satires among the world's great poetry.

Specifically, Pope is directing his wit against the extravagant ostentation of eighteenth-century noblemen and the abominable taste they displayed in building their great country houses. Accordingly, he addresses his epistle to an architect; and in the course of it, he states his own views on building and gardening, so that the poem becomes, incidentally, one of our best illustrations of Augustan taste in landscape architecture. Against

16 Inigo Jones and Andrea Palladio (1518-1580), an Italian architect who adapted the principles of Roman architecture.
17 M. Vitruvius Pollio (*b.* 88? B.C.), the Roman author of *De Architectura.*

Pope's ideal, we have the villa of Lord Timon, a model of all to which the poet stands opposed.

Pope believed that satire must depend upon truth, that its argument must be presented in terms of factual evidence which readers immediately could accept; and for this reason the poem is full of allusions to actual people and places. As the poet makes his initial statement that the rich lord is incapable of appreciating the diverse treasures he collects, he brings in the names of actual collectors of the items he catalogues, from drawings to butterflies: Richard Topham (*d.* 1735), who amassed a famous collection of drawings and engravings; Thomas Herbert, 8th Earl of Pembroke (1656-1733), who devoted his life to amassing "statues, dirty gods, and coins"; Thomas Hearne (1678-1735), the great antiquary noted for his collection of medieval manuscripts, and others. These were names familiar to the sophisticated audience for whom the poet wrote, and they establish at the outset the sense of verisimilitude which Pope considers essential.

Most of the specific characters against whom the satire is directed— Sir Visto, Villario, and, most notably, Lord Timon—while carefully drawn against a background of truth, are not to be taken as representing identifiable noblemen, although they were often so taken by Pope's contemporaries, to the poet's great chagrin. Only Bubo seems closely modeled upon an actual person, George Bubb Doddington, Baron Melcombe (1691-1762), a Whig politician for whom Pope had a strong dislike. The others are composite portraits, each modeled upon some dozen figures who might illustrate the foibles Pope wished to attack. Similarly, none of the great estates he describes can be identified with any single house or park, although he draws details for all from such actual places as Blenheim Palace, the house of Lord Chandos in Edgeware, and the estate of Benjamin Styles at Moor Park, Rickmansworth. The final effect is of general moral statement conveyed in terms of a dramatis personae which allows full play to the poet's imagination but nevertheless has the unmistakable ring of truth.

Since the poem is based upon contrast between the ideal and the actual, the poet's most effective satiric instrument is his skillful use of antithesis, a constant juxtaposition of images which evoke the ideal against those which remind the reader of sordid reality. In the description of Timon's villa, for instance, we have in one couplet a swelling accumulation of images of size and grandeur:

> To compass this, his building is a town,
> His pond an ocean, his parterre a down:

But this is followed by an antithetical reminder of the littleness of the lord:

> Who but must laugh, the master when he sees,
> A puny insect, shivering at a breeze!

And then in a single line the greatness of the first couplet and the smallness of the second are brought together:

> Lo, what huge heaps of littleness around!

Not only in adjacent couplets but in the connotations of single words within a line, this effect of ironic contrast is maintained. "Two cupids squirt before" gives us in the first two words the connotation of formal statuary in a Roman garden, in the second two a reminder of a bodily function which places the Roman garden in a rather tasteless perspective.

The description of the chapel service shows this technique at its most effective:

> And now the chapel's silver bell you hear,
> That summons you to all the pride of prayer:
> Light quirks of music, broken and uneven,
> Make the soul dance upon a jig to heaven.

The first line with its "silver bell" leads us to expect a portrayal of true devotion, but in the second line *pride* is used to qualify *prayer* and relate it to the ostentation which has marked every aspect of Timon's house; what follows is not harmonious religious song but "Light quirks of music, broken and uneven." The entire service is reduced to mockery by the *jig* which the soul must *dance* to heaven.

The description of the dinner reverses expectations in the same manner. We hear first "the chiming clocks to dinner call," but in the *scrape* of the next line—"A hundred footsteps scrape the marble hall"—a note of discord is immediately introduced. The "gaping Tritons" are the elaborate faucets of the Roman bath, but when they "spew to wash your face," their grandeur is lost in the crass function of washing and in the connotations of the verb *spew*. This device of ironic contrast, both through the direct statements of whole couplets and through the conflicting connotations of words within a single line, is repeated throughout the poem and is Pope's primary satiric instrument.

The poet depends also upon subtle allusions to earlier literature. The name *Timon,* for instance, is that of a traditional symbol of profligacy and display whom the reader might have met in Lucian's dialogue *Timon, the Misanthrope* or in Shakespeare's tragedy *Timon of Athens.* When Pope writes of this Timon advancing "Smit with the mighty pleasure, to be seen," we think of Milton's line, "Smit with the love of sacred song," in the third book of *Paradise Lost,* and our recollection of Milton's heroic tone renders Timon's desire "to be seen" all the more petty.

The satire is carried also in the precision with which the poet constructs neat parallels of word and meaning within single lines. In a line like "Trees cut to statues, statues thick as trees," the repetition of *statues* and *trees* in the second half of the line, carefully reversing their order in the first, renders ridiculous both the trees and the statues. And in a line like "You drink by measure, and to minutes eat," the sense of the second half underscores the pun in the first half, for the *measure* is not only the drinking vessel but also the rigid allotment of time within which, in the lord's formal household, the drinking must be confined. The entire dinner service is rendered absurd, and we end with an effective couplet of summation:

> In plenty starving, tantalized in state,
> And complaisantly helped to all I hate,

with its antitheses of *plenty starving, helped* and *hate,* and all the implications of the classical legend of Tantalus, who the reader would know was tortured in hell with hunger and thirst, as the poet is tortured at this dinner where there is nothing to feast upon but display.

We must note also Pope's skillful placing of the *caesura,* the major break in each of the lines. He achieves variety by shifting the position of his caesura from line to line but places it at the end of the fifth syllable more often than elsewhere, having observed that whenever several such lines follow one upon another, there is less monotony than when the caesura is at any other point. Note the following passage:

> But hark! ‖ the chiming clocks to dinner call;
> A hundred footsteps scrape ‖ the marble hall:
> The rich buffet ‖ well-colored serpents grace,
> And gaping Tritons spew ‖ to wash your face.
> Is this a dinner? ‖ this a genial room?
> No, 'tis a temple, ‖ and a hecatomb.
> A solemn sacrifice, ‖ performed in state,
> You drink by measure, ‖ and to minutes eat.
> So quick retires each flying course, ‖ you'd swear
> Sancho's dread doctor ‖ and his wand were there.

The first four lines show a clever variation, the caesura being placed after the second syllable of the first line, after the sixth syllable of the second line, after the fourth syllable of the third line, and again after the sixth syllable of the fourth line. Then for three of the four lines containing the strongest satiric impact of the passage, we have the caesura placed each time after the fifth syllable. This is followed by the variety of a line with a caesura after the eighth syllable, rhyming with a line with a fifth-syllable caesura again, as a kind of echo of the preceding lines. It is by this adroit use of the caesura that Pope keeps his closed heroic couplets from the

monotonous singsong to which they might easily fall in the hands of a
lesser poet. Pope never includes an unnecessary word, and his metrical dexterity accords perfectly with the brilliance of his wit. His satire represents
a highly complex and sophisticated poetic genre.

JOHN GAY

THE TOILET: A TOWN ECLOGUE
LYDIA

Now twenty springs had clothed the park with green,
Since Lydia knew the blossom of fifteen;
No lovers now her morning hours molest,
And catch her at her toilet half undrest;
The thund'ring knocker wakes the street no more,
No chairs, no coaches crowd her silent door;
Her midnights once at cards and Hazard fled,
Which now, alas! she dreams away in bed.
Around her wait Shocks, monkeys and macaws,
To fill the place of fops, and perjured beaux;
In these she views the mimickry of man,
And smiles when grinning Pug gallants her fan;
When Poll repeats, the sounds deceive her ear,
For sounds, like his, once told her Damon's care.
With these alone her tedious mornings pass;
Or at the dumb devotion of her glass,
She smooths her brow, and frizzles forth her hairs,
And fancies youthful dress gives youthful airs;
With crimson wool she fixes every grace,
That not a blush can discompose her face.
Reclined upon her arm she pensive sate,
And cursed th' inconstancy of youth too late.
    O youth! O spring of life! forever lost!
No more my name shall reign the fav'rite toast,
On glass no more the diamond grave my name,
And rhymes mispelled record a lover's flame:
Nor shall the side-boxes watch my restless eyes,

JOHN GAY (1685-1732), best remembered for his play *The Beggar's Opera,*
had no university education but managed to make his way as a writer and secure
the support of wealthy patrons. Although unsound investments robbed him of most
of the profits from his poems, he continued to compose lively lyrics and high-
spirited satires.

And as they catch the glance in rows arise
With humble bows; nor white-gloved beaux encroach
In crowds behind, to guard me to my coach.
Ah hapless nymph! such conquests are no more,
For Chloe's now what Lydia was before!
    'Tis true, this Chloe boasts the peach's bloom.
But does her nearer whisper breathe perfume?
I own her taper shape is formed to please.
Yet if you saw her unconfined by stays!
She doubly to fifteen may make pretence,
Alike we read it in her face and sense.
Her reputation! but that never yet
Could check the freedoms of a young coquet.
Why will ye then, vain fops, her eyes believe?
Her eyes can, like your perjured tongues, deceive.
    What shall I do? how spend the hateful day?
At chapel shall I wear the morn away?
Who there frequents at these unmodish hours,
But ancient matrons with their frizzled towers,
And gray religious maids? my presence there
Amid that sober train would own despair;
Nor am I yet so old; nor is my glance
As yet fixed wholly to devotion's trance.
    Strait then I'll dress, and take my wonted range
Through ev'ry Indian shop, through all the Change;
Where the tall jar erects his costly pride,
With antic shapes in China's azure dyed;
There careless lies the rich brocade unrolled,
Here shines a cabinet with burnished gold;
But then remembrance will my grief renew,
'Twas there the raffling dice false Damon threw;
The raffling dice to him decide the prize.
'Twas there he first conversed with Chloe's eyes;
Hence sprung th' ill-fated cause of all my smart,
To me the toy he gave, to her his heart.
But soon thy perjury in the gift was found,
The shivered China dropt upon the ground;
Sure omen that thy vows would faithless prove;
Frail was thy present, frailer is thy love.
    O happy Poll, in wiry prison pent;
Thou ne'er hast known what love or rivals meant,
And Pug with pleasure can his fetters bear,
Who ne'er believed the vows that lovers swear!

How am I curst! (unhappy and forlorn)
With perjury, with love, and rival's scorn!
False are the loose coquet's inveigling airs,
False is the pompous grief of youthful heirs,
False is the cringing courtier's plighted word,
False are the dice when gamesters stamp the board,
False is the sprightly widow's public tear;
Yet these to Damon's oaths are all sincere.
    Fly from perfidious man, the sex disdain;
Let servile Chloe wear the nuptial chain.
Damon is practised in the modish life,
Can hate, and yet be civil to a wife.
He games; he swears; he drinks; he fights; he roves;
Yet Chloe can believe he fondly loves.
Mistress and wife can well supply his need,
A miss for pleasure, and a wife for breed.
But Chloe's air is unconfined and gay,
And can perhaps an injured bed repay;
Perhaps her patient temper can behold
The rival of her love adorned with gold,
Powdered with diamonds; free from thought and care,
A husband's sullen humors she can bear.
    Why are these sobs? and why these streaming eyes?
Is love the cause? no, I the sex despise;
I hate, I loath his base perfidious name.
Yet if he should but feign a rival flame?
But Chloe boasts and triumphs in my pains,
To her he's faithful, 'tis to me, he feigns.
    Thus love-sick Lydia raved. Her maid appears;
A band-box in her steady hand she bears.
How well this ribband's gloss becomes your face,
She crys, in raptures! then, so sweet a lace!
How charmingly you look! so bright! so fair!
'Tis to your eyes the head-dress owes its air.
Strait Lydia smiled; the comb adjusts her locks,
And at the play-house Harry keeps her box.

IV
THE RESTORATION
AND THE EIGHTEENTH CENTURY

THE AUGUSTAN LYRIC

THE most highly respected form of lyric poetry in the Augustan Age was the great ode, of which Dryden's *Alexander's Feast* is not only a superb example but also one which served as a model for later poets. The form had its origins in the Pindaric imitations of Jonson and Cowley in the seventeenth century, and it was inevitable that poets like Dryden should depart from imitation of the Greek and seek to attain the same kind of effect in original English measures. Among the classical works of criticism most studied by Augustans was Longinus' treatise *On the Sublime,* which dealt with the elevation of spirit that great poetry must attain, its power to transcend the ordinary limits of artistic form by a freedom of imagination which becomes its own reason and justification. Such a notion of poetry was essentially antithetical to the neoclassical reverence for rigid genres, but in the elevation of the ode to a genre itself, this opposition was reconciled. The essential quality of the ode was its varying line lengths, its sudden shifts in meter and in mood. The final effect was prescribed: it must be elevated and heroic, but to attain this effect the poet could rely as he pleased upon his own intuitive sense of sound. It was accorded a place in the eighteenth-century poetic hierarchy next to the epic itself, and in it Dryden and Pope achieved some of their greatest successes.

The love poetry of the Restoration and the eighteenth century carries on the courtly tradition of the mid-seventeenth-century Cavalier poets; and in the works of Sir Charles Sedley, himself a gay-living rake, we see much of their careless disdain and flippant play of wit. This Cavalier tradition persisted largely in song, for which, in spite of its classical predilections, the Augustan Age had a genuine fondness. Perhaps the finest writer in this vein was Matthew Prior, who infused into the traditional quatrains of an earlier age much of neoclassical wit and sophistication. Prior may have come closer than any of his contemporaries to the playful and witty urbanity of Horace. The eighteenth century was capable also of the unsophisticated charm which Thomas Parnell attained in the simple ballad stanzas of *My Days Have Been So Wond'rous Free.* The form of this poem relates it to the tradition of popular literature, which survived in spite of Augustan classicism and which appears notably in such homely verse as Henry Carey's *Ballad of Sally in Our Alley.*

The eighteenth century is also an age of religious poetry, ranging from the simple, classical statement of personal piety in Joseph Addison's *The*

Spacious Firmament on High to the homiletic hymns of Isaac Watts and the profound and moving anthems of John and Charles Wesley. These are products of the religious revival which was also a part of the eighteenth century, a revival inspired by the need to counteract the almost mechanical rationalism of the Church of England with a religion based on personal emotion and a sense of oneness with God. But even the Wesleyan hymns are marked by the clarity of direct statement which is so much a part of eighteenth-century poetry. There is in this poetry none of the subdued passion of Southwell or the metaphysical tension of Donne or Herbert. It is the expression of public rather than of private devotion, of common acceptance of the Deity rather than of personal search for salvation; and as such it is much a part of its age.

FOR FURTHER READING:

MacLean, Norman. "From Action to Image: Theories of the Lyric in the Eighteenth Century," *Critics and Criticism,* ed. R. S. Crane. Chicago, 1952.
Monk, S. H. *The Sublime, A Study of Critical Theories in XVIII-Century England.* New York, 1935.
Shuster, G. N. *The English Ode from Milton to Keats.* New York, 1940.
Spears, M. K. "Some Ethical Aspects of Matthew Prior's Poetry," *Studies in Philology,* VL (1948), 606-629.

JOHN DRYDEN

ALEXANDER'S FEAST;
OR, THE POWER OF MUSIQUE. AN ODE,
IN HONOUR OF ST. CECILIA'S DAY

'Twas at the royal feast for Persia won
By Philip's warlike son:
Aloft in awful state

JOHN DRYDEN (1631-1700) was in the service of Oliver Cromwell during the Commonwealth, but after the Restoration he firmly supported the Stuarts. He turned to the theater as a means of support and established himself as England's leading dramatist as well as poet and critic. He was buried in the Poets' Corner of Westminster Abbey.

The God-like hero sat
On his imperial throne;
His valiant peers were placed around;
Their brows with roses and with myrtles bound.
(So should desert in arms be crowned.)
The lovely Thaïs, by his side,
Sate like a blooming Eastern bride,
In flower of youth and beauty's pride.
Happy, happy, happy pair!
None but the brave,
None but the brave,
None but the brave deserves the fair!

Chorus

Happy, happy, happy pair!
None but the brave,
None but the brave,
None but the brave deserves the fair.

Timotheus, placed on high
Amid the tuneful quire,
With flying fingers touched the lyre;
The trembling notes ascend the sky,
And heavenly joys inspire.
The song began from Jove,
Who left his blissful seats above—
Such is the power of mighty love!
A dragon's fiery form belied the god;
Sublime on radiant spires he rode
When he to fair Olympia pressed,
And while he sought her snowy breast;
Then round her slender waist he curled,
And stamped an image of himself, a sovereign of the world.
The listening crowd admire the lofty sound,
A present deity! they shout around;
A present deity! the vaulted roofs rebound:
With ravished ears
The monarch hears,
Assumes the god,
Affects to nod,
And seems to shake the spheres.

Chorus

With ravished ears
The monarch hears,
Assumes the god,
Affects to nod,
And seems to shake the spheres.

The praise of Bacchus then the sweet musician sung,
Of Bacchus ever fair and ever young.
The jolly god in triumph comes;
Sound the trumpets, beat the drums!
Flushed with a purple grace
He shows his honest face.
Now give the hautboys breath; he comes, he comes.
Bacchus, ever fair and young,
Drinking joys did first ordain;
Bacchus' blessings are a treasure,
Drinking is the soldier's pleasure;
Rich the treasure,
Sweet the pleasure,
Sweet is pleasure after pain.

Chorus

Bacchus' blessings are a treasure,
Drinking is the soldier's pleasure;
Rich the treasure,
Sweet the pleasure,
Sweet is pleasure after pain.

Soothed with the sound, the king grew vain;
Fought all his battles o'er again;
And thrice he routed all his foes, and thrice he slew
the slain!
The master saw the madness rise,
His glowing cheeks, his ardent eyes;
And while he heaven and earth defied,
Changed his hand and checked his pride.
He chose a mournful Muse
Soft pity to infuse.
He sung Darius great and good,
By too severe a fate

Fallen, fallen, fallen, fallen,
   Fallen from his high estate,
And weltering in his blood;
Deserted at his utmost need
By those his former bounty fed;
On the bare earth exposed he lies
With not a friend to close his eyes.
With downcast looks the joyless victor sate,
   Revolving in his altered soul
     The various turns of chance below;
   And now and then a sigh he stole,
   And tears began to flow.

Chorus

   Revolving in his altered soul
     The various turns of chance below;
   And, now and then, a sigh he stole,
   And tears began to flow.

The mighty master smiled to see
That love was in the next degree;
'Twas but a kindred-sound to move,
For pity melts the mind to love.
   Softly sweet, in Lydian measures,
   Soon he soothed his soul to pleasures.
War, (he sung) is toil and trouble;
Honor but an empty bubble;
   Never ending, still beginning,
Fighting still, and still destroying;
   If the world be worth thy winning,
Think, O think, it worth enjoying.
   Lovely Thaïs sits beside thee,
   Take the good the gods provide thee!
The many rend the skies with loud applause;
So love was crowned, but music won the cause.
   The prince, unable to conceal his pain,
     Gazed on the fair
     Who caused his care,
   And sighed and looked, sighed and looked,
   Sighed and looked, and sighed again;
At length, with love and wine at once oppressed,
The vanquished victor sunk upon her breast.

Chorus

The prince, unable to conceal his pain,
Gazed on the fair
Who caused his care,
And sighed and looked, sighed and looked,
Sighed and looked, and sighed again.
At length, with love and wine at once oppressed,
The vanquished victor sunk upon her breast.

Now strike the golden lyre again,
A louder yet, and yet a louder strain!
Break his bands of sleep asunder
And rouse him like a rattling peal of thunder.
Hark, hark! the horrid sound
Has raised up his head;
As awaked from the dead
And amazed he stares around.
"Revenge, revenge!" Timotheus cries;
"See the Furies arise!
See the snakes that they rear,
How they hiss in their hair,
And the sparkles that flash from their eyes!
Behold a ghastly band,
Each a torch in his hand!
Those are Grecian ghosts that in battle were slain,
And unburied remain
Inglorious on the plain.
Give the vengeance due
To the valiant crew!
Behold how they toss their torches on high,
How they point to the Persian abodes
And glittering temples of their hostile gods!"
The princes applaud with a furious joy;
And the King seized a flambeau with zeal to destroy;
Thaïs led the way,
To light him to his prey,
And, like another Helen, fired another Troy!

Chorus

And the King seized a flambeau with zeal to destroy;
Thaïs led the way,

To light him to his prey,
And, like another Helen, fired another Troy.

Thus, long ago,
Ere heaving bellows learned to blow,
While organs yet were mute,
Timotheus, to his breathing flute
And sounding lyre,
Could swell the soul to rage, or kindle soft desire.
At last divine Cecilia came,
Inventress of the vocal frame;
The sweet enthusiast from her sacred store
Enlarged the former narrow bounds,
And added length to solemn sounds,
With nature's mother-wit, and arts unknown before.
Let old Timotheus yield the prize
Or both divide the crown;
He raised a mortal to the skies;
She drew an angel down!

Grand Chorus

At last divine Cecilia came,
Inventress of the vocal frame;
The sweet enthusiast from her sacred store
Enlarged the former narrow bounds,
And added length to solemn sounds,
With nature's mother-wit, and arts unknown before.
Let old Timotheus yield the prize,
Or both divide the crown;
He raised a mortal to the skies;
She drew an angel down!

A SONG FROM THE ITALIAN

By a dismal cypress lying,
Damon cried, all pale and dying,
Kind is death that ends my pain,
But cruel she I loved in vain.
The mossy fountains
Murmur my trouble,
And hollow mountains
My groans redouble:
Every nymph mourns me,

Thus while I languish;
She only scorns me,
Who caus'd my anguish.
No love returning me, but all hope denying;
By a dismal cypress lying,
Like a swan, so sung he dying:
Kind is death that ends my pain,
But cruel she I loved in vain.

SONG

No, no, poor suff'ring heart no change endeavor,
Choose to sustain the smart, rather than leave her;
My ravished eyes behold such charms about her,
I can die with her, but not live without her.
One tender sigh of hers to see me languish,
Will more than pay the price of my past anguish:
Beware, O cruel fair, how you smile on me,
'Twas a kind look of yours that has undone me.

Love has in store for me one happy minute,
And she will end my pain who did begin it;
Then no day void of bliss, or pleasure leaving,
Ages shall slide away without perceiving:
Cupid shall guard the door the more to please us,
And keep out time and death when they would seize us:
Time and death shall depart, and say in flying,
Love has found out a way to live by dying.

SIR CHARLES SEDLEY

SONG

Smooth was the water, calm the air,
 The evening-sun deprest,
Lawyers dismissed the noisy bar,
 The laborer at rest,

SIR CHARLES SEDLEY (1639?-1701) succeeded to his family's title and estate in Kent while still at Oxford. After the Restoration, he lived a gay life in London and was the cause of much scandal.

When Strephon, with his charming fair,
   Cross'd the proud river Thames,
And to a garden did repair,
   To quench their mutual flames.

The crafty waiter soon espied
   Youth sparkling in her eyes;
He brought no ham, nor neats-tongues dried,
   But cream and strawberries.

The amorous Strephon asked the maid,
   What's whiter than this cream?
She blushed, and could not tell, she said:
   Thy teeth, my pretty lamb.

What's redder than these berries are?
   I know not, she replied:
Those lips, which I'll no longer spare,
   The burning shepherd cried.

And straight began to hug her:
   This kiss, my dear,
Is sweeter far
   Than strawberries, cream and sugar.

MATTHEW PRIOR

AN ODE

The merchant, to secure his treasure,
   Conveys it in a borrowed name:
Euphelia serves to grace my measure;
   But Cloe is my real flame.

My softest verse, my darling lyre,
   Upon Euphelia's toilet lay;
When Cloe noted her desire,
   That I should sing, that I should play.

MATTHEW PRIOR (1664-1721) spent most of his career in the diplomatic service. He was imprisoned for two years after the accession of King George I but upon his release was given the money for an estate in Essex, where he spent his remaining days.

My lyre I tune, my voice I raise;
 But with my numbers mix my sighs:
And whilst I sing Euphelia's praise,
 I fixed my soul on Cloe's eyes.

Fair Cloe blushed: Euphelia frowned:
 I sung and gazed: I played and trembled:
And Venus to the loves around
 Remarked, how ill we all dissembled.

AN ODE Matthew Prior's society verse, of which this ode is an excellent example, is marked by urbane wit and sophistication. His poems show how the satiric spirit of the Augustan Age affected the love lyric. In Prior we have the spirit of Horace perhaps most perfectly captured in English. When we compare the verse of a poet like Prior with the lyrics of the Tudor and Stuart periods, we find that the neoclassical lyric usually has a higher polish, a harder surface, and a more sparkling wit, though it may be inferior to the earlier poetry in intellectual depth and emotional sincerity.

This poem turns upon the unending possibilities for deceit suggested by the final line. Up to that point the poet appears to have been guilty of but a single deceit, against Euphelia. Although he sings all his songs to her, using her name in his verses, it is to Cloe, he tells us, that all are really directed. But when Venus observes that all three persons involved in this love triangle are dissemblers, we realize that even the supposed heartfelt sighs for Cloe may not be genuine. Taking the poem a few steps further, we see that the cynical poet does not even exempt himself from being among the deceived. If Cloe's blushes are faked, obviously she is no more deeply involved in her desire for the poet than he is in his desire for her. All these lovers, then, are playing an elaborate game, and the number of men for whom Cloe blushes or the women for whom the poet sighs is endless. Finally we are able to conclude the poem without feeling sorry for Euphelia, for we know now that it is her part in this triangle to appear hurt, to frown; but in some other set of three in another drawing room, she probably plays the desired one and therefore can afford to frown at Cloe's success in this one.

If there is any underlying seriousness in the poem at all—and we suspect that there is, since the age was quick to discern the price of folly—it may be in the realization that no genuine emotions exist anywhere, that no lover can ever trust his beloved for fear that the passion is dissembled. This cynical attitude is prepared for in the commercial metaphor of the opening stanza, which sets the tone of the poem. The deceit of the lover is likened to the precaution of the merchant, and the love which is disguised is as free from spiritual value as the cargo shipped with false labels. That love is just a game is conveyed also in the word *secure,* for the poet by his elaborate stratagem is merely safeguarding his winnings, as the merchant by deceit safeguards his profits.

Much of the poem's charm springs from its metrical dexterity. The simple iambic tetrameter quatrains, rhyming *abab,* are remarkably regular, and a swift pace is maintained by the placing of caesura so that lines echo the music of one another in a perfect harmony. The exact cadence of "My softest verse,|| my darling lyre" is repeated in "That I should sing,|| that I should play," with *sing* corresponding appropriately to *verse* and *play* to *lyre.* Then the order is pleasantly reversed: "My lyre I tune,|| my voice I raise," although the caesura is still kept after the fourth syllable of the line. The device of rhetorical repetition within individual lines is used for emphasis, and it is particularly effective in the final stanza:

> Fair Cloe blushed: Euphelia frowned:
> I sung and gazed: I played and trembled:

We have throughout the poem the fast-moving tempo of a light-hearted song.

PHYLLIS'S AGE

> How old may Phyllis be, you ask,
>   Whose beauty thus all hearts engages?
> To answer is no easy task;
>   For she has really two ages.
>
> Stiff in Brocard, and pinched in stays,
>   Her patches, paint, and jewels on;
> All day let envy view her face;
>   And Phyllis is but twenty-one.
>
> Paint, patches, jewels laid aside,
>   At night astronomers agree,
> That evening has the day belied;
>   And Phyllis is some forty-three.

TO A CHILD OF QUALITY FIVE YEARS OLD THE AUTHOR SUPPOSED FORTY

> Lords, knights, and squires, the numerous band
>   That wear the fair Miss Mary's fetters,

Were summoned by her high command,
  To show their passion by their letters.

My pen amongst the rest I took,
  Lest those bright eyes that cannot read,
Should dart their kindling fire, and look
  The power they have to be obeyed.

Nor quality, nor reputation,
  Forbid me yet my flame to tell;
Dear Five-years-old befriends my passion,
  And I may write till she can spell.

For, while she makes her silkworms beds
  With all the tender things I swear;
Whilst all the house my passion reads,
  In papers round her baby's hair;

She may receive and own my flame;
  For though the strictest prudes should know it,
She'll pass for a most virtuous dame,
  And I for an unhappy poet.

Then too, alas! when she shall tear
  The lines some younger rival sends,
She'll give me leave to write, I fear,
  And we shall still continue friends.

For, as our different ages move,
  'Tis so ordained, would fate but mend it,
That I shall be past making love
  When she begins to comprehend it.

ALEXANDER POPE

ODE ON SOLITUDE

Happy the man whose wish and care
  A few paternal acres bound,
Content to breathe his native air,
      In his own ground.

Whose herds with milk, whose fields with bread,
Whose flocks supply him with attire,
Whose trees in summer yield him shade,
In winter fire.

Blest, who can unconcern'dly find
Hours, days, and years slide soft away,
In health of body, peace of mind,
Quiet by day,

Sound sleep by night; study and ease,
Together mixt; sweet recreation;
And Innocence, which most does please
With meditation.

Thus let me live, unseen, unknown,
Thus unlamented let me die,
Steal from the world, and not a stone
Tell where I lie.

JOSEPH ADDISON

HYMN

The spacious firmament on high,
With all the blue ethereal sky,
And spangled heavens, a shining frame,
Their great Original proclaim.
Th' unwearied sun from day to day
Does his Creator's power display;
And publishes to every land
The work of an almighty hand.

Soon as the evening shades prevail,
The moon takes up the wondrous tale;
And nightly to the listening earth

JOSEPH ADDISON (1672-1719) early distinguished himself as a classical scholar. He was a member of Parliament from 1708 to his death and is important as the editor, with Richard Steele, of the *Tatler* and *Spectator* papers.

Repeats the story of her birth:
Whilst all the stars that round her burn,
And all the planets in their turn,
Confirm the tidings as they roll,
And spread the truth from pole to pole.

What though in solemn silence all
Move round the dark terrestrial ball;
What though nor real voice nor sound
Amid their radiant orbs be found?
In reason's ear they all rejoice,
And utter forth a glorious voice;
For ever singing as they shine,
"The hand that made us is divine."

THOMAS PARNELL

SONG

My days have been so wond'rous free,
   The little birds that fly
With careless ease from tree to tree,
   Were but as blessed as I.

Ask gliding waters, if a tear
   Of mine encreased their stream?
Or ask the flying gales, if e'er
   I lent one sigh to them?

But now my former days retire,
   And I'm by beauty caught,
The tender chains of sweet desire
   Are fixed upon my thought.

Ye nightingales, ye twisting pines!
   Ye swains that haunt the grove!
Ye gentle echoes, breezy winds!
   Ye close retreats of love!

THOMAS PARNELL (1679-1718), an Anglo-Irish poet, spent his life in
the service of the Anglican Church in Ireland.

With all of nature, all of art,
　　Assist the dear design;
O teach a young, unpracticed heart,
　　To make my Nancy mine.

The very thought of change I hate,
　　As much as of despair;
Nor ever covet to be great,
　　Unless it be for her.

'Tis true, the passion in my mind
　　Is mixed with soft distress;
Yet while the fair I love is kind,
　　I cannot wish it less.

HENRY CAREY

THE BALLAD OF SALLY IN OUR ALLEY

Of all the girls that are so smart
　　There's none like pretty Sally;
She is the darling of my heart,
　　And she lives in our alley.
There is no lady in the land
　　Is half so sweet as Sally;
She is the darling of my heart,
　　And she lives in our alley.

Her father he makes cabbage-nets,
　　And through the streets does cry 'em;
Her mother she sells laces long,
　　To such as please to buy 'em;
But sure such folks could ne'er beget
　　So sweet a girl as Sally!
She is the darling of my heart,
　　And she lives in our alley.

HENRY CAREY (d. 1743) was educated at a school kept by his mother in Yorkshire. He earned his living as a teacher of music and was noted as a composer as well as a poet.

When she is by, I leave my work
    (I love her so sincerely);
My master comes, like any Turk,
    And bangs me most severely;
But let him bang his bellyful,
    I'll bear it all for Sally;
She is the darling of my heart,
    And she lives in our alley.

Of all the days that's in the week,
    I dearly love but one day,
And that's the day that comes betwixt
    A Saturday and Monday;
For then I'm dressed, all in my best,
    To walk abroad with Sally;
She is the darling of my heart,
    And she lives in our alley.

My master carries me to church,
    And often am I blamed,
Because I leave him in the lurch,
    As soon as text is named:
I leave the church in sermon time,
    And slink away to Sally;
She is the darling of my heart,
    And she lives in our alley.

When Christmas comes about again,
    O then I shall have money;
I'll hoard it up, and box and all
    I'll give it to my honey:
And, would it were ten thousand pounds,
    I'd give it all to Sally;
She is the darling of my heart,
    And she lives in our alley.

My master and the neighbours all
    Make game of me and Sally;
And (but for her) I'd better be
    A slave, and row a galley:
But when my seven long years are out,
    O then I'll marry Sally!

O then we'll wed and then we'll bed;
But not in our alley!

WILLIAM WALSH

THE DESPAIRING LOVER

Distracted with care,
For Phyllis the Fair;
Since nothing could move her,
Poor Damon, her Lover,
Resolves in despair
No longer to languish,
Nor bear so much anguish;

But, mad with his love,
To a precipice goes;
Where, a leap from above
Would soon finish his woes.

When in rage he came there,
Beholding how steep
The sides did appear,
And the bottom how deep;
His torments projecting,
And sadly reflecting,
That a lover forsaken
A new love may get;
But a neck, when once broken,
Can never be set:
And, that he could die
Whenever he would;
But, that he could live
But as long as he could:
How grievous soever
The torment might grow,
He scorned to endeavor
To finish it so.

WILLIAM WALSH (1663-1708) served as a member of Parliament and as Gentleman of the Horse to Queen Anne.

But bold, unconcerned
At thoughts of the pain,
He calmly returned
To his cottage again.

ISAAC WATTS

AGAINST IDLENESS AND MISCHIEF

How doth the little busy bee
  Improve each shining hour,
And gather honey all the day
  From every opening flower!

How skilfully she builds her cell!
  How neat she spreads the wax;
And labors hard to store it well
  With the sweet food she makes.

In works of labor or of skill
  I would be busy too:
For Satan finds some mischief still
  For idle hands to do.

In books, or work, or healthful play
  Let my first years be past,
That I may give for every day
  Some good account at last.

CHARLES WESLEY

FOR EASTER-DAY

"Christ the Lord is risen to-day,"
Sons of men and angels say.

ISAAC WATTS (1674-1748), pastor of the Independent Congregation in Mark Lane, was a writer of hymns and didactic poetry for children.
CHARLES WESLEY (1707-1788), a leader of the Methodist movement, was educated at Oxford, where he formed a group of religious dissenters. He accompanied his brother John to Georgia and upon his return to England lived as an itinerant preacher.

Raise your joys and triumphs high;
Sing, ye heavens, and earth reply.

Love's redeeming work is done,
Fought the fight, the battle won.
Lo! our Sun's eclipse is o'er;
Lo! He sets in blood no more.

Vain the stone, the watch, the seal;
Christ has burst the gates of hell!
Death in vain forbids His rise:
Christ has opened Paradise.

Lives again our glorious King;
Where, O death, is now thy sting?
Dying once, He all doth save;
Where thy victory, O grave?

Soar we now where Christ has led,
Following our exalted Head:
Made like Him, like Him we rise;
Ours the cross, the grave, the skies!

What though once we perished all,
Partners in our parents' fall:
Second life we all receive,
In our heavenly Adam live.

Risen with Him, we upward move,
Still we seek the things above,
Still pursue, and kiss the Son,
Seated on His Father's throne.

Scarce on earth a thought bestow;
Dead to all we leave below:
Heaven our aim, and loved abode,
Hid our life with Christ in God.

Hid, till Christ our life appear,
Glorious in His members here:
Joined to Him, we then shall shine
All immortal, all divine.

Hail, the Lord of earth and heaven!
Praise to Thee by both be given:
Thee we greet triumphant now;
Hail, the resurrection Thou!

King of glory, soul of bliss,
Everlasting life is this,
Thee to know, Thy power to prove,
Thus to sing, and thus to love.

The Romantic Period V

THE Romantic movement, which had its beginnings probably in the second half of the eighteenth century and grew to major proportions following the publication in 1798 of the *Lyrical Ballads* of Wordsworth and Coleridge, has continued into the literature of our own day. As a philosophy of life, Romanticism represents the culmination of the belief in human perfectibility which emerged in the Augustan Age. Perhaps the strongest element in Romanticism is faith in the potentialities of mankind, which runs counter to the sense of human sin, guilt, and insignificance that is characteristic of so much earlier literature. Although this faith is related to Augustan glorification of man's rational powers, which were regarded as capable of revealing and controlling the mysteries of nature, the Romantics emphasize rather man's power of feeling, his soaring imagination, and his intuitive communion with nature as the sources of his understanding. Admiration for and belief in the fundamental goodness of man led to new theories of political and social liberalism; and the freeing of the imagination sent poets in search of exotic materials, taking them sometimes back to the Middle Ages, sometimes to distant lands—journeys of the mind in time and space.

The Romantic faith expresses itself in a near-deification of the individual and a total belief in nature as a manifestation of God and His wisdom; the basic urge of the poet is to display the human being in all his aspects but primarily as a creature of feeling and imagination whose emotions hold vitality, significance, and truth. In nature the Romantic finds a universal goodness and a reminder of his own grandeur as well as direct emanations from the presence of God. H. N. Fairchild, himself a bitter foe as well as an acute student of the Romantic spirit, has written that its essence is to be found in "man's desire to feel independently good, strong, wise, and creative, his thirst for boundless expansion of being in a universe which echoes back to him his assertion of self-sufficient power." The Romantics sought to find in the very nature of man—his feelings, his aspirations, even his confusions—a new basis for value.

The development of Romantic poetry We are concerned here only with the manner in which the Romantic movement developed in poetry, and in this respect we must beware of oversimplification. We must not think of poets like Blake, Wordsworth, Coleridge, Byron, Shelley, and Keats as representing a homogeneous group or as having any awareness that they belonged to a common school. Indeed, some of these men had little respect for the work of the others, and they did not champion a common critical point of view. On the other hand, while the Romantic movement produced only one critical theorist of distinction, Samuel Taylor Coleridge, it is true that to his ideal of poetry all the Romantic poets in their own ways may be seen to adhere. Coleridge's most important doctrine was that of the organic unity of the work of art—that every poem exhibits a perfect fusion of form and content, which is the result of the poet's personal reaction to his subject. Coleridge maintained also that most poems are self-contained and self-sufficient entities, which must be considered without relation to external laws, the "rules" and "genres" so dear to the age of Pope. The Romantic poet need have as the guiding spirit of his work only his own artistic integrity. The effect of such a critical view was to lift many of the traditional restraints from the artist and to allow a freedom of expression such as the poet had never known before.

Wordsworth's theory of poetry The Romantic idea of poetry was perhaps most notably stated in the *Preface* which William Wordsworth wrote for the second edition of *Lyrical Ballads* in 1800. His poetry, he said, was to deal with humble life, and it was to be expressed in the language of common speech so that it might be understood by unsophisticated people. Wordsworth, in theory, rejected "poetic diction," with its personified abstractions, metaphors, and rhetorical elegance—those devices developed from the beginnings of English poetry up to his own time. Ordinary language in his poetry would be given importance by the emotion, accuracy, and truth with which he was able to infuse it. It would be made distinct from prose by meter rather than diction, for the key to the pleasure and excitement of poetry for Wordsworth lay primarily in recurring metrical patterns. Although his practice did not always support his claims, Wordsworth's new theory of diction represented his most radical break with the past.

Wordsworth believed that all good poetry resulted from "the spontaneous overflow of powerful emotions . . . recollected in tranquillity." To him, the poet stands apart from other men in his high moral and ethical purpose, in his superior powers of feeling and expression, and in his ability to infuse his emotion into language and to convey the highest truth—the truth of feeling. Two important Romantic ideals are implicit in this view: the poet as a moral teacher of the highest order, and the poet as a special creature endowed with mystical powers. For Wordsworth, both these qualities sprang from the poet's close contact with nature, from which he derived his moral truth and the power to convey it. In his *Preface* he was attempting to describe his own poetry, not to make general prescriptions for all poetry, but the principles he stated had a profound effect on poets who followed him.

Verse forms Although they reacted against traditional poetic diction, the Romantic poets did not completely scorn traditional poetic genres. They expressed their opposition to the rigid Augustan heroic couplet by a return to earlier verse forms, particularly the Elizabethan, for in the Tudor poets they thought they recognized a sense of freedom, of man's boundless horizons, which was particularly congenial to them. There was a revival of the Spenserian stanza, as in Keats' *Eve of St. Agnes,* of rhyme royal, and of the sonnet, which had been largely ignored throughout the eighteenth century but which was given new life by Wordsworth, Shelley, and Keats and put to new uses. There was also a great revival of blank verse, which, except in James Thomson's *Seasons,* had been little used in the eighteenth century. It became the principal vehicle for the long reflective poems of Wordsworth and Shelley and attained a smoothness and a simplicity of diction which it had not known since Shakespeare. When iambic pentameter couplets were used, it was not with the epigrammatic end-stopped lines of Pope but with the run-on lines and smooth-flowing verse paragraphs of Keats.

The Romantic poets were responsible for a great revival of interest in the folk ballad, a literary type which appealed to their own esthetics and philosophy. As the product of simple people, written in their simple language, it was a "democratic" poetic form, and its spontaneity seemed to reflect that overflow of powerful feeling which poets like Wordsworth sought to capture. Admiration for the old ballads led to their imitation, and the literary ballad, such as Coleridge's *Rime of the Ancient Mariner* and Keats' *La Belle Dame sans Merci,* is one of the most important developments of the early nineteenth century.

Nature and morality Augustan poetry, in its adherence to the classical principles of Horace, had been highly didactic. The Romantics are no less serious in their faith in poetry's power to uplift mankind, but the poet's function is no longer to express a generally accepted "truth" in the most elegant terms. His function is to be true to himself, and the moral value of his work stems from his power of inspiration, his ability to respond to the forces of nature and to express a poetic vision that has the truth of personal feeling rather than of received precept. Such poetry would be truly moral, rather than moralistic. The high moral mission of the poet was perhaps most consciously and deliberately assumed by Wordsworth. To him, nature was the greatest teacher, and the truth of feeling was the profoundest truth. The excellence of Wordsworth as a moral teacher was later recognized by the Victorian Matthew Arnold, who made the power of poetry to effect the moral elevation of humanity a cornerstone of his own very influential critical theory.

Much of Romantic poetry is nature poetry. Nature means different things to different poets, but to all of them it is actual observable nature which is important, not the conventions of earlier pastoral poetry. The glorification of trees, hills, rocks, and streams may have sprung in part from the revulsion aroused in Romantic poets by the sordid, misery-ridden cities of their time, for we must remember that the early nineteenth century is the period of the worst human degradation ever wrought by the Industrial Revolution. Nature poetry was one reaction against the new factory system and the growth of urban slums. Nature for many poets comes to represent the continuity of some earlier way of life to which they long to return, and the joys of nature come to be associated nostalgically with the joys of childhood, freedom, vitality, and the rapture of enthrallment by simple things. In Wordsworth's *Ode on the Intimations of Immortality* childhood is seen as man's closest link to an ideal existence which he knew before birth; through nature he is able to have some sense of this unattainable past state of perfection.

All the Romantic poets see nature as closely attuned to mankind. Nature may reflect, as in Shelley's *Ode to the West Wind,* man's own feelings and frustrations. It is a force with which man is always in close communion, and when he lives with nature he is happiest. Nature becomes the great source of education, for from it man derives all he really needs to know—the simple virtues of love and kindness as well as oneness with his fellow men and with all creation. Through nature, also, one may come to an awareness of God and the perfect order of His creation. Nature for some poets comes to be the source of all virtue, all wisdom, and all meaning in human life. It provides the evidence of the immortality of man's soul and teaches him how to live in the present world. We find as distinctive facets of Romantic nature poetry two philosophical assumptions which had not usually been a part of traditional pastoral poetry. One is the Platonic doctrine which sees the present world as an imperfect reflection of an ideal world known only before birth and after death. The other is a pantheistic religion, most notable in the early Wordsworth, which sees God as existing not only in some heaven but also in nature, his presence being felt in every stone, tree, and blade of grass.

Supernaturalism A concern with the importance of man and the permanence of the human spirit may have contributed to the interest in the supernatural which is a fundamental aspect of Romantic poetry. Poets showed a constant tendency to explore the mysterious world outside of man's sensory perception. Often this interest manifests itself in the grotesque and exotic, as in Coleridge's *Rime of the Ancient Mariner* and *Christabel,* which borrow from the spirit of Gothic romance so much in vogue at the end of the eighteenth century. Often it appears in the love of magic and enchantment, as in some of the greatest work of Keats. Romantic poetry was concerned, in short, with an intense awareness of the real world and with an imaginative exploration of whatever worlds may lie outside the grasp of man's reason.

The Romantic poets We usually divide the major English Romantic poets into two groups, with Blake as their most important forerunner. The first group includes Coleridge, Wordsworth, and Robert Southey, who were closely associated with one another and who came to maturity in the era of the French Revolution, reflecting in their early poetry the revolutionary optimism for the future of mankind. Coleridge and Southey dreamed of founding a new society in America, but like most of their hopes, this one never came to fruition. All suffered the inevitable frustration of their youthful plans and, as they grew older, turned away from the idealistic causes of their youth. Wordsworth changed his early nature philosophy for conservative adherence to the Anglican Church and his political radicalism for a staid adherence to the status quo which won him the poet laureateship from a conservative government. Southey turned to the writing of history, and Coleridge became more and more absorbed in German metaphysics and the problems of literary criticism.

The second group consists of Byron, Shelley, and Keats, also personally known to one another, although Keats' connection with the other two was very slight. Byron and Shelley lived as exiles in Italy, and Keats journeyed there to die. All these men inherited the hopes and aspirations of a revolutionary era but saw them frustrated by the realities of crass political interests and what they regarded as a degenerate society. They tend to reflect melancholy and despair, and none came to the peace and tranquillity which Wordsworth at last achieved. All died very young, Keats of tuberculosis at twenty-six, Shelley by drowning at thirty, and Byron of fever contracted during a futile battle for Greek independence at thirty-six.

FOR FURTHER READING:

Abrams, M. H. *The Mirror and the Lamp.* New York, 1953.

Bowra, C. M. *The Romantic Imagination.* Cambridge, Mass., 1949.

Beach, J. W. *The Concept of Nature in Nineteenth Century English Poetry.* New York, 1936.

Bate, W. J. *From Classic to Romantic.* Cambridge, Mass., 1946.

Bush, Douglas. *Mythology and the Romantic Tradition in English Poetry.* Cambridge, Mass., 1937.

Fairchild, H. N. *The Romantic Quest.* New York, 1931.

Gérard, Albert. "On the Logic of Romanticism," *Essays in Criticism,* VII (July 1957), 262-273.

Lovejoy, A. O. "On the Discrimination of Romanticisms," *PMLA,* XXXIX (June 1924), 229-253.

Wellek, René. "The Concept of 'Romanticism' in Literary History," *Comparative Literature,* I (Winter 1949), 1-23, and (Spring 1950), 147-172.

V

THE ROMANTIC PERIOD

THE PRE-ROMANTIC

I F literary historians date the beginnings of the Romantic period from
the publication of *Lyrical Ballads* in 1798, it is more for historical convenience than anything else. The Romantic period in England is one of the
most difficult of literary movements to delineate with precision, for it
marks the dominance of attitudes and interests every one of which was
present, at least to some extent, in earlier literary periods. We have come
to apply the term *pre-Romantic,* as a matter of course, to those writers
who, while living in the eighteenth century and sharing most of the values
of Alexander Pope and Samuel Johnson, reveal tendencies which are opposed to the neoclassicism of their time and point toward what is to be
more surely realized in the poetry of Wordsworth and his fellows.

Few corners of eighteenth-century life and art were untouched by the
pre-Romantic spirit. We find it in the growth of the drama and the novel
of sensibility, which emphasized human feelings and stressed an inherent
"moral sense" which could lead man naturally to seek virtue. It appears
in the cult of the "noble savage" with its glorification of the simple, unsophisticated being as one most subject to the control of a native, instinc-
tive goodness. It finds expression in the poetry of Robert Burns, written
deliberately in a simple, untutored Ayrshire dialect so as to support the
legend that its author was a simple plowboy touched with inherent genius.
The dialect poetry of Burns and of the slightly earlier Allan Ramsay was
to be imitated throughout the nineteenth century, even by Tennyson.

There is also in the eighteenth century a revival of interest in the strange
and exotic, in the tale of horror, and in the legendry of Scandinavia. English
and Scottish folklore receives new attention. Even Joseph Addison, an
apostle of neoclassic taste, wrote an appreciation of the medieval ballad
Chevy Chase, and Bishop Thomas Percy and others began their system-
atic exploration of folk balladry. The interest in the Middle Ages is shown
in the popularity of imitations of medieval verse written by the gifted, unfortunate Thomas Chatterton and presented as authentic survivals from
the past.

There is probably no period in English history when nature was not a
subject for poetry, and we must not forget that alongside the artificial
pastorals of Ambrose Philips and Thomas Tickell, we have the celebrations of nature in blank verse of James Thomson's *Seasons.* Thomson, a
contemporary of Pope, looks forward to the Romantic era also in the
Spenserian stanzas of his *Castle of Indolence.* We may find an even more
emotional, almost mystical celebration of nature in the poetry of William

Collins, and in William Cowper there is a meditative reflection upon the simple joys of rural life which is not far removed from the poetry of Words-worth. In the eighteenth-century vogue for melancholy, which gave rise to Gray's *Elegy Written in a Country Churchyard,* with its soulful musings on death and decay, we have the beginnings of a poetic mood that we associate more fully with Keats and Shelley.

Standing upon the threshold of the Romantic movement is William Blake, whom recent critics have come to see as the most important poet of the last quarter of the eighteenth century. A painter and engraver by profession, he had almost no academic or literary training, but early in life he was deeply imbued with the mystical Christianity of Swedenborg. In the poetry of Blake, Romanticism takes the form of a revelation of inner experience and of mystical communion with departed spirits and with God. The poetry contains also an intense reaction against the English social order, which Blake, who was of the working class, expressed in the elabo-rate allegory of his prophetic books. Blake is linked to the Romantic move-ment by his imagination and his emphasis upon the individual's mystical union with divine reality.

FOR FURTHER READING:

Erdman, D. V. *Blake, Prophet against Empire.* Princeton, 1954.

Frey, Northrup. *Fearful Symmetry.* Princeton, 1947.

Percival, M. O. *William Blake's Circle of Destiny.* New York, 1938.

Schorer, Mark. *William Blake: The Politics of Vision.* New York, 1946.

Gleckner, R. F. *The Piper and the Bard.* Detroit, 1959.

WILLIAM COLLINS

ODE TO EVENING

If aught of oaten stop, or pastoral song,
May hope, chaste Eve, to soothe thy modest ear,

WILLIAM COLLINS (1721-1759) published his *Persian Eclogues* at seven-teen and his beautiful *Odes* five years later. For a time he lived a literary life in London; but his productivity soon ceased, and a rapid mental and physical decline led to insanity and death.

Like thy own solemn springs,
Thy springs and dying gales.

O nymph reserved, while now the bright-haired sun
Sits in yon western tent, whose cloudy skirts,
 With brede ethereal wove,
 O'erhang his wavy bed:

Now air is hushed, save where the weak-eyed bat
With short, shrill shriek, flits by on leathern wing;
 Or where the beetle winds
 His small but sullen horn,

As oft he rises 'midst the twilight path,
Against the pilgrim borne in heedless hum:
 Now teach me, maid composed,
 To breathe some softened strain,

Whose numbers, stealing through thy darkening vale,
May, not unseemly, with its stillness suit,
 As, musing slow, I hail
 Thy genial loved return!

For when thy folding-star arising shows
His paly circlet, at his warning lamp
 The fragrant Hours, and elves
 Who slept in flowers the day,

And many a nymph who wreathes her brows with sedge,
And sheds the freshening dew, and, lovelier still,
 The pensive Pleasures sweet,
 Prepare thy shadowy car.

Then lead, calm votaress, where some sheety lake
Cheers the lone heath, or some time-hallowed pile,
 Or upland fallows gray
 Reflect its last cool gleam.

But when chill blustering winds, or driving rain,
Forbid my willing feet, be mine the hut,
 That from the mountain's side,
 Views wilds, and swelling floods,

And hamlets brown, and dim-discovered spires;
And hears their simple bell, and marks o'er all
    Thy dewy fingers draw
    The gradual dusky veil.

While Spring shall pour his showers, as oft he wont,
And bathe thy breathing tresses, meekest Eve!
    While Summer loves to sport
    Beneath thy lingering light;

While sallow Autumn fills thy lap with leaves;
Or Winter, yelling through the troublous air,
    Affrights thy shrinking train,
    And rudely rends thy robes;

So long, sure-found beneath the sylvan shed,
Shall Fancy, Friendship, Science, rose-lipped Health,
    Thy gentlest influence own,
    And hymn thy favorite name!

THOMAS GRAY

ELEGY WRITTEN IN A COUNTRY CHURCHYARD

The curfew tolls the knell of parting day,
    The lowing herd wind slowly o'er the lea,
The plowman homeward plods his weary way,
    And leaves the world to darkness and to me.

Now fades the glimmering landscape on the sight,
    And all the air a solemn stillness holds,
Save where the beetle wheels his droning flight,
    And drowsy tinklings lull the distant folds;

Save that from yonder ivy-mantled tower
    The moping owl does to the moon complain

THOMAS GRAY (1716-1771) began his career as a devoted neoclassicist but was guided by temperament to produce a small body of poems which fit the Romantic tradition. His mother worked to pay for his education at Eton and Cambridge. By 1757 his poems had won such acclaim that he was offered the post of poet laureate—which he refused—and in 1768 he was appointed professor of history and modern languages at Cambridge.

Of such as, wandering near her secret bower,
    Molest her ancient solitary reign.

Beneath those rugged elms, that yew-tree's shade,
    Where heaves the turf in many a moldering heap,
Each in his narrow cell forever laid,
    The rude forefathers of the hamlet sleep.

The breezy call of incense-breathing Morn,
    The swallow twittering from the straw-built shed,
The cock's shrill clarion, or the echoing horn,
    No more shall rouse them from their lowly bed.

For them no more the blazing hearth shall burn,
    Or busy housewife ply her evening care:
No children run to lisp their sire's return,
    Or climb his knees the envied kiss to share.

Oft did the harvest to their sickle yield,
    Their furrow oft the stubborn glebe has broke:
How jocund did they drive their team afield!
    How bowed the woods beneath their sturdy stroke!

Let not Ambition mock their useful toil,
    Their homely joys, and destiny obscure;
Nor Grandeur hear, with a disdainful smile,
    The short and simple annals of the poor.

The boast of heraldry, the pomp of power,
    And all that beauty, all that wealth e'er gave,
Awaits alike the inevitable hour:
    The paths of glory lead but to the grave.

Nor you, ye proud, impute to these the fault,
    If Memory o'er their tomb no trophies raise,
Where through the long-drawn aisle and fretted vault
    The pealing anthem swells the note of praise.

Can storied urn or animated bust
    Back to its mansion call the fleeting breath?
Can Honor's voice provoke the silent dust,
    Or Flattery soothe the dull cold ear of Death?

Perhaps in this neglected spot is laid
   Some heart once pregnant with celestial fire;
Hands that the rod of empire might have swayed,
   Or waked to ecstasy the living lyre.

But Knowledge to their eyes her ample page
   Rich with the spoils of time did ne'er unroll;
Chill Penury repressed their noble rage,
   And froze the genial current of the soul.

Full many a gem of purest ray serene
   The dark unfathomed caves of ocean bear;
Full many a flower is born to blush unseen,
   And waste its sweetness on the desert air.

Some village Hampden that with dauntless breast
   The little tyrant of his fields withstood;
Some mute inglorious Milton here may rest,
   Some Cromwell guiltless of his country's blood.

The applause of listening senates to command,
   The threats of pain and ruin to despise,
To scatter plenty o'er a smiling land,
   And read their history in a nation's eyes.

Their lot forbade; nor circumscribed alone
   Their growing virtues, but their crimes confined;
Forbade to wade through slaughter to a throne,
   And shut the gates of mercy on mankind,

The struggling pangs of conscious truth to hide,
   To quench the blushes of ingenuous shame,
Or heap the shrine of Luxury and Pride
   With incense kindled at the Muse's flame.

Far from the madding crowd's ignoble strife,
   Their sober wishes never learned to stray;
Along the cooling sequestered vale of life
   They kept the noiseless tenor of their way.

Yet ev'n these bones from insult to protect
   Some frail memorial still erected nigh,

With uncouth rhymes and shapeless sculpture decked,
   Implores the passing tribute of a sigh.

Their name, their years, spelt by the unlettered Muse,
   The place of fame and elegy supply;
And many a holy text around she strews,
   That teach the rustic moralist to die.

For who, to dumb Forgetfulness a prey,
   This pleasing anxious being e'er resigned,
Left the warm precincts of the cheerful day,
   Nor cast one longing, lingering look behind?

On some fond breast the parting soul relies,
   Some pious drops the closing eye requires;
Ev'n from the tomb the voice of Nature cries,
   Ev'n in our ashes live their wonted fires.

For thee, who, mindful of the unhonoured dead
   Dost in these lines their artless tale relate;
If chance, by lonely Contemplation led,
   Some kindred spirit shall inquire thy fate,

Haply some hoary-headed swain may say,
   "Oft have we seen him at the peep of dawn
Brushing with hasty steps the dews away
   To meet the sun upon the upland lawn.

"There at the foot of yonder nodding beech,
   That wreathes its old fantastic roots so high,
His listless length at noontide would he stretch,
   And pore upon the brook that babbles by.

"Hard by yon wood, now smiling as in scorn,
   Muttering his wayward fancies he would rove,
Now drooping, woeful wan, like one forlorn,
   Or crazed with care, or crossed in hopeless love.

"One morn I missed him on the customed hill,
   Along the heath, and near his favorite tree;
Another came; nor yet beside the rill,
   Nor up the lawn, nor at the wood was he;

"The next with dirges due in sad array
    Slow through the church-way path we saw him borne.
Approach and read (for thou can'st read) the lay,
    Graved on the stone beneath yon aged thorn."

The Epitaph

Here rests his head upon the lap of Earth
    A youth to Fortune and to Fame unknown.
Fair Science frowned not on his humble birth,
    And Melancholy marked him for her own.

Large was his bounty, and his soul sincere,
    Heaven did a recompense as largely send:
He gave to Misery all he had, a tear,
    He gained from Heaven ('twas all he wished) a friend.

No farther seek his merits to disclose,
    Or draw his frailties from their dread abode,
(There they alike in trembling hope repose),
    The bosom of his Father and his God.

THOMAS CHATTERTON

O SING UNTO MY ROUNDELAY

O sing unto my roundelay,
O drop the briny tear with me;
Dance no more at holyday,
Like a running river be:
    My love is dead,
      Gone to his death-bed
All under the willow-tree.

Black his cryne as the winter night,
White his rode as the summer snow,
Red his face as the morning light,
Cold he lies in the grave below:

THOMAS CHATTERTON (1752-1770) won a place in literary history by presenting poems of his own creation as the work of a fifteenth-century monk and then, penniless and without hope, committing suicide at the age of seventeen. Despite his attempts to defraud, his poetry reveals that he had remarkable talent.

> My love is dead,
>   Gone to his death-bed
> All under the willow-tree.

Sweet his tongue as the throstle's note,
Quick in dance as thought can be,
Deft his tabor, cudgel stout;
O he lies by the willow-tree!
    My love is dead,
        Gone to his death-bed
    All under the willow-tree.

Hark! the raven flaps his wing
In the brier'd dell below;
Hark! the death-owl loud doth sing
To the nightmares, as they go:
    My love is dead,
        Gone to his death-bed
    All under the willow-tree.

See! the white moon shines on high;
Whiter is my true-love's shroud:
Whiter than the morning sky,
Whiter than the evening cloud:
    My love is dead,
        Gone to his death-bed
    All under the willow-tree.

Here upon my true-love's grave
Shall the barren flowers be laid;
Not one holy saint to save
All the coldness of a maid:
    My love is dead,
        Gone to his death-bed
    All under the willow-tree.

With my hands I'll dent the briers
Round his holy corse to gre:
Ouph and fairy, light your fires,
Here my body still shall be:
    My love is dead,
        Gone to his death-bed
    All under the willow-tree.

Come, with acorn-cup and thorn,
Drain my heartès blood away;
Life and all its good I scorn,
Dance by night, or feast by day:
    My love is dead,
      Gone to his death-bed
All under the willow-tree.

WILLIAM COWPER

THE POPLAR FIELD

The poplars are felled; farewell to the shade
And the whispering sound of the cool colonnade;
The winds play no longer and sing in the leaves,
Nor Ouse on his bosom their image receives.

Twelve years have elapsed since I first took a view
Of my favorite field, and the bank where they grew;
And now in the grass behold they are laid,
And the tree is my seat that once lent me a shade.

The blackbird has fled to another retreat,
Where the hazels afford him a screen from the heat,
And the scene where his melody charmed me before,
Resounds with his sweet-flowing ditty no more.

My fugitive years are all hasting away,
And I must ere long lie as lowly as they,
With a turf on my breast, and a stone at my head,
Ere another such grove shall arise in its stead.

'Tis a sight to engage me, if anything can,
To muse on the perishing pleasures of man;
Though his life be a dream, his enjoyments, I see,
Have a being less durable even than he.

WILLIAM COWPER (1731-1800) was barred from public life by mental illness, which flared at times into attacks of extreme irrationality. During the more peaceful periods in his troubled life, he produced some famous hymns and many poems, including *The Task,* a long celebration of humble life, written in blank verse.

WILLIAM BLAKE

SONG

How sweet I roamed from field to field,
And tasted all the summer's pride,
Till I the prince of love beheld,
Who in the sunny beams did glide!

He shewed me lillies for my hair,
And blushing roses for my brow;
He led me through his gardens fair,
Where all his golden pleasures grow.

With sweet May dews my wings were wet,
And Phoebus fired my vocal rage;
He caught me in his silken net,
And shut me in his golden cage.

He loves to sit and hear me sing,
Then, laughing, sports and plays with me;
Then stretches out my golden wing,
And mocks my loss of liberty.

AH, SUN-FLOWER

Ah, Sun-flower! weary of time,
Who countest the steps of the Sun,
Seeking after that sweet golden clime
Where the traveller's journey is done:

Where the Youth pined away with desire,
And the pale Virgin shrouded in snow
Arise from their graves, and aspire
Where my Sun-flower wishes to go.

INTRODUCTION to
SONGS OF INNOCENCE

Piping down the valleys wild,
Piping songs of pleasant glee,

WILLIAM BLAKE (1757-1827) received no schooling, except in art, and
earned a meager living as an engraver; today he is recognized for his unique genius
both as an artist and as a poet. A true mystic, Blake experienced religious visions
throughout a generally calm and quiet life.

On a cloud I saw a child,
And he laughing said to me:

"Pipe a song about a Lamb!"
So I piped with merry cheer.
"Piper, pipe that song again;"
So I piped: he wept to hear.

"Drop thy pipe, thy happy pipe;
"Sing thy songs of happy cheer:"
So I sung the same again,
While he wept with joy to hear.

"Piper, sit thee down and write
"In a book, that all may read."
So he vanished from my sight,
And I plucked a hollow reed,

And I made a rural pen,
And I stained the water clear,
And I wrote my happy songs
Every child may joy to hear.

THE SICK ROSE

O Rose, thou art sick!
The invisible worm
That flies in the night,
In the howling storm,

Has found out thy bed
Of crimson joy,
And his dark secret love
Does thy life destroy.

THE TIGER

Tiger! Tiger! burning bright
In the forests of the night,
What immortal hand or eye
Could frame thy fearful symmetry?

In what distant deeps or skies
Burnt the fire of thine eyes?

On what wings dare he aspire?
What the hand dare seize the fire?

And what shoulder, and what art,
Could twist the sinews of thy heart?
And when thy heart began to beat,
What dread hand? and what dread feet?

What the hammer? what the chain?
In what furnace was thy brain?
What the anvil? what dread grasp
Dare its deadly terrors clasp?

When the stars threw down their spears
And watered heaven with their tears,
Did he smile his work to see?
Did he who made the Lamb make thee?

Tiger! Tiger! burning bright
In the forests of the night,
What immortal hand or eye
Dare frame thy fearful symmetry?

THE TIGER The poetry of William Blake partakes more of mysticism than of other qualities usually associated with the Romantic movement. The symbolism, imagery, and allegory of his later work is so intensely personal that much of it has remained impenetrable even after a great deal of close study by scholars and critics. Blake developed a mythology of his own, peopling his world with private creations and taking on the role of prophet. His mature poems are often called the Prophetic Books; they have some of the lyricism of Isaiah, the fervor of Jeremiah and Ezekiel, and the apocalyptic nature of St. John. They are all religious, but the theology they espouse is highly unorthodox.

A mystical quality comparable to that of the later books may also be found in some of his earliest works. *The Tiger* comes from a volume entitled *Songs of Experience,* which followed his *Songs of Innocence.* As represented by the two volumes, Blake's theme is that experience as well as innocence is in the province of God and that evil belongs in His inscrutable design. *The Tiger* perhaps more than any other *Song of Experience* may be misconstrued if it is not carefully appraised with these beliefs in mind.

In the "Introduction" to *Songs of Innocence* (p. 247) a child on a cloud (symbolic of the infant Christ) commands the poet to "Pipe a song about a Lamb!" The poem which results finds its antithesis in *The Tiger.* These opposites—Lamb and Tiger—are expressions of a more complete ontology than is usually found in orthodox thinkers. Innocence without experience is effete, misguided, even destructive. Experience, confused sometimes by men as degenerative, gives substance and value to existence. Or to put it another way, life that is untouched by experience—by passion, energy, and action—is a life of fetters, is man in his "mind-forged manacles." If, as Blake makes clear, the lamb partakes of the nature of the Godhead, the celestial Lamb, so also the tiger with its strength represents a quality of divinity, the empyreal thunderer.

The natural habitat of the tiger is the forest. Blake extends this archetypal symbol to encompass the abode of error and ignorance. The "forests of the night" remind us of Dante's similar image:

> In the middle of the passage of our life
> I found myself in a dark wood,
> For I had lost the right way.

But Blake's tiger burns bright, bringing light to the darkness. Through his questions, which prove to be rhetorical since there is only one answer, Blake shows that God alone could have created this awesome beast:

> What immortal hand or eye
> Could frame thy fearful symmetry?

Through several images of dread that work to include both the object created and the creator, Blake achieves the singular ambiguities of this poem. The second question—

> In what distant deeps or skies
> Burnt the fire of thine eyes?

does not exclude the possibility that the eyes of the craftsman are being described as well as those of the tiger. The stanza slips into a consideration of the creator—"On what wings dare he aspire?"—and the attributes of the tiger and his maker are inextricably fused. The third and fourth stanzas carry this technique even further. Blake's first draft of this section was cast as follows:

> And what shoulder and what art
> Could twist the sinews of thy heart?
> And when thy heart began to beat
> What dread hand and what dread feet
>
> Could fetch it from the furnace deep [?]

But apparently Blake saw that if he did not immediately complete the question begun in the third stanza, then that question could revert

back to include the tiger as well as the worker at the forge. Of course, the
forge is the mind of God, and the imagery of the fourth stanza becomes
startling in its conception: the second line places the brain of the tiger
inside the brain of God, the anvil upon which God's intellect (the "hammer" and the "chain") tempers the fury of the beast. The final line of
the fifth stanza—"Did he who made the Lamb make thee?"—does much
to establish a real trinity in that the. meekness of Christ is one and the
same with the terror of the Father and with the mystery of the Holy
Ghost, traditionally represented as a dove ("On what wings dare he
aspire?").

The opening couplet of the fifth stanza is one of those images of
mysticism that defy analysis. Clearly, however, some act of rejoicing is
taking place. The weapons (of defense or attack?) are thrown down, and
the tears which follow water heaven. Blake's use of stars here rather than
angels lends itself brilliantly to the dominating image of the forge, in
which they function as sparks struck off the white-hot malleable substance that becomes the tiger.

As in any good poem the meter supports the meaning, so in this one,
the trochaic feet echo the ringing of the hammer on the anvil. In order
to end on a strong beat, the final trochee is shorn of its unaccented syllable. And since no stanza in the poem better sounds the strokes than
the first, it is repeated verbatim at the end.

THE LAMB

Little Lamb, who made thee?
Dost thou know who made thee?
Gave thee life, and bid thee feed
By the stream and o'er the mead;
Gave thee clothing of delight,
Softest clothing, woolly, bright;
Gave thee such a tender voice,
Making all the vales rejoice?
Little Lamb, who made thee?
Dost thou know who made thee?

Little Lamb, I'll tell thee,
Little Lamb, I'll tell thee:
He is callèd by thy name,
For He calls Himself a Lamb,
He is meek, and He is mild;
He became a little child.
I a child, and thou a lamb,

We are callèd by his name.
    Little Lamb, God bless thee!
    Little Lamb, God bless thee!

LONDON

I wander through each chartered street,
Near where the chartered Thames does flow,
And mark in every face I meet
Marks of weakness, marks of woe.

In every cry of every man,
In every infant's cry of fear,
In every voice, in every ban,
The mind-forged manacles I hear:

How the chimney-sweeper's cry
Every blackening church appalls;
And the hapless soldier's sigh
Runs in blood down palace walls.

But most, through midnight streets I hear
How the youthful harlot's curse
Blasts the new-born infant's tear,
And blights with plagues the marriage hearse.

MAD SONG

    The wild winds weep,
    And the night is a-cold;
    Come hither, Sleep,
    And my griefs unfold:
    But lo! the morning peeps
    Over the eastern steeps,
    And the rustling beds of dawn
    The earth do scorn.

    Lo! to the vault
    Of paved heaven,
    With sorrow fraught
    My notes are driven:
    They strike the ear of night,
    Make weep the eyes of day;

They make mad the roaring winds,
And with tempests play.

Like a fiend in a cloud,
With howling woe
After night I do crowd,
And with night will go;
I turn my back to the east
From whence comforts have increased;
For light doth seize my brain
With frantic pain.

THE LITTLE BLACK BOY

My mother bore me in the southern wild,
And I am black, but O! my soul is white;
White as an angel is the English child,
But I am black, as if bereaved of light.

My mother taught me underneath a tree,
And, sitting down before the heat of day,
She took me on her lap and kissèd me,
And, pointing to the east, began to say:

"Look on the rising sun—there God does live,
And gives His light, and gives His heat away;
And flowers and trees and beasts and men receive
Comfort in morning, joy in the noonday.

"And we are put on earth a little space,
That we may learn to bear the beams of love;
And these black bodies and this sunburnt face
Is but a cloud, and like a shady grove.

"For when our souls have learned the heat to bear,
The cloud will vanish; we shall hear His voice,
Saying, 'Come out from the grove, My love and care,
And round my golden tent like lambs rejoice.' "

Thus did my mother say, and kissèd me,
And thus I say to little English boy:
When I from black and he from white cloud free,
And round the tent of God like lambs we joy,

I'll shade him from the heat, till he can bear
To lean in joy upon our Father's knee;
And then I'll stand and stroke his silver hair,
And be like him, and he will then love me.

THE CHIMNEY-SWEEPER

A little black thing among the snow,
Crying "weep! weep!" in notes of woe!
"Where are thy father and mother? Say!"—
"They are both gone up to church to pray.

"Because I was happy upon the heath,
And smiled among the winter's snow,
They clothed me in the clothes of death,
And taught me to sing the notes of woe.

"And because I am happy, and dance and sing,
They think they have done me no injury,
And are gone to praise God and His priest and king,
Who make up a heaven of our misery."

from MILTON

And did those feet in ancient time
  Walk upon England's mountains green?
And was the holy Lamb of God
  On England's pleasant pastures seen?

And did the Countenance Divine
  Shine forth upon our clouded hills?
And was Jerusalem builded here
  Among these dark Satanic Mills?

Bring me my bow of burning gold!
  Bring me my arrows of desire!
Bring me my spear! O clouds, unfold!
  Bring me my chariot of fire!

I will not cease from mental fight,
  Nor shall my sword sleep in my hand
Till we have built Jerusalem
  In England's green and pleasant land.

ROBERT BURNS

TO A MOUSE

On turning her up in her nest with the plow, November, 1785

Wee, sleekit, cowrin, tim'rous beastie,
O, what a panic's in thy breastie!
Thou need na start awa sae hasty,
      Wi' bickering brattle!
I wad be laith to rin an' chase thee,
      Wi' murdering pattle!

I'm truly sorry man's dominion,
Has broken Nature's social union,
An' justifies that ill opinion
      Which makes thee startle
At me, thy poor, earth-born companion,
      An' fellow-mortal!

I doubt na, whyles, but thou may thieve;
What then? poor beastie, thou maun live!
A daimen icker in a thrave
      'S a sma' request:
I'll get a blessin wi' the lave,
      And never miss't!

Thy wee-bit housie, too, in ruin!
Its silly wa's the win's are strewin!
An' naething, now, to big a new ane,
      O' foggage green!
An' bleak December's win's ensuin,
      Baith snell an' keen!

Thou saw the fields laid bare an' waste,
An' weary winter comin' fast,

ROBERT BURNS (1759-1796), Scotland's greatest poet, was born in Ayrshire, the son of a poor farmer. Except for a brief period as the darling of Edinburgh's literary circles, following the publication of his first book, he spent most of his life in the country, creating and adapting dozens of memorable lyrics. Despite his fondness for conviviality, Burns' early death probably resulted more from the hard labor of his youth than from the dissipation of his later years.

An' cozie here, beneath the blast,
    Thou thought to dwell,
Till, crash! the cruel coulter passed
    Out through thy cell.

That wee bit heap o' leaves an' stibble
Has cost thee monie a weary nibble!
Now thou's turned out, for a' thy trouble,
    But house or hald,
To thole the winter's sleety dribble,
    An' cranreuch cauld!

But, Mousie, thou art no thy lane,
In proving foresight may be vain:
The best-laid schemes o' mice an' men
    Gang aft agley,
An' lea'e us naught but grief an' pain,
    For promis'd joy!

Still thou art blest, compared wi' me!
The present only toucheth thee:
But och! I backward cast my e'e,
    On prospects drear!
An' forward, tho' I canna see,
    I guess an' fear!

A RED, RED ROSE

O, my luve is like a red, red rose,
    That's newly sprung in June.
O, my luve is like the melodie
    That's sweetly played in tune.

As fair art thou, my bonie lass,
    So deep in luve am I,
And I will luve thee still, my dear,
    Till a' the seas gang dry.

Till a' the seas gang dry, my dear,
    And the rocks melt wi' the sun!
And I will luve thee still, my dear,
    While the sands o' life shall run.

And fare thee weel, my only luve,
   And fare thee weel a while!
And I will come again, my luve,
   Tho' it were ten thousand mile!

THE SILVER TASSIE

Go, fetch to me a pint o' wine,
   And fill it in a silver tassie,
That I may drink, before I go,
   A service to my bonie lassie!
The boat rocks at the pier o' Leith,
   Fu'loud the wind blaws frae the ferry,
The ship rides by the Berwick-Law,
   And I maun leave my bonie Mary.

The trumpets sound, the banners fly,
   The glittering spears are rankèd ready;
The shouts o' war are heard afar,
   The battle closes deep and bloody.
It's not the roar o' sea or shore
   Wad make me langer wish to tarry;
Nor shouts o' war that's heard afar—
   It's leaving thee, my bonie Mary.

JOHN ANDERSON, MY JO

John Anderson, my jo, John,
   When we were first acquent,
Your locks were like the raven,
   Your bonie brow was brent;
But now your brow is beld, John,
   Your locks are like the snaw;
But blessings on your frosty pow,
   John Anderson, my jo!

John Anderson, my jo, John,
   We clamb the hill thegither;
And monie a cantie day, John,
   We've had wi' ane anither;
Now we maun totter down, John,
   And hand in hand we'll go,

And sleep thegither at the foot,
John Anderson, my jo!

AE FOND KISS

Ae fond kiss, and then we sever!
Ae farewell, and then forever!
Deep in heart-wrung tears I'll pledge thee,
Warring sighs and groans I'll wage thee.
Who shall say that Fortune grieves him,
While the star of hope she leaves him?
Me, nae cheerfu' twinkle lights me,
Dark despair around benights me.

I'll ne'er blame my partial fancy:
Naething could resist my Nancy!
But to see her was to love her,
Love but her, and love for ever.
Had we never loved sae kindly,
Had we never loved sae blindly,
Never met—or never parted—
We had ne'er been broken-hearted.

Fare-thee-weel, thou first and fairest!
Fare-thee-weel, thou best and dearest!
Thine be ilka joy and treasure,
Peace, Enjoyment, Love, and Pleasure!
Ae fond kiss, and then we sever!
Ae farewell, alas, forever!
Deep in heart-wrung tears I'll pledge thee,
Warring sighs and groans I'll wage thee.

BONIE DOON

Ye flowery banks o' bonie Doon,
How can ye blume sae fair?
How can ye chant, ye little birds,
And I sae fu' o' care?

Thou'll break my heart, thou bonie bird,
That sings upon the bough;
Thou minds me o' the happy days
When my fause luve was true.

Thou'll break my heart, thou bonie bird,
    That sings beside thy mate;
For sae I sat, and sae I sang,
    And wist na o' my fate.

Aft hae I rov'd by bonie Doon,
    To see the woodbine twine,
And ilka bird sang o' its luve,
    And sae did I o' mine.

Wi' lightsome heart I pu'd a rose,
    Frae aff its thorny tree;
And my fause luver staw my rose,
    But left the thorn wi' me.

V

THE ROMANTIC PERIOD

INTROSPECTION AND MEDITATION

THE Romantics were convinced that the poet's mission was to convey to humanity the profoundest truths of experience and sensation. Wordsworth assumed the role of philosopher, and we cannot adequately understand his poetry unless we recognize that it was designed to express carefully evolved views of mankind. With poetry regarded as an expression of truth and the poet himself as a man of special vision chosen as the vehicle for truth, it is natural that the poem of calm introspection and meditation should be among the most important phenomena of the Romantic period. Wordsworth felt that great poetry came from powerful emotions recalled in tranquillity, and he was able to give strong feeling a calm tone of philosophic introspection in a manner virtually unique in English poetry. Matthew Arnold strove for the same effect some decades later, but Arnold never was able to reach the kind of resolution and calm that conclude Wordsworth's meditative poems.

Wordsworth was always the poet of faith, but his philosophy developed and changed as he grew older and more mature, and in his philosophical poems we can trace the stages of his growth. This does not mean that he was—as sometimes charged—a sort of turncoat. Little in his later views is inconsistent with his earlier ones. The convictions of his maturity grew naturally out of those of his youth.

In *Lines Composed above Tintern Abbey,* Wordsworth expressed his youthful faith in the power of nature to bring man close to a divine spirit and to fill him with a joy and peace which might produce acts of kindness and love. In his *Ode on Intimations of Immortality,* the poet states his Neoplatonic doctrine of the soul's descent from the ideal world and then poses the question of how man may find compensation for the loss of perfection he must suffer at birth. After letting the poem lie unfinished for many years, he arrived at an answer in the soul's obstinate questioning of outward things—the surest evidence of immortality—and the poem ends with a joyful celebration of human fellowship in harmony with nature. This conclusion is close to the theme of *Tintern Abbey.* and it links the *Ode* to Wordsworth's earlier works.

Coleridge expressed his own spiritual progress and self-questioning primarily in his "Conversation Poems," of which *Frost at Midnight* and *Dejection: An Ode* are excellent examples. These poems are addressed to intimate friends. They are highly personal, beginning usually with a statement of time and place and then passing into self-examination. They end always with a return to the calm mood of the beginning, and like Wordsworth's they are poems of faith and reconciliation. There is a difference, however, in that Coleridge has a sense of the tragic which is not so apparent in Wordsworth; human joy in the "Conversation Poems" is never remote from human suffering.

For their poems of introspection and meditation, the Romantics used every conceivable verse form, from the blank verse of *Tintern Abbey* and *Frost at Midnight* to the false pindaric of Wordsworth's *Ode*. Very notable was the revival of the sonnet, first by Wordsworth and later by Shelley and Keats, as an instrument for the expression of personal philosophy and emotion, springing from immediate experience.

FOR FURTHER READING:

Benziger, James. "Tintern Abbey Revisited," *PMLA,* LXV (March 1950), 154-162.

Danby, J. F. *The Simple Wordsworth.* London, 1960.

Darbishire, Helen. *The Poet Wordsworth.* New York, 1950.

Dunklin, G. T., ed. *Wordsworth; Centenary Studies Presented at Cornell and Princeton Universities.* Princeton, 1951.

Raysor, T. M. "The Themes of Immortality and Natural Piety in Wordsworth's Immortality Ode," *PMLA,* LXIX (September 1954), 861-875.

Read, Herbert. *Wordsworth.* London, 1931.

Stallknecht, N. P. *Strange Seas of Thought.* Durham, N. C., 1945.

Jones, John. *The Egotistical Sublime.* London, 1954.

WILLIAM WORDSWORTH

LINES

Composed a few miles above Tintern Abbey, on revisiting the banks of the Wye during a tour, July 13, 1798

Five years have past; five summers, with the length
Of five long winters! and again I hear

WILLIAM WORDSWORTH (1770-1850) was born in Cockermouth, Cumberland, the son of a well-to-do attorney. After attending St. John's College, Cambridge, he spent a year in revolutionary France and then began his lifetime career as a poet. In 1798 he published *Lyrical Ballads* with his close friend, Samuel Taylor Coleridge. In 1799, with his sister Dorothy, he settled at Grasmere in the beautiful Lake District. He married in 1802 and became poet laureate in 1843.

These waters, rolling from their mountain-springs
With a soft inland murmur.—Once again
Do I behold these steep and lofty cliffs,
That on a wild secluded scene impress
Thoughts of more deep seclusion; and connect
The landscape with the quiet of the sky.
The day is come when I again repose
Here, under this dark sycamore, and view
These plots of cottage-ground, these orchard-tufts,
Which at this season, with their unripe fruits,
Are clad in one green hue, and lose themselves
Mid groves and copses. Once again I see
These hedgerows, hardly hedgerows, little lines
Of sportive wood run wild: these pastoral farms,
Green to the very door; and wreaths of smoke
Sent up, in silence, from among the trees!
With some uncertain notice, as might seem
Of vagrant dwellers in the houseless woods,
Or of some Hermit's cave, where by his fire
The Hermit sits alone.

                    These beauteous forms,
Through a long absence, have not been to me
As is a landscape to a blind man's eye:
But oft, in lonely rooms, and 'mid the din
Of towns and cities, I have owed to them,
In hours of weariness, sensations sweet,
Felt in the blood, and felt along the heart;
And passing even into my purer mind,
With tranquil restoration—feelings too
Of unremembered pleasure: such, perhaps,
As have no slight or trivial influence
On that best portion of a good man's life,
His little, nameless, unremembered acts
Of kindness and of love. Nor less, I trust,
To them I may have owed another gift,
Of aspect more sublime; that blessèd mood,
In which the burthen of the mystery,
In which the heavy and the weary weight
Of all this unintelligible world,
Is lightened—that serene and blessèd mood,
In which the affections gently lead us on—
Until, the breath of this corporeal frame
And even the motion of our human blood

Almost suspended, we are laid asleep
In body, and become a living soul:
While with an eye made quiet by the power
Of harmony, and the deep power of joy,
We see into the life of things.
               If this
Be but a vain belief, yet, oh! how oft—
In darkness and amid the many shapes
Of joyless daylight; when the fretful stir
Unprofitable, and the fever of the world,
Have hung upon the beatings of my heart—
How oft, in spirit, have I turned to thee,
O sylvan Wye! thou wanderer through the woods,
How often has my spirit turned to thee!
   And now, with gleams of half-extinguished thought,
With many recognitions dim and faint,
And somewhat of a sad perplexity,
The picture of the mind revives again:
While here I stand, not only with the sense
Of present pleasure, but with pleasing thoughts
That in this moment there is life and food
For future years. And so I dare to hope,
Though changed, no doubt, from what I was when first
I came among these hills; when like a roe
I bounded o'er the mountains, by the sides
Of the deep rivers, and the lonely streams,
Wherever nature led: more like a man
Flying from something that he dreads than one
Who sought the thing he loved. For nature then
(The coarser pleasures of my boyish days,
And their glad animal movements all gone by)
To me was all in all.—I cannot paint
What then I was. The sounding cataract
Haunted me like a passion: the tall rock,
The mountain, and the deep and gloomy wood,
Their colors and their forms, were then to me
An appetite; a feeling and a love,
That had no need of a remoter charm,
By thought supplied, nor any interest
Unborrowed from the eye.—That time is past,
And all its aching joys are now no more,
And all its dizzy raptures. Not for this
Faint I, nor mourn nor murmur; other gifts

Have followed; for such loss, I would believe,
Abundant recompense. For I have learned
To look on nature, not as in the hour
Of thoughtless youth; but hearing oftentimes
The still, sad music of humanity,
Nor harsh nor grating, though of ample power
To chasten and subdue. And I have felt
A presence that disturbs me with the joy
Of elevated thoughts; a sense sublime
Of something far more deeply interfused,
Whose dwelling is the light of setting suns,
And the round ocean and the living air,
And the blue sky, and in the mind of man:
A motion and a spirit, that impels
All thinking things, all objects of all thought,
And rolls through all things. Therefore am I still
A lover of the meadows and the woods,
And mountains; and of all that we behold
From this green earth; of all the mighty world
Of eye, and ear—both what they half create,
And what perceive; well pleased to recognize
In nature and the language of the sense
The anchor of my purest thoughts, the nurse,
The guide, the guardian of my heart, and soul
Of all my moral being.
                    Nor perchance,
If I were not thus taught, should I the more
Suffer my genial spirits to decay:
For thou art with me here upon the banks
Of this fair river; thou my dearest Friend,
My dear, dear Friend; and in thy voice I catch
The language of my former heart, and read
My former pleasures in the shooting lights
Of thy wild eyes. Oh! yet a little while
May I behold in thee what I was once,
My dear, dear Sister! and this prayer I make,
Knowing that Nature never did betray
The heart that loved her; 'tis her privilege,
Through all the years of this our life, to lead
From joy to joy: for she can so inform
The mind that is within us, so impress
With quietness and beauty, and so feed
With lofty thoughts, that neither evil tongues,

Rash judgments, nor the sneers of selfish men,
Nor greetings where no kindness is, nor all
The dreary intercourse of daily life,
Shall e'er prevail against us, or disturb
Our cheerful faith, that all which we behold
Is full of blessings. Therefore let the moon
Shine on thee in thy solitary walk;
And let the misty mountain-winds be free
To blow against thee: and, in after years,
When these wild ecstasies shall be matured
Into a sober pleasure; when thy mind
Shall be a mansion for all lovely forms,
Thy memory be as a dwelling-place
For all sweet sounds and harmonies; oh! then,
If solitude, or fear, or pain, or grief,
Should be thy portion, with what healing thoughts
Of tender joy wilt thou remember me,
And these my exhortations! Nor, perchance—
If I should be where I no more can hear
Thy voice, nor catch from thy wild eyes these gleams
Of past existence—wilt thou then forget
That on the banks of this delightful stream
We stood together; and that I, so long
A worshiper of Nature, hither came
Unwearied in that service: rather say
With warmer love—oh! with far deeper zeal
Of holier love. Nor wilt thou then forget
That after many wanderings, many years
Of absence, these steep woods and lofty cliffs,
And this green pastoral landscape, were to me
More dear, both for themselves and for thy sake!

THE SOLITARY REAPER

Behold her, single in the field,
Yon solitary Highland lass!
Reaping and singing by herself;
Stop here, or gently pass!
Alone she cuts and binds the grain,
And sings a melancholy strain;
O listen! for the vale profound
Is overflowing with the sound.

No nightingale did ever chaunt
More welcome note to weary bands
Of travelers in some shady haunt,
Among Arabian sands:
A voice so thrilling ne'er was heard
In springtime from the cuckoo-bird,
Breaking the silence of the seas
Among the farthest Hebrides.

Will no one tell me what she sings?—
Perhaps the plaintive numbers flow
For old, unhappy, far-off things,
And battles long ago:
Or is it some more humble lay,
Familiar matter of today?
Some natural sorrow, loss, or pain,
That has been, and may be again?

Whate'er the theme, the maiden sang
As if her song could have no ending;
I saw her singing at her work,
And o'er the sickle bending;—
I listened, motionless and still;
And, as I mounted up the hill,
The music in my heart I bore,
Long after it was heard no more.

THE SOLITARY REAPER was written probably in 1803, during a tour of Scotland by the poet and his sister Dorothy. The piece is a perfect illustration of the kind of poetry announced in the *Preface* to the second edition of *Lyrical Ballads* in 1800, the prolegomena to the literary revolution that established Romanticism:

The principal object, then, proposed in these poems was to choose incidents and situations from common life, and to relate or describe them, throughout, as far as was possible in a selection of language really used by men, and at the same time to throw over them a certain coloring of imagination, whereby ordinary things should be presented to the mind in an unusual aspect; and, further, and above all, to make these incidents and situations interesting by tracing in them, truly though not ostentatiously, the primary laws of our nature: chiefly, as far as regards the manner in which we associate ideas in a state of excitement. Humble and rustic life was generally chosen, because, in that condition, the essential passions of the heart find a better soil in which they can attain their maturity, are less under restraint, and speak a plainer and more emphatic language.

The *Solitary Reaper* meets all the conditions of this paragraph. The Highland lass not only pursues the labors of common life but also represents the humble and rustic. The poet uses simple diction and relatively straightforward word order. Especially noticeable as capturing "language really used by men" are lines like these:

> Will no one tell me what she sings?—
> That has been, and may be again?
> I saw her singing at her work,

A "coloring of imagination" is thrown over the entire situation through reference to the nightingale and the cuckoo-bird in such distant habitats as Arabia and the Hebrides. The mystery of her song and the speculation as to what it may contain add also to the fanciful qualities the poet seeks. As for the most important of the requirements—those that Wordsworth introduces with the modifiers "above all" and "chiefly"—*The Solitary Reaper* traces preëminently one of the "primary laws of our nature" and makes vast "associations" that take flight in the mind of the poet. The law of nature observed is the necessity for the solitary laborer to pass the tedious hours with some thought or pastime that uplifts the spirit. This the girl does through song, song that speaks to her about heroic battles or moving tragedy out of legend and story, or perhaps something that touches her more closely, the domestic sorrows of life like her own. The free associations which Wordsworth makes between the girl's song and that of the nightingale and cuckoo carry him to the near Orient and the far North.

Elsewhere in the *Preface* to *Lyrical Ballads,* Wordsworth states that poetry "takes its origin from emotion recollected in tranquillity." We have clear evidence that the incident which gave rise in Wordsworth's imagination to *The Solitary Reaper* was not recorded on the spot or in the moment of the experience. Dorothy Wordsworth has recorded the encounter which her brother commemorated in verse:

> It was harvest-time, and the fields were quietly . . . enlivened by small companies of reapers. It is not uncommon in the more lonely parts of the Highlands to see a single person so employed. The following poem was suggested to William by a beautiful sentence in Thomas Wilkinson's *Tour in Scotland.*

The poem, then, not only required the observation of the physical scene but also the research, conducted without doubt in "tranquillity," that took him to Wilkinson's book, where he found materials that are worked into the heart of his poem:

Passed a female who was reaping alone; she sung in Erse, as she bended over her sickle; the sweetest human voice I ever heard: her strains were tenderly melancholy, and felt delicious, long after they were heard no more.

Quite obviously, Wordsworth found in Wilkinson a kindred spirit, who treasured, "after they were heard no more," the musical notes of the singer; the poet could almost quote his source in the last line of his own version of the episode: "Long after it was heard no more."

In many poems Wordsworth finds the value of his experiences to be the memory of them that he may carry with him through life, especially when he is in the city, divorced from nature and humble, rustic life. His reminiscences of the river Wye above Tintern Abbey, he tells us, have supported him in tedious city hours:

> But oft, in lonely rooms, and 'mid the din
> Of towns and cities, I have owed to them,
> In hours of weariness, sensations sweet,
> Felt in the blood, and felt along the heart;
> And passing even into my purer mind,
> With tranquil restoration: (p. 262)

But as a poet, Wordsworth goes further than Wilkinson, the traveloguist. His Highland lass has in her song a note of the eternal that may be compared to that of Keats' nightingale (p. 291); her lyric may tell of things far off and long ago or "familiar matter of today," but clearly it is something "That has been, and may be again"; it is a song that can "have no ending." Her "plaintive numbers," like the "plaintive anthem" of Keats' nightingale, record the misery of the human condition, which in itself is eternal and in which every member of the human race can see reflected some portion of his own sorrow. In this thought as well as in the human need for song in hours of labor, Wordsworth has traced a primary law of nature.

LONDON, 1802

> Milton! thou shouldst be living at this hour:
> England hath need of thee; she is a fen
> Of stagnant waters: altar, sword, and pen,
> Fireside, the heroic wealth of hall and bower,
> Have forfeited their ancient English dower
> Of inward happiness. We are selfish men:
> Oh! raise us up, return to us again;
> And give us manners, virtue, freedom, power.

Thy soul was like a Star, and dwelt apart:
Thou hadst a voice whose sound was like the sea,
Pure as the naked heavens, majestic, free;
So didst thou travel on life's common way,
In cheerful godliness; and yet thy heart
The lowliest duties on herself did lay.

THE WORLD IS TOO MUCH WITH US

The world is too much with us; late and soon,
Getting and spending, we lay waste our powers:
Little we see in Nature that is ours;
We have given our hearts away, a sordid boon!
The sea that bares her bosom to the moon;
The winds that will be howling at all hours,
And are up-gathered now like sleeping flowers;
For this, for everything, we are out of tune;
It moves us not.—Great God! I'd rather be
A Pagan suckled in a creed outworn;
So might I, standing on this pleasant lea,
Have glimpses that would make me less forlorn;
Have sight of Proteus rising from the sea;
Or hear old Triton blow his wreathèd horn.

COMPOSED UPON WESTMINSTER BRIDGE

Earth has not anything to show more fair:
Dull would he be of soul who could pass by
A sight so touching in its majesty:
This City now doth, like a garment wear
The beauty of the morning; silent, bare,
Ships, towers, domes, theaters, and temples lie
Open unto the fields, and to the sky;
All bright and glittering in the smokeless air.
Never did sun more beautifully steep
In his first splendor, valley, rock, or hill;
Ne'er saw I, never felt, a calm so deep!
The river glideth at his own sweet will:
Dear God! the very houses seem asleep;
And all that mighty heart is lying still!

IT IS A BEAUTEOUS EVENING, CALM AND FREE

It is a beauteous evening, calm and free,
The holy time is quiet as a Nun,
Breathless with adoration: the broad sun
Is sinking down in its tranquillity;
The gentleness of heaven broods o'er the sea:
Listen! the mighty Being is awake,
And doth with his eternal motion make
A sound like thunder—everlastingly.
Dear Child! dear Girl! that walkest with me here,
If thou appear untouched by solemn thought,
Thy nature is not therefore less divine:
Thou liest in Abraham's bosom all the year,
And worship'st at the Temple's inner shrine,
God being with thee when we know it not.

SURPRISED BY JOY

Surprised by joy—impatient as the Wind
I turned to share the transport—Oh! with whom
But Thee, deep buried in the silent tomb,
That spot which no vicissitude can find?
Love, faithful love, recalled thee to my mind—
But how could I forget thee? Through what power,
Even for the least division of an hour,
Have I been so beguiled as to be blind
To my most grievous loss!—That thought's return
Was the worst pang that sorrow ever bore,
Save one, one only, when I stood forlorn,
Knowing my heart's best treasure was no more;
That neither present time, nor years unborn
Could to my sight that heavenly face restore.

ODE ON INTIMATIONS OF IMMORTALITY FROM RECOLLECTIONS OF EARLY CHILDHOOD

The Child is father of the Man;
And I could wish my days to be
Bound each to each by natural piety.

I

There was a time when meadow, grove, and stream,
The earth, and every common sight,
                To me did seem
                Appareled in celestial light,
The glory and the freshness of a dream.
It is not now as it hath been of yore;—
                Turn wheresoe'er I may,
                By night or day,
The things which I have seen I now can see no more.

II

                The Rainbow comes and goes,
                And lovely is the Rose;
                The Moon doth with delight
Look round her when the heavens are bare;
                Waters on a starry night
                Are beautiful and fair;
                The sunshine is a glorious birth;
                But yet I know, where'er I go,
That there hath past away a glory from the earth.

III

Now, while the birds thus sing a joyous song,
    And while the young lambs bound
                As to the tabor's sound,
To me alone there came a thought of grief:
A timely utterance gave that thought relief,
                And I again am strong:
The cataracts blow their trumpets from the steep;
No more shall grief of mine the season wrong;
I hear the Echoes through the mountains throng,
The Winds come to me from the fields of sleep,
                And all the earth is gay;
                Land and sea
            Give themselves up to jollity,
                And with the heart of May
            Doth every Beast keep holiday;—
                Thou Child of Joy,
Shout round me, let me hear thy shouts, thou
                happy Shepherd-boy!

IV

Ye blessèd Creatures, I have heard the call
  Ye to each other make; I see
The heavens laugh with you in your jubilee;
  My heart is at your festival,
  My head hath its coronal,
The fulness of your bliss, I feel—I feel it all.
  Oh evil day! if I were sullen
  While Earth herself is adorning,
   This sweet May-morning,
  And the Children are culling
   On every side,
  In a thousand valleys far and wide,
Fresh flowers; while the sun shines warm,
And the Babe leaps up on his Mother's arm—
  I hear, I hear, with joy I hear!
  —But there's a Tree, of many, one,
A single Field which I have looked upon,
Both of them speak of something that is gone:
  The Pansy at my feet
  Doth the same tale repeat:
Whither is fled the visionary gleam?
Where is it now, the glory and the dream?

V

Our birth is but a sleep and a forgetting:
The Soul that rises with us, our life's Star,
  Hath had elsewhere its setting,
   And cometh from afar:
  Not in entire forgetfulness,
  And not in utter nakedness,
But trailing clouds of glory do we come
  From God, who is our home:
Heaven lies about us in our infancy!
Shades of the prison-house begin to close
  Upon the growing Boy,
But he beholds the light, and whence it flows,
  He sees it in his joy;
The Youth, who daily farther from the east
  Must travel, still is Nature's priest,
  And by the vision splendid
  Is on his way attended;

At length the Man perceives it die away,
And fade into the light of common day.

VI

Earth fills her lap with pleasures of her .own;
Yearnings she hath in her own natural kind,
And even with something of a Mother's mind,
    And no unworthy aim,
    The homely Nurse doth all she can
To make her Foster-child, her Inmate Man,
    Forget the glories he hath known,
And that imperial palace whence he came.

VII

Behold the Child among his new-born blisses,
A six years' darling of a pigmy size!
See, where 'mid work of his own hand he lies,
Fretted by sallies of his mother's kisses,
With light upon him from his father's eyes!
See, at his feet, some little plan or chart,
Some fragment from his dream of human life,
Shaped by himself with newly-learnèd art;
    A wedding or a festival,
    A mourning or a funeral;
    And this hath now his heart,
    And unto this he frames his song:
    Then will he fit his tongue
To dialogues of business, love, or strife;
    But it will not be long
    Ere this be thrown aside,
    And with new joy and pride
The little Actor cons another part;
Filling from time to time his "humorous stage"
With all the Persons, down to palsied Age,
That Life brings with her in her equipage;
    As if his whole vocation
    Were endless imitation.

VIII

Thou, whose exterior semblance doth belie
    Thy Soul's immensity;

Thou best Philosopher, who yet dost keep
Thy heritage, thou Eye among the blind,
That, deaf and silent, read'st the eternal deep,
Haunted forever by the eternal mind,—
    Mighty Prophet! Seer blest!
    On whom those truths do rest,
Which we are toiling all our lives to find,
In darkness lost, the darkness of the grave;
Thou, over whom thy Immortality
Broods like the Day, a master o'er a slave,
A Presence which is not to be put by;
Thou little Child, yet glorious in the might
Of heaven-born freedom on thy being's height,
Why with such earnest pains dost thou provoke
The years to bring the inevitable yoke,
Thus blindly with thy blessedness at strife?
Full soon thy Soul shall have her earthly freight,
And custom lie upon thee with a weight,
Heavy as frost, and deep almost as life!

IX

    O joy! that in our embers
    Is something that doth live,
    That nature yet remembers
    What was so fugitive!
The thought of our past years in me doth breed
Perpetual benediction: not indeed
For that which is most worthy to be blest;
Delight and liberty, the simple creed
Of Childhood, whether busy or at rest,
With new-fledged hope still fluttering in his breast—
    Not for these I raise
    The song of thanks and praise;
    But for those obstinate questionings
    Of sense and outward things,
    Fallings from us, vanishings;
    Blank misgivings of a Creature
Moving about in worlds not realized,
High instincts before which our mortal nature
Did tremble like a guilty thing surprised:
    But for those first affections,
    Those shadowy recollections,
    Which, be they what they may,

Are yet the fountain light of all our day,
Are yet a master light of all our seeing;
  Uphold us, cherish, and have power to make
Our noisy years seem moments in the being
Of the Eternal Silence: truths that wake,
  To perish never;
Which neither listlessness, nor mad endeavor
  Nor Man nor Boy,
Nor all that is at enmity with joy,
Can utterly abolish or destroy!
  Hence in a season of calm weather
  Though inland far we be,
Our souls have sight of that immortal sea
  Which brought us hither,
  Can in a moment travel thither,
And see the children sport upon the shore,
And hear the mighty waters rolling evermore.

X

Then sing, ye Birds, sing, sing a joyous song!
  And let the young Lambs bound
  As to the tabor's sound!
We in thought will join your throng,
  Ye that pipe and ye that play,
  Ye that through your hearts today
  Feel the gladness of the May!
What though the radiance which was once so bright
Be now forever taken from my sight,
 Though nothing can bring back the hour
Of splendor in the grass, of glory in the flower;
  We will grieve not, rather find
  Strength in what remains behind;
  In the primal sympathy
  Which having been must ever be;
  In the soothing thoughts that spring
  Out of human suffering;
  In the faith that looks through death,
In years that bring the philosophic mind.

XI

And O, ye Fountains, Meadows, Hills, and Groves,
Forebode not any severing of our loves!

Yet in my heart of hearts I feel your might;
I only have relinquished one delight
To live beneath your more habitual sway.
I love the Brooks which down their channels fret,
Even more than when I tripped lightly as they;
The innocent brightness of a new-born Day
           Is lovely yet;
The Clouds that gather round the setting sun
Do take a sober coloring from an eye
That hath kept watch o'er man's mortality.
Another race hath been, and other palms are won.
Thanks to the human heart by which we live,
Thanks to its tenderness, its joys, and fears,
To me the meanest flower that blows can give
Thoughts that do often lie too deep for tears.

SAMUEL TAYLOR COLERIDGE

FROST AT MIDNIGHT

The frost performs its secret ministry,
Unhelped by any wind. The owlet's cry
Came loud—and hark, again! loud as before.
The inmates of my cottage, all at rest,
Have left me to that solitude, which suits
Abstruser musings: save that at my side
My cradled infant slumbers peacefully.
'Tis calm indeed! so calm, that it disturbs
And vexes meditation with its strange
And extreme silentness. Sea, hill, and wood,
This populous village! Sea, and hill, and wood,
With all the numberless goings-on of life,
Inaudible as dreams! the thin blue flame
Lies on my low-burnt fire, and quivers not;
Only that film, which fluttered on the grate,
Still flutters there, the sole unquiet thing.

SAMUEL TAYLOR COLERIDGE (1772-1834), son of a Devonshire clergyman, joined his friend Wordsworth in the publication of *Lyrical Ballads* in 1798. Practically all his best poetry was composed within a few years of that date. At various times a publisher, translator, dramatist, essayist, critic, and lecturer, Coleridge nevertheless failed to live up to his remarkable potentialities. Ill health, combined with an addiction to opium, halted many of his ambitious projects far short of completion.

Methinks, its motion in this hush of nature
Gives it dim sympathies with me who live,
Making it a companionable form,
Whose puny flaps and freaks the idling spirit
By its own moods interprets, everywhere
Echo or mirror seeking of itself,
And makes a toy of thought.

          But O! how oft,
How oft, at school, with most believing mind,
Presageful, have I gazed upon the bars,
To watch that fluttering stranger! and as oft
With unclosed lids, already had I dreamt
Of my sweet birth-place, and the old church-tower,
Whose bells, the poor man's only music, rang
From morn to evening, all the hot Fair-day,
So sweetly, that they stirred and haunted me
With a wild pleasure, falling on mine ear
Most like articulate sounds of things to come!
So gazed I, till the soothing things, I dreamt,
Lulled me to sleep, and sleep prolonged my dreams!
And so I brooded all the following morn,
Awed by the stern preceptor's face, mine eye
Fixed with mock study on my swimming book:
Save if the door half opened, and I snatched
A hasty glance, and still my heart leaped up,
For still I hoped to see the stranger's face,
Townsman, or aunt, or sister more beloved,
My play-mate when we both were clothed alike!

   Dear babe, that sleepest cradled by my side,
Whose gentle breathings, heard in this deep calm,
Fill up the interspersèd vacancies
And momentary pauses of the thought!
My babe so beautiful! it thrills my heart
With tender gladness, thus to look at thee,
And think that thou shalt learn far other lore,
And in far other scenes! For I was reared
In the great city, pent 'mid cloisters dim,
And saw nought lovely but the sky and stars.
But thou, my babe! shall wander like a breeze
By lakes and sandy shores, beneath the crags
   Of ancient mountain, and beneath the clouds,

Which image in their bulk both lakes and shores
And mountain crags: so shalt thou see and hear
The lovely shapes and sounds intelligible
Of that eternal language, which thy God
Utters, who from eternity doth teach
Himself in all, and all things in himself.
Great universal Teacher! he shall mould
Thy spirit, and by giving make it ask.

Therefore all seasons shall be sweet to thee,
Whether the summer clothe the general earth
With greenness, or the redbreast sit and sing
Betwixt the tufts of snow on the bare branch
Of mossy apple-tree, while the nigh thatch
Smokes in the sun-thaw; whether the eave-drops fall
Heard only in the trances of the blast,
Or if the secret ministry of frost
Shall hang them up in silent icicles,
Quietly shining to the quiet moon.

DEJECTION: AN ODE

Late, late yestreen I saw the new Moon
With the old Moon in her arms:
And I fear, I fear, my Master dear!
We shall have a deadly storm.
Ballad of Sir Patrick Spence.

Well! If the bard was weather-wise, who made
  The grand old ballad of Sir Patrick Spence,
  This night, so tranquil now, will not go hence
Unroused by winds, that ply a busier trade
Than those which mold yon cloud in lazy flakes,
Or the dull sobbing draft, that moans and rakes
Upon the strings of this Aeolian lute,
    Which better far were mute;
  For lo! the new-moon winter-bright!
  And overspread with phantom light,
  (With swimming phantom light o'er-spread
  But rimmed and circled by a silver thread)
I see the old moon in her lap, foretelling
  The coming-on of rain and squally blast.
And oh! that even now the gust were swelling,
  And the slant night-shower driving loud and fast!

Those sounds which oft have raised me, whilst they awed,
    And sent my soul abroad,
Might now perhaps their wonted impulse give,
Might startle this dull pain, and make it move and live!

A grief without a pang, void, dark, and drear,
  A stifled, drowsy, unimpassioned grief,
   Which finds no natural outlet, no relief,
     In word, or sigh, or tear—
O Lady! in this wan and heartless mood,
To other thoughts by yonder throstle woo'd,
  All this long eve, so balmy and serene,
Have I been gazing on the western sky,
  And its peculiar tint of yellow green:
And still I gaze—and with how blank an eye!
And those thin clouds above, in flakes and bars,
That give away their motion to the stars;
Those stars, that glide behind them or between,
Now sparkling, now bedimmed, but always seen:
Yon crescent moon, as fixed as if it grew
In its own cloudless, starless lake of blue;
I see them all so excellently fair,
I see, not feel, how beautiful they are!

    My genial spirits fail;
     And what can these avail
To lift the smothering weight from off my breast?
    It were a vain endeavor,
    Though I should gaze forever
On that green light that lingers in the west:
I may not hope from outward forms to win
The passion and the life, whose fountains are within.

O Lady! we receive but what we give,
And in our life alone does Nature live:
Ours is her wedding garment, ours her shroud!
  And would we aught behold, of higher worth,
Than that inanimate cold world allowed
To the poor loveless ever-anxious crowd,
  Ah! from the soul itself must issue forth
A light, a glory, a fair luminous cloud
  Enveloping the earth—
And from the soul itself must there be sent

A sweet and potent voice, of its own birth,
Of all sweet sounds the life and element!

O pure of heart! thou need'st not ask of me
What this strong music in the soul may be!
What, and wherein it doth exist,
This light, this glory, this fair luminous mist,
This beautiful and beauty-making power.
    Joy, virtuous Lady! Joy that ne'er was given,
Save to the pure, and in their purest hour,
Life, and life's effluence, cloud at once and shower,
Joy, Lady! is the spirit and the power,
Which wedding Nature to us gives in dower,
    A new earth and new heaven,
Undreamt of by the sensual and the proud—
Joy is the sweet voice, Joy the luminous cloud—
    We in ourselves rejoice!
And thence flows all that charms or ear or sight,
    All melodies the echoes of that voice,
All colors a suffusion from that light.

There was a time when, though my path was rough,
    This joy within me dallied with distress,
And all misfortunes were but as the stuff
    Whence Fancy made me dreams of happiness:
For Hope grew round me, like the twining vine,
And fruits, and foliage, not my own, seemed mine.
But now afflictions bow me down to earth:
Nor care I that they rob me of my mirth;
    But oh! each visitation
Suspends what nature gave me at my birth,
    My shaping spirit of Imagination.
For not to think of what I needs must feel,
    But to be still and patient, all I can;
And haply by abstruse research to steal
    From my own nature all the natural man—
    This was my sole resource, my only plan:
Till that which suits a part infects the whole,
And now is almost grown the habit of my soul.

Hence, viper thoughts, that coil around my mind,
        Reality's dark dream!

I turn from you, and listen to the wind,
   Which long has raved unnoticed. What a scream
Of agony by torture lengthened out
That lute sent forth! Thou Wind, that rav'st without,
Bare crag, or mountain-tairn, or blasted tree,
Or pine-grove whither woodman never clomb,
Or lonely house, long held the witches' home,
   Methinks were fitter instruments for thee,
Mad Lutanist! who in this month of showers,
Of dark-brown gardens, and of peeping flowers,
Mak'st Devils' yule, with worse than wintry song,
The blossoms, buds, and timorous leaves among.
   Thou actor, perfect in all tragic sounds!
Thou mighty poet, e'en to frenzy bold!
     What tell'st thou now about?
    'Tis of the rushing of an host in rout,
   With groans, of trampled men, with smarting wounds—
At once they groan with pain, and shudder with the cold!
But hush! there is a pause of deepest silence!
   And all that noise, as of a rushing crowd,
With groans, and tremulous shudderings—all is over—
   It tells another tale, with sounds less deep and loud!
     A tale of less affright,
     And tempered with delight,
As Otway's self had framed the tender lay—
     'Tis of a little child
     Upon a lonesome wild,
Not far from home, but she hath lost her way:
And now moans low in bitter grief and fear,
And now screams loud, and hopes to make her mother hear.

'Tis midnight, but small thoughts have I of sleep:
Full seldom may my friend such vigils keep!
Visit her, gentle Sleep! with wings of healing,
   And may this storm be but a mountain-birth,
May all the stars hang bright above her dwelling,
   Silent as though they watched the sleeping earth!
     With light heart may she rise,
     Gay fancy, cheerful eyes,
   Joy lift her spirit, joy attune her voice;
To her may all things live, from pole to pole,
Their life the eddying of her living soul!
   O simple spirit, guided from above,

Dear Lady! friend devoutest of my choice,
Thus mayest thou ever, evermore rejoice.

THOMAS MOORE

OFT, IN THE STILLY NIGHT

Oft, in the stilly night,
    Ere Slumber's chain has bound me,
Fond Memory brings the light
    Of other days around me;
      The smiles, the tears,
      Of boyhood's years,
    The words of love then spoken;
      The eyes that shone,
      Now dimmed and gone,
    The cheerful hearts now broken!
Thus, in the stilly night,
    Ere Slumber's chain has bound me,
Sad Memory brings the light
    Of other days around me.

When I remember all
    The friends, so linked together,
I've seen around me fall,
    Like leaves in wintry weather;
      I feel like one
      Who treads alone
    Some banquet-hall deserted,
      Whose lights are fled,
      Whose garlands dead,
    And all but he departed!
Thus, in the stilly night,
    Ere Slumber's chain has bound me,
Sad Memory brings the light
    Of other days around me.

THOMAS MOORE (1779-1852) achieved great popularity as Ireland's national poet. Born in Dublin, the son of a grocer, he attended Trinity College, held a government post in Bermuda, and became a close friend of Lord Byron. He is best remembered for the love lyrics and patriotic verses he set to Irish folk tunes.

PERCY BYSSHE SHELLEY

OZYMANDIAS

I met a traveller from an antique land
Who said: "Two vast and trunkless legs of stone
Stand in the desert. Near them, on the sand,
Half sunk, a shattered visage lies, whose frown,
And wrinkled lip, and sneer of cold command,
Tell that its sculptor well those passions read
Which yet survive, stamped on these lifeless things,
The hand that mocked them, and the heart that fed:
And on the pedestal these words appear:
'My name is Ozymandias, king of kings:
Look on my works, ye Mighty, and despair!'
Nothing besides remains. Round the decay
Of that colossal wreck, boundless and bare
The lone and level sands stretch far away."

PERCY BYSSHE SHELLEY (1792-1822), son and heir of a wealthy Sussex country squire, began his career as a poet and his battle against conformity while a schoolboy. He was expelled from Oxford for writing a pamphlet in favor of atheism. He deserted his first wife in 1814 and, after her suicide in 1817, lived in exile in Italy with his second wife, Mary Godwin, until his death by drowning.

V

THE ROMANTIC PERIOD

INDIVIDUALISM

THE Romanticist's glorification of the poet as seer or prophet of heightened sensibility gives value to this sensibility itself and is related to a general concern with the condition of humanity. There is interest not only in individual human feeling but in the social milieu, and for the first time we find a considerable body of social and political protest in English verse. The opening years of the nineteenth century are full of the spirit of the French Revolution, with its faith in human progress and perfectibility and its dreams of a freedom such as mankind had never before experienced. These hopes are expressed in the early poems of Wordsworth. But when the second group of Romantics—Byron, Shelley, and Keats—began to write less than two decades later, the hopes had faded, suppressed by the tyranny of the most conservative political regime England had known in many years. These poets reflect the general frustration and disillusion that follow the collapse of a visionary ideal. A common theme of Romantic poetry is the contrast between the sordid reality of actual life and the ideal of what man might be. The plight of the poet caught between these extremes is described in highly personal expressions of melancholy and self-pity. In Keats, despair sometimes leads to a longing for death as the condition where dreams unattainable on earth at last may be realized.

Since many of the greatest poems of the era spring from immediate personal experience, literary biography becomes very important. To perceive the full force of Shelley's *Stanzas Written in Dejection, near Naples,* for instance, we must understand that Shelley's personal sorrow, which is the theme of the poem and is underscored in the title, springs from the death of his beloved daughter Clara and the separation between the poet and his wife, Mary Godwin; both parents were filled with remorse and self-accusation over the death of their child. This tragedy had followed close upon the decision of the English courts to take away the poet's children by his first wife, Harriet Westbrook, who had committed suicide. The poem is an expression of loneliness and longing for death by an exile who knows he can never return to his native land. We cannot share fully the poet's sorrow without awareness of the personal context from which it springs.

Romantic individualism leads to a constant intrusion of the poet himself into his subject, as in Shelley's *Ode to the West Wind.* The wind is the symbol of human regeneration—it preserves while it destroys—but it is always the poet who is the subject of the poem, who is identified with the wind: "Be thou, Spirit fierce,/ My spirit! Be thou me, impetuous one!" His words the wind must scatter among mankind; through him the wind must be "The trumpet of a prophecy!" This egocentricity has alienated many readers from Shelley on the grounds that the man and his thoughts are themselves not sufficiently great or important to justify the poetic emphasis placed upon them.

Recent critics have been inclined to award a higher position as poet to John Keats; his perceptions of reality are generally more profound and his emotions are more deeply felt by the reader because they are better controlled. But Keats' own experiences impinge just as much upon his poems, in which we find the longing of the city boy for the natural beauty of the country and the yearnings of the lower-class youth for recognition in literary circles. In the sonnet *When I Have Fears That I May Cease to Be,* the poet's desire for immortality is linked to that absorption with death which runs through so much of Keats' poetry. In *La Belle Dame sans Merci* there may be fused into a conventional medieval theme some reflection of the poet's frustrating affair with Fanny Brawne, the girl he loved but could not marry because of his poverty and ill health. The final line of *Bright Star, Would I Were Steadfast As Thou Art*—"And so live ever—or else swoon to death"—holds a deeper poignancy when we compare it to the words Keats wrote in a letter to Fanny: "I have two luxuries to brood over in my walks, your loveliness and the hour of death. O that I could have possession of them both in the same moment!" More than the poets of any previous age, the Romantics made their own lives, their fears and their triumphs, the subject of their verse.

FOR FURTHER READING:

Baker, Carlos. *Shelley's Major Poetry.* Princeton, 1948.

Bate, W. J. *The Stylistic Development of Keats.* London, 1945.

Finney, C. L. *The Evolution of Keats's Poetry.* 2 vols. Cambridge, Mass., 1936.

Fogle, R. H. *The Imagery of Keats and Shelley.* Chapel Hill, N. C., 1949.

Garrod, H. W. *Keats.* New York, 1926.

Murry, J. M. *Studies in Keats.* New York, 1930.

Tate, Allan. "A Reading of Keats," *On the Limits of Poetry; Selected Essays 1928-48.* New York, 1948.

Thorpe, C. D. *The Mind of John Keats.* New York, 1926.

Wasserman, Earl. *The Finer Tone: Keats' Major Poems.* Baltimore, 1953.

White, N. I. *A Portrait of Shelley.* New York, 1945.

PERCY BYSSHE SHELLEY

ODE TO THE WEST WIND

I

O wild West Wind, thou breath of Autumn's being,
Thou, from whose unseen presence the leaves dead
Are driven, like ghosts from an enchanter fleeing,

Yellow, and black, and pale, and hectic red,
Pestilence-stricken multitudes: O thou,
Who chariotest to their dark wintry bed

The wingèd seeds, where they lie cold and low,
Each like a corpse within its grave, until
Thine azure sister of the Spring shall blow

Her clarion o'er the dreaming earth, and fill
(Driving sweet buds like flocks to feed in air)
With living hues and odors plain and hill:

Wild Spirit, which art moving everywhere;
Destroyer and preserver; hear! oh, hear!

II

Thou on whose stream, mid the steep sky's commotion,
Loose clouds like earth's decaying leaves are shed,
Shook from the tangled boughs of Heaven and Ocean,

Angels of rain and lightning: there are spread
On the blue surface of thine airy surge,
Like the bright hair uplifted from the head

Of some fierce Maenad, even from the dim verge
Of the horizon to the zenith's height,
The locks of the approaching storm. Thou dirge

Of the dying year, to which this closing night
Will be the dome of a vast sepulcher,
Vaulted with all thy congregated might

Of vapors, from whose solid atmosphere
Black rain, and fire, and hail will burst: oh, hear!

III

Thou who didst waken from his summer dreams
The blue Mediterranean, where he lay,
Lulled by the coil of his crystalline streams,

Beside a pumice isle in Baiae's bay,
And saw in sleep old palaces and towers
Quivering within the wave's intenser day,

All overgrown with azure moss and flowers
So sweet, the sense faints picturing them! thou
For whose path the Atlantic's level powers

Cleave themselves into chasms, while far below
The sea-blooms and the oozy woods which wear
The sapless foliage of the ocean, know

Thy voice, and suddenly grow gray with fear,
And tremble and despoil themselves: oh, hear!

IV

If I were a dead leaf thou mightest bear;
If I were a swift cloud to fly with thee;
A wave to pant beneath thy power, and share

The impulse of thy strength, only less free
Than thou, O, uncontrollable! If even
I were as in my boyhood, and could be

The comrade of thy wanderings over Heaven,
As then, when to outstrip thy skyey speed
Scarce seemed a vision; I would ne'er have striven

As thus with thee in prayer in my sore need.
Oh, lift me as a wave, a leaf, a cloud!
I fall upon the thorns of life! I bleed!

A heavy weight of hours has chained and bowed
One too like thee: tameless, and swift, and proud.

V

Make me thy lyre, even as the forest is:
What if my leaves are falling like its own!
The tumult of thy mighty harmonies

Will take from both a deep, autumnal tone,
Sweet though in sadness. Be thou, Spirit fierce,
My spirit! Be thou me, impetuous one!

Drive my dead thoughts over the universe
Like withered leaves to quicken a new birth!
And, by the incantation of this verse,

Scatter, as from an unextinguished hearth
Ashes and sparks, my words among mankind!
Be through my lips to unawakened earth

The trumpet of a prophecy! O Wind,
If Winter comes, can Spring be far behind?

STANZAS WRITTEN IN DEJECTION, NEAR NAPLES

The sun is warm, the sky is clear,
  The waves are dancing fast and bright,
Blue isles and snowy mountains wear
  The purple noon's transparent might,
  The breath of the moist earth is light,
Around its unexpanded buds;
  Like many a voice of one delight,
  The winds, the birds, the ocean floods,
The City's voice itself, is soft like Solitude's.

I see the Deep's untrampled floor
  With green and purple seaweeds strown;
I see the waves upon the shore,
  Like light dissolved in star-showers, thrown:
  I sit upon the sands alone,—
The lightning of the noontide ocean
  Is flashing round me, and a tone

Arises from its measured motion,
How sweet! did any heart now share in my emotion.

Alas! I have nor hope nor health,
    Nor peace within nor calm around,
Nor that content surpassing wealth
    The sage in meditation found,
    And walked with inward glory crowned—
Nor fame, nor power, nor love, nor leisure.
    Others I see whom these surround—
Smiling they live, and call life pleasure;—
To me that cup has been dealt in another measure.

Yet now despair itself is mild,
    Even as the winds and waters are;
I could lie down like a tired child,
    And weep away the life of care
    Which I have borne and yet must bear,
Till death like sleep might steal on me,
    And I might feel in the warm air
My cheek grow cold, and hear the sea
Breathe o'er my dying brain its last monotony.

Some might lament that I were cold,
    As I, when this sweet day is gone,
Which, my lost heart, too soon grown old,
    Insults with this untimely moan;
    They might lament—for I am one
Whom men love not—and yet regret,
    Unlike this day, which, when the sun
Shall on its stainless glory set,
Will linger, though enjoyed, like joy in memory yet.

THE INDIAN SERENADE

I arise from dreams of Thee
In the first sweet sleep of night,
When the winds are breathing low
And the stars are shining bright:
I arise from dreams of thee,
And a spirit in my feet
Hath led me—who knows how?
To thy chamber-window, Sweet!

The wandering airs, they faint
On the dark, the silent stream—
The champak odors fail
Like sweet thoughts in a dream;
The nightingale's complaint,
It dies upon her heart,
As I must on thine,
Oh, belovèd as thou art!

Oh, lift me from the grass!
I die, I faint, I fail!
Let thy love in kisses rain
On my lips and eyelids pale.
My cheek is cold and white, alas!
My heart beats loud and fast;
Oh! press it close to thine again,
Where it will break at last.

JOHN KEATS

ON FIRST LOOKING INTO CHAPMAN'S HOMER

Much have I traveled in the realms of gold,
And many goodly states and kingdoms seen;
Round many western islands have I been
Which bards in fealty to Apollo hold.
Oft of one wide expanse had I been told
That deep-browed Homer ruled as his demesne;
Yet did I never breathe its pure serene
Till I heard Chapman speak out loud and bold:
Then felt I like some watcher of the skies
When a new planet swims into his ken;
Or like stout Cortez when with eagle eyes
He stared at the Pacific—and all his men
Looked at each other with a wild surmise—
Silent, upon a peak in Darien.

JOHN KEATS (1795-1821), the son of a London livery-stable keeper, was apprenticed to a barber surgeon but gave up a medical career to devote himself to poetry. Troubled by family tragedy, financial problems, a hopeless love affair, and the onslaught of tuberculosis, he nevertheless produced in the last few years of his life some of the most beautiful poems in the English language. He died in Italy.

ODE TO A NIGHTINGALE

My heart aches, and a drowsy numbness pains
   My sense, as though of hemlock I had drunk,
Or emptied some dull opiate to the drains
   One minute past, and Lethe-wards had sunk:
'Tis not through envy of thy happy lot,
   But being too happy in thine happiness,—
      That thou, light-wingèd Dryad of the trees,
         In some melodious plot
   Of beechen green, and shadows numberless,
      Singest of summer in full-throated ease.

O, for a draught of vintage! that hath been
   Cooled a long age in the deep-delvèd earth,
Tasting of Flora and the country green,
   Dance, and Provençal song, and sunburnt mirth!
O for a beaker full of the warm South,
   Full of the true, the blushful Hippocrene,
      With beaded bubbles winking at the brim,
         And purple-stainèd mouth;
   That I might drink, and leave the world unseen,
      And with thee fade away into the forest dim:

Fade far away, dissolve, and quite forget
   What thou among the leaves hast never known,
The weariness, the fever, and the fret
   Here, where men sit and hear each other groan;
Where palsy shakes a few, sad, last gray hairs,
   Where youth grows pale, and spectre-thin, and dies;
      Where but to think is to be full of sorrow
         And leaden-eyed despairs,
   Where Beauty cannot keep her lustrous eyes,
      Or new Love pine at them beyond tomorrow.

Away! away! for I will fly to thee,
   Not charioted by Bacchus and his pards,
But on the viewless wings of Poesy,
   Though the dull brain perplexes and retards:
Already with thee! tender is the night,
   And haply the Queen-Moon is on her throne,
      Cluster'd around by all her starry fays;

But here there is no light,
Save what from heaven is with the breezes blown
Through verdurous glooms and winding mossy ways.

I cannot see what flowers are at my feet,
Nor what soft incense hangs upon the boughs,
But, in embalmèd darkness, guess each sweet
Wherewith the seasonable month endows
The grass, the thicket, and the fruit-tree wild;
White hawthorn, and the pastoral eglantine;
Fast fading violets covered up in leaves;
And mid-May's eldest child,
The coming musk-rose, full of dewy wine,
The murmurous haunt of flies on summer eves.

Darkling I listen; and, for many a time
I have been half in love with easeful Death,
Called him soft names in many a musèd rhyme,
To take into the air my quiet breath;
Now more than ever seems it rich to die,
To cease upon the midnight with no pain,
While thou art pouring forth thy soul abroad
In such an ecstasy!
Still wouldst thou sing, and I have ears in vain—
To thy high requiem become a sod.

Thou wast not born for death, immortal Bird!
No hungry generations tread thee down;
The voice I hear this passing night was heard
In ancient days by emperor and clown:
Perhaps the self-same song that found a path
Through the sad heart of Ruth, when, sick for home,
She stood in tears amid the alien corn;
The same that oft-times hath
Charmed magic casements, opening on the foam
Of perilous seas, in faery lands forlorn.

Forlorn! the very word is like a bell
To toll me back from thee to my sole self,
Adieu! the fancy cannot cheat so well
As she is famed to do, deceiving elf.
Adieu! adieu! thy plaintive anthem fades
Past the near meadows, over the still stream,

Up the hillside; and now 'tis buried deep
  In the next valley glades:
Was it a vision, or a waking dream?
  Fled is that music—do I wake or sleep?

ODE ON A GRECIAN URN

Thou still unravished bride of quietness,
  Thou foster-child of Silence and slow Time,
Sylvan historian, who canst thus express
  A flowery tale more sweetly than our rime:
What leaft-fringed legend haunts about thy shape
  Of deities or mortals, or of both,
    In Tempe or the dales of Arcady?
  What men or gods are these? What maidens loth?
What mad pursuit? What struggle to escape?
    What pipes and timbrels? What wild ecstasy?

Heard melodies are sweet, but those unheard
  Are sweeter; therefore, ye soft pipes, play on;
Not to the sensual ear, but, more endeared,
  Pipe to the spirit ditties of no tone:
Fair youth, beneath the trees, thou canst not leave
  Thy song, nor ever can those trees be bare;
    Bold Lover, never, never canst thou kiss,
Though winning near the goal—yet, do not grieve;
  She cannot fade, though thou hast not thy bliss,
    Forever wilt thou love, and she be fair!

Ah, happy, happy boughs! that cannot shed
  Your leaves, nor ever bid the Spring adieu;
And, happy melodist, unwearièd,
  Forever piping songs forever new;
More happy love! more happy, happy love!
  Forever warm and still to be enjoyed,
    Forever panting, and forever young;
All breathing human passion far above,
  That leaves a heart high-sorrowful and cloyed,
    A burning forehead, and a parching tongue.

Who are these coming to the sacrifice?
  To what green altar, O mysterious priest,
Lead'st thou that heifer lowing at the skies,
  And all her silken flanks with garlands dressed?

What little town by river or seashore,
　　Or mountain-built with peaceful citadel,
　　　　Is emptied of this folk, this pious morn?
And, little town, thy streets forevermore
　　Will silent be; and not a soul to tell
　　　　Why thou art desolate, can e'er return.

O Attic shape! Fair attitude! with brede
　　Of marble men and maidens overwrought,
With forest branches and the trodden weed;
　　Thou, silent form! dost tease us out of thought
As doth eternity: Cold Pastoral!
　　When old age shall this generation waste,
　　　　Thou shalt remain, in midst of other woe
Than ours, a friend to man, to whom thou say'st,
　　"Beauty is truth, truth beauty,"—that is all
　　　　Ye know on earth, and all ye need to know.

ODE ON MELANCHOLY

No, no, go not to Lethe, neither twist
　　Wolf's-bane, tight-rooted, for its poisonous wine;
Nor suffer thy pale forehead to be kissed
　　By nightshade, ruby grape of Proserpine;
Make not your rosary of yew-berries,
　　Nor let the beetle, nor the death-moth be
　　　　Your mournful Psyche, nor the downy owl
A partner in your sorrow's mysteries;
　　For shade to shade will come too drowsily,
　　　　And drown the wakeful anguish of the soul.

But when the melancholy fit shall fall
　　Sudden from heaven like a weeping cloud,
That fosters the droop-headed flowers all,
　　And hides the green hill in an April shroud;
Then glut thy sorrow on a morning rose,
　　Or on the rainbow of the salt sand-wave,
　　　　Or on the wealth of globèd peonies;
Or if thy mistress some rich anger shows,
　　Emprison her soft hand, and let her rave,
　　　　And feed deep, deep upon her peerless eyes.

She dwells with Beauty—Beauty that must die;
　　And Joy, whose hand is ever at his lips

Bidding adieu; and aching Pleasure nigh,
   Turning to poison while the bee-mouth sips:
Ay, in the very temple of Delight
   Veiled Melancholy has her sovran shrine,
     Though seen of none save him whose
         strenuous tongue
   Can burst Joy's grape against his palate fine;
His soul shall taste the sadness of her might,
   And be among her cloudy trophies hung.

ODE ON MELANCHOLY Two distinct biographical events prompted Keats in the composition of the *Ode on Melancholy.* In a letter to Benjamin Robert Haydon, the painter, Keats wrote that he was low in spirits, though he did not think he should "ever come to the rope or the pistol." Possibly to feed this personal mood, Keats took to reading Robert Burton's *Anatomy of Melancholy,* a seventeenth-century pseudoscientific treatise. In his own emotions and his readings, the poet found a theme which would continue to be the chief statement of any major work he would write before his early death: Beauty must die; joy turns first to aching pleasure and then to poison even as we take our first delight in all lovely things.

Keats' great odes all express intimately personal themes, and in them he searched for an equally personal form. In *Ode on Indolence, Ode to a Nightingale, Ode on a Grecian Urn,* and *Ode on Melancholy,* he settled upon a ten-line stanza that combines parts of the English and the Italian sonnet. In these poems Keats opens each stanza with the English quatrain: *abab.* He then employs some variation of the three rhyme letters common to the sestet of the Italian sonnet: *cde, cde; cde, dce;* or *cde, ced.* In the *Ode on Melancholy* the first two stanzas adhere perfectly to the ten-line sequence rhyming *abab, cde, cde,* but the final sestet varies to *cde, dce.* Keats limits himself to iambic pentameter throughout.

Of all his odes, Keats is most free with rhyme in the *Ode on Melancholy.* Although the quatrains are quite conventional, two of the sestets use half rhyme (see glossary) as well as paired masculine and feminine endings. In the first stanza *berries* is made to rhyme with *mysteries,* although within the metrical lines where each appears, both lines impress the ear as though they end with dactyls rather than trochee and iamb respectively. Also in the first stanza Keats rhymes *be,* a strongly stressed word, with *drowsily,* a word indeed ending in a stress but in one far lighter than its counterpart. The final pairing of the first stanza couples *owl* with *soul* in a clear example of half rhyme. In the second stanza the only divergence from standard practice is the rather daring rhyme of *peonies* with *peerless eyes.* These variations are not unwarranted in a poem about melancholy, in which the soul is too weary to be concerned about exact equivalents.

The *Ode on Melancholy* perhaps more than any other ode by Keats follows the classical movements of strophe, antistrophe, and epode. The first stanza tells the victim of melancholy not to seek escape through death. The second stanza urges that he enrich the experience by gazing upon the various masks of beauty. And the third stanza explains how the pursuit of beauty, joy, pleasure, and delight will deepen the melancholy state.

As with so many poems by Keats, the *Ode on Melancholy* achieves its success more by its sensuous imagery than by its intellectual statement. The content we can paraphrase in a few brief sentences, but the chief statement of each stanza is wrapped in a complex of images which brings most of the five senses into an affective response. The commandment of the first stanza is to refrain from suicide, but the poet, in order to make this statement, invokes a vision of the classical underworld by a reference to the river Lethe; he takes us through witch-haunted forests in search of poisonous roots and herbs and back again to hell by way of salutation to its queen, Proserpine. The three poisons are all liquids; two make reference to the sense of taste, the third to the sense of touch: "Nor suffer thy pale forehead to be kissed/ By nightshade." The second half of the stanza employs various traditional symbols of death—yew-berries, the scarab beetle, the death's-head moth, and the owl—all of which appeal to the sight.

In contrast to the dark world of the first stanza, the second evokes a wealth of bright and shining images of the upper world. Although the poet opens with a cloud cover, rain, mist, and drooping flowers, the rainbow soon appears with its magnificent colors reflected in the rose and peonies. These flowers bring into play our sense of smell; and even hearing is called upon to record in our inner mind the ravings of the angry lady. By this point Keats has forced us, in any full experience of his poem, to use all our five senses, and he may devote his last stanza to the full realization of his thematic statement, though here too he does not neglect the sensual: the bee-mouth sips, the tongue bursts Joy's grape, the soul tastes.

The compression of statement in this final stanza almost defies line-by-line coherent paraphrase, and yet it is not difficult to recognize the literal meaning of the words. We might well have trouble in understanding how the personified *Pleasure* turns to poison or why it has a bee-mouth; but we sense the appropriateness of the image, of the use of a creature that takes in honey but exudes a poison in its sting. Without being sure how the poet achieves the effect, we know that somehow the pronoun *She* which opens the stanza refers both to the mistress of stanza

2 and "Veiled Melancholy" that comes after. We may find it impossible to explain in other words exactly what "taste the sadness of her might" means literally, but we approve of the tension in an image that combines an expression of the power of melancholy with a metaphor of how we experience it and what its essence ("taste of sadness") is. The density (see glossary) of the entire stanza helps us to understand that beauty, joy, pleasure, and delight exist simultaneously with death, decay, pain, and sadness, and that at the very moment of any triumph of happiness, we have already laid the foundation for bitter defeat, sorrow, and despair.

Some critics claim that Keats refrains from commenting upon the experiences he records in the odes, that he has observed some episode of life and captured it merely, refusing evaluation—approval or rejection. But in the *Ode on Melancholy* at least, we might note that the final victor is always one of the forces of defeat—death or depression—and that the sentient man's soul hangs among the trophies of his adversary.

KEEN, FITFUL GUSTS ARE WHISPERING HERE AND THERE

Keen, fitful gusts are whispering here and there
　　Among the bushes half leafless, and dry;
　　The stars look very cold about the sky,
And I have many miles on foot to fare,
Yet feel I little of the cool bleak air,
　　Or of the dead leaves rustling drearily,
　　Or of these silver lamps that burn on high,
Or of the distance from home's pleasant lair:
For I am brimful of the friendliness
　　That in a l ttle cottage I have found;
Of fair-haired Milton's eloquent distress,
　　And all his love for gentle Lycid drowned;
Of lovely Laura in her light green dress,
　　And faithful Petrarch gloriously crowned.

LA BELLE DAME SANS MERCI

O what can ail thee, knight-at-arms!
　　Alone and palely loitering!
The sedge has wither'd from the lake,
　　And no birds sing.

O what can ail thee, knight-at-arms!
　　So haggard and so woe-begone?

The squirrel's granary is full,
   And the harvest's done.

I see a lily on thy brow
   With anguish moist and fever dew,
And on thy cheeks a fading rose
   Fast withereth too.

"I met a lady in the meads,
   Full beautiful—a faery's child,
Her hair was long, her foot was light,
   And her eyes were wild.

"I made a garland for her head,
   And bracelets too, and fragrant zone;
She looked at me as she did love,
   And made sweet moan.

"I set her on my pacing steed,
   And nothing else saw all day long,
For sideways would she lean, and sing
   A faery's song.

"She found me roots of relish sweet,
   And honey wild, and manna-dew;
And sure in language strange she said,
   'I love thee true.'

"She took me to her elfin grot,
   And there she wept, and sighed full sore,
And there I shut her wild, wild eyes,
   With kisses four.

"And there she lullèd me asleep,
   And there I dreamed—ah! woe betide!—
The latest dream I ever dreamed
   On the cold hillside.

"I saw pale kings, and princes too,
   Pale warriors, death-pale were they all:
They cried—'La Belle Dame sans Merci
   Hath thee in thrall!'

"I saw their starved lips in the gloam,
  With horrid warning gapèd wide;
And I awoke, and found me here
  On the cold hillside.

"And this is why I sojourn here
  Alone and palely loitering,
Though the sedge is wither'd from the lake,
  And no birds sing."

WHEN I HAVE FEARS THAT I MAY CEASE TO BE

When I have fears that I may cease to be
Before my pen has gleaned my teeming brain,
Before high-pilèd books, in charactry,
Hold like rich garners the full-ripened grain;
When I behold, upon the night's starred face,
Huge cloudy symbols of a high romance,
And think that I may never live to trace
Their shadows, with the magic hand of chance;
And when I feel, fair creature of an hour,
That I shall never look upon thee more,
Never have relish in the faery power
Of unreflecting love!—then on the shore
Of the wide world I stand alone, and think
Till Love and Fame to nothingness do sink.

TO ONE WHO HAS BEEN LONG IN CITY PENT

To one who has been long in city pent
'Tis very sweet to look into the fair
And open face of heaven—to breathe a prayer
Full in the smile of the blue firmament.
Who is more happy, when, with heart's content,
Fatigued he sinks into some pleasant lair
Of wavy grass, and reads a debonair
And gentle tale of love and languishment?
Returning home at evening, with an ear
Catching the notes of Philomel—an eye
Watching the sailing cloudlet's bright career,
He mourns that day so soon has glided by:
E'en like the passage of an angel's tear
That falls through the clear ether silently.

BRIGHT STAR, WOULD I WERE
STEADFAST AS THOU ART

Bright star, would I were steadfast as thou art!
  Not in lone splendor hung aloft the night,
And watching, with eternal lids apart,
  Like Nature's patient, sleepless eremite,
The moving waters at their priestlike task
  Of pure ablution round earth's human shores,
Or gazing on the new soft-fallen mask
  Of snow upon the mountains and the moors:
No—yet still steadfast, still unchangeable,
  Pillowed upon my fair love's ripening breast,
To feel forever its soft fall and swell,
  Awake forever in a sweet unrest.
Still, still to hear her tender-taken breath,
And so live ever—or else swoon to death.

V

THE ROMANTIC PERIOD

THE DISTANT AND EXOTIC

WHILE one aspect of the Romantic imagination showed itself in a concern with the simple details of ordinary life, another aspect appears in a devotion to the distant, strange, and exotic. A faith in the importance of the imagination lent an interest and validity to whatever the imagination might reveal, and there were no such inhibiting canons of "good taste" in this matter as the Augustan writers had valued. Romantic poets liked to write of distant places and ancient times, perhaps in reaction against that neoclassical devotion to the rational and ordinary life of a London which represented the best of all possible places in the highest age of civilization. The sordid realities of the nineteenth-century Industrial Revolution may have led poets also to dream of distant lands with magic pleasure domes, and the bent bodies of laboring women and children in the new English factories may have rendered very appealing visions of Abyssinian maidens playing upon their dulcimers. Whatever its origins, this escape from reality is an important part of Romantic poetry.

Interest in the unusual ranges from flights into supernatural fantasy to an extension of the poet's awareness of his actual world. Travel literature had been popular since the sixteenth century, and even the Middle Ages had had their mythical voyages of saints; but with the Romantics, the glamour of distant lands becomes a subject for poetry. Coleridge especially was absorbed with the magical, the occult, and the exotic. He wrote of a vampire-haunted castle in *Christabel* and of enchanted oceans in *The Rime of the Ancient Mariner*. He is said to have written *Kubla Khan* while in a trance induced by opium, but whether this be true or not, the poem captures the essence of a dream-vision. The poet who catered most fully to the Romantic interest in foreign lands was probably Lord Byron, who in his poetry recorded his intensely personal impressions of the many places he visited in his wanderings throughout Europe. He retold in skillful narrative poetry exotic tales of the Middle East and the Orient.

The interest in the Middle Ages which is so strong among the Romantic poets is in part a reflection of their absorption with the strange and distant, but it is also a reflection of Romantic primitivism, the belief lands was probably Lord Byron, who in his poetry recorded his intensely descendants because his life was simpler and less marred by the debilitating effects of civilization. The Romantic poets had little real understanding of the Middle Ages, however. To them it was a fairy-tale era of wonder, of syrups, jellies, spices, of successful love and fierce storybook lords such as Keats describes in his *Eve of St. Agnes.* Romantic medievalism was a flight from reality, not concerned with historical truth.

The interest in the distant and strange sometimes led to an absorption in the morbid and unnatural. This facet of Romanticism appears in the Gothic tales of horror so popular near the turn of the nineteenth century; it later found its most masterful expression in the works of an American, Edgar Allan Poe. In his poetry Poe used an extraordinary skill in metrics to capture, as in his *Ulalume,* the tone and feeling of a time and place entirely remote from the world we know.

While Augustan poetry had been centered in the enclosed society of London and had placed its confidence in human reason and the validity of the actual, Romantic poetry reveals an extension of time and space; all human experience is its domain, all history and geography. It never hesitates to move from the real to the fantastic, from the ordinary to the grotesque. It allows an unrestricted range to the poet's imagination.

FOR FURTHER READING:

Fogle, R. H. "The Romantic Unity of Kubla Khan," *College English,* XIII (October 1951), 13-18.
Lowes, J. L. *The Road to Xanadu.* New York, 1930.
Schneider, Elizabeth. *Coleridge, Opium, and Kubla Khan.* Chicago, 1953.

SAMUEL TAYLOR COLERIDGE

KUBLA KHAN: OR, A VISION IN A DREAM

A Fragment

> In Xanadu did Kubla Khan
> A stately pleasure-dome decree:
> Where Alph, the sacred river, ran
> Through caverns measureless to man
> Down to a sunless sea.
> So twice five miles of fertile ground
> With walls and towers were girdled round:

And here were gardens bright with sinuous rills,
Where blossomed many an incense-bearing tree;
And here were forests ancient as the hills,
Enfolding sunny spots of greenery.
But oh! that deep romantic chasm which slanted
Down the green hill athwart a cedarn cover!
A savage place! as holy and enchanted
As e'er beneath a waning moon was haunted
By woman wailing for her demon-lover!
And from this chasm, with ceaseless turmoil seething,
As if this earth in fast thick pants were breathing
A mighty fountain momently was forced;
Amid whose swift half-intermitted burst
Huge fragments vaulted like rebounding hail,
Or chaffy grain beneath the thresher's flail:
And 'mid these dancing rocks at once and ever
It flung up momently the sacred river.
Five miles meandering with a mazy motion
Through wood and dale the sacred river ran,
Then reached the caverns measureless to man,
And sank in tumult to a lifeless ocean:
And 'mid this tumult Kubla heard from far
Ancestral voices prophesying war!

    The shadow of the dome of pleasure
    Floated midway on the waves;
    Where was heard the mingled measure
    From the fountain and the caves.
It was a miracle of rare device,
A sunny pleasure-dome with caves of ice!
    A damsel with a dulcimer
    In a vision once I saw:
    It was an Abyssinian maid,
    And on her dulcimer she played,
    Singing of Mount Abora.
    Could I revive within me
    Her symphony and song,
    To such a deep delight 'twould win me,
That with music loud and long,
I would build that dome in air,
That sunny dome! those caves of ice!
And all who heard should see them there,
And all should cry, Beware! Beware!

His flashing eyes, his floating hair!
Weave a circle round him thrice,
And close your eyes with holy dread,
For he on honey-dew hath fed,
And drunk the milk of Paradise.

KUBLA KHAN Coleridge's explanation of the composition of Kubla Khan is one of the more fascinating stories in literary history. A visitor interrupted the poet after he had awakened from a visionary dream and was in the act of putting on paper the two to three hundred lines which he claimed had fashioned themselves in his image-ridden sleep and which at that moment he still retained clearly in his mind. When the visitor left, Coleridge found that he could not remember enough of the dream or the verse written while in the subconscious state to conclude satisfactorily the fifty-four lines he had already committed to paper. We need not comment on the truth of this story other than to say that it has been called seriously into question. What is more important for the poetry reader is that Coleridge has captured the effect of a poem such as might have issued from a dream, full of the exotic and the strange which so appealed to the Romantic imagination.

Before he had fallen asleep, Coleridge had been reading—so he tells us—a passage in an early seventeenth-century travel book called *Purchas His Pilgrims.* Coleridge's memory of the sentence was faulty, for he misquotes it in his preface to the printed poem. These are the lines over which he fell asleep:

In Xamdu did Cublai Can build a stately Pallace, encompassing sixteene miles of plaine ground with a wall, wherein are fertile Meddowes, pleasant Springs, delightful Streames, and all sorts of beasts of chase and game, and in the middest thereof a sumptuous house of pleasure.

John Livingston Lowes has shown that Coleridge borrowed not only from *Purchas His Pilgrims* but also from at least eight other travel books. In all these works we find the generative images that served as points of departure for the poet; but they are only a small part of the poem. The palace, walls, springs, meadows, streams, and pleasure-house are all confined to the first part of the poem, where they merely free Coleridge's imagination, which goes on to evoke the "romantic chasm," "a waning moon," and "woman wailing for her demon-lover." The first part of the poem describes, with elaborations, an actual scene from Purchas and other writers. In the second part Coleridge recalls a vision he once had and relates it to what he has just described. To understand the poem, we must perceive fully the interplay between its two parts, which together probe the very nature of poetry and its composition. Too often readers of *Kubla Khan* are carried away by the exotic imagery and fail to see that the poem is a unified statement.

The real mistake they make is to think that both parts are dream-vision. Even if the poem were distilled in the alembic of an opium sleep, that does not mean that what went down on paper was supposed to betray its origins. The poem from line 1 to line 36 is a description of what should be taken as a concrete and historical setting, similar to that in such poems as Wordsworth's *Tintern Abbey* or Yeats' *The Lake Isle of Innisfree*. It is the poet's attempt to describe, as objectively as possible, a pleasure-dome built by a great Khan of antiquity. The central point is that the Khan achieved something magnificent and placed his delicate architectural jewel in a natural setting that was worthy of the stone:

> The shadow of the dome of pleasure
> Floated midway on the waves;
> Where was heard the mingled measure
> From the fountain and the caves.
> It was a miracle of rare device,
> A sunny pleasure-dome with caves of ice!

Only the second part of the poem is admittedly concerned with a vision. The dream took place some time ago ("In a vision once I saw"), and part of it was a singing lesson:

> Could I revive within me
> Her symphony and song,
> To such a deep delight 'twould win me,
> That with music loud and long,
> I would build . . . .

And except for the fact that in his vision there was a damsel singing of Mount Abora while playing on her dulcimer, we know nothing more about the dream. But could the poet sing like that maid, he would try to achieve in poetry what the Khan had decreed in Xanadu. The act of creativity for the poet, however—and this is what Coleridge is telling us about the nature of poetry—requires more than a little magic. We know that Coleridge is talking about poetry, for through "music loud and long" he wants to rebuild Kubla's dome not on earth in some substantial way but "in air." We know that magic will have been used if the poet succeeds to the height of his ambition, because all who hear will cry

> Beware! Beware!
> His flashing eyes, his floating hair!

> Weave a circle round him thrice,
> And close your eyes with holy dread,
> For he on honey-dew hath fed,
> And drunk the milk of Paradise.

Part two savors of necromancy; we are reminded very strongly of Shakespeare's Prospero, the magician in *The Tempest*:

> But this rough magic
> I here abjure, and, when I have required
> Some heavenly music, which even now I do,
> To work mine end upon their senses that
> This airy charm is for, I'll break my staff.

Part two is linked to part one in two important ways. There is, of course, the repetition of "That sunny dome! those caves of ice!" but, more excitingly, the poet-magician reminds us of the demon-lover. The unmistakable imagery of sexual excitement that follows the reference to "woman wailing for her demon-lover" (lines 17 to 28) suggests that Alph the sacred river stands symbolically for poetry and that the creation of poetry is like all procreative acts. When the poetry is great, when the river comes to its furthest reaches, it probes regions beyond the rational: the "caverns measureless to man."

It would seem from such a reading of the poem that Coleridge produced a finished work rather than the fragment he calls *Kubla Khan* in the subtitle. There are a sizable number of critics and readers who disagree gently with the poet and argue that while *Kubla Khan* may not be what Coleridge intended or what he saw in his dream, the second part nevertheless brings the work to a close simply by explaining why he could not go on with part one. Other critics, with greater subtlety, point out that part one is neatly rounded off by the recapitulating image of the dome and caves and that part two is really a modest little joke which tells us that the poet is incapable of doing the very thing he has just completed in part one. Both these arguments have considerable merit, but both leave out any reference to lines 29 and 30:

> And 'mid this tumult Kubla heard from far
> Ancestral voices prophesying war!

To rephrase a famous dictum by Chekhov, when a poet fires the opening salvo of a war in the first part of his work, he had better bring about a truce, a victory, or a defeat by the end. Coleridge's statement must be honored; the work is fragmentary.

An interesting sidelight of literary history indicates that at least one reader perceived that Coleridge in writing *Kubla Khan* was a magician, for part of the poem was magic. Kipling has written that

in all the millions permitted there are no more than five—five
little lines—of which one can say, "These are the magic. These
are the vision. The rest is only poetry."

Two of the five belong to Keats, but the remaining three are the fourteenth, fifteenth, and sixteenth lines of *Kubla Khan*:

> A savage place! as holy and enchanted
> As e'er beneath a waning moon was haunted
> By woman wailing for her demon-lover!

GEORGE NOEL GORDON, LORD BYRON

THE DESTRUCTION OF SENNACHERIB

The Assyrian came down like the wolf on the fold,
And his cohorts were gleaming in purple and gold;
And the sheen of their spears was like stars on the sea,
When the blue wave rolls nightly on deep Galilee.

Like the leaves of the forest when Summer is green,
That host with their banners at sunset were seen:
Like the leaves of the forest when Autumn hath blown,
That host on the morrow lay withered and strown.

For the Angel of Death spread his wings on the blast,
And breathed in the face of the foe as he passed;
And the eyes of the sleepers waxed deadly and chill,
And their hearts but once heaved, and forever grew still!

And there lay the steed with his nostril all wide,
But through it there rolled not the breath of his pride;
And the foam of his gasping lay white on the turf,
And cold as the spray of the rock-beating surf.

And there lay the rider distorted and pale,
With the dew on his brow, and the rust on his mail:

GEORGE NOEL GORDON, LORD BYRON (1788-1824), son of a
profligate father and a neurotic mother, inherited a great estate while still a minor and
published his first poems while at Cambridge. By 1812 he was a literary sensation; in
1816, after the scandal which followed the collapse of his marriage, he left England
forever. Living in Italy, he produced many of his major works. Byron died of a fever
while preparing to fight for Greek independence from Turkey.

And the tents were all silent—the banners alone—
The lances unlifted—the trumpet unblown.

And the widows of Ashur are loud in their wail,
And the idols are broke in the temple of Baal;
And the might of the Gentile, unsmote by the sword,
Hath melted like snow in the glance of the Lord!

THE ISLES OF GREECE

(From *Don Juan, Canto III*)

The isles of Greece, the isles of Greece!
    Where burning Sappho loved and sung,
Where grew the arts of war and peace,
    Where Delos rose, and Phoebus sprung!
Eternal summer gilds them yet,
But all, except their sun, is set.

The Scian and the Teian muse,
    The hero's harp, the lover's lute,
Have found the fame your shores refuse:
    Their place of birth alone is mute
To sounds which echo further west
Than your sires' "Islands of the Blest."

The mountains look on Marathon—
    And Marathon looks on the sea;
And musing there an hour alone,
    I dream'd that Greece might still be free;
For standing on the Persians' grave,
I could not deem myself a slave.

A king sate on the rocky brow
    Which looks o'er sea-born Salamis;
And ships, by thousands, lay below,
    And men in nations;—all were his!
He counted them at break of day—
And when the sun set, where were they?

And where are they? and where art thou,
    My country? On thy voiceless shore
The heroic lay is tuneless now—
    The heroic bosom beats no more!

And must thy lyre, so long divine,
Degenerate into hands like mine?

'Tis something, in the dearth of fame,
    Though linked among a fettered race,
To feel at least a patriot's shame,
    Even as I sing, suffuse my face;
For what is left the poet here?
For Greeks a blush—for Greece a tear.

Must *we* but weep o'er days more blest?
    Must *we* but blush?—Our fathers bled.
Earth! render back from out thy breast
    A remnant of our Spartan dead!
Of the three hundred grant but three,
To make a new Thermopylae!

What, silent still? and silent all?
    Ah! no;—the voices of the dead
Sound like a distant torrent's fall,
    And answer, "Let one living head,
But one arise,—we come, we come!"
'Tis but the living who are dumb.

In vain—in vain: strike other chords;
    Fill high the cup with Samian wine!
Leave battles to the Turkish hordes,
    And shed the blood of Scio's vine!
Hark! rising to the ignoble call—
How answers each bold Bacchanal!

You have the Pyrrhic dance as yet;
    Where is the Pyrrhic phalanx gone?
Of two such lessons, why forget
    The nobler and the manlier one?
You have the letters Cadmus gave—
Think ye he meant them for a slave?

Fill high the bowl with Samian wine!
    We will not think of themes like these!
It made Anacreon's song divine:
    He served—but served Polycrates—
A tyrant; but our masters then
Were still, at least, our countrymen.

The tyrant of the Chersonese
  Was freedom's best and bravest friend;
That tyrant was Miltiades!
  Oh! that the present hour would lend
Another despot of the kind!
Such chains as his were sure to bind.

Fill high the bowl with Samian wine!
  On Suli's rock, and Parga's shore,
Exists the remnant of a line
  Such as the Doric mothers bore;
And there, perhaps, some seed is sown,
The Heracleidan blood might own.

Trust not for freedom to the Franks—
  They have a king who buys and sells;
In native swords, and native ranks,
  The only hope of courage dwells:
But Turkish force, and Latin fraud,
Would break your shield, however broad.

Fill high the bowl with Samian wine!
  Our virgins dance beneath the shade—
I see their glorious black eyes shine;
  But gazing on each glowing maid,
My own the burning tear-drop laves,
To think such breasts must suckle slaves.

Place me on Sunium's marbled steep,
  Where nothing, save the waves and I,
May hear our mutual murmurs sweep;
  There, swan-like, let me sing and die:
A land of slaves shall ne'er be mine—
Dash down yon cup of Samian wine!

JOHN KEATS

THE EVE OF ST. AGNES

St. Agnes' Eve—Ah, bitter chill it was!
The owl, for all his feathers, was a-cold;

The hare limped trembling through the frozen grass,
And silent was the flock in woolly fold:
Numb were the Beadsman's fingers, while he told
His rosary, and while his frosted breath,
Like pious incense from a censer old,
Seemed taking flight for heaven, without a death,
Past the sweet Virgin's picture, while his prayer he saith.

His prayer, he saith, this patient, holy man;
Then takes his lamp, and riseth from his knees,
And back returneth, meagre, barefoot, wan,
Along the chapel aisle by slow degrees:
The sculptured dead, on each side, seem to freeze,
Emprisoned in black, purgatorial rails:
Knights, ladies, praying in dumb orat'ries,
He passeth by; and his weak spirit fails
To think how they may ache in icy hoods and mails.

Northward he turneth through a little door,
And scarce three steps, ere Music's golden tongue
Flattered to tears this aged man and poor;
But no—already had his death-bell rung:
The joys of all his life were said and sung:
His was harsh penance on St. Agnes' Eve:
Another way he went, and soon among
Rough ashes sat he for his soul's reprieve,
And all night kept awake, for sinner's sake to grieve.

That ancient Beadsman heard the prelude soft;
And so it chanced, for many a door was wide,
From hurry to and fro. Soon, up aloft,
The silver, snarling trumpets 'gan to chide:
The level chambers, ready with their pride,
Were glowing to receive a thousand guests:
The carvèd angels, ever eager-eyed,
Stared, where upon their heads the cornice rests,
With hair blown back, and wings put cross-wise on
    their breasts.

At length burst in the argent revelry,
With plume, tiara, and all rich array,
Numerous as shadows haunting faerily
The brain, new-stuffed, in youth, with triumphs gay

Of old romance. These let us wish away,
And turn, sole-thoughted, to one Lady there,
Whose heart had brooded, all that wintry day,
On love, and winged St. Agnes' saintly care,
As she had heard old dames full many times declare.

They told her how, upon St. Agnes' Eve,
Young virgins might have visions of delight,
And soft adorings from their loves receive
Upon the honeyed middle of the night,
If ceremonies due they did aright;
As, supperless to bed they must retire,
And couch supine their beauties, lily white;
Nor look behind, nor sideways, but require
Of Heaven with upward eyes for all that they desire.

Full of this whim was thoughtful Madeline:
The music, yearning like a god in pain,
She scarcely heard: her maiden eyes divine,
Fixed on the floor, saw many a sweeping train
Pass by—she heeded not at all: in vain
Came many a tiptoe, amorous cavalier,
And back retired; not cooled by high disdain,
But she saw not: her heart was otherwhere;
She sighed for Agnes' dreams, the sweetest of the year.

She danced along with vague, regardless eyes,
Anxious her lips, her breathing quick and short:
The hallowed hour was near at hand: she sighs
Amid the timbrels, and the thronged resort
Of whispers in anger, or in sport;
'Mid looks of love, defiance, hate, and scorn,
Hoodwinked with faery fancy; all amort,
Save to St. Agnes and her lambs unshorn,
And all the bliss to be before tomorrow morn.

So, purposing each moment to retire,
She lingered still. Meantime, across the moors,
Had come young Porphyro, with heart on fire
For Madeline. Beside the portal doors,
Buttressed from moonlight, stands he, and implores
All saints to give him sight of Madeline,
But for one moment in the tedious hours,

That he might gaze and worship all unseen;
Perchance speak, kneel, touch, kiss—in sooth such things
    have been.

He ventures in: let no buzzed whisper tell:
All eyes be muffled, or a hundred swords
Will storm his heart, Love's fev'rous citadel:
For him, those chambers held barbarian hordes,
Hyena foemen, and hot-blooded lords,
Whose very dogs would execrations howl
Against his lineage: not one breast affords
Him any mercy, in that mansion foul,
Save one old beldame, weak in body and in soul.

Ah, happy chance! the aged creature came,
Shuffling along with ivory-headed wand,
To where he stood, hid from the torch's flame,
Behind a broad hall-pillar, far beyond
The sound of merriment and chorus bland:
He startled her; but soon she knew his face,
And grasp'd his fingers in her palsied hand,
    Saying, "Mercy, Porphyro! hie thee from this place;
They are all here tonight, the whole blood-thirsty race!

"Get hence! get hence! there's dwarfish Hildebrand;
He had a fever late, and in the fit
He cursèd thee and thine, both house and land:
Then there's that old Lord Maurice, not a whit
More tame for his gray hairs—Alas me! flit!
Flit like a ghost away."—"Ah, Gossip dear,
We're safe enough; here in this armchair sit,
And tell me how"—"Good Saints! not here, not here;
Follow me, child, or else these stones will be thy bier."

He follow'd through a lowly archèd way,
Brushing the cobwebs with his lofty plume;
And as she muttered, "Well-a—well-a-day!"
He found him in a little moonlight room,
Pale, latticed, chill, and silent as a tomb.
"Now tell me where is Madeline," said he,
"O tell me, Angela, by the holy loom
Which none but secret sisterhood may see,
When they St. Agnes' wool are weaving piously."

"St. Agnes! Ah! it is St. Agnes' Eve—
Yet men will murder upon holy days:
Thou must hold water in a witch's sieve,
And be liege-lord of all the Elves and Fays,
To venture so: it fills me with amaze
To see thee, Porphyro!—St. Agnes' Eve!
God's help! my lady fair the conjuror plays
This very night: good angels her deceive!
But let me laugh awhile, I've mickle time to grieve."

Feebly she laugheth in the languid moon,
While Porphyro upon her face doth look,
Like puzzled urchin on an aged crone
Who keepeth closed a wond'rous riddle-book,
As spectacled she sits in chimney nook.
But soon his eyes grew brilliant, when she told
His lady's purpose; and he scarce could brook
Tears, at the thought of those enchantments cold,
And Madeline asleep in lap of legends old.

Sudden a thought came like a full-blown rose,
Flushing his brow, and in his painèd heart
Made purple riot: then doth he propose
A stratagem, that makes the beldame start:
"A cruel man and impious thou art:
Sweet lady, let her pray, and sleep, and dream
Alone with her good angels, far apart
From wicked men like thee. Go, go!—I deem
Thou canst not surely be the same that thou didst seem."

"I will not harm her, by all saints I swear,"
Quoth Porphyro: "Oh may I ne'er find grace
When my weak voice shall whisper its last prayer,
If one of her soft ringlets I displace,
Or look with ruffian passion in her face:
Good Angela, believe me by these tears;
Or I will, even in a moment's space,
Awake, with horrid shout, my foemen's ears,
And beard them, though they be more fanged than
        wolves and bears."

"Ah! why wilt thou affright a feeble soul?
A poor, weak, palsy-stricken, churchyard thing,
Whose passing-bell may ere the midnight toll;

Whose prayers for thee, each morn and evening,
Were never missed."—Thus plaining, doth she bring
A gentler speech from burning Porphyro;
So woeful, and of such deep sorrowing,
That Angela gives promise she will do
Whatever he shall wish, betide her weal or woe.

Which was, to lead him, in close secrecy,
Even to Madeline's chamber, and there hide
Him in a closet, of such privacy
That he might see her beauty unespied,
And win perhaps that night a peerless bride,
While legioned faeries paced the coverlet,
And pale enchantment held her sleepy-eyed.
Never on such a night have lovers met,
Since Merlin paid his Demon all the monstrous debt.

"It shall be as thou wishest," said the Dame:
All cates and dainties shall be storèd there
Quickly on this feast-night: by the tambour frame
Her own lute thou wilt see: no time to spare,
For I am slow and feeble, and scarcely dare
On such a catering trust my dizzy head.
Wait here, my child, with patience; kneel in prayer
The while: Ah! thou must needs the lady wed,
Or may I never leave my grave among the dead."

So saying, she hobbled off with busy fear.
The lover's endless minutes slowly passed;
The Dame returned, and whispered in his ear
To follow her—with agèd eyes aghast
From fright of dim espial. Safe at last,
Through many a dusky gallery, they gain
The maiden's chamber, silken, hushed, and chaste;
Where Porphyro took covert, pleas'd amain.
His poor guide hurried back with agues in her brain.

Her faltering hand upon the balustrade,
Old Angela was feeling for the stair,
When Madeline, St. Agnes' charmèd maid,
Rose, like a missioned spirit, unaware:
With silver taper's light, and pious care,
She turn'd, and down the aged gossip led
To a safe level matting. Now prepare,

Young Porphyro, for gazing on that bed;
She comes, she comes again, like ring-dove frayed and fled.

Out went the taper as she hurried in;
Its little smoke, in pallid moonshine, died:
She closed the door, she panted, all akin
To spirits of the air, and visions wide:
No uttered syllable, or woe, betide!
But to her heart, her heart was voluble,
Paining with eloquence her balmy side;
As though a tongueless nightingale should swell
Her throat in vain, and die, heart-stifled in her dell.

A casement high and triple-arched there was,
All garlanded with carven imag'ries
Of fruits, and flowers, and bunches of knot-grass,
And diamonded with panes of quaint device,
Innumerable of stains and splendid dyes,
As are the tiger-moth's deep-damasked wings;
And in the midst, 'mong thousand heraldries,
And twilight saints, and dim emblazonings,
A shielded scutcheon blushed with blood of queens and
        kings.

Full on this casement shone the wintry moon,
And threw warm gules on Madeline's fair breast,
As down she knelt for heaven's grace and boon;
Rose-bloom fell on her hands, together pressed,
And on her silver cross soft amethyst,
And on her hair a glory, like a saint:
She seem'd a splendid angel, newly dressed,
Save wings, for heaven—Porphyro grew faint:
She knelt, so pure a thing, so free from mortal taint.

Anon his heart revives: her vespers done,
Of all its wreathèd pearls her hair she frees;
Unclasps her warmèd jewels one by one;
Loosens her fragrant bodice; by degrees
Her rich attire creeps rustling to her knees:
Half-hidden, like a mermaid in sea-weed,
Pensive awhile she dreams awake, and sees,
In fancy, fair St. Agnes in her bed,
But dares not look behind, or all the charm is fled.

Soon, trembling, in her soft and chilly nest,
In sort of wakeful swoon, perplexed she lay,
Until the poppied warmth of sleep oppressed
Her soothèd limbs, and soul fatigued away;
Flown, like a thought, until the morrow-day;
Blissfully havened both from joy and pain;
Clasped like a missal where swart Paynims pray;
Blinded alike from sunshine and from rain,
As though a rose should shut, and be a bud again.

Stol'n to this paradise, and so entranced,
Porphyro gazed upon her empty dress,
And listen'd to her breathing, if it chanced
To wake into a slumberous tenderness;
Which when he heard, that minute did he bless,
And breathed himself: then from the closet crept,
Noiseless as fear in a wide wilderness,
And over the hushed carpet, silent, stepped,
And 'tween the curtains peep'd, where, lo!—how fast
    she slept.

Then by the bedside, where the faded moon
Made a dim, silver twilight, soft he set
A table, and, half anguished, threw thereon
A cloth of woven crimson, gold, and jet:—
O for some drowsy Morphean amulet!
The boisterous, midnight, festive clarion,
The kettle-drum, and far-heard clarinet,
Affray his ears, though but in dying tone—
The hall door shuts again, and all the noise is gone.

And still she slept an azure-lidded sleep,
In blanchèd linen, smooth, and lavendered,
While he from forth the closet brought a heap
Of candied apple, quince, and plum, and gourd;
With jellies smoother than the creamy curd,
And lucent syrups, tinct with cinnamon;
Manna and dates, in argosy transferred
From Fez; and spicèd dainties, every one,
From silken Samarcand to cedared Lebanon.

These delicates he heaped with glowing hand
On golden dishes and in baskets bright

Of wreathèd silver: sumptuous they stand
In the retirèd quiet of the night,
Filling the chilly room with perfume light.—
"And now, my love, my seraph fair, awake!
Thou art my heaven, and I thine eremite:
Open thine eyes, for meek St. Agnes' sake,
Or I shall drowse beside thee, so my soul doth ache."

Thus whispering, his warm, unnervèd arm
Sank in her pillow. Shaded was her dream
By the dusk curtains:—'twas a midnight charm
Impossible to melt as icèd stream:
The lustrous salvers in the moonlight gleam;
Broad golden fringe upon the carpet lies:
It seemed he never, never could redeem
From such a stedfast spell his lady's eyes;
So mused awhile, entoiled in woofèd phantasies.

Awakening up, he took her hollow lute,—
Tumultuous,—and, in chords that tenderest be,
He played an ancient ditty, long since mute,
In Provence called, "La belle dame sans merci";
Close to her ear touching the melody;—
Wherewith disturbed, she uttered a soft moan:
He ceased—she panted quick—and suddenly
Her blue affrayèd eyes wide open shone:
Upon his knees he sank, pale as smooth-sculptured stone.

Her eyes were open, but she still beheld,
Now wide awake, the vision of her sleep:
There was a painful change, that nigh expelled
The blisses of her dream so pure and deep
At which fair Madeline began to weep,
And moan forth witless words with many a sigh;
While still her gaze on Porphyro would keep;
Who knelt, with joinèd hands and piteous eye,
Fearing to move or speak, she look'd so dreamingly.

"Ah, Porphyro!" said she, "but even now
Thy voice was at sweet tremble in mine ear,
Made tuneable with every sweetest vow;
And those sad eyes were spiritual and clear:
How changed thou art! how pallid, chill, and drear!

Give me that voice again, my Porphyro,
Those looks immortal, those complainings dear!
Oh leave me not in this eternal woe,
For if thou diest, my Love, I know not where to go."

Beyond a mortal man impassioned far
At these voluptuous accents, he arose,
Ethereal, flushed, and like a throbbing star
Seen mid the sapphire heaven's deep repose;
In her dream he melted, as the rose
Blendeth its odor with the violet—
Solution sweet: meantime the frost-wind blows
Like Love's alarum pattering the sharp sleet
Against the window-panes; St. Agnes' moon hath set.

'Tis dark: quick pattereth the flaw-blown sleet;
"This is no dream, my bride, my Madeline!"
'Tis dark: the icèd gusts still rave and beat;
"No dream, alas! alas! and woe is mine!
Porphyro will leave me here to fade and pine.—
Cruel! what traitor could thee hither bring?
I curse not, for my heart is lost in thine.
Though thou forsakest a deceivèd thing;—
A dove forlorn and lost with sick unprunèd wing."

"My Madeline! sweet dreamer! lovely bride!
Say, may I be for aye thy vassal blest?
Thy beauty's shield, heart-shap'd and vermeil-dyed?
Ah, silver shrine, here will I take my rest
After so many hours of toil and quest,
A famished pilgrim,—saved by miracle.
Though I have found, I will not rob thy nest
Saving of thy sweet self; if thou think'st well
To trust, fair Madeline, to no rude infidel.

"Hark! 'tis an elfin-storm from faery land,
Of haggard seeming, but a boon indeed:
Arise—arise! the morning is at hand—
The bloated wassaillers will never heed—
Let us away, my love, with happy speed;
There are no ears to hear, or eyes to see—
Drowned all in Rhenish and the sleepy mead:
Awake! arise! my love, and fearless be,
For o'er the southern moors I have a home for thee."

She hurried at his words, beset with fears,
For there were sleeping dragons all around,
At glaring watch, perhaps, with ready spears—
Down the wide stairs a darkling way they found.—
In all the house was heard no human sound.
A chain-drooped lamp was flickering by each door;
The arras, rich with horseman, hawk, and hound,
Flutter'd in the besieging wind's uproar;
And the long carpets rose along the gusty floor.

They glide, like phantoms, into the wide hall;
Like phantoms, to the iron porch they glide,
Where lay the Porter, in uneasy sprawl,
With a huge empty flagon by his side;
The wakeful bloodhound rose, and shook his hide,
But his sagacious eye an inmate owns:
By one, and one, the bolts full easy slide—
The chains lie silent on the footworn stones—
The key turns, and the door upon its hinges groans.

And they are gone: aye, ages long ago
These lovers fled away into the storm.
That night the Baron dreamt of many a woe,
And all his warrior-guests, with shade and form
Of witch, and demon, and large coffin-worm,
Were long be-nightmared. Angela the old
Died palsy-twitched, with meagre face deform;
The Beadsman, after thousand aves told,
For aye unsought-for slept among his ashes cold.

EDGAR ALLAN POE

TO HELEN

Helen, thy beauty is to me
Like those Nicèan barks of yore

EDGAR ALLAN POE (1809-1849), the son of traveling actors, was orphaned at the age of two. Brought up by John Allan of Virginia, he was a student for a time at both the University of Virginia and West Point. After breaking with his foster father in 1832, Poe earned a precarious livelihood as editor, critic, poet, and storywriter, achieving fame but neither financial security nor happiness.

That gently, o'er a perfumed sea,
  The weary way-worn wanderer bore
  To his own native shore.

On desperate seas long wont to roam,
  Thy hyacinth hair, thy classic face,
Thy Naiad airs have brought me home
  To the glory that was Greece
And the grandeur that was Rome.

Lo, in yon brilliant window-niche
  How statue-like I see thee stand,
  The agate lamp within thy hand,
Ah! Psyche, from the regions which
  Are holy land!

ULALUME

The skies they were ashen and sober;
  The leaves they were crispèd and sere—
  The leaves they were withering and sere;
It was night in the lonesome October
  Of my most immemorial year;
It was hard by the dim lake of Auber,
  In the misty mid region of Weir—
It was down by the dank tarn of Auber,
  In the ghoul-haunted woodland of Weir.

Here once, through an alley Titanic,
  Of cypress, I roamed with my Soul—
  Of cypress, with Psyche, my Soul.
These were days when my heart was volcanic
  As the scoriac rivers that roll—
  As the lavas that restlessly roll
Their sulphurous currents down Yaanek
  In the ultimate climes of the pole—
That groan as they roll down Mount Yaanek
  In the realms of the boreal pole.

Our talk had been serious and sober,
  But our thoughts they were palsied and sere—
  Our memories were treacherous and sere—
For we knew not the month was October,

And we marked not the night of the year—
  (Ah, night of all nights in the year!)
We noted not the dim lake of Auber—
  (Though once we had journeyed down here)—
Remembered not the dank tarn of Auber
Nor the ghoul-haunted woodland of Weir.

And now, as the night was senescent
  And star-dials pointed to morn—
  As the star-dials hinted of morn—
At the end of our path a liquescent
  And nebulous lustre was born,
Out of which a miraculous crescent
  Arose with a duplicate horn—
Astarte's bediamonded crescent
  Distinct with its duplicate horn.

And I said—"She is warmer than Dian:
  She rolls through an ether of sighs—
  She revels in a region of sighs:
She has seen that the tears are not dry on
  These cheeks, where the worm never dies
And has come past the stars of the Lion
  To point us the path to the skies—
  To the Lethean peace of the skies—
Come up, in despite of the Lion,
  To shine on us with her bright eyes—
Come up through the lair of the Lion,
  With love in her luminous eyes."

But Psyche, uplifting her finger,
  Said—"Sadly this star I mistrust—
  Her pallor I strangely mistrust:—
Oh, hasten!—oh, let us not linger!
  Oh, fly!—let us fly!—for we must."
In terror she spoke, letting sink her
  Wings till they trailed in the dust—
In agony sobbed, letting sink her
  Plumes till they trailed in the dust—
  Till they sorrowfully trailed in the dust.

I replied—"This is nothing but dreaming:
  Let us on by this tremulous light!

Let us bathe in this crystalline light!
Its Sibyllic splendor is beaming
    With Hope and in Beauty to-night:—
        See!—it flickers up the sky through the night!
Ah, we safely may trust to its gleaming,
    And be sure it will lead us aright—
We safely may trust to a gleaming
    That cannot but guide us aright,
        Since it flickers up to Heaven through the night."

Thus I pacified Psyche and kissed her,
    And tempted her out of her gloom—
    And conquered her scruples and gloom;
And we passed to the end of the vista,
    But were stopped by the door of a tomb—
    By the door of a legended tomb;
And I said—"What is written, sweet sister,
    On the door of this legended tomb?"
    She replied—"Ulalume—Ulalume!—
    'Tis the vault of thy lost Ulalume!"

Then my heart it grew ashen and sober
    As the leaves that were crispèd and sere—
    As the leaves that were withering and sere,
And I cried—"It was surely October
    On *this* very night of last year
    That I journeyed—I journeyed down here—
    That I brought a dread burden down here—
    On this night of all nights in the year,
    Ah, what demon has tempted me here?
Well I know, now, this dim lake of Auber—
    This misty mid region of Weir—
Well I know, now, this dank tarn of Auber,
    This ghoul-haunted woodland of Weir."

The
Victorian VI
Period

T HE distinction between Romantic and Victorian poetry is one that is made chiefly for the sake of historical convenience, so that the poetry of the disciples of Romanticism may be set apart from that of the pioneers. The dominant critical force behind the work of such men as Tennyson, Browning, Arnold, and Rossetti is their veneration for Wordsworth, Coleridge, Shelley, and Keats and their determination to carry on the poetic modes of their masters. Much of the poetry of Matthew Arnold, for instance, may be explained by the powerful effect upon him of the poems of Wordsworth and Shelley, which he read in his adolescence; and Keats was one of the most important early influences upon Tennyson.

While the continuity of the Victorians with the Romantics deserves major emphasis, the universal tendency of the younger to react against the elder cannot be ignored. Among the Victorians a strain of reaction against their earlier nineteenth-century forebears existed, and it is from this strain, growing stronger and stronger, that the poetic revolution of the 1920's is to emerge. For one thing, there is a reaction, even in Matthew Arnold, against the self-revelation found in Romantic poetry— the concept of poetry as the pouring out of one's own soul. Arnold and others are influenced by a doctrine widespread in the criticism of nineteenth-century France, that the function of the poet is not to display himself but to paint the world around him, that the poet himself is finally unimportant, and that self-revelation is in bad taste. While he wrote such romantic outpourings of the soul as *Dover Beach* and *A Summer Night,* Arnold sought also for objectivity in *The Scholar-Gypsy* and in his longer narrative poems.

Realism in Victorian poetry A concern with depicting the world outside the poet led to the growth of realism, also influenced by French examples, and already affecting the nineteenth-century novel. We note this most strongly in the poems of Robert Browning, who portrayed not so much himself as fully drawn characters of his own time and of earlier periods of history. Browning knew how to recreate the sights and sounds of Renaissance Italy—in a poem like *My Last Duchess,* how to capture the aristocratic disdain and the hidden evil of the lavish court of the Este princes at Ferrara. William Morris is one of the first poets to convey a portrait of the Middle Ages authentic to the degree of contemporary historical knowledge and to escape at last from the artificial "medievalism" of the Romantic poets.

Psychological themes The Victorian is also the first great age of psychological poetry, reflecting an interest important also in such Victorian novels as those of the Brontë sisters. Tennyson, Browning, Clough, and, toward the end of the century, George Meredith and Thomas Hardy, all probe deeply into the psychology of the individual. They give us characters designed to express philosophical points of view consonant with psychological states. Among the major examples of this type of verse are Browning's *Rabbi Ben Ezra* and his longer dramatic monologues such as *Andrea Del Sarto* and *Fra Lippo Lippi*. Victorian poetry exhibits a concern with the details of present reality, which is linked in the work of the greater poets with a quest for the distant, unattainable ideal.

The concern with realism and individual psychology is seen best perhaps in the development of the dramatic monologue, one of the Victorian age's distinctive poetic forms. Such poems had been written earlier; Byron's *Prisoner of Chillon* is a good example. But never was the form more widely used than in the latter half of the nineteenth century, and in Victorian hands it became a more flexible instrument than ever before, using the cadences of actual speech and probing psychological depths far beyond the scope of Byron. Although Browning was the dramatic monologue's greatest practitioner, such poems were written also by Tennyson, Arnold, Morris, Swinburne, and others. Perhaps we may say that the form reconciled the romantic self-revelatory tendency of the Victorians with their belief in the need for good taste and objectivity.

The techniques of Victorian poets There are few other poetic forms which can be called distinctively Victorian, but Victorian poets varied Romantic forms and extended their range. While using all the conventional stanzaic patterns of earlier poetry, they introduced original ones as well, such as those which Browning developed in poems like *Love Among the Ruins, A Grammarian's Funeral, A Toccata of Galuppi's,* and others. Tennyson, one of the most skillful versifiers in all English poetry, loved complex, controlled stanzaic patterns like that of *The Lady of Shalott,* where he could display his ingenuity in the handling of multiple rhymes and attain unusual effects of sound. His blank verse flows with an ease and naturalness which probably never has been equaled and which sets it apart from that of Robert Browning, who was also a master in this form. Swinburne took delight in long lines of controlled alliteration, in the use of the anapest, and in stanzas calling for the maximum of ingenuity in the number of required rhymes. He loved to adapt in English such elaborate Provençal and Italian forms as the canzone and sestina (see glossary). Arnold was probably one of the first experimenters with free verse (see glossary), although it was given its greatest currency by Walt Whitman in America. Poe's experiments with repetition and refrain were not always successful, but though *Ulalume* is not a great poem, it is an interesting illustration of the metrical experimentation in which he delighted. The metrical experiments of the Victorians were to culminate toward the end of the century in the sprung rhythm (see glossary) of Gerard Manley Hopkins.

Browning is important for the changes he effected in the language of poetry. In his dramatic monologues, he used blank verse which captured the cadences of ordinary speech in order to portray the shifts and stops of thought going through the human mind. The seeming harshness of his blank verse lines is a consciously developed poetic instrument, as is his use of a diction in marked contrast to the elevated language of the Romantic poets and of most of his Victorian contemporaries. Walt Whitman extended poetic diction to include a vocabulary closely linked to American democratic ideals and an expanding frontier. He sought a deliberate break from the poetic media of the old world.

Victorian poets, like their Romantic predecessors, conceived of poetry as a vehicle for philosophy, and much of their work is deliberately didactic. Matthew Arnold regarded poetry as the perfect instrument for the moral elevation of mankind, and he valued Wordsworth for this power in him. The intellectual concerns of Victorian poetry reflect very closely the conflicts and dilemmas of the time, and even those poems which are not deliberately didactic in intent show the effects of deep spiritual questioning.

The challenging of old beliefs Although it is true that in every age there has been a challenging of traditional ideas and values—for old beliefs must always face the competition of the new—the spiritual questioning and the intellectual conflicts of the Victorian age are acute. The settled values of rural England were disappearing under the impact of the accelerating Industrial Revolution, with peaceful villages giving way to crowded city slums and human values yielding to an expanding imperial economy. There is a literature of vehement social protest, most marked perhaps in the novel but an important force also in poetry. William Morris and others express their social dissatisfaction in a nostalgia for the Middle Ages, with its simple system of hand craftsmanship in which the laborer could maintain his self-respect. The Victorian era is one in which poetry comes to be used as an instrument for attack upon the established system. In this the poets had Shelley as their example. Much of Morris' later poetry, written for socialist newspapers, is frankly propagandistic and of little value. Perhaps only in Elizabeth Barrett Browning and the early Swinburne do we find a true poetic quality in political and social protest.

Even more marked in Victorian poetry is the reflection of two great challenges to accepted religious belief—the doctrine of evolution expressed by Charles Darwin in his *On the Origin of Species* (1859) and the new higher criticism of the Bible, which, for some Victorians, was destroying the essential bases of Christianity. By the mid-nineteenth century the paleological and archaeological techniques of classical scholarship had developed to a high degree, and it was perhaps inevitable that these techniques for determining the age and authenticity of Greek and Latin texts should be applied to the Bible. The movement began in Germany and spread to England, bearing its most sensational fruit in the work of John William Colenso, Bishop of Natal. The Biblical critics were themselves religious men, but their conclusions about the reliability of parts of Scripture seemed to many to destroy the value of all Scripture, for they dealt with the mysterious and unassailable word of God in terms of the writings of men, with their human errors of copying and translating. The growth of religious skepticism to which it gave rise was furthered by the appearance in France in 1863 of Ernest Renan's *Life of Jesus,* with its shocking conclusion that Jesus, though the greatest man in history, was nevertheless mortal.

Much of Victorian poetry reflects a search for belief in the face of this new skepticism and an awareness of the problems created by science and Biblical criticism. In Tennyson and Browning we have a constant reaffirmation of the old values with an acceptance of the new science and the potentialities for mankind inherent in it. Browning ignored the question of the Bible's authenticity, regarding it as unimportant, for he believed that Christianity's justification lay in its value for mankind, and of this value he had no doubt. Yet in poem after poem he explored the implications of the new Biblical scholarship. In Tennyson's *Ulysses* is recorded, perhaps most notably, the poet's determination to follow knowledge wherever it may lead. In Matthew Arnold the conflict between the old and the new is most marked. We have in the Victorian age much poetry which is profoundly Christian—some of the best of Browning, Tennyson, Coventry Patmore, Arthur Hugh Clough, Christina Rossetti, and Gerard Manley Hopkins. Indeed the age is also one of great religious reawakening, with its Oxford movement and its growth of evangelicalism. But we have also poetry which is deliberately unchristian, most notably that of Meredith and Swinburne and, toward the close of the century, that of A. E. Housman.

The Victorian age is remarkable not only for the great quantity of poetry which it produced but also for the number of long, sustained poetic enterprises. Tennyson's *In Memoriam* is the triumph of a lifetime. Another of the great poetic achievements of the age is Browning's *The Ring and the Book,* but even one of its twelve books would be far too long for inclusion here. Almost all the poets wrote long narratives: Arnold his *Tristram and Iseult* and *Sohrab and Rustum,* Tennyson his *Idylls of the King* and many others, and Morris his book-length Norse saga,

Sigurd the Volsung, his *Life and Death of Jason,* and the collection of versified tales from medieval and classical legendry which he gathered together as *The Earthly Paradise.* Many sonnet sequences were written, such as those of E. B. Browning and D. G. Rossetti. Victorian poets were confident in their craft, aware of the long tradition of English poetry which they inherited, willing to use it, and unafraid to enlarge it. The number of skillful poets was vast, and they wrote for a reading public larger than ever before.

FOR FURTHER READING:

Buckley, Jerome H. *The Victorian Temper.* Cambridge, Mass., 1951.

Irvine, William. *Apes, Angels and Victorians.* New York, 1955.

Faverty, F. E. *The Victorian Poets: A Guide to Research.* Cambridge, Mass., 1956.

Johnson, E. D. H. *The Alien Vision of Victorian Poetry.* Princeton, 1952.

Lucas, F. L. *Ten Victorian Poets.* 2nd ed. New York, 1940.

VI

THE VICTORIAN PERIOD

THE DRAMATIC MONOLOGUE

THE dramatic monologue has its origins perhaps in the soliloquy which Elizabethan dramatists developed as a means of making clear to an audience what could not be presented directly through action and dialogue, most notably the conscience of a character. As perfected by Browning, the dramatic monologue does much more than this. While it reveals the mind of the speaker, its focus usually is upon some other person, and there is often an auditor whose presence gives additional depth and meaning to what the speaker is saying, by unspoken but clearly understood responses. In *My Last Duchess,* for instance, the duke's words are conditioned by the behavior of the visiting emissary he is entertaining, and the focus is upon the dead duchess whose portrait furnishes the occasion for her husband's speech. In *Soliloquy of the Spanish Cloister* Brother Lawrence emerges as fully as the vituperative speaker, although in this poem there is no imaginary auditor. We have a total dramatic situation. We see Brother Lawrence at the other end of the garden, watering his flowerpots, and the speaker muttering to himself in envy while he waits for the bell to call him to prayer. So also, in *The Bishop Orders His Tomb at Saint Praxed's Church,* the presence of the unfilial sons about the bed of the dying bishop provides a dramatic context for his thoughts and gives poignancy and meaning to the manner in which he finally begs for his tomb. Out of this situation, we gradually learn the details of his long, sordid career.

We must note also that while the Elizabethan dramatic soliloquy made its point by direct statement, the principal device of Browning's dramatic monologue is dramatic irony (see glossary). The speaker is never fully aware of the implications of what he is saying or thinking and reveals to the reader dimensions of his own personality which were better hid; the duke of *My Last Duchess* shows his own cruelty and avarice, laying them bare to the go-between in the new marriage settlement he is trying so eagerly to arrange. The speaker of *Soliloquy of the Spanish Cloister,* while priding himself on his piety, makes clear that he is a religious hypocrite. Browning's dramatic monologues draw their effect not from the mere revelation of an individual mind but from an entire dramatic context, which is established by the words of a single speaker and supplemented by setting, audience, and the adept use of the nuances of language.

Tennyson's dramatic monologues are much simpler than Browning's. They also depend upon setting, but for his dramatic context Tennyson is content usually to rely upon the reader's familiarity with the classical legend from which the speaker is drawn, as in *Ulysses* and *Tithonus*. Unlike Browning, Tennyson does not create original characters in original situations. Tennyson also relies more fully than Browning upon direct statement to make his points. *Ulysses,* for instance, is a didactic poem in which a classical hero is used to proclaim a view of life which is the reason for the poem: mankind's need to pursue knowlege and experience in spite of danger. For this purpose Tennyson uses not the Ulysses of Homer, who wished only to reach home and rest, but the Ulysses who appears in *Dante's Inferno,* urging his men to voyage onward forever, because it is in the nature of mankind never to rest from travel and adventure. Here is Tennyson's answer to the conflict raised by Darwin and evolution.

FOR FURTHER READING:

DeVane, William C. *Browning's Parleying: The Autobiography of a Mind.* New Haven, Conn., 1927.

Honan, Park. *Browning's Characters: A Study in Technique.* New Haven, Conn., 1961.

Langbaum, Robert. *The Poetry of Experience.* New York, 1957.

Raymond, W. O. *The Infinite Moment and Other Essays in Robert Browning.* Toronto, 1950.

ALFRED, LORD TENNYSON

ULYSSES

It little profits that an idle king,
By this still hearth, among these barren crags,
Matched with an agèd wife, I mete and dole

ALFRED, LORD TENNYSON (1809-1892) was educated at Trinity College, Cambridge, where he associated with young men of literary tastes, including Arthur Henry Hallam, whose early death was one of the most profoundly moving events in the poet's life. In 1850 he was appointed poet laureate of England, and in 1883 he was elevated to the peerage.

Unequal laws unto a savage race,
That hoard, and sleep, and feed, and know not me.
I cannot rest from travel; I will drink
Life to the lees: All times I have enjoyed
Greatly, have suffered greatly, both with those
That loved me, and alone; on shore, and when
Through scudding drifts the rainy Hyades
Vext the dim sea; I am become a name;
For always roaming with a hungry heart
Much have I seen and known; cities of men,
And manners, climates, councils, governments,
Myself not least, but honored of them all;
And drunk delight of battle with my peers,
Far on the ringing plains of windy Troy.
I am a part of all that I have met.
Yet all experience is an arch wherethrough
Gleams that untraveled world whose margin fades
Forever and forever when I move.
How dull it is to pause, to make an end,
To rust unburnished, not to shine in use!
As though to breathe were life! Life piled on life
Were all too little, and of one to me
Little remains; but every hour is saved
From that eternal silence, something more,
A bringer of new things; and vile it were
For some three suns to store and hoard myself,
And this gray spirit yearning in desire
To follow knowledge like a sinking star,
Beyond the utmost bound of human thought.
　　This is my son, mine own Telemachus,
To whom I leave the sceptre and the isle—
Well-loved of me, discerning to fulfill
This labor, by slow prudence to make mild
A rugged people, and thro' soft degrees
Subdue them to the useful and the good.
Most blameless is he, centred in the sphere
Of common duties, decent not to fail
In offices of tenderness, and pay
Meet adoration to my household gods,
When I am gone. He works his work, I mine.
　　There lies the port; the vessel puffs her sail:
There gloom the dark broad seas. My mariners,
Souls that have toiled, and wrought, and thought with me—

That ever with a frolic welcome took
The thunder and the sunshine, and opposed
Free hearts, free foreheads—you and I are old;
Old age hath yet his honor and his toil.
Death closes all; but something ere the end,
Some work of noble note, may yet be done,
Not unbecoming men that strove with gods.
The lights begin to twinkle from the rocks;
The long day wanes; the slow moon climbs; the deep
Moans round with many voices. Come, my friends,
'Tis not too late to seek a newer world.
Push off, and sitting well in order smite
The sounding furrows; for my purpose holds
To sail beyond the sunset, and the baths
Of all the western stars, until I die.
It may be that the gulfs will wash us down:
It may be we shall touch the Happy Isles,
And see the great Achilles, whom we knew.
Tho' much is taken, much abides; and tho'
We are not now that strength which in old days
Moved earth and heaven, that which we are, we are—
One equal temper of heroic hearts,
Made weak by time and fate, but strong in will
To strive, to seek, to find, and not to yield.

TITHONUS

The woods decay, the woods decay and fall,
The vapors weep their burthen to the ground,
Man comes and tills the field and lies beneath,
And after many a summer dies the swan.
Me only cruel immortality
Consumes; I wither slowly in thine arms,
Here at the quiet limit of the world,
A white-haired shadow roaming like a dream
The ever-silent spaces of the East,
Far-folded mists, and gleaming halls of morn.
   Alas! for this gray shadow, once a man—
So glorious in his beauty and thy choice,
Who madest him thy chosen, that he seemed
To his great heart none other than a god!

I asked thee, "Give me immortality."
Then didst thou grant mine asking with a smile,
Like wealthy men who care not how they give.
But thy strong Hours indignant worked their wills,
And beat me down and marred and wasted me,
And though they could not end me, left me maimed
To dwell in presence of immortal youth,
Immortal age beside immortal youth,
And all I was in ashes. Can thy love,
Thy beauty, make amends, though even now,
Close over us, the silver star, thy guide,
Shines in those tremulous eyes that fill with tears
To hear me? Let me go; take back thy gift.
Why should a man desire in any way
To vary from the kindly race of men,
Or pass beyond the goal of ordinance
Where all should pause, as is most meet for all?
    A soft air fans the cloud apart; there comes
A glimpse of that dark world where I was born.
Once more the old mysterious glimmer steals
From thy pure brows, and from thy shoulders pure,
And bosom beating with a heart renewed.
Thy cheek begins to redden through the gloom,
Thy sweet eyes brighten slowly close to mine,
Ere yet they blind the stars, and the wild team
Which love thee, yearning for thy yoke, arise
And shake the darkness from their loosened manes,
And beat the twilight into flakes of fire.
    Lo! ever thus thou growest beautiful
In silence; then, before thine answer given,
Departest, and thy tears are on my cheek.
    Why wilt thou ever scare me with thy tears,
And make me tremble lest a saying learnt,
In days far-off, on that dark earth, be true?
"The gods themselves cannot recall their gifts."
    Ay me! ay me! with what another heart
In days far-off, and with what other eyes
I used to watch—if I be he that watched—
The lucid outline forming round thee; saw
The dim curls kindle into sunny rings;
Changed with thy mystic change, and felt my blood
Glow with the glow that slowly crimsoned all
Thy presence and thy portals, while I lay,

Mouth, forehead, eyelids, growing dewy-warm
With kisses balmier than half-opening buds
Of April, and could hear the lips that kissed
Whispering I knew not what of wild and sweet,
Like that strange song I heard Apollo sing,
While Ilion like a mist rose into towers.

Yet hold me not forever in thine East;
How can my nature longer mix with thine?
Coldly thy rosy shadows bathe me, cold
Are all thy lights, and cold my wrinkled feet
Upon thy glimmering thresholds, when the steam
Floats up from those dim fields about the homes
Of happy men that have the power to die,
And grassy barrows of the happier dead.
Release me, and restore me to the ground.
Thou seest all things, thou wilt see my grave;
Thou wilt renew thy beauty morn by morn,
I earth in earth forget these empty courts,
And thee returning on thy silver wheels.

TITHONUS is a dramatic monologue based on an elemental Greek myth. The story is told by various classical writers, but its outline is always the same. The goddess of the dawn, called Eos by the Greeks and Aurora by the Romans, fell in love with the young mortal, Tithonus. When the handsome youth was sure of the goddess' love, he requested the gift of immortality, which she willingly granted. She forgot, however, to give him eternal youth as well. Tennyson's poem begins at a point when Tithonus has aged cruelly, and youth has given way to palsy, rheum, and decrepitude. The entire poem is a plea for death, in iambics so calm that they reflect at once the unending eons of life that Tithonus already has lived and must continue to live, and the peace of death for which he so eloquently pleads. Nature itself reflects the dilemma of Tithonus. It constantly allows death to its creatures and plants, but in its renewal it is always there in much the same way that Keats' nightingale is eternal. The very image of the trees, dew, man, and the swan creates a vision of the stooped and tearful Tithonus, bent toward the earth in longing for oblivion:

The woods decay, the woods decay and fall,
The vapors weep their burthen to the ground,

$$\acute{\text{M}}\text{an}\ \overset{/}{\text{comes}}\ \overset{\cup}{\text{and}}\ \overset{/}{\text{tills}}\ \overset{\cup}{\text{the}}\ \overset{/}{\text{field}}\ \overset{\cup}{\text{and}}\ \overset{/}{\text{lies}}\ \overset{\cup}{\text{be}}\overset{/}{\text{neath,}}$$

Man comes and tills the field and lies beneath,
And after many a summer dies the swan.

The movement of the verse is achieved not by regularity of measure nor by the selection of any of the several feet available to the poet in English. Instead, the desired effect is gained by the cadence of units of language larger than the poetic foot. This we call rhythm, and its careful control can produce limitless variation within a single metrical pattern. As can be seen from the scansion above, the four lines of pentameter verse contain at most only two variations from strict iambics; yet we can compare these lines to those of Robert Southwell's *I Die Alive* (p. 99), another example of almost unvaried iambics, and find immense difference in the pace of the lines, the creation of mood, the pitch of emotion, and the support given to meaning. Tennyson's lines are made up of larger word groupings, in general, than Southwell's. The Renaissance poet uses a strong caesura, with the majority of his lines breaking near the middle. These phrases, clauses, and sentences are in careful balance or antithesis, and they establish a highly emotional state. In Tennyson's first four lines, only the initial one is broken at all. Each group of words represents a main clause, and all four lines comprise one tightly knit compound sentence. As the poem develops, Tennyson lengthens out this already elongated syntactical unit, to work primarily in verse paragraphs. He avoids caesura as much as possible and employs run-on lines or enjambment so that often a grammatical sequence will encompass two complete lines without a major break:

> A white-haired shadow roaming like a dream
> The ever-silent spaces of the East,

> Why should a man desire in any way
> To vary from the kindly race of men,

>   . . . and felt my blood
> Glow with the glow that slowly crimsoned all
> Thy presence and thy portals.

Even where there is punctuation in mid-line or at line-end, it is minor punctuation which barely slows the movement.

A second factor which contributes to serenity and calm is the poet's use of vowels. Again taking the first four lines, we find nine uses of short *a* and only three of the long vowel. Wherever the *o* is used, either alone or doubled or in diphthongs, the value is short rather than long. We can go through the entire poem in this way and find that the short vowels predominate to a marked degree; and in the frequent recurrence of vowels of similar sound, Tennyson is able to capture a delicate half-rhyme, sometimes internal, sometimes at line endings. Added to this is a considerable amount of repetition. Together these provide the effect of rhyme, but in a half-felt and distant way, not intruding upon the effects which the poet wishes to gain through his selection of blank verse:

> Ay me! ay me! *with what another* heart
>
> In days far-off, and *with what other* eyes
>
> I used to *watch*—If I be he that *watched*—
>
> The lucid outline forming round thee saw
>
> The dim curls kindle into sunny rings;
>
> *Changed* with thy mys tic *change,* and felt my blood
>
> *Glow* with the *glow* that slow ly crimsoned all
>
> Thy presence and thy portals, while I lay,
>
> Mouth, forehead, eyelids, grow ing dewy warm
>
> With *kissed* balm ier than half-opening buds
>
> Of April, and could hear the lips that *kissed*
>
> Whis pering I knew not what of wild and sweet,
>
> Like that strange song I heard Apollo sing,
>
> While Ilion like a mist rose into towers.

In this one sentence of fourteen lines we have *italicized* words and their variants which approximate repetition and have circled and connected words in which letter groupings provide the effect of rhyme. It is clear that Tennyson, though he repudiates conventional rhyme, does not neglect that aspect of his craft completely.

Tithonus is a dramatic monologue different from *Ulysses* but like *My Last Duchess* and *The Bishop Orders His Tomb at Saint Praxed's Church* in that there is an auditor to whom the monologist speaks. Even in *Soliloquy of the Spanish Cloister,* though the monk growls only to himself, we observe in the background the saintly figure of Brother Lawrence. A second figure in the monologue increases its dramatic quality and adds by his reaction further commentary on the speaker. The tears of the immortal Eos, which she weeps out of pity for Tithonus, add to our belief in the pathos of his situation.

The situation, however, is unique, and we wonder what may have prompted Tennyson's choice of subject. What may we learn from Tithonus' plight? No reader will ever be faced with immortality, nor do we wish to be taught how to ask for death. It is believed that part of the poet's urge to write such a poem came from Tennyson's melancholy over the death of his friend, Arthur Hallam, for whom he wrote *In Memoriam.* The search for rest and peace was strong in Tennyson. But Tithonus is also the poet's essay upon the very human longing for immortality. The poem is a commentary not upon men who have gone to dwell with goddesses but upon this life in this world: "Why should a man desire in any way/ To vary from the kindly race of men." Immortality is not possible for man, despite the myth of Tithonus; his aging but never dying is of no interest to us. We must read in his story the implication that it is experience and the world which age around us as we ourselves move toward death. Experience and the world grow tedious in the same way that the body of the mythical Tithonus grows wrinkled and bent. We see then that even if we could live forever, the prospect would not be bright. We would continue to live after all our friends had departed, after the life we knew had altered, and after the cultures we understood and admired had passed away. Without the things we love, existence— even in the midst of a paradise and in sight of transcendent beauty—is inexpressibly wearisome:

> Thou wilt renew thy beauty morn by morn,
> I earth in earth forget these empty courts,
> And thee returning on thy silver wheels.

Even if eternal youth were granted with eternal life, these same conditions would obtain. Tennyson shows us this through the figure of Eos, who weeps tears upon the cheeks of her beloved and who leaves his side speechless because she cannot bear the agony of telling him that "The gods themselves cannot recall their gifts." The commentary on immortality is then complete: to live forever among the race of men is not under any conditions to be desired.

ROBERT BROWNING

MY LAST DUCHESS

Ferrara

That's my last Duchess painted on the wall,
Looking as if she were alive. I call
That piece a wonder, now: Frà Pandolf's hands
Worked busily a day, and there she stands.
Will't please you sit and look at her? I said
"Frà Pandolf" by design, for never read
Strangers like you that pictured countenance,
The depth and passion of its earnest glance,
But to myself they turned (since none puts by
The curtain I have drawn for you, but I)
And seemed as they would ask me, if they durst,
How such a glance came there; so, not the first
Are you to turn and ask thus. Sir 'twas not
Her husband's presence only, called that spot
Of joy into the Duchess' cheek: perhaps
Frà Pandolf chanced to say, "Her mantle laps
Over my lady's wrist too much," or "Paint
Must never hope to reproduce the faint
Half-flush that dies along her throat." Such stuff
Was courtesy, she thought, and cause enough
For calling up that spot of joy. She had
A heart—how shall I say?—too soon made glad,
Too easily impressed; she liked whate'er
She looked on, and her looks went everywhere.
Sir, 'twas all one! My favor at her breast,
The drooping of the daylight in the West,
The bough of cherries some officious fool
Broke in the orchard for her, the white mule
She rode with round the terrace—all and each
Would draw from her alike the approving speech,
Or blush, at least. She thanked men,—good! but thanked
Somehow—I know not how—as if she ranked

ROBERT BROWNING (1812-1889), born in a suburb of London, was educated by private tutors and spent six months at the University of London. His earliest works were plays and obscure, difficult, long poems. In 1846 Browning eloped to Italy with the poetess Elizabeth Barrett; he spent most of the remainder of his life abroad, where he produced his finest poetry. He died in Venice.

My gift of a nine-hundred-years-old name
With anybody's gift. Who'd stoop to blame
This sort of trifling? Even had you skill
In speech—which I have not—to make your will
Quite clear to such an one, and say, "Just this
Or that in you disgusts me; here you miss,
Or there exceed the mark"—and if she let
Herself be lessoned so, nor plainly set
Her wits to yours, forsooth, and made excuse—
E'en then would be some stooping; and I choose
Never to stoop. Oh, sir, she smiled, no doubt,
Whene'er I passed her; but who passed without
Much the same smile? This grew; I gave commands;
Then all smiles stopped together. There she stands
As if alive. Will't please you rise? We'll meet
The company below, then. I repeat,
The Count your master's known munificence
Is ample warrant that no just pretense
Of mine for dowry will be disallowed;
Though his fair daughter's self, as I avowed
At starting, is my object. Nay, we'll go
Together down, sir. Notice Neptune, though,
Taming a sea-horse, thought a rarity,
Which Claus of Innsbruck cast in bronze for me!

SOLILOQUY OF THE SPANISH CLOISTER

Gr-r-r—there go, my heart's abhorrence!
　　Water your damned flower-pots, do!
If hate killed men, Brother Lawrence,
　　God's blood, would not mine kill you!
What? your myrtle-bush wants trimming?
　　Oh, that rose has prior claims—
Needs its leaden vase filled brimming?
　　Hell dry you up with its flames!

At the meal we sit together:
　　Salve tibi! I must hear
Wise talk of the kind of weather,
　　Sort of season, time of year:
Not a plenteous cork-crop; scarcely
　　Dare we hope oak-galls, I doubt;

What's the Latin name for "parsley"?
　　What's the Greek name for Swine's Snout?

Whew! We'll have our platter burnished,
　　Laid with care on our own shelf!
With a fire-new spoon we're furnished,
　　And a goblet for ourself,
Rinsed like something sacrificial
　　Ere 'tis fit to touch our chaps—
Marked with L for our initial!
　　(He-he! There his lily snaps!)

Saint, forsooth! While brown Dolores
　　Squats outside the Convent bank
With Sanchicha, telling stories,
　　Steeping tresses in the tank,
Blue-black, lustrous, thick like horsehairs
　　—Can't I see his dead eye glow,
Bright as 'twere a Barbary corsair's?
　　(That is, if he'd let it show!)

When he finishes refection,
　　Knife and fork he never lays
Cross-wise, to my recollection,
　　As do I, in Jesu's praise.
I the Trinity illustrate,
　　Drinking watered orange-pulp—
In three sips the Arian frustrate;
　　While he drains his at one gulp.

Oh, those melons! If he's able
　　We're to have a feast! so nice!
One goes to the Abbot's table,
　　All of us get each a slice.
How go on your flowers? None double?
　　Not one fruit-sort can you spy?
Strange!—And I, too, at such trouble
　　Keep them close-nipped on the sly!

There's a great text in Galatians,
　　Once you trip on it, entails
Twenty-nine distinct damnations,
　　One sure, if another fails:

If I trip him just a-dying,
    Sure of heaven as sure can be,
Spin him round and send him flying
    Off to hell, a Manichee?

Or, my scrofulous French novel
    On gray paper with blunt type!
Simply glance at it, you grovel
    Hand and foot in Belial's gripe;
If I double down its pages
    At the woeful sixteenth print,
When he gathers his greengages,
    Ope a sieve and slip it in 't?

Or, there's Satan!—one might venture
    Pledge one's soul to him, yet leave
Such a flaw in the indenture
    As he'd miss till, past retrieve,
Blasted lay that rose-acacia
    We're so proud of! *Hy, Zy, Hine* . . .
'St, there's Vespers! *Plena gratiâ,*
    Ave, Virgo! Gr-r-r—you swine!

THE BISHOP ORDERS HIS TOMB AT SAINT PRAXED'S CHURCH

Rome, 15—

Vanity, saith the preacher, vanity!
Draw round my bed; is Anselm keeping back?
Nephews—sons mine . . . ah, God, I know not! Well—
She, men would have to be your mother once,
Old Gandolf envied me, so fair she was!
What's done is done, and she is dead beside,
Dead long ago, and I am Bishop since,
And as she died so must we die ourselves,
And thence ye may perceive the world's a dream.
Life, how and what is it? As here I lie
In this state-chamber, dying by degrees,
Hours and long hours in the dead night, I ask
"Do I live, am I dead?" Peace, peace seems all.
Saint Praxed's ever was the church for peace;
And so, about this tomb of mine. I fought

With tooth and nail to save my niche, ye know—
Old Gandolf cozened me, despite my care;
Shrewd was that snatch from out the corner South
He graced his carrion with, God curse the same!
Yet still my niche is not so cramped but thence
One sees the pulpit o' the epistle-side,
And somewhat of the choir, those silent seats,
And up into the aery dome where live
The angels, and a sunbeam's sure to lurk;
And I shall fill my slab of basalt there,
And 'neath my tabernacle take my rest,
With those nine columns round me, two and two,
The odd one at my feet where Anselm stands:
Peach-blossom marble all, the rare, the ripe
As fresh-poured red wine of a mighty pulse.
—Old Gandolf with his paltry onion-stone,
Put me where I may look at him! True peach,
Rosy and flawless: how I earned the prize!
Draw close; that conflagration of my church—
What then? So much was saved if aught were missed!
My sons, ye would not be my death? Go dig
The white-grape vineyard where the oil-press stood,
Drop water gently till the surface sink,
And if ye find . . . Ah, God, I know not, I! . . .
Bedded in store of rotten fig-leaves soft,
And corded up in a tight olive-frail,
Some lump, ah God, of *lapis lazuli,*
Big as a Jew's head cut off at the nape,
Blue as a vein o'er the Madonna's breast. . . .
Sons, all have I bequeathed you, villas, all,
That brave Frascati villa with its bath,
So, let the blue lump poise between my knees,
Like God the Father's globe on both his hands
Ye worship in the Jesu Church so gay,
For Gandolf shall not choose but see and burst!
Swift as a weaver's shuttle fleet our years:
Man goeth to the grave, and where is he?
Did I say basalt for my slab, sons? Black—
'Twas ever antique-black I meant! How else
Shall ye contrast my frieze to come beneath?
The bas-relief in bronze ye promised me,
Those Pans and Nymphs ye wot of, and perchance
Some tripod, thyrsus, with a vase or so,

The Saviour at his sermon on the mount,
Saint Praxed in a glory, and one Pan
Ready to twitch the Nymph's last garment off,
And Moses with the tables . . . but I know
Ye mark me not! What do they whisper thee,
Child of my bowels, Anselm? Ah, ye hope
To revel down my villas while I gasp
Bricked o'er with beggar's moldy travertine
Which Gandolf from his tomb-top chuckles at!
Nay, boys, ye love me—all of jasper, then!
'Tis jasper ye stand pledged to, lest I grieve.
My bath must needs be left behind, alas!
One block, pure green as a pistachio-nut,
There's plenty jasper somewhere in the world—
And have I not Saint Praxed's ear to pray
Horses for ye, and brown Greek manuscripts,
And mistresses with great smooth marbly limbs?
—That's if ye carve my epitaph aright,
Choice Latin, picked phrase, Tully's every word,
No gaudy ware like Gandolf's second line—
Tully, my masters? Ulpian serves his need!
And then how I shall lie through centuries,
And hear the blessed mutter of the Mass,
And see God made and eaten all day long,
And feel the steady candle-flame, and taste
Good strong thick stupefying incense-smoke!
For as I lie here, hours of the dead night,
Dying in state and by such slow degrees,
I fold my arms as if they clasped a crook,
And stretch my feet forth straight as stone can point,
And let the bedclothes, for a mortcloth, drop
Into great laps and folds of sculptor's-work;
And as yon tapers dwindle, and strange thoughts
Grow, with a certain humming in my ears,
About the life before I lived this life,
And this life too, popes, cardinals and priests,
Saint Praxed at his sermon on the mount,
Your tall pale mother with her talking eyes,
And new-found agate urns as fresh as day,
And marble's language, Latin pure, discreet—
Aha, ELUCESCEBAT quoth our friend?
No Tully, said I, Ulpian at the best!
Evil and brief hath been my pilgrimage.

All *lapis,* all sons! Else I give the Pope
My villas! Will ye ever eat my heart?
Ever your eyes were as a lizard's quick,
They glitter like your mother's for my soul,
Or ye would heighten my impoverished frieze,
Piece out its starved design, and fill my vase
With grapes, and add a visor and a term,
And to the tripod ye would tie a lynx
That in his struggle throws the thyrsus down,
To comfort me on my entablature
Whereon I am to lie till I must ask
"Do I live, am I dead?" There, leave me, there!
For ye have stabbed me with ingratitude
To death—ye wish it—God, ye wish it! Stone—
Gritstone, a-crumble! Clammy squares which sweat
As if the corpse they keep were oozing through—
And no more *lapis* to delight the world!
Well; go! I bless ye. Fewer tapers there,
But in a row; and, going, turn your backs—
Aye, like departing altar-ministrants,
And leave me in my church, the church for peace,
That I may watch at leisure if he leers—
Old Gandolf—at me, from his onion-stone,
As still he envied me, so fair she was!

VI

THE VICTORIAN PERIOD

SPIRITUAL QUESTIONING

THAT large segment of Victorian poetry which reflects the artist's search for identity and for stability in a world of conflicting values appears in many forms: in the musings of the imaginary persons of dramatic monologues, in the reinterpretation of ancient legends, in long philosophical poems, and in such brief lyrical statements as Tennyson's *Flower in the Crannied Wall,* which in its six lines reflects the poet's longing to understand all things earthly and spiritual. The most monumental work of this search for the meaning of life is *In Memoriam,* a kind of autobiography of the soul, which Tennyson began upon the death of his friend Arthur Henry Hallam in 1833 and did not complete until 1850. In sections which he wrote at various times, the poet reflects his own doubt, despair, and disillusion, moving finally to a triumphant affirmation of traditional religion to which only a blind faith can bring him. In the short fragment *Oh Yet We Trust,* we have one of Tennyson's most lyrical statements of his need for faith, coupled with an awareness of his own smallness in the universe.

The spiritual affirmation at which Tennyson finally arrived and which Browning proclaimed throughout his career is missing from the poetry of Matthew Arnold. Arnold is the poet between two worlds, the one dead and the other incapable of being born, and his poetry is a record of his melancholy failure of belief. In later life Arnold did resolve his spiritual conflicts, but by that time he had virtually ceased to write poetry. Poems like *To Marguerite, Dover Beach,* and *A Summer Night* are the products of his youth, and in their tone of *Weltschmerz,* or worldpain (the German cannot really be translated), they reflect a state of the Victorian mind common also to the French and German poets Arnold admired.

In America the note of affirmation is struck most forcefully by Walt Whitman, but it is an affirmation not so much of God as of the dream of America, the dignity of the individual in a land of expanding horizons, the perfection of nature and the goodness of all mankind. Whitman and Arnold, writing at much the same time on opposite sides of the Atlantic, are perfect antitheses: Arnold, the sophisticated, intellectual European, steeped in classical learning, unable to find direction in human life; Whitman, the coarse, bluff, profane, self-educated, egotistical American, voicing the unrestrained optimism of the frontier, unplagued by any of Arnold's doubt or despair. Whitman's *When Lilacs Last in the Dooryard Bloom'd,* his elegy on the death of President Lincoln and one of his most sustained poetic achievements, is perhaps the finest example of how free verse can be used in English. While it mourns the death of a loved one, it is itself an affirmation of life. It may be compared in this respect with the quiet longing for death of Swinburne's *Garden of Proserpine,* a perfect example of the negation and longing for escape with which some poets met the spiritual conflicts of the Victorian age.

FOR FURTHER READING :

Buckley, Jerome H. *Tennyson, The Growth of a Poet.* Cambridge, Mass., 1960.

Eliot, T. S. "In Memoriam," *Selected Essays.* New York, 1950.

Johnson, W. Stacy. *The Voices of Matthew Arnold.* New Haven, Conn., 1961.

Nicolson, Harold. *Tennyson: Aspects of his Life, Character and Poetry.* Boston, 1923.

Tinker, C. B., and H. F. Lowry. *The Poetry of Matthew Arnold: A Commentary.* New York, 1940.

Trilling, Lionel. *Matthew Arnold,* 2nd ed. New York, 1949.

ALFRED, LORD TENNYSON

from IN MEMORIAM

I

I held it truth, with him who sings
    To one clear harp in divers tones,
    That men may rise on stepping-stones
Of their dead selves to higher things.

But who shall so forecast the years
    And find in loss a gain to match?
    Or reach a hand through time to catch
The far-off interest of tears?

Let Love clasp Grief lest both be drowned,
    Let darkness keep her raven gloss.
    Ah, sweeter to be drunk with loss,
To dance with Death, to beat the ground,

Than that the victor Hours should scorn
The long result of love, and boast,
"Behold the man that loved and lost,
But all he was is overworn."

II

Old yew, which graspest at the stones
That name the underlying dead,
Thy fibers net the dreamless head,
Thy roots are wrapped about the bones.

The seasons bring the flower again,
And bring the firstling to the flock;
And in the dusk of thee the clock
Beats out the little lives of men.

O not for thee the glow, the bloom,
Who changest not in any gale,
Nor branding summer suns avail
To touch thy thousand years of gloom;

And gazing on thee, sullen tree,
Sick for thy stubborn hardihood,
I seem to fail from out my blood
And grow incorporate into thee.

VII

Dark house, by which once more I stand
Here in the long unlovely street,
Doors, where my heart was used to beat
So quickly, waiting for a hand,

A hand that can be clasped no more—
Behold me, for I cannot sleep,
And like a guilty thing I creep
At earliest morning to the door.

He is not here; but far away
The noise of life begins again,
And ghastly through the drizzling rain
On the bald street breaks the blank day.

XXVIII

The time draws near the birth of Christ.
　The moon is hid; the night is still;
　The Christmas bells from hill to hill
Answer each other in the mist.

Four voices of four hamlets round,
　From far and near, on mead and moor,
　Swell out and fail, as if a door
Were shut between me and the sound;

Each voice four changes on the wind,
　That now dilate, and now decrease,
　Peace and goodwill, goodwill and peace,
Peace and goodwill, to all mankind.

This year I slept and woke with pain,
　I almost wished no more to wake,
　And that my hold on life would break
Before I heard those bells again.

But they my troubled spirit rule,
　For they controlled me when a boy;
　They bring me sorrow touched with joy,
The merry merry bells of Yule.

L

Be near me when my light is low,
　When the blood creeps, and the nerves prick
　And tingle; and the heart is sick,
And all the wheels of being slow.

Be near me when the sensuous frame
　Is racked with pangs that conquer trust;
　And Time, a maniac scattering dust,
And Life, a Fury slinging flame.

Be near me when my faith is dry,
　And men the flies of latter spring,
　That lay their eggs, and sting and sing
And weave their petty cells and die.

Be near me when I fade away,
 To point the term of human strife,
 And on the low dark verge of life
The twilight of eternal day.

LIV

O yet we trust that somehow good
 Will be the final goal of ill,
 To pangs of nature, sins of will,
Defects of doubt, and taints of blood;

That nothing walks with aimless feet;
 That not one life shall be destroyed,
 Or cast as rubbish to the void,
When God hath made the pile complete;

That not a worm is cloven in vain;
 That not a moth with vain desire
 Is shriveled in a fruitless fire,
Or but subserves another's gain.

Behold, we know not anything;
 I can but trust that good shall fall
 At last—far off—at last, to all,
And every winter change to spring.

So runs my dream; but what am I?
 An infant crying in the night;
 An infant crying for the light,
And with no language but a cry.

CIV

The time draws near the birth of Christ;
 The moon is hid, the night is still;
 A single church below the hill
Is pealing, folded in the mist.

A single peal of bells below,
 That wakens at this hour of rest
 A single murmur in the breast,
That these are not the bells I know.

Like strangers' voices here they sound,
  In lands where not a memory strays,
  Nor landmark breathes of other days,
But all is new unhallowed ground.

CVI

Ring out, wild bells, to the wild sky,
  The flying cloud, the frosty light;
  The year is dying in the night;
Ring out, wild bells, and let him die.

Ring out the old, ring in the new,
  Ring, happy bells, across the snow;
  The year is going, let him go;
Ring out the false, ring in the true.

Ring out the grief that saps the mind,
  For those that here we see no more;
  Ring out the feud of rich and poor,
Ring in redress to all mankind.

Ring out a slowly dying cause,
  And ancient forms of party strife;
  Ring in the nobler modes of life,
With sweeter manners, purer laws.

Ring out the want, the care, the sin,
  The faithless coldness of the times;
  Ring out, ring out my mournful rimes,
But ring the fuller minstrel in.

Ring out false pride in place and blood,
  The civic slander and the spite;
  Ring in the love of truth and right,
Ring in the common love of good.

Ring out old shapes of foul disease;
  Ring out the narrowing lust of gold;
  Ring out the thousand wars of old,
Ring in the thousand years of peace.

Ring in the valiant man and free,
  The larger heart, the kindlier hand;

Ring out the darkness of the land,
Ring in the Christ that is to be.

FLOWER IN THE CRANNIED WALL

Flower in the crannied wall,
I pluck you out of the crannies,
I hold you here, root and all, in my hand,
Little flower—but *if* I could understand
What you are, root and all, and all in all,
I should know what God and man is.

ARTHUR HUGH CLOUGH

SAY NOT THE STRUGGLE NAUGHT AVAILETH

Say not the struggle naught availeth,
    The labor and the wounds are vain,
The enemy faints not, nor faileth,
    And as things have been they remain.

If hopes were dupes, fears may be liars;
    It may be, in yon smoke concealed,
Your comrades chase e'en now the fliers,
    And, but for you, possess the field.

For while the tired waves, vainly breaking,
    Seem here no painful inch to gain,
Far back, through creeks and inlets making,
    Comes silent, flooding in, the main.

And not by eastern windows only,
    When daylight comes, comes in the light,
In front, the sun climbs slow, how slowly,
    But westward, look, the land is bright.

ARTHUR HUGH CLOUGH (1819-1861) was born in Liverpool and spent part of his childhood in the United States. Upon his return to England, he was educated under Thomas Arnold at Rugby and later at Balliol College, Oxford. First a fellow of Oriel College, Oxford, he served later as professor of English at University College, London. He died in Florence, Italy, where he had journeyed for his health.

THE LATEST DECALOGUE

Thou shalt have one God only; who
Would be at the expense of two?
No graven images may be
Worshiped, except the currency.
Swear not at all; for, for thy curse
Thine enemy is none the worse.
At church on Sunday to attend
Will serve to keep the world thy friend.
Honor thy parents; that is, all
From whom advancement may befall.
Thou shalt not kill; but need'st not strive
Officiously to keep alive.
Do not adultery commit;
Advantage rarely comes of it.
Thou shalt not steal; an empty feat,
When it's so lucrative to cheat.
Bear not false witness; let the lie
Have time on its own wings to fly.
Thou shalt not covet, but tradition
Approves all forms of competition.

MATTHEW ARNOLD

DOVER BEACH

The sea is calm tonight,
The tide is full, the moon lies fair
Upon the straits;—on the French coast the light
Gleams and is gone; the cliffs of England stand,
Glimmering and vast, out in the tranquil bay.
Come to the window, sweet is the night-air!
Only, from the long line of spray
Where the sea meets the moon-blanched land,
Listen! you hear the grating roar
Of pebbles which the waves draw back, and fling,

MATTHEW ARNOLD (1822-1888) was the son of the famous educator, Dr. Thomas Arnold, headmaster of Rugby School. Matthew was educated at Rugby and at Balliol College, Oxford, and, like his good friend Arthur Hugh Clough, succeeded to a fellowship at Oriel College. In 1851 he was appointed an inspector of schools, in which position he spent most of the remainder of his career.

At their return, up the high strand,
Begin, and cease, and then again begin,
With tremulous cadence slow, and bring
The eternal note of sadness in.

Sophocles long ago
Heard it on the Ægæan, and it brought
Into his mind the turbid ebb and flow
Of human misery; we
Find also in the sound a thought,
Hearing it by this distant northern sea.

The Sea of Faith
Was once, too, at the full, and round earth's shore
Lay like the folds of a bright girdle furled.
But now I only hear
Its melancholy, long, withdrawing roar,
Retreating, to the breath
Of the night-wind, down the vast edges drear
And naked shingles of the world.

Ah, love, let us be true
To one another! for the world, which seems
To lie before us like a land of dreams,
So various, so beautiful, so new,
Hath really neither joy, nor love, nor light,
Nor certitude, nor peace, nor help for pain;
And we are here as on a darkling plain
Swept with confused alarms of struggle and flight,
Where ignorant armies clash by night.

TO MARGUERITE

Yes! in the sea of life enisled,
With echoing straits between us thrown,
Dotting the shoreless watery wild,
We mortal millions live *alone*.
The islands feel the enclasping flow,
And then their endless bounds they know.

But when the moon their hollows lights,
And they are swept by balms of spring,
And in their glens, on starry nights,

The nightingales divinely sing;
And lovely notes, from shore to shore,
Across the sounds and channels pour—

Oh! then a longing like despair
Is to their farthest caverns sent;
For surely once, they feel, we were
Parts of a single continent!
Now round us spreads the watery plain—
Oh, might our marges meet again!

Who ordered, that their longing's fire
Should be, as soon as kindled, cooled?
Who renders vain their deep desire?—
A god, a god their severance ruled!
And bade betwixt their shores to be
The unplumbed, salt, estranging sea.

A SUMMER NIGHT

In the deserted moon-blanched street,
How lonely rings the echo of my feet!
Those windows, which I gaze at, frown,
Silent and white, unopening down,
Repellent as the world—but see,
A break between the housetops shows
The moon! and, lost behind her, fading dim
Into the dewy dark obscurity
Down at the far horizon's rim,
Doth a whole tract of heaven disclose!

And to my mind the thought
Is on a sudden brought
Of a past night, and a far different scene.
Headlands stood out into the moonlit deep
As clearly as at noon;
The spring-tide's brimming flow
Heaved dazzlingly between;
Houses, with long white sweep,
Girdled the glistening bay;
Behind, through the soft air,
The blue haze-cradled mountains spread away.
That night was far more fair—

But the same restless pacings to and fro,
And the same vainly throbbing heart was there,
And the same bright, calm moon.

And the calm moonlight seems to say:
Hast thou then still the old unquiet breast,
Which neither deadens into rest,
Nor ever feels the fiery glow
That whirls the spirit from itself away,
But fluctuates to and fro,
Never by passion quite possessed
And never quite benumbed by the world's sway?—
And I, I know not if to pray
Still to be what I am, or yield and be
Like all the other men I see.

For most men in a brazen prison live,
Where, in the sun's hot eye,
With heads bent o'er their toil, they languidly
Their lives to some unmeaning taskwork give,
Dreaming of naught beyond their prison-wall.
And as, year after year,
Fresh products of their barren labor fall
From their tired hands, and rest
Never yet comes more near,
Gloom settles slowly down over their breast;
And while they try to stem
The waves of mournful thought by which
            they are prest
Death in their prison reaches them,
Unfreed, having seen nothing, still unblest.

And the rest, a few,
Escape their prison and depart
On the wide ocean of life anew.
There the freed prisoner, where'er his heart
Listeth, will sail;
Nor doth he know how there prevail,
Despotic on that sea,
Trade-winds which cross it from eternity.
Awhile he holds some false way, undebarred
By thwarting signs, and braves
The freshening wind and blackening waves,

And then the tempest strikes him; and between
The lightning-bursts is seen
Only a driving wreck,
And the pale master on his spar-strewn deck
With anguished face and flying hair
Grasping the rudder hard,
Still bent to make some port he knows not where,
Still standing for some false, impossible shore.
And sterner comes the roar
Of sea and wind, and through the deepening gloom
Fainter and fainter wreck and helmsman loom,
And he too disappears, and comes no more.

Is there no life, but these alone?
Madman or slave, must man be one?

Plainness and clearness without shadow of stain!
Clearness divine!

Ye heavens, whose pure dark regions have no sign
Of languor, though so calm, and, though so great,
Are yet untroubled and unpassionate;
Who, though so noble, share in the world's toil,
And, though so tasked, keep free from dust and soil!
I will not say that your mild deeps retain
A tinge, it may be, of their silent pain
Who have longed deeply once, and longed in vain—
But I will rather say that you remain
A world above man's head, to let him see
How boundless might his soul's horizons be,
How vast, yet of what clear transparency!
How it were good to abide there, and breathe free;
How fair a lot to fill
Is left to each man still!

A SUMMER NIGHT is a good example of the philosophic, reflective poem, infused with deep personal emotion, which the Victorians loved and wherein Arnold revealed the distinctive qualities of his mind and art. In this poem he expresses his own sense of alienation from society and at the same time his romantic longing for a beauty which he sees in the heavens above him. The poem, by its constant juxtaposition of images that reveal the sordidness of actual life against those that evoke the beauty of the summer night, maintains its opposition between a melancholy awareness of what man is and a fond longing for what he might be.

In the first paragraph, the alienation of the poet and the beauty of the night are held simultaneously before us. The street is "deserted," but it is also "moon-blanched." The windows are closed to him, indicating the inaccessibility of fellow human beings, but behind the housetops is the moon with its reminder of something beautiful beyond humanity— which "Doth a whole tract of heaven disclose!" We have melancholy but not despair, loneliness and alienation but an awareness also of something in the world greater and more beautiful than mankind or human fellowship.

The second paragraph restates in other terms the antithesis of the first. The moon reminds the poet of another beautiful night when he stood in the south of France and gazed out on the Mediterranean. This is the same moon, unchanging, and his sorrow is the same, constant:

> But the same restless pacings to and fro,
> And the same vainly throbbing heart was there,
> And the same bright, calm moon.

The image of moonlight serves also as a transition to the next paragraph; the poet's alienation from humanity begins to be explained through the poet's dilemma:

> And I, I know not if to pray
> Still to be what I am, or yield and be
> Like all the other men I see.

The succeeding paragraph is devoted to a moving description of what these "other men" are like. Arnold cannot be a part of society, "For most men in a brazen prison live," but he cannot any more live with the "unquiet breast," the restless anxiety which must accompany his isolation. Although he cannot accept the slavery of a mankind which lives in a perpetual prison and dies "Unfreed, having seen nothing, still unblest," he can find no real alternative.

Then one possibility is explored—blind, passionate rejection of the human condition and surrender to whatever forces may sweep man where they will. It is essentially a surrender of mind, and in this road lurks inevitable disaster. The paragraph is remarkable for the manner in which Arnold draws out the traditional metaphor of the ship at sea to indicate first the sense of freedom of the escaped prisoner and then the "Trade-winds which cross it from eternity," connoting the forces that mold man's destiny whether he will or not. The tension between the sense of freedom and the foreboding of inevitable destruction is maintained in the contrast between "freshening wind" and "blackening waves." In the final wreck we see the futility of the voyage, with the pale master.

> Still bent to make some port he knows not where,
> Still standing for some false, impossible shore.

This vivid picture of the madness of such escape prepares for the striking couplet in which Arnold puts in opposition such madness and the slavery which seems its only alternative:

> Is there no life, but these alone?
> Madman or slave, must man be one?

In the final paragraph the calmness of the summer moon is again contrasted to the turbulence of the shipwreck. The "plainness and clearness without shadow of stain" recalls the divinity in which the poet longs to believe and of which the beauty of the heavens above him seems to give some evidence. But the heavens, though pure and beautiful, are remote from mankind, "free from dust and soil." The heavens retain nothing of the pain of the men who gaze upon them, but they offer always a vision of the beauty and freedom to which the poet vainly aspires: "How boundless might his soul's horizons be." In this hope is the poet's only consolation.

A Summer Night presents a highly controlled and unified expression of the poet's frustration and poignant longing for an ideal which he sees reflected always above him but which he cannot attain. The poem is direct and straightforward in its expression, generally avoiding verbal ambiguities; although rich in imagery, much of it is of a traditional nature. The resources of metrics further the poem's simple expository tone. Although we may no longer share entirely the premises about mankind from which the poem springs, we can still be moved by the melancholy which it so superbly conveys.

WALT WHITMAN

WHEN LILACS LAST IN THE DOORYARD BLOOM'D

I

> When lilacs last in the dooryard bloom'd,
> And the great star early droop'd in the western sky in the night,
> I mourn'd, and yet shall mourn with ever-returning spring.

WALT WHITMAN (1819-1892) was born on Long Island, New York, the son of a carpenter. He served as a journalist in Brooklyn and New Orleans. His *Leaves of Grass*, published in 1855, attracted the attention of Ralph Waldo Emerson but otherwise received little notice. During the Civil War Whitman served indefatigably as a volunteer nurse; his health was impaired and he remained a partial invalid the rest of his life.

Ever-returning spring, trinity sure to me you bring,
Lilac blooming perennial and drooping star in the west,
And thought of him I love.

II

O powerful western fallen star!
O shades of night—O moody, tearful night!
O great star disappear'd—O the black murk that hides the star!
O cruel hands that hold me powerless—O helpless soul of me!
O harsh surrounding cloud that will not free my soul.

III

In the dooryard fronting an old farm-house near the white-wash'd palings,
Stands the lilac-bush tall-growing with heart-shaped leaves of rich green,
With many a pointed blossom rising delicate, with the perfume strong I
     love,
With every leaf a miracle—and from this bush in the dooryard,
With delicate-color'd blossoms and heart-shaped leaves of rich green,
A sprig with its flower I break.

IV

In the swamp in secluded recesses,
A shy and hidden bird is warbling a song.
Solitary the thrush,
The hermit withdrawn to himself, avoiding the settlements,
Sings by himself a song.

Song of the bleeding throat,
Death's outlet song of life, (for well dear brother I know,
If thou wast not granted to sing thou would'st surely die.)

V

Over the breast of the spring, the land, amid cities,
Amid lanes and through old woods, where lately the violets peep'd from
     the ground, spotting the gray debris,
Amid the grass in the fields each side of the lanes, passing the endless
     grass,
Passing the yellow-spear'd wheat, every grain from its shroud in the dark-
     brown fields uprisen,

Passing the apple-tree blows of white and pink in the orchards,
Carrying a corpse to where it shall rest in the grave,
Night and day journeys a coffin.

VI

Coffin that passes through lanes and streets,
Through day and night with the great cloud darkening the land,
With the pomp of the inloop'd flags with the cities draped in black,
With the show of the States themselves as of crape-veil'd women standing,
With processions long and winding and the flambeaus of the night,
With the countless torches lit, with the silent sea of faces and the unbared
      heads,
With the waiting depot, the arriving coffin, and the sombre faces,
With dirges through the night, with the thousand voices rising strong and
      solemn,
With all the mournful voices of the dirges pour'd around the coffin,
The dim-lit churches and the shuddering organs—where amid these you
      journey,
With the tolling tolling bells' perpetual clang,
Here, coffin that slowly passes,
I give you my sprig of lilac.

VII

(Nor for you, for one alone,
Blossoms and branches green to coffins all I bring,
For fresh as the morning, thus would I chant a song for you
      O sane and sacred death.

All over bouquets of roses,
O death, I cover you over with roses and early lilies,
But mostly and now the lilac that blooms the first,
Copious I break, I break the sprigs from the bushes,
With loaded arms I come, pouring for you,
For you and the coffins all of you O death.)

VIII

O western orb sailing the heaven,
Now I know what you must have meant as a month since I walk'd,
As I walk'd in silence the transparent shadowy night,
As I saw you had something to tell as you bent to me night after night,

As you droop'd from the sky low down as if to my side, (while the other
 stars all look'd on,)
As we wander'd together the solemn night, (for something I know not
 what kept me from sleep,)
As the night advanced, and I saw on the rim of the west how full you were
 of woe,
As I stood on the rising ground in the breeze in the cool transparent night,
As I watch'd where you pass'd and was lost in the netherward black of the
 night,
As my soul in its trouble dissatisfied sank, as where you sad orb,
Concluded, dropt in the night, and was gone.

IX

Sing on there in the swamp,
O singer bashful and tender, I hear your notes, I hear your call,
I hear, I come presently, I understand you,
But a moment I linger, for the lustrous star has detain'd me,
The star my departing comrade holds and detains me.

X

O how shall I warble myself for the dead one there I loved?
And how shall I deck my song for the large sweet soul that has gone?
And what shall my perfume be for the grave of him I love?

Sea-winds blown from east and west,
Blown from the Eastern sea and blown from the Western sea, till there on
 the prairies meeting,
These and with these and the breath of my chant,
I'll perfume the grave of him I love.

XI

O what shall I hang on the chamber walls?
And what shall the pictures be that I hang on the walls,
To adorn the burial-house of him I love?

Pictures of growing spring and farms and homes,
With the Fourth-month eve at sundown, and the gray smoke lucid and
 bright,
With floods of the yellow gold of the gorgeous, indolent, sinking sun,
 burning, expanding the air,

With the fresh sweet herbage under foot, and the pale green leaves of the
    trees prolific,
In the distance the flowing glaze, the breast of the river, with a wind-
    dapple here and there,
With ranging hills on the banks, with many a line against the sky, and
    shadows,
And the city at hand with dwellings so dense, and stacks of chimneys,
And all the scenes of life and the workshops, and the workmen home-
    ward returning.

XII

Lo, body and soul—this land,
My own Manhattan with spires, and the sparkling and hurrying tides, and
    the ships,
The varied and ample land, the South and the North in the light, Ohio's
    shores and flashing Missouri,
And ever the far-spreading prairies cover'd with grass and corn.
Lo, the most excellent sun so calm and haughty,
The violet and purple morn with just-felt breezes,
The gentle soft-born measureless light,
The miracle spreading bathing all, the fulfill'd noon,
The coming eve delicious, the welcome night and the stars,
Over my cities shining all, enveloping man and land.

XIII

Sing on, sing on you gray-brown bird,
Sing from the swamps, the recesses, pour your chant from the bushes,
Limitless out of the dusk, out of the cedars and pines.

Sing on dearest brother, warble your reedy song,
Loud human song, with voice of uttermost woe.
O liquid and free and tender!
O wild and loose to my soul—O wondrous singer!
You only I hear—yet the star holds me, (but will soon depart,)
Yet the lilac with mastering odor holds me.

XIV

Now while I sat in the day and look'd forth,
In the close of the day with its light and the fields of spring, and the
    farmers preparing their crops,

In the large unconscious scenery of my land with its lakes and forests,
In the heavenly aerial beauty (after the perturb'd winds and the storms,)
Under the arching heavens of the afternoon swift passing, and the voices
    of children and women,
The many-moving sea-tides, and I saw the ships how they sail'd,
And the summer approaching with richness, and the fields all busy with
    labor,
And the infinite separate houses, how they all went on, each with its
    meals and minutia of daily usages,
And the streets how their throbbings throbb'd, and the cities pent—lo,
    then and there,
Falling upon them all and among them all, enveloping me with the rest,
Appear'd the cloud, appear'd the long black trail,
And I knew death, its thought, and the sacred knowledge of death.

Then with the knowledge of death as walking one side of me,
And the thought of death close-walking the other side of me,
And I in the middle as with companions, and as holding the hands of
    companions,
I fled forth to the hiding receiving night that talks not,
Down to the shores of the water, the path by the swamp in the dimness,
To the solemn shadowy cedars and ghostly pines so still.

And the singer so shy to the rest receiv'd me,
The gray-brown bird I know receiv'd us comrades three,
And he sang the carol of death, and a verse for him I love.

From deep secluded recesses,
From the fragrant cedars and the ghostly pines so still
Came the carol of the bird.

And the charm of the carol rapt me,
As I held as if by their hands my comrades in the night,
And the voice of my spirit tallied the song of the bird.

Come lovely and soothing death,
Undulate round the world, serenely arriving, arriving,
In the day, in the night, to all, to each,
Sooner or later delicate death.

Prais'd be the fathomless universe,
For life and joy, and for objects and knowledge curious,
And for love, sweet love—but praise! praise! praise!
For the sure-enwinding arms of cool-enfolding death.

Dark mother always gliding near with soft feet,
Have none chanted for thee a chant of fullest welcome?
Then I chant it for thee, I glorify thee above all,
I bring thee a song that when thou must indeed come, come unfalteringly.

Approach strong deliveress,
When it is so, when thou hast taken them I joyously sing the dead,
Lost in the loving floating ocean of thee,
Laved in the flood of thy bliss, O death.

From me to thee glad serenades,
Dances for thee I propose saluting thee, adornments and feastings for
       thee,
And the sights of the open landscape and the high-spread sky are fitting,
And life and the fields, and the huge and thoughtful night.

The night in silence under many a star,
The ocean shore and the husky whispering wave whose voice I know,
And the soul turning to thee, O vast and well-veil'd death,
And the body gratefully nestling close to thee.

Over the tree-tops I float thee a song,
Over the rising and sinking waves, over the myriad fields and the prairies
       wide,
Over the dense-pack'd cities all and the teeming wharves and ways,
I float this carol with joy, with joy to thee, O death.

XV

To the tally of my soul,
Loud and strong kept up the gray-brown bird,
With pure deliberate notes spreading filling the night.

Loud in the pines and cedars dim,
Clear in the freshness moist and the swamp-perfume,
And I with my comrades there in the night.

While my sight that was bound in my eyes unclosed,
As to long panoramas of visions.

And I saw askant the armies,
I saw as in noiseless dreams hundreds of battle-flags,
Borne through the smoke of the battles and pierc'd with missiles I saw
       them,

And carried hither and yon through the smoke, and torn and bloody,
And at last but a few shreds left on the staffs, (and all in silence,)
And the staffs all splinter'd and broken.

I saw battle-corpses, myriads of them,
And the white skeletons of young men, I saw them,
I saw the debris and debris of all the slain soldiers of the war,
But I saw they were not as was thought,
They themselves were fully at rest, they suffer'd not,
The living remain'd and suffer'd, the mother suffer'd,
And the wife and the child and the musing comrade suffer'd,
And the armies that remain'd suffer'd.

XVI

Passing the visions, passing the night,
Passing, unloosing the hold of my comrades' hands,
Passing the song of the hermit bird and the tallying song of my soul,
Victorious song, death's outlet song, yet varying ever-altering song,
As low and wailing, yet clear the notes, rising and falling, flooding the
    night,
Sadly sinking and fainting, as warning and warning, and yet again
    bursting with joy,
Covering the earth and filling the spread of the heaven,
As that powerful psalm in the night I heard from recesses,
Passing, I leave thee lilac with heart-shaped leaves,
I leave thee there in the door-yard, blooming, returning with spring.

I cease from my song for thee,
From my gaze on thee in the west, fronting the west, communing with
    thee,
O comrade lustrous with silver face in the night.

Yet each to keep and all, retrievements out of the night,
The song, the wondrous chant of the gray-brown bird,
And the tallying chant, the echo arous'd in my soul,
With the lustrous and drooping star with the countenance full of woe,
With the holders holding my hand nearing the call of the bird,
Comrades mine and I in the midst, and their memory ever to keep, for the
    dead I loved so well,
For the sweetest, wisest soul of all my days and lands—and this for his
    dear sake,
Lilac and star and bird twined with the chant of my soul,
There in the fragrant pines and the cedars dusk and dim.

ALGERNON CHARLES SWINBURNE

THE GARDEN OF PROSERPINE

Here, where the world is quiet;
   Here, where all trouble seems
Dead winds' and spent waves' riot
   In doubtful dreams of dreams;
I watch the green field growing
For reaping folk and sowing,
For harvest-time and mowing,
   A sleepy world of streams.

I am tired of tears and laughter,
   And men that laugh and weep,
Of what may come hereafter
   For men that sow to reap;
I am weary of days and hours,
Blown buds of barren flowers,
Desires and dreams and powers
   And everything but sleep.

Here life has death for neighbor,
   And far from eye or ear
Wan waves and wet winds labor,
   Weak ships and spirits steer;
They drive adrift, and whither
They wot not who make thither;
But no such winds blow hither,
   And no such things grow here.

No growth of moor or coppice,
   No heather-flower or vine,
But bloomless buds of poppies,
   Green grapes of Proserpine,
Pale beds of blowing rushes
Where no leaf blooms or blushes
Save this whereout she crushes
   For dead men deadly wine.

ALGERNON CHARLES SWINBURNE (1837-1909) was born in London and educated at Eton and Balliol College, Oxford. His health began to fail in 1876, and he spent the remainder of his life under the care of his friend Theodore Watts-Duncan. He was a prolific writer both before and after his physical decline—an untiring experimenter in verse and a vigorous critic in prose.

Pale, without name or number,
  In fruitless fields of corn,
They bow themselves and slumber
  All night till light is born;
And like a soul belated,
In hell and heaven unmated,
By cloud and mist abated
  Comes out of darkness morn.

Though one were strong as seven,
  He too with death shall dwell,
Nor wake with wings in heaven,
  Nor weep for pains in hell;
Though one were fair as roses,
His beauty clouds and closes;
And well though love reposes,
  In the end it is not well.

Pale, beyond porch and portal,
  Crowned with calm leaves, she stands
Who gathers all things mortal
  With cold immortal hands;
Her languid lips are sweeter
Than love's who fears to greet her
To men that mix and meet her
  From many times and lands.

She waits for each and other,
  She waits for all men born;
Forgets the earth her mother,
  The life of fruits and corn;
And spring and seed and swallow
Take wing for her and follow
Where summer song rings hollow
  And flowers are put to scorn.

There go the loves that wither,
  The old loves with wearier wings;
And all dead years draw thither,
  And all disastrous things;
Dead dreams of days forsaken,
Blind buds that snows have shaken,
Wild leaves that winds have taken,
  Red strays of ruined springs.

We are not sure of sorrow,
  And joy was never sure;
Today will die tomorrow;
  Time stoops to no man's lure;
And love, grown faint and fretful,
With lips but half regretful
Sighs, and with eyes forgetful
  Weeps that no loves endure.

From too much love of living,
  From hope and fear set free,
We thank with brief thanksgiving
  Whatever gods may be
That no life lives forever;
That dead men rise up never;
That even the weariest river
  Winds somewhere safe to sea.

Then star nor sun shall waken,
  Nor any change of light;
Nor sound of waters shaken,
  Nor any sound or sight;
Nor wintry leaves nor vernal,
Nor days nor things diurnal;
Only the sleep eternal
  In an eternal night.

VI

THE VICTORIAN PERIOD

CLASSICAL AND MEDIEVAL LEGEND

THE interest of the Romantic poets in the Middle Ages continued well into the second half of the nineteenth century, and with it continued also a fondness for the extended narrative poem, so that the Victorian becomes one of the most prolific of all ages in its poetic renditions of traditional legends. Although the legends represent diverse sources, the poems reflect the tastes and attitudes of the age which produced them.

Tennyson showed an interest in Arthurian legend throughout his career, from the finely controlled stanzas of *The Lady of Shalott* written in his youth through the smooth-flowing blank verse of *The Idylls of the King,* a product of his maturity. Tennyson liked to use medieval and classical story as a vehicle for ideas, as we have noted in *Ulysses;* in *The Lady of Shalott* the story of Lancelot and Elaine is used to express the poet's own philosophy of art. The lady weaving in isolation is a symbol of the artist interpreting life in his ivory tower, separate from the ordinary concerns of humanity; and the tragedy that befalls the lady is what must also befall such an artist when reality intrudes, as it always must. Arnold also used traditional stories as a means to express his ideas.

Poets like Arnold and Tennyson carried on a romantic conception of the Middle Ages. In the poems of D. G. Rossetti and, above all, of William Morris, the true quality of the medieval world is recaptured. This authenticity came from a deep absorption in medieval life. The Pre-Raphaelite artists with whom Rossetti was associated attempted to recapture the simplicity of medieval art and devoted themselves to the mystical and religious themes of the medieval artists they admired, as *The Blessed Damozel* illustrates. Morris was interested in this movement, although he never joined the brotherhood which Rossetti and his friends formed. Morris saw in the Middle Ages a way of life which in its simplicity and respect for individual labor was the antithesis of the Victorian life he despised. The great drive of Morris' life was to escape the consequences of the Industrial Revolution, and of this drive his conscious medievalism is one reflection. It is part of his tragedy that he pursued an ideal which could never be realized.

Morris was also a supreme storyteller. Calling himself "the idle singer of an empty day," he ransacked classical and medieval legend for tales which he turned into poetry with consummate skill and with little purpose other than to amuse. His *Earthly Paradise,* which appeared in four volumes between 1868 and 1870, is perhaps his age's greatest collection of romantic narrative poetry. From Norse folklore he took his *Sigurd the Volsung.* His *Life and Death of Jason,* although drawn from a classical source, is told in a medieval manner; Morris deliberately assumes the guise of the medieval troubadour and fills his long poem with characteristically medieval symbols. For *The Haystack in the Floods* there is no source. The story is Morris' own invention, but few poems have better captured the spirit of the Middle Ages, its chivalry and brutality commingled.

Victorian poets resorted to medieval and classical legendry as a vehicle for ideas and as a means of escape from the sordid reality of their industrialized England. They turned to it also in a spirit of romance, searching traditional literature for perennially fascinating stories in order that a wide poetry-reading audience might indulge its fancy for adventure and romance.

FOR FURTHER READING:

Beerbohm, Max. *Rossetti and His Circle.* London, 1922.

Drinkwater, John. *William Morris, A Study.* London, 1912.

Evans, B. I. *William Morris and His Poetry.* London, 1925.

MacCallum, M. W. *Tennyson's Idylls of the King and Arthurian Story from the Sixteenth Century.* Glasgow, 1894.

ALFRED, LORD TENNYSON

THE LADY OF SHALOTT

Part I

On either side the river lie
Long fields of barley and of rye,
That clothe the wold and meet the sky;
And through the field the road runs by
    To many-towered Camelot;
And up and down the people go,
Gazing where the lilies blow
Round an island there below,
    The island of Shalott.

Willows whiten, aspens quiver,
Little breezes dusk and shiver

Through the wave that runs forever
By the island in the river
      Flowing down to Camelot.
Four gray walls, and four gray towers,
Overlook a space of flowers,
And the silent isle embowers
      The Lady of Shalott.

By the margin, willow-veiled,
Slide the heavy barges trailed
By slow horses; and unhailed
The shallop flitteth silken-sailed
      Skimming down to Camelot:
But who hath seen her wave her hand?
Or at the casement seen her stand?
Or is she known in all the land,
      The Lady of Shalott?

Only reapers, reaping early
In among the bearded barley,
Hear a song that echoes cheerly
From the river winding clearly,
      Down to towered Camelot;
And by the moon the reaper weary,
Piling sheaves in uplands airy,
Listening, whispers, " 'Tis the fairy
      Lady of Shalott."

Part II

There she weaves by night and day
A magic web with colors gay.
She has heard a whisper say,
A curse is on her if she stay
      To look down to Camelot.
She knows not what the curse may be,
And so she weaveth steadily,
And little other care hath she,
      The Lady of Shalott.

And moving through a mirror clear
That hangs before her all the year,
Shadows of the world appear.

There she sees the highway near
       Winding down to Camelot;
There the river eddy whirls,
And there the surly village-churls,
And the red cloaks of market girls,
       Pass onward from Shalott.

Sometimes a troop of damsels glad,
An abbot on an ambling pad,
Sometimes a curly shepherd-lad,
Or long-haired page in crimson clad,
       Goes by to towered Camelot;
And sometimes through the mirror blue
The knights come riding two and two;
She hath no loyal knight and true,
       The Lady of Shalott.

But in her web she still delights
To weave the mirror's magic sights,
For often through the silent nights
A funeral, with plumes and lights
       And music, went to Camelot;
Or when the moon was overhead,
Came two young lovers lately wed;
"I am half sick of shadows," said
       The Lady of Shalott.

Part III

A bow-shot from her bower-eaves,
He rode between the barley-sheaves;
The sun came dazzling through the leaves,
And flamed upon the brazen greaves
       Of bold Sir Lancelot.
A red-cross knight forever kneeled
To a lady in his shield,
That sparkled on the yellow field,
       Beside remote Shalott.

The gemmy bridle glittered free,
Like to some branch of stars we see
Hung in the golden Galaxy.
The bridle bells rang merrily

As he rode down to Camelot;
And from his blazoned baldric slung
A mighty silver bugle hung,
And as he rode his armor rung,
  Beside remote Shalott.

All in the blue unclouded weather
Thick-jewelled shone the saddle-leather,
The helmet and the helmet-feather
Burned like one burning flame together
  As he rode down to Camelot;
As often through the purple night,
Below the starry clusters bright,
Some bearded meteor, trailing light,
  Moves over still Shalott.

His broad clear brow in sunlight glowed;
On burnished hooves his war-horse trode;
From underneath his helmet flowed
His coal-black curls as on he rode,
  As he rode down to Camelot.
From the bank and from the river
He flashed into the crystal mirror,
"Tirra lirra," by the river
  Sang Sir Lancelot.

She left the web, she left the loom,
She made three paces through the room,
She saw the water-lily bloom,
She saw the helmet and the plume,
  She looked down to Camelot.
Out flew the web and floated wide;
The mirror cracked from side to side;
"The curse is come upon me," cried
  The Lady of Shalott.

Part IV

In the stormy east-wind straining,
The pale yellow woods were waning,
The broad stream in his banks complaining,
Heavily the low sky raining
  Over towered Camelot;
Down she came and found a boat

Beneath a willow left afloat,
And round about the prow she wrote
   The Lady of Shalott.

And down the river's dim expanse
Like some bold seer in a trance,
Seeing all his own mischance—
With a glassy countenance
     Did she look to Camelot.
And at the closing of the day
She loosed the chain, and down she lay;
The broad stream bore her far away,
   The Lady of Shalott.

Lying, robed in snowy white
That loosely flew to left and right—
The leaves upon her falling light—
Through the noises of the night
     She floated down to Camelot;
And as the boat-head wound along
The willowy hills and fields among,
They heard her singing her last song,
   The Lady of Shalott.

Heard a carol, mournful, holy,
Chanted loudly, chanted lowly,
Till her blood was frozen slowly,
And her eyes were darkened wholly,
     Turned to towered Camelot.
For ere she reached upon the tide
The first house by the water-side,
Singing in her song she died,
   The Lady of Shalott.

Under tower and balcony,
By garden-wall and gallery,
A gleaming shape she floated by,
Dead-pale between the houses high,
     Silent into Camelot.
Out upon the wharfs they came,
Knight and burgher, lord and dame,
And round the prow they read her name,
   The Lady of Shalott.

Who is this? and what is here?
And in the lighted palace near
Died the sound of royal cheer;
And they crossed themselves for fear,
　　　All the knights at Camelot.
But Lancelot mused a little space;
He said, "She has a lovely face;
God in his mercy lend her grace,
　　　The Lady of Shalott."

THE LOTOS-EATERS

"Courage!" he said, and pointed toward the land,
"This mounting wave will roll us shoreward soon."
In the afternoon they came unto a land
In which it seemed always afternoon.
All round the coast the languid air did swoon,
Breathing like one that hath a weary dream.
Full-faced above the valley stood the moon;
And, like a downward smoke, the slender stream
Along the cliff to fall and pause and fall did seem.

A land of streams! some, like a downward smoke,
Slow-dropping veils of thinnest lawn, did go;
And some through wavering lights and shadows broke,
Rolling a slumbrous sheet of foam below.
They saw the gleaming river seaward flow
From the inner land; far off, three mountain-tops,
Three silent pinnacles of aged snow,
Stood sunset-flushed; and, dewed with showery drops,
Up-clomb the shadowy pine above the woven copse.

The charmed sunset lingered low adown
In the red West; through mountain clefts the dale
Was seen far inland, and the yellow down
Bordered with palm, and many a winding vale
And meadow, set with slender galingale;
A land where all things always seemed the same!
And round about the keel with faces pale,
Dark faces pale against that rosy flame,
The mild-eyed melancholy Lotos-eaters came.

Branches they bore of that enchanted stem,
Laden with flower and fruit, whereof they gave

To each, but whoso did receive of them
And taste, to him the gushing of the wave
Far far away did seem to mourn and rave
On alien shores; and if his fellow spake,
His voice was thin, as voices from the grave;
And deep-asleep he seemed, yet all awake,
And music in his ears his beating heart did make.

They sat them down upon the yellow sand
Between the sun and moon upon the shore;
And sweet it was to dream of Fatherland,
Of child, and wife, and slave; but evermore
Most weary seemed the sea, weary the oar,
Weary the wandering fields of barren foam.
Then someone said, "We will return no more";
And all at once they sang, "Our island home
Is far beyond the wave; we will no longer roam."

Choric Song

There is sweet music here that softer falls
Than petals from blown roses on the grass,
Or night-dews on still waters between walls
Of shadowy granite, in a gleaming pass;
Music that gentlier on the spirit lies,
Than tired eyelids upon tired eyes;
Music that brings sweet sleep down from the blissful skies.
Here are cool mosses deep,
And through the moss the ivies creep,
And in the stream the long-leaved flowers weep,
And from the craggy ledge the poppy hangs in sleep.

Why are we weighed upon with heaviness,
And utterly consumed with sharp distress,
While all things else have rest from weariness?
All things have rest; why should we toil alone,
We only toil, who are the first of things,
And make perpetual moan,
Still from one sorrow to another thrown;
Nor ever fold our wings,
And cease from wanderings,
Nor steep our brows in slumber's holy balm;
Nor harken what the inner spirit sings,

"There is no joy but calm!"—
Why should we only toil, the roof and crown of things?

Lo! in the middle of the wood,
The folded leaf is wooed from out the bud
With winds upon the branch, and there
Grows green and broad, and takes no care,
Sun-steeped at noon, and in the moon
Nightly dew-fed; and turning yellow
Falls, and floats adown the air.
Lo! sweetened with the summer light,
The full-juiced apple, waxing over-mellow,
Drops in a silent autumn night.
All its allotted length of days
The flower ripens in its place,
Ripens and fades, and falls, and hath no toil,
Fast-rooted in the fruitful soil.

Hateful is the dark-blue sky,
Vaulted o'er the dark-blue sea.
Death is the end of life; ah, why
Should life all labor be?
Let us alone. Time driveth onward fast,
And in a little while our lips are dumb.
Let us alone. What is it that will last?
All things are taken from us, and become
Portions and parcels of the dreadful past.
Let us alone. What pleasure can we have
To war with evil? Is there any peace
In ever climbing up the climbing wave?
All things have rest, and ripen toward the grave
In silence—ripen, fall, and cease;
Give us long rest or death, dark death, or dreamful ease.

How sweet it were, hearing the downward stream
With half-shut eyes ever to seem
Falling asleep in a half-dream!
To dream and dream, like yonder amber light,
Which will not leave the myrrh-bush on the height;
To hear each other's whispered speech;
Eating the Lotos day by day,
To watch the crisping ripples on the beach,
And tender curving lines of creamy spray;

To lend our hearts and spirits wholly
To the influence of mild-minded melancholy;
To muse and brood and live again in memory,
With those old faces of our infancy
Heaped over with a mound of grass,
Two handfuls of white dust, shut in an urn of brass!

Dear is the memory of our wedded lives,
And dear the last embraces of our wives
And their warm tears; but all hath suffered change;
For surely now our household hearths are cold,
Our sons inherit us, our looks are strange,
And we should come like ghosts to trouble joy.
Or else the island princes over-bold
Have eat our substance, and the minstrel sings
Before them of the ten years' war in Troy,
And our great deeds, as half-forgotten things.
Is there confusion in the little isle?
Let what is broken so remain.
The gods are hard to reconcile;
'Tis hard to settle order once again.
There *is* confusion worse than death,
Trouble on trouble, pain on pain,
Long labor unto aged breath,
Sore task to hearts worn out by many wars
And eyes grown dim with gazing on the pilot-stars.

But, propped on beds of amaranth and moly,
How sweet—while warm airs lull us, blowing lowly—
With half-dropped eyelid still,
Beneath a heaven dark and holy,
To watch the long bright river drawing slowly
His waters from the purple hill—
To hear the dewy echoes calling
From cave to cave through the thick-twined vine—
To watch the emerald-colored water falling
Through many a woven acanthus-wreath divine!
Only to hear and see the far-off sparkling brine,
Only to hear were sweet, stretched out beneath the pine.

The Lotos blooms below the barren peak,
The Lotos blows by every winding creek;
All day the wind breathes low with mellower tone;

Through every hollow cave and alley lone
Round and round the spicy downs the yellow Lotos-dust
    is blown.
We have had enough of action, and of motion we,
Rolled to starboard, rolled to larboard, when the surge
     was seething free,
Where the wallowing monster spouted his foam-fountains
    in the sea.
Let us swear an oath, and keep it with an equal mind,
In the hollow Lotos-land to live and lie reclined
On the hills like gods together, careless of mankind.
For they lie beside their nectar, and the bolts are hurled
Far below them in the valleys, and the clouds are
     lightly curled
Round their golden houses, girdled with the gleaming world;
Where they smile in secret, looking over wasted lands,
Blight and famine, plague and earthquake, roaring deeps
     and fiery sands,
Clanging fights, and flaming towns, and sinking ships,
     and praying hands.
But they smile, they find a music centered in a doleful song
Steaming up, a lamentation and an ancient tale of wrong,
Like a tale of little meaning though the words are strong;
Chanted from an ill-used race of men that cleave the soil,
Sow the seed, and reap the harvest with enduring toil,
Storing yearly little dues of wheat, and wine and oil;
Till they perish and they suffer—some, 'tis whispered—down in hell
Suffer endless anguish, others in Elysian valleys dwell,
Resting weary limbs at last on beds of asphodel.
Surely, surely, slumber is more sweet than toil, the shore
Than labor in the deep mid-ocean, wind and wave and oar;
O rest ye, brother mariners, we will not wander more.

MATTHEW ARNOLD

THE FORSAKEN MERMAN

Come, dear children, let us away;
Down and away below!
Now my brothers call from the bay,

Now the great winds shoreward blow,
Now the salt tides seaward flow;
Now the wild white horses play,
Champ and chafe and toss in the spray.
Children dear, let us away!
This way, this way!

Call her once before you go—
Call once yet!
In a voice that she will know:
"Margaret! Margaret!"
Children's voices should be dear
(Call once more) to a mother's ear;
Children's voices, wild with pain—
Surely she will come again!
Call her once and come away;
This way, this way!
"Mother dear, we cannot stay!
The wild white horses foam and fret."
Margaret! Margaret!

Come, dear children, come away down;
Call no more!
One last look at the white-walled town,
And the little gray church on the windy shore,
Then come down!
She will not come though you call all day;
Come away, come away!

Children dear, was it yesterday
We heard the sweet bells over the bay?
In the caverns where we lay,
Through the surf and through the swell,
The far-off sound of a silver bell?
Sand-strewn caverns, cool and deep,
Where the winds are all asleep;
Where the spent lights quiver and gleam,
Where the salt weed sways in the stream,
Where the sea-beasts, ranged all round,
Feed in the ooze of their pasture-ground;
Where the sea-snakes coil and twine,
Dry their mail and bask in the brine;
Where great whales come sailing by,

Sail and sail, with unshut eye,
Round the world for ever and aye?
When did music come this way?
Children dear, was it yesterday?

Children dear, was it yesterday
(Call yet once) that she went away?
Once she sate with you and me,
On a red gold throne in the heart of the sea,
And the youngest sate on her knee.
She combed its bright hair, and she tended it well,
When down swung the sound of a far-off bell.
She sighed, she looked up through the clear green sea;
She said: "I must go, for my kinsfolk pray
In the little gray church on the shore today.
'Twill be Easter-time in the world—ah me!
And I lose my poor soul, Merman! here with thee."
I said: "Go up, dear heart, through the waves;
Say thy prayer, and come back to the kind sea-caves!"
She smiled, she went up through the surf in the bay.
Children dear, was it yesterday?

 Children dear, were we long alone?
"The sea grows stormy, the little ones moan;
Long prayers," I said, "in the world they say;
Come!" I said; and we rose through the surf in the bay.
We went up the beach, by the sandy down
Where the sea-stocks bloom, to the white-walled town;
Through the narrow paved streets, where all was still,
To the little gray church on the windy hill.
From the church came a murmur of folk at their prayers,
But we stood without in the cold blowing airs.
We climbed on the graves, on the stones worn with rains,
And we gazed up the aisle through the small leaded panes.
She sate by the pillar; we saw her clear:
"Margaret, hist! come quick, we are here!
Dear heart," I said, "we are long alone;
The sea grows stormy, the little ones moan."
But, ah, she gave me never a look,
For her eyes were sealed to the holy book!
Loud prays the priest; shut stands the door.
Come away, children, call no more!
Come away, come down, call no more!

Down, down, down!
Down to the depths of the sea!
She sits at her wheel in the humming town,
Singing most joyfully.
Hark what she sings: "O joy, O joy,
For the humming street, and the child with its toy!
For the priest, and the bell, and the holy well;
For the wheel where I spun,
And the blessed light of the sun!"
And so she sings her fill,
Singing most joyfully,
Till the spindle drops from her hand,
And the whizzing wheel stands still.
She steals to the window, and looks at the sand,
And over the sand at the sea;
And her eyes are set in a stare;
And anon there breaks a sigh,
And anon there drops a tear,
From a sorrow-clouded eye,
And a heart sorrow-laden,
A long, long sigh;
For the cold strange eyes of a little Mermaiden
And the gleam of her golden hair.

Come away, away children;
Come children, come down!
The hoarse wind blows coldly;
Lights shine in the town.
She will start from her slumber
When gusts shake the door;
She will hear the winds howling,
Will hear the waves roar.
We shall see, while above us
The waves roar and whirl,
A ceiling of amber,
A pavement of pearl.
Singing: "Here came a mortal,
But faithless was she.
And alone dwell forever
The kings of the sea."

But, children, at midnight,
When soft the winds blow,

When clear falls the moonlight,
When spring-tides are low;
When sweet airs come seaward
From heaths starred with broom,
And high rocks throw mildly
On the blanched sands a gloom;
Up the still, glistening beaches,
Up the creeks we will hie,
Over banks of bright seaweed
The ebb-tide leaves dry.
We will gaze, from the sand-hills,
At the white, sleeping town;
At the church on the hillside—
And then come back down.
Singing: "There dwells a loved one,
But cruel is she!
She left lonely forever
The kings of the sea."

DANTE GABRIEL ROSSETTI

TROY TOWN

Heavenborn Helen, Sparta's queen,
      (O Troy Town!)
Had two breasts of heavenly sheen,
The sun and moon of the heart's desire;
All Love's lordship lay between.
      (O Troy's down,
      Tall Troy's on fire!)

Helen knelt at Venus' shrine,
      (O Troy Town!)
Saying, "A little gift is mine,
A little gift for a heart's desire.
Hear me speak and make me a sign!
      (O Troy's down,
      Tall Troy's on fire!)

DANTE GABRIEL ROSSETTI (1828-1882) was born in London, the son of an Italian political exile. After finishing his study at British art schools, he became one of the founders of the Pre-Raphaelite Brotherhood, a group opposed to contemporary conventions in literature and art. His poems represent the best expression of Pre-Raphaelite theories in verse.

"Look, I bring thee a carven cup;
                    (O Troy Town!)
See it here as I hold it up—
Shaped it is to the heart's desire,
Fit to fill when the gods would sup.
                    (O Troy's down,
                    Tall Troy's on fire!)

"It was molded like my breast;
                    (O Troy Town!)
He that sees it may not rest,
Rest at all for his heart's desire.
O give ear to my heart's behest!
                    (O Troy's down,
                    Tall Troy's on fire!)

"See my breast, how like it is;
                    (O Troy Town!)
See it bare for the air to kiss!
Is the cup to thy heart's desire?
O for the breast, O make it his!
                    (O Troy's down,
                    Tall Troy's on fire!)

"Yea, for my bosom here I sue;
                    (O Troy Town!)
Thou must give it where 'tis due,
Give it there to the heart's desire.
Whom do I give my bosom to?
                    (O Troy's down,
                    Tall Troy's on fire!)

"Each twin breast is an apple sweet!
                    (O Troy Town!)
Once an apple stirred the beat
Of thy heart with the heart's desire;
Say, who brought it then to thy feet?
                    (O Troy's down,
                    Tall Troy's on fire!)

"They that claimed it then were three;
                    (O Troy Town!)
For thy sake two hearts did he

Make forlorn of the heart's desire.
Do for him as he did for thee!
(O Troy's down,
Tall Troy's on fire!)

"Mine are apples grown to the south,
(O Troy Town!)
Grown to taste in the days of drouth,
Taste and waste to the heart's desire;
Mine are apples meet for his mouth!"
(O Troy's down,
Tall Troy's on fire!)

Venus looked on Helen's gift,
(O Troy Town!)
Looked and smiled with subtle drift,
Saw the work of her heart's desire—
"There thou kneel'st for Love to lift!"
(O Troy's down,
Tall Troy's on fire!)

Venus looked in Helen's face,
(O Troy Town!)
Knew far off an hour and place,
And fire lit from the heart's desire;
Laughed and said, "Thy gift hath grace!"
(O Troy's down,
Tall Troy's on fire!)

Cupid looked on Helen's breast,
(O Troy Town!)
Saw the heart within its nest,
Saw the flame of the heart's desire—
Marked his arrow's burning crest.
(O Troy's down,
Tall Troy's on fire!)

Cupid took another dart,
(O Troy Town!)
Fledged it for another heart,
Winged the shaft with the heart's desire,
Drew the string and said, "Depart!"
(O Troy's down,
Tall Troy's on fire!)

Paris turned upon his bed,
>   *(O Troy Town!)*
Turned upon his bed and said,
Dead at heart with the heart's desire—
"O to clasp her golden head!"
>   *(O Troy's down,*
>   *Tall Troy's on fire!)*

THE BLESSED DAMOZEL

The blessed damozel leaned out
>   From the gold bar of heaven;
Her eyes were deeper than the depth
>   Of waters stilled at even;
She had three lilies in her hand,
>   And the stars in her hair were seven.

Her robe, ungirt from clasp to hem,
>   No wrought flowers did adorn,
But a white rose of Mary's gift,
>   For service meetly worn;
Her hair that lay along her back
>   Was yellow, like ripe corn.

Herseemed she scarce had been a day
>   One of God's choristers;
The wonder was not yet quite gone
>   From that still look of hers;
Albeit, to them she left, her day
>   Had counted as ten years.

(To *one*, it is ten years of years.
>   ... Yet now, and in this place,
Surely she leaned o'er me—her hair
>   Fell all about my face. . . .
Nothing: the autumn fall of leaves.
>   The whole year sets apace.)

It was the rampart of God's house
>   That she was standing on;
By God built over the sheer depth
>   The which is Space begun;
So high, that looking downward thence
>   She scarce could see the sun.

It lies in heaven, across the flood
   Of ether, as a bridge.
Beneath the tides of day and night
   With flame and darkness ridge
The void, as low as where this earth
   Spins like a fretful midge.

Around her, lovers, newly met
   'Mid deathless love's acclaims,
Spoke evermore among themselves
   Their heart-remembered names;
And the souls mounting up to God
   Went by her like thin flames.

And still she bowed herself and stooped
   Out of the circling charm;
Until her bosom must have made
   The bar she leaned on warm,
And the lilies lay as if asleep
   Along her bended arm.

From the fixed place of heaven she saw
   Time like a pulse shake fierce
Through all the worlds. Her gaze still strove
   Within the gulf to pierce
Its path; and now she spoke as when
   The stars sang in their spheres.

The sun was gone now; the curled moon
   Was like a little feather
Fluttering far down the gulf; and now
   She spoke through the still weather.
Her voice was like the voice the stars
   Had when they sang together.

(Ah, sweet! Even now, in that bird's song,
   Strove not her accents there,
Fain to be harkened? When those bells
   Possessed the mid-day air,
Strove not her steps to reach my side
   Down all the echoing stair?)

"I wish that he were come to me,
   For he will come," she said.

"Have I not prayed in heaven?—on earth,
  Lord, Lord, has he not prayed?
Are not two prayers a perfect strength?
  And shall I feel afraid?

"When round his head the aureole clings,
  And he is clothed in white,
I'll take his hand and go with him
  To the deep wells of light;
As unto a stream we will step down,
  And bathe there in God's sight.

"We two will stand beside that shrine,
  Occult, withheld, untrod,
Whose lamps are stirred continually
  With prayers sent up to God;
And see our old prayers, granted, melt
  Each like a little cloud.

"We two will lie i' the shadow of
  That living mystic tree
Within whose secret growth the Dove
  Is sometimes felt to be,
While every leaf that His plumes touch
  Saith His Name audibly.

"And I myself will teach to him,
  I myself, lying so,
The songs I sing here; which his voice
  Shall pause in, hushed and slow,
And find some knowledge at each pause,
  Or some new thing to know."

(Alas! we two, we two, thou say'st!
  Yea, one wast thou with me
That once of old. But shall God lift
  To endless unity
The soul whose likeness with thy soul
  Was but its love for thee?)

"We two," she said, "will seek the groves
  Where the lady Mary is,
With her five handmaidens, whose names
  Are five sweet symphonies,

Cecily, Gertrude, Magdalen,
   Margaret and Rosalys.

"Circlewise sit they, with bound locks
   And foreheads garlanded;
Into the fine cloth white like flame
   Weaving the golden thread,
To fashion the birth-robes for them
   Who are just born, being dead.

"He shall fear, haply, and be dumb;
   Then will I lay my cheek
To his, and tell about our love,
   Not once abashed or weak;
And the dear Mother will approve
   My pride, and let me speak.

"Herself shall bring us, hand in hand,
   To Him round whom all souls
Kneel, the clear-ranged unnumbered heads
   Bowed with their aureoles;
And angels meeting us shall sing
   To their citherns and citoles.

"There will I ask of Christ the Lord
   Thus much for him and me—
Only to live as once on earth
   With Love, only to be,
As then awhile, forever now,
   Together, I and he."

She gazed and listened and then said,
   Less sad of speech than mild—
"All this is when he comes." She ceased.
   The light thrilled toward her, filled
With angels in strong, level flight.
   Her eyes prayed, and she smiled.

(I saw her smile.) But soon their path
   Was vague in distant spheres;
And then she cast her arms along
   The golden barriers,
And laid her face between her hands,
   And wept. (I heard her tears.)

WILLIAM MORRIS

THE HAYSTACK IN THE FLOODS

Had she come all the way for this,
To part at last without a kiss?
Yea, had she borne the dirt and rain
That her own eyes might see him slain
Beside the haystack in the floods?

Along the dripping, leafless woods,
The stirrup touching either shoe,
She rode astride as troopers do;
With kirtle kilted to her knee,
To which the mud splashed wretchedly;
And the wet dripped from every tree
Upon her head and heavy hair,
And on her eyelids broad and fair;
The tears and rain ran down her face.

By fits and starts they rode apace,
And very often was his place
Far off from her; he had to ride
Ahead, to see what might betide
When the roads crossed; and sometimes, when
There rose a murmuring from his men,
Had to turn back with promises.
Ah me! she had but little ease;
And often for pure doubt and dread
She sobbed, made giddy in the head
By the swift riding; while, for cold,
Her slender fingers scarce could hold
The wet reins; yea, and scarcely, too,
She felt the foot within her shoe
Against the stirrup: all for this,
To part at last without a kiss
Beside the haystack in the floods.

For when they neared that old soaked hay,
They saw across the only way

WILLIAM MORRIS (1834-1896), the son of a wealthy merchant, made up his mind to devote his life to art while a student at Oxford. As one of the initiators of the Pre-Raphaelite Brotherhood, he shaped English taste through the beautiful publications of his Kelmscott Press, his furniture and tapestry designs, and his haunting poetry.

That Judas, Godmar, and the three
Red running lions dismally
Grinned from his pennon, under which
In one straight line along the ditch,
They counted thirty heads.

    So then
While Robert turned round to his men,
She saw at once the wretched end,
And, stooping down, tried hard to rend
Her coif the wrong way from her head,
And hid her eyes; while Robert said,
"Nay, love, 'tis scarcely two to one;
At Poictiers where we made them run
So fast—why, sweet my love, good cheer,
The Gascon frontier is so near,
Naught after us."

    But: "O!" she said,
"My God! my God! I have to tread
The long way back without you; then
The court at Paris; those six men;
The gratings of the Chatelet;
The swift Seine on some rainy day
Like this, and people standing by,
And laughing, while my weak hands try
To recollect how strong men swim.
All this, or else a life with him,
For which I should be damned at last;
Would God that this next hour were past!"

He answered not, but cried his cry,
"St. George for Marny!" cheerily;
And laid his hand upon her rein.
Alas! no man of all his train
Gave back that cheery cry again;
And, while for rage his thumb beat fast
Upon his sword-hilt, someone cast
About his neck a kerchief long,
And bound him.

    Then they went along
To Godmar; who said: "Now, Jehane,
Your lover's life is on the wane
So fast, that, if this very hour

You yield not as my paramour,
He will not see the rain leave off;
Nay, keep your tongue from gibe and scoff,
Sir Robert, or I slay you now."

She laid her hand upon her brow,
Then gazed upon the palm, as though
She thought her forehead bled, and "No!"
She said, and turned her head away,
As there was nothing else to say,
And everything was settled; red
Grew Godmar's face from chin to head—
"Jehane, on yonder hill there stands
My castle, guarding well my lands;
What hinders me from taking you,
And doing that I list to do
To your fair willful body, while
Your knight lies dead?"

        A wicked smile
Wrinkled her face, her lips grew thin,
A long way out she thrust her chin:
"You know that I should strangle you
While you were sleeping; or bite through
Your throat, by God's help; ah!" she said,
"Lord Jesus, pity your poor maid!
For in such wise they hem me in,
I cannot choose but sin and sin,
Whatever happens; yet I think
They could not make me eat or drink,
And so should I just reach my rest."

"Nay, if you do not my behest,
O Jehane! though I love you well,"
Said Godmar, "would I fail to tell
All that I know?" "Foul lies," she said.
"Eh? lies, my Jehane? by God's head,
At Paris folks would deem them true!
Do you know, Jehane, they cry for you:
'Jehane the brown! Jehane the brown!
Give us Jehane to burn or drown!'
Eh!—gag me Robert!—sweet my friend,
This were indeed a piteous end

For those long fingers, and long feet,
And long neck, and smooth shoulders sweet;
An end that few men would forget
That saw it. So, an hour yet—
Consider, Jehane, which to take
Of life or death!"

                So, scarce awake,
Dismounting, did she leave that place,
And totter some yards; with her face
Turned upward to the sky she lay,
Her head on a wet heap of hay,
And fell asleep; and while she slept,
And did not dream, the minutes crept
Round to the twelve again; but she,
Being waked at last, sighed quietly,
And strangely childlike came, and said:
"I will not." Straightway Godmar's head,
As though it hung on strong wires, turned
Most sharply round, and his face burned.

For Robert, both his eyes were dry—
He could not weep—but gloomily
He seemed to watch the rain; yea, too,
His lips were firm; he tried once more
To touch her lips; she reached out, sore
And vain desire so tortured them,
The poor gray lips, and now the hem
Of his sleeve brushed them.

                With a start
Up Godmar rose, thrust them apart;
From Robert's throat he loosed the bands
Of silk and mail; with empty hands
Held out, she stood and gazed, and saw,
The long bright blade without a flaw
Glide out from Godmar's sheath, his hand
In Robert's hair; she say him bend
Back Robert's head; she saw him send
The thin steel down; the blow told well—
Right backward the knight Robert fell,
And moaned as dogs do, being half dead,
Unwitting, as I deem; so then

Godmar turned grinning to his men,
Who ran, some five or six, and beat
His head to pieces at their feet.

Then Godmar turned again and said:
"So, Jehane, the first fitte is read!
Take note, my lady, that your way
Lies backward to the Chatelet!"
She shook her head and gazed awhile
At her cold hands with a rueful smile,
As though this thing had made her mad.

This was the parting that they had
Beside the haystack in the floods.

THE HAYSTACK IN THE FLOODS There is no source for *The Hay-stack in the Floods;* Morris seems to have made up the story, framing it not as the usual romantic legend of medieval chivalry but so that it would have the ring of verisimilitude and read like a true account of a medieval event, with the superstition, pathos, and sadistic brutality typical of the fourteenth century. The story seems a simple one, of an escaping girl and her lover, trapped by their pursuer. The knight is savagely be-headed and his lady, close to madness, faces return to a Paris prison and probable death. But as we read the poem closely, we discover that the story is far more complex, made so by the insertion of judicious detail to suggest a tangled skein of relationships and to supply a symbolic commentary on the plight of all mortal sufferers.

Much of the poet's artistry lies in a subtle narrative technique that furthers the illusion of historical truth while it develops a religious sub-structure which lends to the narrative a universal significance. The poem's wealth of detail assumes either a knowledge of history on the reader's part or a willingness to obtain the knowledge that will enable him to place the story in an accurate historical context. When Robert, for in-stance, speaks of "Poictiers where we made them run," we learn that he is an Englishman, for at the battle of Poictiers in 1356 the English had scored one of their most memorable victories over the French. The medieval setting which we have already sensed is made specific. We see the events as an episode in the Hundred Years' War; we know that Godmar and his men are either French or in French employ and that the lovers are heading for the "Gascon frontier" because Gascony was in English hands during most of the fourteenth century. This knowledge is reinforced a bit later in the poem when Robert gives his battle cry of

"St. George for Marny!"; St. George is the patron saint of England. We also learn Robert's full name.

The English knight is fleeing toward English territory with a girl who, when she speaks of "The court at Paris; those six men;/The gratings of the Chatelet," indicates that she is French and that she fears imprisonment, perhaps on charges of unchastity. The threat of Godmar to testify against her and the people to taunt her with

> 'Jehane the brown! Jehane the brown!
> Give us Jehane to burn or drown!'

recalls the medieval judicial practice of trial by ordeal. If a suspected person did not sink when thrown into a pool, he was believed to be protected by evil spirits and was therefore burned at the stake.

And what of Godmar? The three lions rampant on his pennant identify him as a knight. He pursues Jehane out of lust, and the alternative he offers upon her capture is either death in Paris or life as his paramour in his hilltop castle. She "cannot choose but sin and sin," for she must either be guilty of illicit love or of murdering Godmar in his sleep. Poignance and pathos are developed about the *kiss* of line 2, a kiss which cannot be had: "sore/ And vain desire so tortured them,/ The poor gray lips." The grayness of the lips which should be red foreshadows the death which awaits Robert. Shocking in its brutal realism is the nature of that death—the striking off of Robert's head and those

> Who ran, some five or six, and beat
> His head to pieces at their feet.

A culmination of the sordid misery which has gone before, it reminds us that we are not in the fairy-tale Middle Ages of Tennyson's *Lady of Shalott* but in the cruel reality of the Hundred Years' War. The promise that Jehane will be led back to the Chatelet rings faintly anticlimactic; her peak of tragedy is her madness. The final couplet recalls the pathos of the five-line opening of the poem; through the repetition Morris achieves a unified effect with the statement of despair at the beginning, its slow explanation in realistic narrative terms, and then its restatement at the end.

No matter how carefully we work out the corners of the narrative suggested by the details we have examined, we feel that the poem has related more than a stirring, if tragic, adventure. Certain words and images have nagged us. Going back, we can gather together a series of statements which give depth to the story because they identify what is for modern readers a distant historical event as something in which all humanity may share. There is a statement beneath the surface which shows us that Jehane's sufferings are similar to those in which other

innocent people have been involved. Morris makes this point by allusion
to original sin and to Christ's betrayal and Crucifixion. *The Haystack
in the Floods* is not, however, an allegory of the passion of Christ, for
Morris does not employ allegory in this poem. Instead, he alludes through
imagery and language, at several points in the narrative, to familiar episodes, situations, and relationships in the New Testament.

The flight of the lovers is made under conditions very much like
those Christ underwent on the path to Golgotha. Jehane is pelted and
bespattered:

> . . . the mud splashed wretchedly;
> And the wet dripped from every tree
> Upon her head and heavy hair,
> And on her eyelids broad and fair;
> The tears and rain ran down her face.

There may be a subtle and unobtrusive reference to the Cross:

> . . . he had to ride
> Ahead, to see what might betide
> When the roads crossed.

No further use is made of Christ imagery until the introduction of "That
Judas, Godmar," who is supported by thirty knights. Not only is the
false knight referred to directly as a Judas, but his name is a composite
of the words *God* and *mar.* Furthermore, his knights number thirty, and
since only their heads may be seen, no doubt gleaming in their metal
helmets, we are reminded of the price for which Judas betrayed his Lord.
That Godmar is a true betrayer and not merely an enemy—and this is
why we suggested that he is perhaps not French but only in French
employ—is implied by his reference to Sir Robert as an old acquaintance:
"Eh!—gag me Robert!—sweet my friend." He has a castle very close
to the Gascon border and is perhaps one of those border knights, of
whom history is full, who cast their lot with whichever side seems to
offer the greater advantages.

The coif that Jehane tries hard to rend from her head, apparently
unsuccessfully, is suggestive of the crown of thorns, especially when we
learn that a coif is not only a medieval cap but also a roll of stiff material that encircles the head. Later we are told that Jehane

> . . . laid her hand upon her brow,
> Then gazed upon the palm, as though
> She thought her forehead bled.

These are the main segments of the argument for sacramental imagery in the poem. There are other, lesser points to consider, natural both to the narrative and to the Christian symbolism and eschatology. The innocent Jehane, for instance, is charged with lechery, but maintains her chastity: " 'Foul lies,' she said." The number of people following Sir Robert give odds to Godmar's thirty of "scarcely two to one." Could that number be twelve, representative of the apostles? Significantly, it is one of his own men who binds Sir Robert and turns him over. Since we are not dealing with true allegory, there is no difficulty in Godmar's serving for Judas at one point and this unnamed follower at another.

Through these means Morris has made a story, interesting in itself, even richer and deeper in meaning and in beauty. On the framework of a romance, he has embroidered a tapestry containing not only the chivalry, brutality, bloodshed, and tragedy of a grim age but also an application to the Christian mysteries which medieval man himself was so fond of making.

The
Twentieth VII
Century

E ACH literary age develops out of its predecessor, partly by continuing tradition, partly by reacting against forces felt to be outmoded. Four major shapers of twentieth-century poetry were inhabitants of the Victorian world. Emily Dickinson, Walt Whitman, and Gerard Manley Hopkins all died between 1886 and 1892; Thomas Hardy, although he lived for many years after the death of the great queen, was more Victorian than the three who died during her reign. Emily Dickinson looks back to New England Puritanism and transcendentalism, but she looks forward to the crisp economy and unique imagery of later moderns. Whitman inherits Yankee optimism, but he bequeaths linear and metrical freedom. Hopkins reverts to the alliterative primitives, but he develops a new tension in language. Hardy lives in the English countryside, but he doubts the gods of his ancestors. In the works of these poets we can see the path along which modern poetry must have traveled, and we can better understand the reasons for the direction it takes into the future.

New influences in twentieth-century poetry Some moderns, however, introduced ingredients that were not part of the immediate past. William Butler Yeats' use of Gaelic myth may have been at first only an extension of the Victorian love for classical myth, medieval legend, and exotic lore, but later Yeats came to use myth for its symbolic appropriateness in the contemporary scene, not merely for its romantic coloring. A. E. Housman's classicism was also different from that of the Victorians. A scholar, Housman understood the pessimism that underlay Sophoclean precision and sparseness. Ezra Pound, too, searched alien literatures for their spirit rather than their myths; his interest in Greek, Roman, Oriental, and Provençal poetry was of a nature far different from Victorian engagement in idyllic myths, oriental tales, Norse sagas, and Arthurian legends. T. S. Eliot resurrected metaphysical poetry and, along with Yeats, resorted to techniques of the French Symbolists.

The major innovators The figure who emerges from this group as perhaps the greatest poet of our century is Yeats. A conventional Victorian in his early poetry, he soon made his way from among his contemporaries; his espousal of Irish nationalism, his involvement in theosophy and Rosicrucianism, and his initiation through Arthur Symons and Ezra Pound into Symbolist expression led to an elaborate private symbology, which he explained in a prose work called *A Vision* (1925, 1937). He had entered ranges of thought and modes of expression where no one seemed able to follow.

Three Americans, born within twelve years of each other and from ten to twenty years after Yeats, have become, like Yeats, difficult to fit into discernible categories, groups, or movements. Robert Frost, born in

1875, had to resort to an English printer in order to get his first volume, *North of Boston,* published. Since 1915 he has grown steadily, in his unique way, recording a wise and wide-embracing philosophy sometimes imbedded in the concerns of a regional writer but always evoking universal beauties and universal themes. As the most eminent living American poet, he was invited, at the age of eighty-five, to deliver a poem at the inauguration of President Kennedy in 1961. He is the first poet to have been thus honored by an American President.

Wallace Stevens, born in 1879, successfully combined a business career with poetry. Whereas we think of Frost as a regionalist of one corner of the earth, we think of Stevens as a regionalist of one corner of the mind—that corner where imagination is most active, where strangeness and rareness are most appreciated. He died in 1955, leaving a rich testament in the more than seven hundred pages of his collected poems to show that living a crowded life in the hurly-burly world need not keep a man from moving widely in the realms of the spirit.

Robinson Jeffers, the youngest of the trio, was born in 1887 and, in contrast to Frost and Stevens, isolated himself from the world on a barren California promontory jutting into the Pacific. Never comfortable in the traditional verse forms, he early broke from them, first to work in simple free forms, then to develop his own distinctive long line, in which most of his best-known works are written. There is not only a severe quality to his landscapes and images but also a crabbedness in his vision—a misanthropy—that developed in the post-World War I era, when it may have been appropriate, and persisted in later years, when most of Jeffers' contemporaries had moved on to some serenity, if not always to affirmation.

Out of the decade that witnessed the first global war came a renaissance of American letters. The early experiment called Imagism had had its moment and was fading. In 1912, Harriet Monroe founded *Poetry: A Magazine of Verse,* which first printed the creations of many of America's greatest poetic imaginations. Poets who have since become the major spokesmen published either their first or their most important early volumes between 1910 and 1920. These include Ezra Pound, T. S. Eliot, Vachel Lindsay, Amy Lowell, Robert Frost, Edgar Lee Masters, Edwin Arlington Robinson, and Carl Sandburg.

There are many other poets who developed in these years, some staying within the traditional modes of expression, others going outside. Among the former are D. H. Lawrence, Conrad Aiken, and Edna St. Vincent Millay; among the latter, John Gould Fletcher, H. D. (Hilda Doolittle), E. E. Cummings, Marianne Moore, and William Carlos Williams. On the whole the experimentalists in this group have left a greater mark on the poetry of their time; E. E. Cummings established the importance of typography, the pattern a poem makes on the page; Marianne Moore investigated with great success the subtler rhythms to be found outside of rhyme, meter, and regular line length; and William Carlos Williams fused lively free forms with disjunctive images and colloquial speech.

Milestones in modern poetry Three seminal poems were the product of the next decade. T. S. Eliot's *The Waste Land* was published in 1922; the first sixteen of Ezra Pound's *Cantos* were published in 1925; and Hart Crane completed *The Bridge* in 1929, although it was not published until 1930. *The Waste Land* revealed a violent reaction to the ornate diction of the Victorians as well as to their sugary optimism. Calling upon vastly disparate literatures, Eliot borrowed from *The Divine Comedy*, the metaphysical poets, the Jacobean playwrights, and the French Symbolists. His poetic diction had undergone a rigorous refining earlier in the important *Love Song of J. Alfred Prufrock*, which along with Pound's early *Ripostes* (1912) had an impact somewhat like that of *Lyrical Ballads* in 1798, in which Wordsworth and Coleridge had proclaimed their desire to bring verse back to the accents of living speech.

Pound's *Cantos* have been added to periodically: there were thirty by 1930, seventy-one by 1940, and eighty-four by 1948 with the publication of *The Pisan Cantos*, written while the poet was imprisoned in Italy at the end of World War II. To date, the *Cantos* have gone over the hundred mark, a number at which they might logically have concluded, in imitation of Dante. Crane, repudiating all ancient myth, all ritual and iconography from the established churches, claimed that in *The Bridge* he was writing the myth of America. He was, in part, rebelling against the negativism, the emptiness, and the dryness of *The Waste Land*.

Of these three men only Eliot exerted an influence that has prevailed in any real sense. Crane, having made an astounding contribution to modern letters, died in 1932, too soon to gain the kind of discipleship that is needed if a poet is to become a potent force. Pound has moved further and further away from the mainstream of modern poetry by his continued use of esoteric knowledge, extreme rightist philosophies, and foreign languages, including the Chinese ideogram. Eliot, after the nihilism of *The Waste Land*, moved into the affirmation of organized religion. Since the highly influential *Ash Wednesday* and *Four Quartets*, however, he has turned his hand to verse dramas, which, except for *Murder in the Cathedral*, seem to have had little or no influence on his contemporaries.

Poetry in the thirties, like every other dimension of intellectual activity or thought, saw a rise of leftist sentiment. Chiefly British, this verse found its best expression in the early works of W. H. Auden, Stephen Spender, and C. Day Lewis; its influence has persisted in more measured social comment. In the forties and fifties, Auden became the most vigorous poet of our age. Experimental in the best sense of the word, he has tried most of the verse forms that the tradition allows; but also he has invented new forms in such works as *For the Time Being,* a Christmas oratorio, and *The Sea and the Mirror,* a verse and prose critique of Shakespeare's *Tempest.* Spender and Lewis have not developed as broadly, but both have labored greatly in the cause of modern poetry, Lewis by writing a long prose essay entitled *A Hope for Poetry* and Spender by making many public appearances on radio and television and at cultural congresses.

The Southern Agrarians While Eliot, Pound, and Crane were having successes with free forms in the 1920's, in the American South several men at Tennessee's Vanderbilt University—called variously the Southern Agrarians, the Fugitives, or the Nashville group—were winning considerable reputations with established forms. Gathered about John Crowe Ransom, their leader, Allen Tate, Robert Penn Warren, and others wrote poetry as part of their broad attempts to re-create order within the framework of old Southern values. They extended their interests to politics, economics, religion, and especially to literary criticism, helping to create what for some time now has been called the New Criticism. Never attempting anything of great scope or range, Ransom has produced some of the most impressive short poems of his time. Tate, with greater ambition, spent ten years in perfecting his *Ode to the Confederate Dead* and more recently has labored long on a second major work, only part of which has yet appeared. Robert Penn Warren has found greater recognition in prose fiction but has never given up what would appear to be his favorite medium, poetry. In 1953 he published a book-length narrative poem, *Brother to Dragons,* and in 1958 he won the Pulitzer Prize for a collection called *Promises.*

Poetry in the forties and fifties The poetry of the forties is difficult to observe whole. In the first half of the decade both England and America were engaged in a world war, and at its end so many new poets appeared, so many old ones wrote in new ways, that we cannot yet assess the period. Older poets such as Tate, Cummings, Auden, Spender, and MacLeish contributed important verse either of protest or of patriotism, while younger men sharpened their talents in experience of war: Karl Shapiro, Randall Jarrell, Richard Eberhart, Theodore Roethke, and John Berryman in America; John Manifold in Australia; and Roy Fuller, Dunstan Thompson, Alex Comfort, and George Barker in England. A dominant voice, speaking importantly first during the war in such a poem as *A Refusal to Mourn the Death, by Fire, of a Child in London,* was that of Dylan Thomas. He introduced new rhythms, new imagery, and new forms—in fact, a kind of poetry never encountered in English before but obviously indebted to Welsh culture. His growth during the rest of the forties and on until his tragic death in 1953 has led John Crowe Ransom to call him a "major-minor" poet.

Other young poets of the forties and fifties illustrate a rather strange phenomenon: the period is one of tremendous poetic activity, producing scores of highly competent and gifted writers, but with the possible exception of Robert Lowell, no poet of true major status is developed. The list of talented poets who hit their stride in the forties would fill more space than is here allowed. Those outstanding include Delmore Schwartz, Elizabeth Bishop, Jean Garrigue, Muriel Rukeyser, Theodore Spencer, and Richard Wilbur. Those emerging from the host of competent poets in the fifties with something more than mere competence include Louis Simpson, James Wright, W. D. Snodgrass, Donald Davie, Philip Larkin, Ted Hughes, and many, many others.

What direction poetry will take in the sixties and beyond is, of course, impossible to determine. In general, there seems to be in store a period of consolidation, during which little if any experimentation will be conducted. The experiments in typography, in the throwing off of all the traditional restrictions of verse, have been taken over, for the most part, by the so-called "beat" poets. Their addition of jazz backgrounds to oral reading is only a further development of the experiments of Vachel Lindsay, who in marginal notations, or "stage directions," called for instrumental accompaniment in poems written fifty years ago. Most of the young poets have returned to traditional forms with a kind of vengeance. They have outlawed obscurantism and simplified their metaphysics. They try for great affective responses with a commensurate lessening of intellectual display. Rather than finding the generation "beat," as their freer contemporaries do, they find it faced with immense problems—problems that require thoughtful examination, not self-pitying despair.

FOR FURTHER READING:

Deutsch, Babette. *This Modern Poetry*. London, 1936.
Isaacs, J. *The Background of Modern Poetry*. New York, 1952.
Brooks, Cleanth. *Modern Poetry and the Tradition*. Chapel Hill, 1939.
Drew, Elizabeth, and J. L. Sweeney. *Directions in Modern Poetry*. New York, 1940.
Shapiro, Karl. *English Prosody and Modern Poetry*. Lincoln, Neb., 1947.
Tate, Allen. *The Man of Letters in the Modern World*. New York, 1955.
Blackmur, R. P. *The Double Agent*. New York, 1935.

VII

THE TWENTIETH CENTURY

THE TRANSITIONAL PERIOD

A T the close of the nineteenth century, Romanticism was still an unflagging literary movement even though it had undergone changes at the hands of the Victorians. The subjectivity of writers in the first great wave of Romantics—Wordsworth, Coleridge, Byron, Keats, and Shelley—had given way to heightened awareness of expanding horizons, of new science, of religious questionings, and of social change; but nature provided solace still, God was in his heaven, the eternal verities showed that science would not change things too greatly, and the best themes for poetry came still from Greek myth (*Ulysses, Tithonus, The Garden of Proserpine*) and medieval legend (*The Idylls of the King*). The diction of the established poets—Tennyson, Browning, Arnold, and Swinburne—was still eloquent or poetic; their forms and meters were traditional; their sensibilities were decorous and cultured. However, in little more than thirty years, vast changes took place.

We may designate the years from 1885 to 1919 as the transitional period in which the poets of Victorianism gave way to new writers with new themes, new accents, and new cadences. In these years Emily Dickinson and Gerard Manley Hopkins died. Robert Bridges developed interests that took him in new directions, away from his old dependence on the Victorians. Yeats immersed himself deeply in Irish mythology and cult mysticism; he was also lured, somewhat reluctantly, into the Irish national movement. Hardy turned from his successes as a novelist and devoted himself again to the medium he preferred—poetry. Housman offered a first book of poems under the pseudonym of Terence Hearsay.

By 1890, four years after her death, Emily Dickinson's short, stark stanzas had reached print. In quick succession came Robert Bridges' *Shorter Poems* (1894), A. E. Housman's *A Shropshire Lad* (1896), and Thomas Hardy's *Wessex Poems* (1898). Yeats had published verse before the turn of the century—*The Wanderings of Oisin* (1889) and *The Countess Kathleen and Various Lyrics* (1892)—but poems in his new idiom did not appear in any great number until *The Wild Swans at Coole* (1919). *The Poems of Gerard Manley Hopkins* (1918) remained unpublished until thirty years after the death of their author.

The break with tradition was sharper, the cleavage greater, than perhaps in any other poetic revolution in English literary history. No poet of the past ever exhibited a cynicism quite like Hardy's. Hopkins' sprung rhythm, for all his claim that its origins were in English alliterative measures, presented to the reader lines, stresses, dissonances, images, compressions, and ellipses never encountered before. Emily Dickinson's kaleidoscopic stanzas, her startling metaphors, shifting tones, and surprising rhythms—all contained in tight, clipped, short-line quatrains—were also unique. Housman's pessimism struck a familiar note chiefly for students of classical Latin.

Although none of these writers conferred with one another, there seemed to be an agreement to simplify diction, to bring it closer again to colloquial speech, to use the unexpected word, to seek out the images of precision rather than of mystery, shadow, and blurred outline. Of course, romantic elements were there in abundance—consider the poetry of Stephen Crane—and it may be questioned even at this late date whether the Romantic movement has yet reached the end of the line. But by the end of the First World War, young poets were seizing upon precisely those practices in the works of the transitional figures that became the chief ingredients of a new poetry. The horrors of war and the destruction of values that both preceded it and followed it caused writers like T. S. Eliot to see the world as a cruel, dry, shallow, spiritless desert. Gertrude Stein's "lost generation" lived in Eliot's *The Waste Land* and had the same lack of intense conviction that characterized his J. Alfred Prufrock (see p. 425) and his Hollow Men. Hart Crane probably owed some literary debts to Emily Dickinson—a sort of poetic shorthand and startling images. Many poets borrowed Hopkins' torment of soul and his tortured language (*see The Windhover* and *Thou Art Indeed Just, Lord,* pp. 411 and 412). And Yeats, who had been abandoned by James Joyce as already too old to help, became, in his final twenty years, one of the chief models for younger writers who were repudiating most of their immediate predecessors.

The influence of Dickinson, Yeats, and Hopkins has not yet disappeared. Some part of it has not even diminished. These three writers especially have become objects of the most penetrating criticism of our time; they have been given overwhelming attention by scholars. Thomas Hardy's reputation as a poet has grown to the point where it almost surpasses his fame as a novelist. Even Bridges and Housman have won new laurels as contributors to the modernist movement. All seem to have looked more consistently toward the future than over their shoulders at the past.

FOR FURTHER READING:

Leavis, F. R. *New Bearings in English Poetry.* London, 1932. (On Hopkins.)
Van Doren, Mark. "The Poems of Thomas Hardy," *Four Poets on Poetry.* Baltimore, 1959.

Unterecker, John. *A Reader's Guide to William Butler Yeats*. New York, 1959.

Guérard, Albert. *Robert Bridges, A Study of Traditionalism in Poetry*. Cambridge, Mass., 1942.

Wilson, Edmund. *The Triple Thinkers*. New York, 1938. (On Housman.)

Chase, Richard. *Emily Dickinson*. New York, 1951.

EMILY DICKINSON

BECAUSE I COULD NOT STOP FOR DEATH

Because I could not stop for Death—
He kindly stopped for me—
The Carriage held but just Ourselves—
And Immortality.

We slowly drove—He knew no haste
And I had put away
My labor and my leisure too,
For His Civility—

We passed the School, where Children strove
At Recess—in the Ring—
We passed the Fields of Gazing Grain—
We passed the Setting Sun—

Or rather—He passed Us—
The Dews drew quivering and chill—
For only Gossamer, my Gown—
My Tippet—only Tulle—

We paused before a House that seemed
A Swelling of the Ground—
The Roof was scarcely visible—
The Cornice—in the Ground—

EMILY DICKINSON (1830-1886) was born in Amherst, Massachusetts. She began writing in the winter of 1861 but published only seven of the seventeen hundred poems she wrote. It has been said that two men—Benjamin Newton and Charles Wadsworth—exerted strong influences on her. When they were removed from her life, by varying circumstances, she became something of a recluse in the house of her birth, where she died.

Since then—'tis Centuries—and yet
Feels shorter than the Day
I first surmised the Horses' Heads
Were toward Eternity—

THE BRAIN, WITHIN ITS GROOVE

The Brain, within its Groove
Runs evenly—and true—
But let a Splinter swerve—
'Twere easier for You—

To put a Current back—
When Floods have slit the Hills—
And scooped a Turnpike for Themselves—
And trodden out the Mills—

HOW MANY TIMES THESE LOW FEET STAGGERED

How many times these low feet staggered—
Only the soldered mouth can tell—
Try—can you stir the awful rivet—
Try—can you lift the hasps of steel!

Stroke the cool forehead—hot so often—
Lift—if you care—the listless hair—
Handle the adamantine fingers
Never a thimble—more—shall wear—

Buzz the dull flies—on the chamber window—
Brave—shines the sun through the freckled pane—
Fearless—the cobweb swings from the ceiling—
Indolent Housewife—in Daisies—lain!

AFTER GREAT PAIN, A FORMAL FEELING COMES

After great pain, a formal feeling comes—
The stiff Heart questions was it He, that bore,
The Nerves sit ceremonious, like Tombs—
And Yesterday, or Centuries before?

The Feet, mechanical, go round—
Of Ground, or Air, or Ought—

A Wooden way
Regardless grown,
A Quartz contentment, like a stone—

This is the Hour of Lead—
Remembered, if outlived,
As Freezing persons, recollect the Snow—
First—Chill—then Stupor—then the letting go—

GERARD MANLEY HOPKINS

THE WINDHOVER

To Christ Our Lord

I caught this morning morning's minion, kingdom of daylight's
    dauphin, dapple-dawn-drawn Falcon, in his riding
Of the rolling level underneath him steady air, and striding
High there, how he rung upon the rein of a wimpling wing
In his ecstasy! then off, off forth on swing,
    As a skate's heel sweeps smooth on a bow-bend: the hurl
    and gliding
Rebuffed the big wind. My heart in hiding
Stirred for a bird,—the achieve of, the mastery of the thing!

Brute beauty and valor and act, oh, air, pride, plume, here
    Buckle! AND the fire that breaks from thee then, a billion
Times told lovelier, more dangerous, O my chevalier!

No wonder of it: shéer plód makes plough down sillion
Shine, and blue-bleak embers, ah my dear,
    Fall, gall themselves, and gash gold-vermilion.

FELIX RANDAL

Felix Randal the farrier, O he is dead then? my duty all ended,
Who have watched his mould of man, big-boned and hardy-handsome
Pining, pining, till time when reason rambled in it and some
Fatal four disorders, fleshed there, all contended?

GERARD MANLEY HOPKINS (1844-1889) was born in Essex. He was converted to Roman Catholicism in 1866 and entered Jesuit orders two years later, finally becoming Professor of Greek at Dublin University. Not until thirty years after his death were his poems published.

Sickness broke him. Impatient he cursed at first, but mended
Being anointed and all; though a heavenlier heart began some
Months earlier, since I had our sweet reprieve and ransom
Tendered to him. Ah well, God rest him all road ever he offended!

This seeing the sick endears them to us, us too it endears.
My tongue had taught thee comfort, touch had quenched thy tears,
Thy tears that touched my heart, child, Felix, poor Felix Randal;

How far from then forethought of, all thy more boisterous years,
When thou at the random grim forge, powerful amidst peers,
Didst fettle for the great gray drayhorse his bright and battering
    sandal!

THOU ART INDEED JUST, LORD

*Justus quidem tu es, Domine, si disputem tecum: verumtamen justa lo-
quar ad te: Quare via impiorum prosperatur? etc.*

Thou art indeed just, Lord, if I contend
With thee; but, sir, so what I plead is just.
Why do sinners' ways prosper? and why must
Disappointment all I endeavour end?
Wert thou my enemy, O thou my friend,
How wouldst thou worse, I wonder, than thou dost
Defeat, thwart me? Oh, the sots and thralls of lust
Do in spare hours more thrive than I that spend,
Sir, life upon thy cause. See, banks and brakes
Now, leavèd how thick! lacèd they are again
With fretty chervil, look, and fresh wind shakes
Them; birds build—but not I build; no, but strain,
Time's eunuch, and not breed one work that wakes.
Mine, O thou lord of life, send my roots rain.

RIBBLESDALE

Earth, sweet Earth, sweet landscape, with leavès throng
And louchèd low grass, heaven that dost appeal
To, with no tongue to plead, no heart to feel;
That canst but only be, but dost that long—

Thou canst but be, but that thou well dost; strong
Thy plea with him who dealt, nay does now deal,

Thy lovely dale down thus and thus bids reel
Thy river, and o'er gives all to rack or wrong.

   And what is Earth's eye, tongue, or heart else, where
Else, but in dear and dogged man?—Ah, the heir
To his own selfbent so bound, so tied to his turn,
To thriftless reave both our rich round world bare
And none reck of world after, this bids wear
Earth brows of such care, care and dear concern.

ROBERT BRIDGES

CHEDDAR PINKS

Mid the squander'd colour
    idling as I lay
Reading the Odyssey
    in my rock-garden
I espied the cluster'd
    tufts of Cheddar pinks
Burgeoning with promise
    of their scented bloom
All the modish motley
    of their bloom to-be
Thrust up in narrow buds
    on the slender stalks
Thronging springing urgent
    hasting (so I thought)
As if they feared to be
    too late for summer—
Like schoolgirls overslept
    waken'd by the bell
Leaping from bed to don
    their muslin dresses
      On a May morning:

Then felt I like to one
    indulging in sin

ROBERT BRIDGES (1844-1930) was born at Walmer, in Kent. He studied for a career in medicine but gave it up for literature in 1882. In 1913 he was named poet laureate.

(Whereto Nature is oft
    a blind accomplice)
Because my aged bones
    so enjoyed the sun
There as I lay along
    idling with my thoughts
Reading an old poet
    while the busy world
Toil'd moil'd fuss'd and scurried
    worried bought and sold
Plotted stole and quarrel'd
    fought and God knows what.
I had forgotten Homer
    dallying with my thoughts
Till I fell to making
    these little verses
Communing with the flowers
    in my rock-garden
        On a May morning.

ALFRED EDWARD HOUSMAN

EPITAPH ON AN ARMY OF MERCENARIES

These, in the day when heaven was falling,
    The hour when earth's foundations fled,
Followed their mercenary calling
    And took their wages and are dead.

Their shoulders held the sky suspended;
    They stood, and earth's foundations stay;
What God abandoned, these defended,
    And saved the sum of things for pay.

I HOED AND TRENCHED AND WEEDED

I hoed and trenched and weeded,
    And took the flowers to fair:

ALFRED EDWARD HOUSMAN (1859-1936) was one of the greatest of recent classical scholars, holding the post of professor of Latin at Cambridge University. He published only two slim volumes of verse during his life.

I brought them home unheeded;
    The hue was not the wear.

So up and down I sow them
    For lads like me to find,
When I shall lie below them,
    A dead man out of mind.

Some seed the birds devour,
    And some the season mars,
But here and there will flower
    The solitary stars,

And fields will yearly bear them
    As light-leaved spring comes on,
And luckless lads will wear them
    When I am dead and gone.

ON WENLOCK EDGE

On Wenlock Edge the wood's in trouble;
    His forest fleece the Wrekin heaves;
The gale, it plies the saplings double,
    And thick on Severn snow the leaves.

'Twould blow like this through holt and hanger
    When Uricon the city stood:
'Tis the old wind in the old anger,
    But then it threshed another wood.

Then, 'twas before my time, the Roman
    At yonder heaving hill would stare:
The blood that warms an English yeoman,
    The thoughts that hurt him, they were there.

There, like the wind through woods in riot,
    Through him the gale of life blew high;
The tree of man was never quiet:
    Then 'twas the Roman, now 'tis I.

The gale, it plies the saplings double,
    It blows so hard, 'twill soon be gone:
To-day the Roman and his trouble
    Are ashes under Uricon.

THOMAS HARDY

THE OXEN

Christmas Eve, and twelve of the clock,
  "Now they are all on their knees,"
An elder said as we sat in a flock
  By the embers in hearthside ease.

We pictured the meek mild creatures where
  They dwelt in their strawy pen.
Nor did it occur to one of us there
  To doubt they were kneeling then.

So fair a fancy few would weave
  In these years! Yet, I feel,
If someone said on Christmas Eve,
  "Come; see the oxen kneel

"In the lonely barton by yonder coomb
  Our childhood used to know,"
I should go with him in the gloom,
  Hoping it might be so.

AFTER THE LAST BREATH

There's no more to be done, or feared, or hoped;
None now need watch, speak low, and list, and tire;
No irksome crease outsmoothed, no pillow sloped
    Does she require.

Blankly we gaze. We are free to go or stay;
Our morrow's anxious plans have missed their aim;
Whether we leave to-night or wait till day
    Counts as the same.

The lettered vessels of medicaments
Seem asking wherefore we have set them here;

THOMAS HARDY (1840-1928) began his career as an architect but soon turned to literature. Poetry was his first love, but prose fiction afforded him fame and money. He returned to poetry after extraordinary success as a novelist and published his first volume of verse in 1898.

> Each palliative its silly face presents
> As useless gear.

> And yet we feel that something savours well;
> We note a numb relief withheld before;
> Our well-beloved is prisoner in the cell
> Of Time no more.

> We see by littles now the deft achievement
> Whereby she has escaped the Wrongers all,
> In view of which our momentary bereavement
> Outshapes but small.

AFTER THE LAST BREATH was written by Hardy sometime in 1904, following the death of his mother on April 3. It was first published in *Time's Laughingstocks* (1909) without identification of whom it commemorated. In subsequent editions Hardy added his mother's initials and dates—J. H. (Jemima Hardy), 1813-1904. The poem is singularly modern in its tone and treatment and as such is different from many of Hardy's other poems. A flaw common to much of his work is looseness of construction, which comes from unnecessary repetition or from the padding out of a line to meet metrical requirements. The diction of his early poems, while frequently colloquial, folksy, and dialectal, is often blurred, worn, sentimental, and "poetic" in the sense that it strays from the accents of spoken speech. *After the Last Breath* escapes these shortcomings by the use of understatement, fresh language, and exceedingly careful formal control.

The poem's modernity may best be shown by comparison with two other poems on the same topic, the death of a lady: E. A. Robinson's *For a Dead Lady* (p. 472) and John Crowe Ransom's *Here Lies a Lady* (p. 483). It would seem either that Robinson's poem influenced Hardy or Hardy's poem Robinson, since both start with similar negative constructions:

> There's no more to be done

> No more with overflowing light

but interrelation between the poems is not likely, since both were published in 1909 and it is hardly possible that either poet saw the other's poem before publication. Ransom's poem did not appear until 1924.

Although both Robinson and Hardy are known for their pessimism and these two elegies carry a heavy burden of gloom, there is at least some sense of triumph in Hardy's poem, for the lady, his mother, has out-witted the malignant forces of destiny:

> . . . the deft achievement
> Whereby she has escaped the Wrongers all,

The cynical reflection that only through death can these "Wrongers" be escaped still remains, but Robinson's poem is even more pessimistic, for here there is no sense of victory of any kind. He gives us the feeling that the dead lady has been overcome by the "Wrongers all":

> The beauty, shattered by the laws
> That have creation in their keeping,

In many ways Hardy's poem is more modern than Robinson's, which uses diction that is traditional in elegies on beautiful women. Robinson's lady moved with "flowing wonder"; she had divine, definitive grace, and roses withered at her breast. Hardy avoids these poetic commonplaces. Some of the differences in diction may be traced to the relation of mourner to lady in the two poems. Hardy's mother lived to be ninety-one, and death was as much a release to her as it must have been to her children and other relatives forced to give her care and nursing. Her death was not as tragic to others as the death of Robinson's lady apparently was.

But even while we pose this explanation, we still find a distinctively modern quality in such phrases as "irksome crease," "lettered vessels of medicaments," or "Each palliative its silly face presents/ As useless gear." Their modernity of tone is comparable to that achieved by Ransom in *Here Lies a Lady* with such terms as "medicos marveling sweetly," or "she sat in a maze/ Of old scraps of laces" and "After six little spaces of chill, and six of burning." Neither Hardy nor Ransom neglects the honest appearance of the sickroom, and the language of both poets matches the incongruities always present at the grim, great act of dying. A word as harsh as *gear* in the way Hardy uses it looks all the way forward to W. H. Auden's "The words of a dead man/ Are modified in the guts of the living" (see p. 456).

The increase in economy which Hardy shows in the lines of *After the Last Breath* is impossible to illustrate without reference to his other poems. One must have read widely in the eight hundred pages of his collected poems to appreciate the success of these stanzas. But even without such comparison, we can observe that Hardy has captured most of the emotions and activities of the sickroom in two crisp lines:

> There's no more to be done, or feared, or hoped;
> None now need watch, speak low, and list, and tire;

The frequent punctuation with its frequent pauses in some way re-creates the start and stop of grief and bewilderment, the confusion and questioning in the minds of those intimately involved. The antithesis of shock and relief is carried out by the remaining four stanzas. Stanzas 2 and 3 explore the aimlessness of lives that have had one of their most important concerns removed and the uselessness of the efforts to thwart death:

> Blankly we gaze. We are free to go or stay;
> . . . .
> . . . vessels of medicaments
> Seem asking wherefore we have set them here;

Stanzas 4 and 5 express the reconcilement, the consolation that is not long in coming when the person who has died was very old. Grief gives way not out of selfish relief that an ordeal is over but because

> Our well-beloved is prisoner in the cell
> Of Time no more.

This mood carries something of the old pastoral elegy, as in Milton's *Lycidas* (p. 178): "Weep no more, woeful shepherds, weep no more." Although Hardy does not see death in terms of his mother's soul going to heaven—the reason for which Milton ceases to mourn for Lycidas—he welcomes the release it offers her.

STEPHEN CRANE

ONCE I SAW MOUNTAINS ANGRY

> Once I saw mountains angry,
> And ranged in battle-front.
> Against them stood a little man;
> Ay, he was no bigger than my finger.
> I laughed, and spoke to one near me,
> "Will he prevail?"
> "Surely," replied this other;
> "His grandfathers beat them many times."
> Then did I see much virtue in grandfathers—

STEPHEN CRANE (1871-1900) was born in Newark, New Jersey. Beginning a journalistic career as a free-lance writer, he became a war correspondent and covered actions in Cuba and Greece. His first novel, *Maggie: A Girl of the Streets,* was published under a pseudonym at his own expense when he was twenty-one; *The Red Badge of Courage,* published the following year, made him famous. His two volumes of verse appeared in 1895 and 1899.

At least, for the little man
Who stood against the mountains.

WILLIAM BUTLER YEATS

THE LAKE ISLE OF INNISFREE

I will arise and go now, and go to Innisfree,
And a small cabin build there, of clay and wattles made;
Nine bean rows will I have there, a hive for the honey bee,
And live alone in the bee-loud glade.

And I shall have some peace there, for peace comes dropping slow,
Dropping from the veils of the morning to where the cricket sings;
There midnight's all a glimmer, and noon a purple glow,
And evening full of the linnet's wings.

I will arise and go now, for always night and day
I hear lake water lapping with low sounds by the shore;
While I stand on the roadway, or on the pavements gray,
I hear it in the deep heart's core.

THE SONG OF WANDERING AENGUS

I went out to the hazel wood,
Because a fire was in my head,
And cut and peeled a hazel wand,
And hooked a berry to a thread;
And when white moths were on the wing,
And moth-like stars were flickering out,
I dropped the berry in a stream
And caught a little silver trout.

When I had laid it on the floor
I went to blow the fire a-flame,
But something rustled on the floor,
And some one called me by my name:
It had become a glimmering girl

WILLIAM BUTLER YEATS (1865-1939) was born near Dublin, the son of a Pre-Raphaelite painter. Yeats played an important part in the organization of the Abbey Theater as well as a role in Irish politics. He served as a senator from 1922 to 1928. The Nobel Prize for literature was accorded him in 1923.

With apple blossom in her hair
Who called me by my name and ran
And faded through the brightening air.

Though I am old with wandering
Through hollow lands and hilly lands,
I will find out where she has gone,
And kiss her lips and take her hands;
And walk among long dappled grass,
And pluck till time and times are done,
The silver apples of the moon,
The golden apples of the sun.

VII

THE TWENTIETH CENTURY

SYMBOLISM

T HE greatest single influence upon the poetry of the twentieth century has been the Symbolist movement as it developed in France and as it was incorporated into English verse through the writings of William Butler Yeats, T. S. Eliot, and Hart Crane. In France, Symbolism was a reaction against the form of realism called naturalism. It had its origins in the writings of Baudelaire, which in turn were influenced by the tales of Edgar Allan Poe. But the high priest of French Symbolism was Stephen Mallarmé, who saw in this movement a means of liberating French literature from the flatness he found in naturalism and from traditional restraints. As high priest he developed a text that gave the law: poetry must be freed in order to capture more fully, more exactly, the sensations and emotions of the poet; all emotions, all experiences are unique, and they require unique expression to record them.

The symbols used by the Symbolists mark a break with poetic tradition. Conventional symbols were fixed and widely understood, but the new poetry required new symbols, and often these were arbitrary, obscure, and even impenetrable. Although not always ultimately successful, the ambiguities thus obtained often supplied richness to the poetic texture, depth to the poem as a whole, and density or compactness to the individual line or lesser units of the poem. The Symbolists believed in stating things only indirectly: mystery was desirable; the implicit is always more exciting than the explicit. Logic and the grammar of clear communication were discarded. In their place was used a language that expressed the free associations of the mind, and images and symbols that captured emotions which are sometimes beyond language. Among those writing in English, Hart Crane comes closer to the French Symbolists in method than does any other poet.

Comparable to the new freedom in language was a new freedom in verse forms. It was the French Symbolists who, in their practice of *vers libre,* gave greatest impetus to the prosodic innovations of Walt Whitman. These were taken back again into English practice by Ezra Pound, by the Imagists, and by T. S. Eliot. The writers of free verse substituted for the counting of syllable and foot a concern for larger units of the poem: cadence, rhythm, balance of phrase, clause, verb cluster, and items in a series. Much new poetry of value came from these experiments in form, and freedom from artificial restraints of line length and rhyme gave the poet new breadth in which to create exciting new effects. E. E. Cummings spread his poems all over the page in in-

teresting typographical patterns that were supposed to support meaning.
Wilfred Owen experimented with slant rhyme (see glossary). Less ad-
venturous poets were content merely to vary line length, but they too
intended that their variations should be functional and organic, that they
should grow out of the demands of content, out of the scope of the
images. H. D. (Hilda Doolittle) was preëminent in refining and sharpening
her precision-cut Imagist poems through a brilliant harmony of symbol
and form. As late as the 1960's, Marianne Moore was still achieving remarkable effects through similar methods (see *O To Be a Dragon*, p.
454). However, too many poets accepted the freedom of unrestricted
forms without taking on also the responsibility of finding suitable substitutes for traditional modes of expression. The result was a great many
poems that were no more than flat, inchoate, and disjunctive prose. Robert
Frost derided the practice as similar to playing tennis without a net.

In the works of Yeats and Eliot the search for new symbols became
a reëxamination of myth. Yeats went frequently to Irish legend and folklore but also ransacked classical materials and medieval storehouses (*Leda
and the Swan, Sailing to Byzantium*). Eliot used that great compilation
of comparative mythology, *The Golden Bough,* gathered by the anthro-
pologist J. G. Frazer in 1890. Yeats found Mallarmé important and
wrote that "translations from Mallarmé may have given elaborate form
to my verses of these years, to the latter poems of 'The Wind Among
the Reeds.'" Following Mallarmé's charge to the poets to create arbitrary symbols in order to capture unique thoughts, Yeats developed a
personal mythology; having little or no association with the established
patterns of existence, it was a private interpretation of the entire cosmos, given definitive expression in his prose treatise of 1925, *A Vision.*

Eliot found his inspiration not so much in Mallarmé as in Tristan
Corbière and Jules Laforgue. Their method of free rhythms, of disso-
ciated imagery, of mixing the high with the low, the serious with the
banal, was the method of *The Love Song of J. Alfred Prufrock* (1917)
and led into the greater complexities of *The Waste Land* (1922). But
Eliot wanted answers also, and although he did not develop a set of
private symbols such as those of *A Vision,* his search among the established symbols was for a similar purpose—to find meaning in a world
that seemed fragmented, brutal, sterile, and divorced from spiritual belief. Eliot's reliance upon myth of wide acceptance was therefore an
attempt to link the present with the past, to find value in the lessons
of history, to give order to modern experience. The *locus criticus* for
this belief is perhaps his essay on James Joyce's *Ulysses:*

> In using the myth, in manipulating a continuous parallel between
> contemporaneity and antiquity, Mr. Joyce is pursuing a method which

others must pursue after him. They will not be imitators, any more than the scientist who uses the discoveries of an Einstein in pursuing his own, independent, further investigations. It is simply a way of controlling, of ordering, of giving a shape and a significance to the immense panorama of futility and anarchy which is contemporary history. It is a method already adumbrated by Mr. Yeats, and of the need for which I believe Mr. Yeats to have been the first contemporary to be conscious. It is a method for which the horoscope is auspicious. Psychology (such as it is, and whether our reaction to it be comic or serious), ethnology, and *The Golden Bough* have concurred to make possible what was impossible even a few years ago. Instead of narrative method, we may now use the mythical method. It is, I seriously believe, a step toward making the modern world possible for art. [1923]

After the pessimism—the "futility and anarchy"—of *The Waste Land* and *The Hollow Men* (1925), the increasing need for order led Eliot to the rigorous authoritarianism of a church of elaborate ritual, complex symbolism, and time-rooted sacraments, to poetry such as *Ash Wednesday* (1930), *Journey of the Magi* (1930), and *Four Quartets* (1943).

Poets such as Hart Crane and Allen Tate used the techniques of Eliot, although Crane, in *The Bridge,* was rebelling against the nihilism of Eliot, and Tate never allowed himself the extreme freedom of form of a poem like *Prufrock* or *The Hollow Men.* Crane used the myth of America; some critics felt that it, like the country, was too young, too unformed, not yet unified enough to explain the complete American experience, and that therefore *The Bridge* never achieved the "unfractured idiom" that Crane saw in his chief symbol—Brooklyn Bridge (see p. 437).

Many other poets practicing their craft in the 1930's and 1940's abandoned the nihilism of the so-called "lost generation" of the twenties; but though they moved in new directions of affirmation and belief, their poetic techniques were still for the most part those of the Symbolists. In the thirties, for example, Auden wrote verse of socialistic reform; in the forties and fifties he veered from the extreme left to the extreme right, the conservatism of the organized and orthodox church; but the rhetoric, the verse forms, the meters, and almost all the other devices of poetry he used were still recognizable as those used by Eliot, Yeats, and Pound in the first three decades of the century.

FOR FURTHER READING:

Bowra, C. M. *The Heritage of Symbolism.* London, 1947.
Fraser, G. S. "W. B. Yeats and T. S. Eliot," *T. S. Eliot: A Symposium.* New York, 1958.

Matthiessen, F. O. *The Achievement of T. S. Eliot.* 3rd ed., with an additional chapter by C. Lombardi Barber. New York, 1958.
Wilson, Edmund. *Axel's Castle.* New York, 1931.
Marcel, Raymond. *From Baudelaire to Surrealism.* New York, 1949.

T. S. ELIOT

THE LOVE SONG OF J. ALFRED PRUFROCK

S'io credesse che mia risposta fosse
A persona che mai tornasse al mondo,
Questa fiamma staria senza piu scosse.
Ma perciocche giammai di questo fondo
Non torno vivo alcum, s'i'odo il vero,
Senza tema d'infamia ti rispondo.

Let us go then, you and I,
When the evening is spread out against the sky
Like a patient etherized upon a table;
Let us go, through certain half-deserted streets,
The muttering retreats
Of restless nights in one-night cheap hotels
And sawdust restaurants with oyster-shells:
Streets that follow like a tedious argument
Of insidious intent
To lead you to an overwhelming question. . . .
Oh, do not ask, "What is it?"
Let us go and make our visit.

In the room the women come and go
Talking of Michelangelo.

The yellow fog that rubs its back upon the window-panes,
The yellow smoke that rubs its muzzle on the window-panes,
Licked its tongue into the corners of the evening,
Lingered upon the pools that stand in drains,

THOMAS STEARNS ELIOT (1888-   ) was born in St. Louis and educated at Harvard, the Sorbonne, and Oxford. He entered the British publishing trade with Faber and Faber and became a director of the company. A naturalized British citizen since 1927, he joined the Anglican Church. He was awarded the Nobel Prize for literature in 1948.

Let fall upon its back the soot that falls from chimneys,
Slipped by the terrace, made a sudden leap,
And seeing that it was a soft October night,
Curled once about the house, and fell asleep.

And indeed there will be time
For the yellow smoke that slides along the street,
Rubbing its back upon the window-panes;
There will be time, there will be time
To prepare a face to meet the faces that you meet;
There will be time to murder and create,
And time for all the works and days of hands
That lift and drop a question on your plate;
Time for you and time for me,
And time yet for a hundred indecisions,
And for a hundred visions and revisions,
Before the taking of a toast and tea.

In the room the women come and go
Talking of Michelangelo.

And indeed there will be time
To wonder, "Do I dare?" and, "Do I dare?"
Time to turn back and descend the stair,
With a bald spot in the middle of my hair—
(They will say: "How his hair is growing thin!")
My morning coat, my collar mounting firmly to the chin,
My necktie rich and modest, but asserted by a simple pin—
(They will say: "But how his arms and legs are thin!")
Do I dare
Disturb the universe?
In a minute there is time
For decisions and revisions which a minute will reverse.

For I have known them all already, known them all:—
Have known the evenings, mornings, afternoons,
I have measured out my life with coffee spoons;
I know the voices dying with a dying fall
Beneath the music from a farther room.
        So how should I presume?

And I have known the eyes already, know them all—
The eyes that fix you in a formulated phrase,

And when I am formulated, sprawling on a pin,
When I am pinned and wriggling on the wall,
Then how should I begin
To spit out all the butt-ends of my days and ways?
    And how should I presume?

And I have known the arms already, know them all—
Arms that are braceleted and white and bare
(But in the lamplight, downed with light brown hair!)
Is it perfume from a dress
That makes me so digress?
Arms that lie along a table, or wrap about a shawl,
    And should I then presume?
    And how should I begin?

        .   .   .   .

Shall I say, I have gone at dusk through narrow streets
And watched the smoke that rises from the pipes
Of lonely men in shirt-sleeves, leaning out of windows? . . .

I should have been a pair of ragged claws
Scuttling across the floors of silent seas.

        .   .   .   .

And the afternoon, the evening, sleeps so peacefully!
Smoothed by long fingers,
Asleep . . . tired . . . or it malingers,
Stretched on the floor, here beside you and me.
Should I, after tea and cakes and ices,
Have the strength to force the moment to its crisis?
But though I have wept and fasted, wept and prayed,
Though I have seen my head (grown slightly bald) brought in upon
    a platter,
I am no prophet—and here's no great matter;
I have seen the moment of my greatness flicker,
And I have seen the eternal Footman hold my coat, and snicker,
And in short, I was afraid.

And would it have been worth it, after all,
After the cups, the marmalade, the tea,
Among the porcelain, among some talk of you and me,
Would it have been worth while,
To have bitten off the matter with a smile,

To have squeezed the universe into a ball
To roll it toward some overwhelming question,
To say: "I am Lazarus, come from the dead,
Come back to tell you all, I shall tell you all"—
If one, settling a pillow by her head,
    Should say: "That is not what I meant at all;
    That is not it, at all."

And would it have been worth it, after all,
Would it have been worth while,
After the sunsets and the dooryards and the sprinkled streets,
After the novels, after the teacups, after the skirts that trail along the
        floor—
And this, and so much more?—
It is impossible to say just what I mean!
But as if a magic lantern threw the nerves in patterns on a screen:
Would it have been worth while
If one, settling a pillow or throwing off a shawl,
And turning toward the window, should say:
    "That is not it at all,
    That is not what I meant, at all."

                    .   .   .   .

No! I am not Prince Hamlet, nor was meant to be;
Am an attendant lord, one that will do
To swell a progress, start a scene or two,
Advise the prince; no doubt, an easy tool,
Deferential, glad to be of use,
Politic, cautious, and meticulous;
Full of high sentence, but a bit obtuse;
At times, indeed, almost ridiculous—
Almost, at times, the Fool.

I grow old. . . . I grow old. . . .
I shall wear the bottoms of my trousers rolled.

Shall I part my hair behind? Do I dare to eat a peach?
I shall wear white flannel trousers, and walk upon the beach.
I have heard the mermaids singing, each to each.

I do not think that they will sing to me.

I have seen them riding seaward on the waves
Combing the white hair of the waves blown back

When the wind blows the water white and black.
We have lingered in the chambers of the sea
By sea-girls wreathed with seaweed red and brown
Till human voices wake us, and we drown.

JOURNEY OF THE MAGI

"A cold coming we had of it,
Just the worst time of the year
For a journey, and such a long journey:
The ways deep and the weather sharp,
The very dead of winter."
And the camels galled, sore-footed, refractory,
Lying down in the melting snow.
There were times we regretted
The summer palaces on slopes, the terraces,
And the silken girls bringing sherbet.
Then the camel men cursing and grumbling
And running away, and wanting their liquor and women,
And the night-fires going out, and the lack of shelters,
And the cities hostile and the towns unfriendly
And the villages dirty and charging high prices:
A hard time we had of it.
At the end we preferred to travel all night,
Sleeping in snatches,
With the voices singing in our ears, saying
That this was all folly.

Then at dawn we came down to a temperate valley,
Wet, below the snow line, smelling of vegetation;
With a running stream and a water-mill beating the darkness,
And three trees on the low sky,
And an old white horse galloped away in the meadow.
Then we came to a tavern with vine-leaves over the lintel,
Six hands at an open door dicing for pieces of silver,
And feet kicking the empty wine-skins.
But there was no information, and so we continued
And arrived at evening, not a moment too soon
Finding the place; it was (you may say) satisfactory.

All this was a long time ago, I remember,
And I would do it again, but set down
This set down

This: were we led all that way for
Birth or Death? There was a Birth, certainly,
We had evidence and no doubt. I had seen birth and death,
But had thought they were different; this Birth was
Hard and bitter agony for us, like Death, our death.
We returned to our places, these Kingdoms,
But no longer at ease here, in the old dispensation,
With an alien people clutching their gods.
I should be glad of another death.

WILFRID OWEN

ARMS AND THE BOY

Let the boy try along this bayonet-blade
How cold steel is, and keen with hunger of blood;
Blue with all malice, like a madman's flash;
And thinly drawn with famishing for flesh.

Lend him to stroke these blind, blunt bullet-heads
Which long to nuzzle in the heart of lads,
Or give him cartridges of fine zinc teeth,
Sharp with the sharpness of grief and death.

For his teeth seem for laughing round an apple.
There lurk no claws behind his fingers supple;
And god will grow no talons at his heels,
Nor antlers through the thickness of his curls.

WALLACE STEVENS

THE EMPEROR OF ICE-CREAM

Call the roller of big cigars,
The muscular one, and bid him whip

WILFRED OWEN (1893-1918) was preëminently a war poet. After fighting in
France and being invalided home in 1917, he was sent back as a company commander
in 1918 and was killed in battle a week before the Armistice. His poems were published posthumously by his poet-friend, Siegfried Sassoon.
WALLACE STEVENS (1879-1955) was born in Reading, Pennsylvania, and
attended Harvard University and the New York Law School. In 1916 he became associated with the Hartford Accident and Indemnity Company; from 1934 until his death
he served as vice-president. He received the Bollingen Award for poetry in 1949, the
National Book Award for poetry twice (in 1951 and in 1955), and the Pulitzer Prize
for poetry in 1955.

In kitchen cups concupiscent curds.
Let the wenches dawdle in such dress
As they are used to wear, and let the boys
Bring flowers in last month's newspapers.
Let be be finale of seem.
The only emperor is the emperor of ice-cream.

Take from the dresser of deal,
Lacking the three glass knobs, that sheet
On which she embroidered fantails once
And spread it so as to cover her face.
If her horny feet protrude, they come
To show how cold she is, and dumb.
Let the lamp affix its beam.
The only emperor is the emperor of ice-cream.

PETER QUINCE AT THE CLAVIER

I

Just as my fingers on these keys
   Make music, so the self-same sounds
   On my spirit make a music, too.

Music is feeling, then, not sound;
   And thus it is that what I feel,
   Here in this room, desiring you,

Thinking of your blue-shadowed silk,
   Is music. It is like the strain
   Waked in the elders by Susanna;

Of a green evening, clear and warm,
   She bathed in her still garden, while
   The red-eyed elders, watching, felt
   The basses of their being throb
   In witching chords, and their thin blood
   Pulse pizzicati of Hosanna.

II

In the green water, clear and warm,
Susanna lay.
She searched

The touch of springs,
And found
Concealed imaginings.
She sighed
For so much melody.

Upon the bank she stood
In the cool
Of spent emotions.
She felt, among the leaves,
The dew
Of old devotions.

She walked upon the grass,
Still quavering.
The winds were like her maids,
On timid feet,
Fetching her woven scarves,
Yet wavering.

A breath upon her hand
Muted the night.
She turned—
A cymbal crashed,
And roaring horns.

III

Soon, with a noise like tambourines,
Came her attendant Byzantines.

They wondered why Susanna cried
Against the elders by her side:

And as they whispered, the refrain
Was like a willow swept by rain.

Anon their lamps' uplifted flame
Revealed Susanna and her shame.

And then the simpering Byzantines,
Fled, with a noise like tambourines.

IV

Beauty is momentary in the mind—
The fitful tracing of a portal;
But in the flesh it is immortal.

The body dies; the body's beauty lives.
So evenings die, in their green going,
A wave, interminably flowing.
So gardens die, their meek breath scenting
The cowl of winter, done repenting.
So maidens die, to the auroral
Celebration of a maiden's choral.

Susanna's music touched the bawdy strings
Of those white elders; but, escaping,
Left only Death's ironic scraping.
Now, in its immortality, it plays
On the clear viol of her memory,
And makes a constant sacrament of praise.

SUNDAY MORNING

I

Complacencies of the peignoir, and late
Coffee and oranges in a sunny chair,
And the green freedom of a cockatoo
Upon a rug mingle to dissipate
The holy hush of ancient sacrifice.
She dreams a little, and she feels the dark
Encroachment of that old catastrophe,
As a calm darkens among water-lights.
The pungent oranges and bright, green wings
Seem things in some procession of the dead,
Winding across wide water, without sound.
The day is like wide water, without sound,
Stilled for the passing of her dreaming feet
Over the seas, to silent Palestine,
Dominion of the blood and sepulchre.

II

Why should she give her bounty to the dead?
What is divinity if it can come
Only in silent shadows and in dreams?
Shall she not find in comforts of the sun,
In pungent fruit and bright, green wings, or else
In any balm or beauty of the earth,
Things to be cherished like the thought of heaven?
Divinity must live within herself:
Passions of rain, or moods in falling snow;
Grievings in loneliness, or unsubdued
Elations when the forest blooms; gusty
Emotions on wet roads on autumn nights;
All pleasures and all pains, remembering
The bough of summer and the winter branch.
These are the measures destined for her soul.

III

Jove in the clouds had his inhuman birth.
No mother suckled him, no sweet land gave
Large-mannered motions to his mythy mind.
He moved among us, as a muttering king,
Magnificent, would move among his hinds,
Until our blood, commingling, virginal,
With heaven, brought such requital to desire
The very hinds discerned it, in a star.
Shall our blood fail? Or shall it come to be
The blood of paradise? And shall the earth
Seem all of paradise that we shall know?
The sky will be much friendlier then than now,
A part of labor and a part of pain,
And next in glory to enduring love,
Not this dividing and indifferent blue.

IV

She says, "I am content when wakened birds,
Before they fly, test the reality
Of misty fields, by their sweet questionings;

But when the birds are gone, and their warm fields
Return no more, where, then, is paradise?"
There is not any haunt of prophecy,
Nor any old chimera of the grave,
Neither the golden underground, nor isle
Melodious, where spirits gat them home,
Nor visionary south, nor cloudy palm
Remote on heaven's hill, that has endured
As April's green endures; or will endure
Like her remembrance of awakened birds,
Or her desire for June and evening, tipped
By the consummation of the swallow's wings.

V

She says, "But in contentment I still feel
The need of some imperishable bliss."
Death is the mother of beauty; hence from her,
Alone, shall come fulfilment to our dreams
And our desires. Although she strews the leaves
Of sure obliteration on our paths,
The path sick sorrow took, the many paths
Where triumph rang its brassy phrase, or love
Whispered a little out of tenderness,
She makes the willow shiver in the sun
For maidens who were wont to sit and gaze
Upon the grass, relinquished to their feet.
She causes boys to pile new plums and pears
On disregarded plate. The maidens taste
And stray impassioned in the littering leaves.

VI

Is there no change of death in paradise?
Does ripe fruit never fall? Or do the boughs
Hang always heavy in that perfect sky,
Unchanging, yet so like our perishing earth,
With rivers like our own that seek for seas
They never find, the same receding shores
That never touch with inarticulate pang?
Why set the pear upon those river-banks

Or spice the shores with odors of the plum?
Alas, that they should wear our colors there,
The silken weavings of our afternoons,
And pick the strings of our insipid lutes!
Death is the mother of beauty, mystical,
Within whose burning bosom we devise
Our earthly mothers waiting, sleeplessly.

VII

Supple and turbulent, a ring of men
Shall chant in orgy on a summer morn
Their boisterous devotion to the sun,
Not as a god, but as a god might be,
Naked among them, like a savage source.
Their chant shall be a chant of paradise,
Out of their blood, returning to the sky;
And in their chant shall enter, voice by voice,
The windy lake wherein their lord delights,
The trees, like serafin, and echoing hills,
That choir among themselves long afterward.
They shall know well the heavenly fellowship
Of men that perish and of summer morn.
And whence they came and whither they shall go
The dew upon their feet shall manifest.

VIII

She hears, upon that water without sound,
A voice that cries, "The tomb in Palestine
Is not the porch of spirits lingering.
It is the grave of Jesus, where He lay."
We live in an old chaos of the sun,
Or old dependency of day and night,
Or island solitude, unsponsored, free,
Of that wide water, inescapable.
Deer walk upon our mountains, and the quail
Whistle about us their spontaneous cries;
Sweet berries ripen in the wilderness;
And, in the isolation of the sky,
At evening, casual flocks of pigeons make
Ambiguous undulations as they sink,
Downward to darkness, on extended wings.

ROBINSON JEFFERS

SHINE, PERISHING REPUBLIC

While this America settles in the mold of its vulgarity, heavily
    thickening to empire,
And protest, only a bubble in the molten mass, pops and sighs out,
    and the mass hardens,

I sadly smiling remember that the flower fades to make fruit, the
    fruit rots to make earth.
Out of the mother; and through the spring exultances, ripeness and
    decadence; and home to the mother.

You make haste haste on decay: not blameworthy; life is good, be it
    stubbornly long or suddenly
A mortal splendor: meteors are not needed less than mountains: shine,
    perishing republic.

But for my children, I would have them keep their distance from the
    thickening center; corruption
Never has been compulsory, when the cities lie at the monster's feet
    there are left the mountains.

And boys, be in nothing so moderate as in love of man, a clever
    servant, insufferable master.
There is the trap that catches noblest spirits, that caught—they say—
    God, when he walked on earth.

HART CRANE

THE BRIDGE: To Brooklyn Bridge

How many dawns, chill from his rippling rest
The seagull's wings shall dip and pivot him,

ROBINSON JEFFERS (1887-1962) was born in Pittsburgh but moved to California in his youth and graduated from Occidental College. He spent most of his life on the California coast, near the Point Lobos that figures in many of his poems. HAROLD HART CRANE (1899-1932), son of an Ohio candy manufacturer, published only two volumes of poetry—*White Buildings* (1926) and *The Bridge* (1930)—but these established him as one of the most individual voices in American poetry since the First World War. He is believed to have jumped to his death from the deck of a steamer in the Gulf of Mexico.

Shedding white rings of tumult, building high
Over the chained bay waters Liberty—

Then, with inviolate curve, forsake our eyes
As apparitional as sails that cross
Some page of figures to be filed away;
—Till elevators drop us from our day. . . .

I think of cinemas, panoramic sleights
With multitudes bent toward some flashing scene
Never disclosed, but hastened to again,
Foretold to other eyes on the same screen;

And Thee, across the harbor, silver-paced
As though the sun took step of thee, yet left
Some motion ever unspent in thy stride—
Implicitly thy freedom staying thee!

Out of some subway scuttle, cell or loft
A bedlamite speeds to thy parapets,
Tilting there momently, shrill shirt ballooning,
A jest falls from the speechless caravan.

Down Wall, from girder into street noon leaks,
A rip-tooth of the sky's acetylene;
All afternoon the cloud-flown derricks turn . . .
Thy cables breathe the North Atlantic still.

And obscure as that heaven of the Jews,
Thy guerdon . . . Accolade thou dost bestow
Of anonymity time cannot raise:
Vibrant reprieve and pardon thou dost show.

O harp and altar, of the fury fused,
(How could mere toil align thy choiring strings!)
Terrific threshold of the prophet's pledge,
Prayer of pariah, and the lover's cry,—

Again the traffic lights that skim thy swift
Unfractioned idiom, immaculate sigh of stars,
Beading thy path—condense eternity:
And we have seen night lifted in thine arms.

Under thy shadow by the piers I waited;
Only in darkness is thy shadow clear.
The City's fiery parcels all undone,
Already snow submerges an iron year . . .

O Sleepless as the river under thee,
Vaulting the sea, the prairies' dreaming sod,
Unto us lowliest sometime sweep, descend
And of the curveship lend a myth to God.

AT MELVILLE'S TOMB

Often beneath the wave, wide from this ledge
The dice of drowned men's bones he saw bequeath
An embassy. Their numbers as he watched,
Beat on the dusty shore and were obscured.

And wrecks passed without sound of bells,
The calyx of death's bounty giving back
A scattered chapter, livid hieroglyph,
The portent wound in corridors of shells.

Then in the circuit calm of one vast coil,
Its lashings charmed and malice reconciled,
Frosted eyes there were that lifted altars;
And silent answers crept across the stars.

Compass, quadrant and sextant contrive
No farther tides . . . High in the azure steeps
Monody shall not wake the mariner.
This fabulous shadow only the sea keeps.

THE MERMEN

And if
Thy banished trunk be found in our dominions—
—King Lear

Buddhas and engines serve us undersea;
Though why they bide here, only hell that's sacked
Of every blight and ingenuity—
Can solve.

> The Cross alone has flown the wave.
> But since the Cross sank, much that's warped and cracked
> Has followed in its name, has heaped its grave.
>
> Oh—
>
> Gallows and guillotines to hail the sun
> And smoking racks for penance when day's done!
>
> No—
>
> Leave us you idols of Futurity—alone,
> Here where we finger moidores of spent grace
> And ponder the bright stains that starred His Throne
> —This Cross, agleam still with a human face!

THE MERMEN Both the title and the epigraph of Crane's poem supply literary associations that must be examined before the text itself can be read intelligently. While the idea of a mermaid is familiar to us, that of a merman is not; therefore, Crane's title causes us to think immediately of another poem in the language that takes as its subject this fabled creature—Matthew Arnold's *The Forsaken Merman*. Although much of the pathos of Arnold's poem comes from the merman's being forsaken by a mortal woman who has loved him and borne his children, additional pity is found in his plight as a supernatural creature who is denied the church and salvation; as such he is like the female water spirit called the undine, who in the same manner is banished from the Christian community. Crane's epigraph from *King Lear* refers also to banishment; Lear pronounces this heavy judgment upon Kent. In both cases—that of the forsaken merman and that of the banished Kent—the exile wishes humbly to be allowed into the forbidden kingdom.

Crane's mermen become understandable against this literary background. They too are banished from Christianity, but in a somewhat different manner. They have known the Cross because once it had sunk beneath the waves; now it "has flown," but the atrocities that have been practiced in the name of the Cross have remained. The inhumanities of "Gallows and guillotines" are used apparently upon the mermen, their administrators claiming them perhaps as tools of salvation. "Smoking racks" as well, instruments of torture, are used inhumanly to purify the soul, as they were used historically by the Inquisition. These thoughts— the realization that the Cross has fled, that evil has replaced it, and the awareness that pain and death have been substituted for love and light— lead the mermen to cry "Oh" and "No."

Since no true Christianity remains, the mermen ask that these substitutes for the Cross—the "idols of Futurity"—leave them. Instead, the sea-dwellers will meditate on merciful Christianity, the "bright stains" that symbolize God's gentleness, His compassion, His mercy. They will think instead of the Cross of the Crucifixion, glowing still with the humanity of Christ's benevolent gaze. It is apparent that the mermen do not want to rid their undersea world of the Cross; they desire it still, as poignantly as the forsaken merman desires his Margaret, as the banished Kent desires to serve Lear.

The larger implications of the poem are clear. Crane is not confining his picture of spiritual barrenness to an undersea realm; he is suggesting that mankind is drowned under a flood of cruelty and intolerance, that it suffers under a tyrannic deputy instead of glorying under a beneficent God. The world suffers on, supported weakly with shreds of other faiths ("Buddhas") and with mechanical contrivances ("engines"), even though its people cannot understand why these things will remain in a place which, they recognize, has sacked hell "Of every blight and ingenuity." All that men can do is finger the golden coins ("moidores") of grace that they have spent through spiritual profligacy and think about the blessings ("bright stains") they have lost.

Crane's technique in *The Mermen* tells us something about modern poetry in general. It is highly intellectualized poetry, depending frequently upon literary allusion. It is considered by its practitioners to be part of an unbroken tradition of English poetry: part of time and part of history. (See T. S. Eliot's essay, *Tradition and the Individual Talent.*) But Crane takes many of his images and symbols from contemporary life also, sometimes to stress the mechanistic quality of the twentieth century. This practice is seen more clearly in *The Bridge,* Crane's most ambitious work, but it is discernible in *The Mermen* in the use of such symbols as "engines" and "idols of Futurity."

Modern poetry has attempted many experiments in versification; we might almost say that it has been overly conscious of metrical innovation. Walt Whitman, in the second half of the nineteenth century, was instrumental in freeing English verse from the restraints of the conventional forms of older poetry. His free verse pointed the way to further divestment of constraint. In the poetry of writers like E. E. Cummings and William Carlos Williams we can see the extremes to which metrical experimentation has sometimes led. Crane, too, has attempted new forms and has written verse (tone poems, prose poems, free verse) that is divorced from all artificial limitations. In his later work he returns to formal poetry, though still experimenting within the traditional types.

In *The Mermen* Crane attempts an interesting though ultimately unsuccessful experiment. He works with the iambic line of five feet, the commonest line of English poetry, but though the poem rhymes in recognizable patterns, it is not built upon conventional stanzas. Crane's experimentation is with the extra syllables at the end of the second and third divisions: the "Oh" and the "No." Both these syllables are stressed and in effect turn the pentameter line into a six stress unit. Their function is both outside the poem and within it. In order to draw the syllables more strongly into the poem, Crane first ends the couplet that is between them with a short *u* rhyme (s*u*n, *done*); then he picks up the long *o* of the expletives themselves in the first line of the quatrain that follows them, in the vowel sound of *alone*. Note also that a dash separates this word typographically from the line in which it is printed, but it is not separated from the syntax of the line in the same way that "Oh" and "No" are separated from their lines. Furthermore, the word *alone* supplies the sixth foot to its line, another feature to combine it with the "exiled" words above and another attempt to draw them back into the poem.

Perhaps in this verse experiment Crane was trying to support the meaning of the lyric. The tension established between the mermen who live in one world but desire to be in another is reflected in the tension of these syllables that are both outside the traditional form and yet drawn strongly to it. The experiment is unsuccessful at the last because the rhythm and cadence of the poem have been dealt a severer blow than they can stand. The extra syllables seem ametrical and are so far outside the poem that they are never brought back into it effectively.

ALLEN TATE

DEATH OF LITTLE BOYS

When little boys grow patient at last, weary,
Surrender their eyes immeasurably to the night,
The event will rage terrific as the sea;
Their bodies fill a crumbling room with light.

Then you will touch at the bedside, torn in two,
Gold curls now deftly intricate with gray
As the windowpane extends a fear to you
From one peeled aster drenched with the wind all day.

And over his chest the covers, in an ultimate dream,
Will mount to the teeth, ascend the eyes, press back

ALLEN TATE (1899-   ) was born in Kentucky. He attended Vanderbilt University, where he met John Crowe Ransom and worked with him to found and edit *The Fugitive*. Active as critic as well as poet, he has written some of the most incisive literary essays of his time. Since 1951 he has taught at the University of Minnesota.

The locks—while round his sturdy belly gleam
The suspended breaths, white spars above the wreck:

Till all the guests, come in to look, turn down
Their palms; and delirium assails the cliff
Of Norway where you ponder, and your little town
Reels like a sailor drunk in his rotten skiff. . . .

The bleak sunshine shrieks its chipped music then
Out to the milkweed amid the fields of wheat.
There is a calm for you where men and women
Unroll the chill precision of moving feet.

THE WOLVES

There are wolves in the next room waiting
With heads bent low, thrust out, breathing
At nothing in the dark; between them and me
A white door patched with light from the hall
Where it seems never (so still is the house)
A man has walked from the front door to the stair.
It has all been forever. A beast claws the floor.
I have brooded on angels and archfiends
But no man has ever sat where the next room's
Crowded with wolves, and for the honor of man
I affirm that never have I before. Now while
I have looked for the evening star at a cold window
And whistled when Arcturus spilt his light,
I've heard the wolves scuffle, and said: So this
Is man; so—what better conclusion is there—
The day will not follow night, and the heart
Of man has a little dignity, but less patience
Than a wolf's, and a duller sense that cannot
Smell its own mortality. (This and other
Meditations will be suited to other times
After dog silence howls my epitaph)
Now remember courage, go to the door,
Open it and see whether coiled on the bed
Or cringing by the wall, a savage beast
Maybe with golden hair, with deep eyes
Like a bearded spider on a sunlit floor,
Will snarl—and man can never be alone.

WILLIAM BUTLER YEATS

AMONG SCHOOL CHILDREN

I walk through the long schoolroom questioning;
A kind old nun in a white hood replies;
The children learn to cipher and to sing,
To study reading-books and history,
To cut and sew, be neat in everything
In the best modern way—the children's eyes
In momentary wonder stare upon
A sixty-year-old smiling public man.

I dream of a Ledaean body, bent
Above a sinking fire, a tale that she
Told of a harsh reproof, or trivial event
That changed some childish day to tragedy—
Told, and it seemed that our two natures blent
Into a sphere from youthful sympathy,
Or else, to alter Plato's parable,
Into the yolk and white of the one shell.

And thinking of that fit of grief or rage
I look upon one child or t'other there
And wonder if she stood so at that age—
For even daughters of the swan can share
Something of every paddler's heritage—
And had that colour upon cheek or hair,
And thereupon my heart is driven wild:
She stands before me as a living child.

Her present image floats into the mind—
Did Quattrocento finger fashion it
Hollow of cheek as though it drank the wind
And took a mess of shadows for its meat?
And I though never of Ledaean kind
Had pretty plumage once—enough of that,
Better to smile on all that smile, and show
There is a comfortable kind of scarecrow.

What youthful mother, a shape upon her lap
Honey of generation had betrayed,

And that must sleep, shriek, struggle to escape
As recollection or the drug decide,
Would think her son, did she but see that shape
With sixty or more winters on its head,
A compensation for the pang of his birth,
Or the uncertainty of his setting forth?

Plato thought nature but a spume that plays
Upon a ghostly paradigm of things;
Solider Aristotle played the taws
Upon the bottom of a king of kings;
World-famous golden-thighed Pythagoras
Fingered upon a fiddle-stick or strings
What a star sang and careless Muses heard:
Old clothes upon old sticks to scare a bird.

Both nuns and mothers worship images,
But those the candles light are not as those
That animate a mother's reveries,
But keep a marble or a bronze repose.
And yet they too break hearts—O Presences
That passion, piety or affection knows,
And that all heavenly glory symbolize—
O self-born mockers of man's enterprise;

Labor is blossoming or dancing where
The body is not bruised to pleasure soul,
Nor beauty born out of its own despair,
Nor blear-eyed wisdom out of midnight oil.
O chestnut-tree, great-rooted blossomer,
Are you the leaf, the blossom or the bole?
O body swayed to music, O brightening glance,
How can we know the dancer from the dance?

SAILING TO BYZANTIUM

That is no country for old men. The young
In one another's arms, birds in the trees,
—Those dying generations—at their song,
The salmon-falls, the mackerel-crowded seas,
Fish, flesh, or fowl, commend all summer long
Whatever is begotten, born, and dies.
Caught in that sensual music all neglect
Monuments of unaging intellect.

An aged man is but a paltry thing,
A tattered coat upon a stick, unless
Soul clap its hands and sing, and louder sing
For every tatter in its mortal dress,
Nor is there singing school but studying
Monuments of its own magnificence;
And therefore I have sailed the seas and come
To the holy city of Byzantium.

O sages standing in God's holy fire
As in the gold mosaic of a wall,
Come from the holy fire, perne in a gyre,
And be the singing-masters of my soul.
Consume my heart away, sick with desire
And fastened to a dying animal
It knows not what it is; and gather me
Into the artifice of eternity.

Once out of nature I shall never take
My bodily form from any natural thing,
But such a form as Grecian goldsmiths make
Of hammered gold and gold enamelling
To keep a drowsy Emperor awake;
Or set upon a golden bough to sing
To lords and ladies of Byzantium
Of what is past, or passing, or to come.

LEDA AND THE SWAN

A sudden blow: the great wings beating still
Above the staggering girl, her thighs caressed
By the dark webs, her nape caught in his bill,
He holds her helpless breast upon his breast.

How can those terrified vague fingers push
The feathered glory from her loosening thighs?
And how can body, laid in that white rush,
But feel the strange heart beating where it lies?

A shudder in the loins engenders there
The broken wall, the burning roof and tower
And Agamemnon dead.

Being so caught up,
So mastered by the brute blood of the air,
Did she put on his knowledge with his power
Before the indifferent beak could let her drop?

TWO SONGS FROM A PLAY

I

I saw a staring virgin stand
Where holy Dionysus died,
And tear the heart out of his side,
And lay the heart upon her hand
And bear that beating heart away;
And then did all the Muses sing
Of Magnus Annus at the spring,
As though God's death were but a play.

Another Troy must rise and set,
Another lineage feed the crow,
Another Argo's painted prow
Drive to a flashier bauble yet.
The Roman Empire stood appalled:
It dropped the reins of peace and war
When that fierce virgin and her Star
Out of the fabulous darkness called.

II

In pity for man's darkening thought
He walked that room and issued thence
In Galilean turbulence;
The Babylonian starlight brought
A fabulous, formless darkness in;
Odor of blood when Christ was slain
Made all Platonic tolerance vain
And vain all Doric discipline.

Everything that man esteems
Endures a moment or a day.
Love's pleasure drives his love away,
The painter's brush consumes his dreams;
The herald's cry, the soldier's tread
Exhaust his glory and his might:

Whatever flames upon the night
Man's own resinous heart has fed.

THE SECOND COMING

Turning and turning in the widening gyre
The falcon cannot hear the falconer;
Things fall apart: the centre cannot hold;
Mere anarchy is loosed upon the world,
The blood-dimmed tide is loosed, and everywhere
The ceremony of innocence is drowned;
The best lack all conviction, while the worst
Are full of passionate intensity.

Surely some revelation is at hand;
Surely the Second Coming is at hand.
The Second Coming! Hardly are those words out
When a vast image out of *Spiritus Mundi*
Troubles my sight: somewhere in sands of the desert
A shape with lion body and the head of a man,
A gaze blank and pitiless as the sun,
Is moving its slow thighs, while all about it
Reel shadows of the indignant desert birds.
The darkness drops again; but now I know
That twenty centuries of stony sleep
Were vexed to nightmare by a rocking cradle,
And what rough beast, its hour come round at last,
Slouches towards Bethlehem to be born?

D. H. LAWRENCE

CHERRY ROBBERS

Under the long dark boughs, like jewels red
In the hair of an Eastern girl
Hang strings of crimson cherries, as if had bled
Blood-drops beneath each curl.

DAVID HERBERT LAWRENCE (1885-1930) was born in Nottingham. His first novel was published in 1911, his first volume of verse in 1914. In the last fifteen years of his life his work became greatly influenced by a study of psychoanalytical doctrine and by his wide travels in search of a climate where he might bolster his failing health.

Under the glistening cherries, with folded wings
    Three dead birds lie:
Pale-breasted throstles and a blackbird, robberlings
    Stained with red dye.

Against the haystack a girl stands laughing at me,
    Cherries hung round her ears.
Offers me her scarlet fruit: I will see
    If she has any tears.

EZRA POUND

BALLAD FOR GLOOM

For God, our God is a gallant foe
That playeth behind the veil.

I have loved my God as a child at heart
That seeketh deep bosoms for rest,
I have loved my God as a maid to man—
But lo, this thing is best:
To love your God as a gallant foe that plays behind the veil;
To meet your God as the night winds meet beyond Arcturus' pale.

    I have played with God for a woman,
    I have staked with my God for truth,
    I have lost to my God as a man, clear-eyed—
        His dice be not of ruth.

For I am made as a naked blade,
    But hear ye this thing in sooth:

Who loseth to God as man to man
    Shall win at the turn of the game.
I have drawn my blade where the lightnings meet
    But the ending is the same:
Who loseth to God as the sword blades lose
    Shall win at the end of the game.

EZRA LOOMIS POUND (1885-   ) was born in Hailey, Idaho, and was educated at Hamilton College and the University of Pennsylvania. He went to London to live in 1908. In 1945 United States Army forces arrested him in Italy upon a charge of treason. Returned to the United States, he was declared insane and restricted to a mental hospital until 1958. He then took up residence with his daughter in Italy.

For God, our God is a gallant foe that playeth behind the veil.
Whom God deigns not to overthrow hath need of triple mail.

CANTO XLV

With *Usura*

With usura hath no man a house of good stone
each block cut smooth and well fitting
that design might cover their face,
with usura
hath no man a painted paradise on his church wall
harpes et luthes
or where virgin receiveth message
and halo projects from incision,
with usura
seeth no man Gonzaga his heirs and his concubines
no picture is made to endure nor to live with
but it is made to sell and sell quickly
with usura, sin against nature,
is thy bread ever more of stale rags
is thy bread dry as paper,
with no mountain wheat, no strong flour
with usura the line grows thick
with usura is no clear demarcation
and no man can find site for his dwelling.
Stone cutter is kept from his stone
weaver is kept from his loom
WITH USURA
wool comes not to the market
sheep bringeth no gain with usura
Usura is a murrain, usura
blunteth the needle in the maid's hand
and stoppeth the spinner's cunning. Pietro Lombardo
Came not by usura
Duccio came not by usura
nor Pier della Francesca; Zuan Bellin' not by usura
nor was 'La Calunnia' painted.
Came not by usura Angelico; came not Ambrogio Praedis,
came no church of cut stone signed: *Adamo me fecit.*
Not by usura St Trophime
Not by usura Saint Hilaire,
Usura rusteth the chisel

It rusteth the craft and the craftsman
It gnaweth the thread in the loom
None learneth to weave gold in her pattern;
Azure hath a canker by usura; cramoisi is unbroidered
Emerald findeth no Memling
Usura slayeth the child in the womb
It stayeth the young man's courting
It hath brought palsey to bed, lyeth
between the young bride and her bridegroom
            CONTRA NATURAM
They have brought whores for Eleusis
Corpses are set to banquet
at behest of usura.

A VIRGINAL

No, no! Go from me. I have left her lately.
I will not spoil my sheath with lesser brightness,
For my surrounding air has a new lightness;
Slight are her arms, yet they have bound me straitly
And left me cloaked as with a gauze of ether;
As with sweet leaves; as with a subtle clearness.
Oh, I have picked up magic in her nearness
To sheathe me half in half the things that sheathe her.

No, no! Go from me. I have still the flavor,
Soft as spring wind that's come from birchen bowers.
Green come the shoots, aye April in the branches,
As winter's wound with her sleight hand she staunches,
Hath of the trees a likeness of the savor:
As white their bark, so white this lady's hours.

ELINOR WYLIE

THE EAGLE AND THE MOLE

Avoid the reeking herd,
Shun the polluted flock,

ELINOR WYLIE (1885-1928) was born in Somerville, New Jersey. Her first volume of verse, *Nets to Catch the Wind* (1921), established her as one of the noteworthy poets of her time, and eventually she became known for her novels as well. Definitive editions of her work have been edited by her husband, William Rose Benét.

Live like that stoic bird,
The eagle of the rock.

The huddled warmth of crowds
Begets and fosters hate;
He keeps, above the clouds,
His cliff inviolate.

When flocks are folded warm
And herds to shelter run,
He sails above the storm,
He stares into the sun.

If in the eagle's track
Your sinews cannot leap,
Avoid the lathered pack,
Turn from the steaming sheep.

If you would keep your soul
From spotted sight or sound,
Live like the velvet mole;
Go burrow underground.

And there hold intercourse
With roots of trees and stones,
With rivers at their source
And disembodied bones.

WILLIAM CARLOS WILLIAMS

TRAGIC DETAIL

The day before I died
I noticed the maple tree
how its bark curled
against the November blaze

There was some work
to do and three birds

WILLIAM CARLOS WILLIAMS (1883-   ) was born in Rutherford, New Jersey, and practiced medicine there throughout his career. The American Academy of Arts and Letters awarded him its prize in 1948.

stopped awkwardly abreast
upon the bare lawn

Only the country-woman's
lip soft with down
black as her hair was black
against the white skin

comforted me but the twins
and their sister
excluded me dragging
insistent upon the loose gown.

MARIANNE MOORE

WHAT ARE YEARS?

What is our innocence,
what is our guilt? All are
    naked, none is safe. And whence
is courage: the unanswered question,
the resolute doubt,—
    dumbly calling, deafly listening—that
in misfortune, even death,
        encourages others
        and in its defeat, stirs

    the soul to be strong? He
sees deep and is glad; who
    accedes to mortality
and in his imprisonment, rises
upon himself as
the sea in a chasm, struggling to be
free and unable to be,
        in its surrendering
        finds its continuing.

    So he who strongly feels,
behaves. The very bird,

MARIANNE MOORE (1887-   ) was born in St. Louis. She received her
B.A. degree from Bryn Mawr in 1909. By 1926 she was editor of *The Dial*, a post she
held until the magazine ceased publication three years later. She won the Bollingen
Award in 1951, and her *Collected Poems* won the 1952 Pulitzer Prize.

grown taller as he sings, steels
his form straight up. Though he is captive,
his mighty singing
says, satisfaction is a lowly
thing, how pure a thing is joy.
    This is mortality,
    this is eternity.

O TO BE A DRAGON

        If I, like Solomon, . . .
        could have my wish—

my wish . . . O to be a dragon,
a symbol of the power of Heaven—of silkworm
size or immense; at times invisible.
    Felicitous phenomenon!

E. E. CUMMINGS

SINCE FEELING IS FIRST

since feeling is first
who pays any attention
to the syntax of things
will never wholly kiss you;

wholly to be a fool
while Spring is in the world

my blood approves,
and kisses are a better fate
than wisdom
lady i swear by all flowers. Don't cry
—the best gesture of my brain is less than
your eyelids' flutter which says

EDWARD ESTLIN CUMMINGS (1894-   ) was born in Cambridge, Massachusetts, and educated at Harvard. His experiences as an ambulance driver during World War I and as a prisoner of the French furnished the material for his novel *The Enormous Room* (1922). His first volume of poetry was published the next year

we are for each other:then
laugh,leaning back in my arms
for life's not a paragraph

And death i think is no parenthesis

ARCHIBALD MACLEISH

STARVED LOVERS

Chrysanthemums last too long for these ravenous ladies.
The flowers they prefer are brief, unfold
At evening filling the cool room then fade,
Budded at pleasure and at pleasure old.

Chrysanthemums stand too still for these starved ladies.
Staring like Vincent's sunlight, bright and still,
They burn until these feasters are afraid
Hunger may leave them and their lives be filled.

The ravenous ladies in the still-starved lives
Strip off the ever-burning leaves with silver knives.

W. H. AUDEN

IN MEMORY OF W. B. YEATS

(d. Jan. 1939)

I

He disappeared in the dead of winter:
The brooks were frozen, the air-ports almost deserted,

ARCHIBALD MACLEISH (1892-   ) was born in Glencoe, Illinois, and graduated from Yale University and Harvard Law School. He served as Librarian of Congress from 1939 to 1944 and the following year as Undersecretary of State. In 1949 he was appointed professor at Harvard. He twice has been the recipient of the Pulitzer Prize for poetry, in 1933 and in 1953.
WYSTAN HUGH AUDEN (1907-   ) was born in York. During the Spanish Civil War, he was an ambulance driver for the Loyalist forces. In 1939 he came to the United States, where he became a citizen. For many years chief judge in the Yale Series of Younger Poets competition, he withdrew in order to take the chair of poetry at Oxford for 1959-1960.

And snow disfigured the public statues;
The mercury sank in the mouth of the dying day.
O all the instruments agree
The day of his death was a dark cold day.

Far from his illness
The wolves ran on through the evergreen forests,
The peasant river was untempted by the fashionable quays;
By mourning tongues
The death of the poet was kept from his poems.

But for him it was his last afternoon as himself,
An afternoon of nurses and rumours;
The provinces of his body revolted,
The squares of his mind were empty,
Silence invaded the suburbs,
The current of his feeling failed: he became his admirers.

Now he is scattered among a hundred cities
And wholly given over to unfamiliar affections;
To find his happiness in another kind of wood
And be punished under a foreign code of conscience.
The words of a dead man
Are modified in the guts of the living.

But in the importance and noise of to-morrow
When the brokers are roaring like beasts on the floor of the Bourse,
And the poor have the sufferings to which they are fairly accustomed,
And each in the cell of himself is almost convinced of his freedom;
A few thousand will think of this day
As one thinks of a day when one did something slightly unusual.
O all the instruments agree
The day of his death was a dark cold day.

II

You were silly like us: your gift survived it all;
The parish of rich women, physical decay,
Yourself; mad Ireland hurt you into poetry.
Now Ireland has her madness and her weather still,
For poetry makes nothing happen: it survives

In the valley of its saying where executives
Would never want to tamper; it flows south
From ranches of isolation and the busy griefs,
Raw towns that we believe and die in; it survives,
A way of happening, a mouth.

III

Earth, receive an honoured guest;
William Yeats is laid to rest:
Let the Irish vessel lie
Emptied of its poetry.

Time that is intolerant
Of the brave and innocent,
And indifferent in a week
To a beautiful physique,

Worships language and forgives
Everyone by whom it lives;
Pardons cowardice, conceit,
Lays its honours at their feet.

Time that with this strange excuse
Pardoned Kipling and his views,
And will pardon Paul Claudel,
Pardons him for writing well.

In the nightmare of the dark
All the dogs of Europe bark,
And the living nations wait,
Each sequestered in its hate;

Intellectual disgrace
Stares from every human face,
And the seas of pity lie
Locked and frozen in each eye.

Follow, poet, follow right
To the bottom of the night,
With your unconstraining voice
Still persuade us to rejoice;

With the farming of a verse
Make a vineyard of the curse,
Sing of human unsuccess
In a rapture of distress;

In the deserts of the heart
Let the healing fountain start,
In the prison of his days
Teach the free man how to praise.

BALLAD

O what is that sound which so thrills the ear
      Down in the valley drumming, drumming?
Only the scarlet soldiers, dear,
      The soldiers coming.

O what is that light I see flashing so clear
      Over the distance brightly, brightly?
Only the sun on their weapons, dear,
      As they step lightly.

O what are they doing with all that gear;
      What are they doing this morning, this morning?
Only the usual maneuvers, dear,
      Or perhaps a warning.

O why have they left the road down there;
      Why are they suddenly wheeling, wheeling?
Perhaps a change in the orders, dear;
      Why are you kneeling?

O haven't they stopped for the doctor's care;
      Haven't they reined their horses, their horses?
Why, they are none of them wounded, dear,
      None of these forces.

O is it the parson they want, with white hair;
      Is it the parson, is it, is it?
No, they are passing his gateway, dear,
      Without a visit.

O it must be the farmer who lives so near,
  It must be the farmer, so cunning, cunning;
They have passed the farm already, dear,
  And now they are running.

O where are you going? stay with me here.
  Were the vows you swore me deceiving, deceiving?
No, I promised to love you, my dear,
  But I must be leaving.

O it's broken the lock and splintered the door,
  O it's the gate where they're turning, turning;
Their feet are heavy on the floor
  And their eyes are burning.

ROBERT GRAVES

IN THE WILDERNESS

Christ of His gentleness
Thirsting and hungering,
Walked in the wilderness;
Soft words of grace He spoke
Unto lost desert-folk
That listened wondering.
He heard the bitterns call
From ruined palace-wall,
Answered them brotherly.
He held communion
With the she-pelican
Of lonely piety.
Basilisk, cockatrice,
Flocked to his homilies,
With mail of dread device,
With monstrous barbed slings,
With eager dragon-eyes;

ROBERT GRAVES (1895-) was born in London. He left Oxford to enlist in the British army during World War I. Since 1929 he has lived in Majorca. In 1961 he was elected to the poetry chair at Oxford University.

Great bats on leathern wings
And poor blind broken things,
Foul in their miseries.
And ever with Him went,
Of all His wanderings
Comrade, with ragged coat,
Gaunt ribs—poor innocent—
Bleeding foot, burning throat,
The guileless old scapegoat;
For forty nights and days
Followed in Jesus' ways,
Sure guard behind Him kept,
Tears like a lover wept.

DELMORE SCHWARTZ

TIRED AND UNHAPPY, YOU THINK OF HOUSES

Tired and unhappy, you think of houses
Soft-carpeted and warm in the December evening,
While snow's white pieces fall past the window,
And the orange firelight leaps.
                          A young girl sings
That song of Gluck where Orpheus pleads with Death;
Her elders watch, nodding their happiness
To see time fresh again in her self-conscious eyes:
The servants bring the coffee, the children retire,
Elder and younger yawn and go to bed,
The coals fade and glow, rose and ashen,
It is time to shake yourself! and break this
Banal dream, and turn your head
Where the underground is charged, where the weight
Of the lean buildings is seen,
Where close in the subway rush, anonymous
In the audience, well-dressed or mean,
So many surround you, ringing your fate,
Caught in an anger exact as a machine!

DELMORE SCHWARTZ (1913-   ) was born in Brooklyn and educated at New York University and Harvard, to which he later returned as a teacher. He has been poetry editor for *Partisan Review* and *New Republic*.

KARL SHAPIRO

TRAVELOGUE FOR EXILES

Look and remember. Look upon this sky;
Look deep and deep into the sea-clean air,
The unconfined, the terminus of prayer.
Speak now and speak into the hallowed dome.
What do you hear? What does the sky reply?
The heavens are taken: this is not your home.

Look and remember. Look upon this sea;
Look down and down into the tireless tide.
What of a life below, a life inside,
A tomb, a cradle in the curly foam?
The waves arise; sea-wind and sea agree
The waters are taken: this is not your home.

Look and remember. Look upon this land,
Far, far across the factories and the grass.
Surely, there, surely, they will let you pass.
Speak then and ask the forest and the loam.
What do you hear? What does the land command?
The earth is taken: this is not your home.

GEORGE BARKER

ON THE DEATH OF MANOLETE

You, king, die. Mithra. Where was death
Hiding for those ten hours when you lay
Endowing Lenares with that great red legend?
The Monster. Dead. Drag the bright corpse away.

Did the sword shriek in his hand? The sand
Wept as he fell. You, king, die. The Miura

KARL SHAPIRO (1913-   ) was born in Baltimore, Maryland, and attended the University of Virginia and Johns Hopkins. His *V-Letter and Other Poems*, published in 1944 while he was with the army in the South Pacific, won him the Pulitzer Prize. He edited *Poetry* magazine in 1950-1956, and since 1956 has been professor of English at the University of Nebraska.
GEORGE BARKER (1913-   ) was educated in London. He taught at the Imperial Tohoku University in Japan, returning to England in 1943 via the United States. He has been publishing verse since the age of twenty.

Groaned as he gored his god. But the long
Face of a stone and a saint only set surer

Into the calm that had always crowned it. You,
King, die. The killer with a bull's hair on his belly
Goes towering to his death under a cape.
Black that Islero honours the place where he fell.

O expiation! The king and the bull, kissing,
Enter and share a kingdom. The sword and horn
Sleep side by side. Justice. You, kings, die.
Between this man and this bull a myth is born.

DYLAN THOMAS

THE HUNCHBACK IN THE PARK

The hunchback in the park
A solitary mister
Propped between trees and water
From the opening of the garden lock
That lets the trees and water enter
Until the Sunday sombre bell at dark,

Eating bread from a newspaper
Drinking water from the chained cup
That the children filled with gravel
In the fountain basin where I sailed my ship
Slept at night in a dog kennel
But nobody chained him up.

Like the park birds he came early
Like the water he sat down
And Mister they called Hey mister
The truant boys from the town
Running when he had heard them clearly
On out of sound

DYLAN THOMAS (1914-1953) was born in Swansea, Wales, and published
his first book of poetry at the age of twenty. After the Second World War he spent a
great deal of time in the United States, making extensive reading tours. He died in
New York City at the age of thirty-nine.

Past lake and rockery
Laughing when he shook his paper
Hunchbacked in mockery
Through the loud zoo of the willow groves
Dodging the park keeper
With his stick that picked up leaves.

And the old dog sleeper
Alone between nurses and swans
While the boys among willows
Made the tigers jump out of their eyes
To roar on the rockery stones
And the groves were blue with sailors

Made all day until bell time
A woman figure without fault
Straight as a young elm
Straight and tall from his crooked bones
That she might stand in the night
After the locks and chains

All night in the unmade park
After the railings and shrubberies
The birds the grass the trees the lake
Had followed the hunchback
And the wild boys innocent as strawberries
To his kennel in the dark.

A REFUSAL TO MOURN THE DEATH, BY FIRE, OF A CHILD IN LONDON

Never until the mankind making
Bird beast and flower
Fathering and all humbling darkness
Tells with silence the last light breaking
And the still hour
Is come of the sea tumbling in harness

And I must enter again the round
Zion of the water bead
And the synagogue of the ear of corn
Shall I let pray the shadow of a sound
Or sow my salt seed
In the least valley of sackcloth to mourn

The majesty and burning of the child's death.
I shall not murder
The mankind of her going with a grave truth
Nor blaspheme down the stations of the breath
With any further
Elegy of innocence and youth.

Deep with the first dead lies London's daughter.
Robed in the long friends,
The grains beyond age, the dark veins of her mother,
Secret by the unmourning water
Of the riding Thames.
After the first death, there is no other.

FERN HILL

Now as I was young and easy under the apple boughs
About the lilting house and happy as the grass was green,
        The night above the dingle starry,
            Time let me hail and climb
        Golden in the heydays of his eyes,
And honoured among wagons I was prince of the apple towns
And once below a time I lordly had the trees and leaves
            Trail with daisies and barley
        Down the rivers of the windfall light.

And as I was green and carefree, famous among the barns
About the happy yard and singing as the farm was home,
        In the sun that is young once only,
            Time let me play and be
        Golden in the mercy of his means,
And green and golden I was huntsman and herdsman, the calves
Sang to my horn, the foxes on the hills barked clear and cold,
            And the sabbath rang slowly
        In the pebbles of the holy streams.

All the sun long it was running, it was lovely, the hay-
Fields high as the house, the tunes from the chimneys, it was air
            And playing, lovely and watery
                And fire green as grass.
        And nightly under the simple stars
As I rode to sleep the owls were bearing the farm away,
All the moon long I heard, blessed among stables, the nightjars
            Flying with the ricks, and the horses
                Flashing into the dark.

And then to awake, and the farm, like a wanderer white
With the dew, come back, the cock on his shoulder: it was all
  Shining, it was Adam and maiden,
   The sky gathered again
  And the sun grew round that very day.
So it must have been after the birth of the simple light
In the first, spinning place, the spellbound horses walking warm
  Out of the whinnying green stable
   On to the fields of praise.

And honoured among foxes and pheasants by the gay house
Under the new made clouds and happy as the heart was long,
  In the sun born over and over,
   I ran my heedless ways,
  My wishes raced through the house-high hay
And nothing I cared, at my sky blue trades, that time allows
In all his tuneful turning so few and such morning songs
  Before the children green and golden
   Follow him out of grace,

Nothing I cared, in the lamb white days, that time would take me
Up to the swallow thronged loft by the shadow of my hand,
  In the moon that is always rising,
   Nor that riding to sleep
  I should hear him fly with the high fields
And wake to the farm forever fled from the childless land.
Oh as I was young and easy in the mercy of his means,
  Time held me green and dying
  Though I sang in my chains like the sea.

THEODORE ROETHKE

ELEGY FOR JANE

(My student, thrown by a horse)

I remember the neckcurls, limp and damp as tendrils;
And her quick look, a sidelong pickerel smile;
And how, once startled into talk, the light syllables leaped for her,

THEODORE ROETHKE (1908-) was born in Saginaw, Michigan, and was educated at the University of Michigan and at Harvard. He has spent his career teaching, at Lafayette, Pennsylvania State, Bennington, and the University of Washington. His verse has won him the Pulitzer Prize (1953) and the Bollingen Award (1958).

And she balanced in the delight of her thought,
A wren, happy, tail into the wind,
Her song trembling the twigs and small branches.
The shade sang with her;
The leaves, their whispers turned to kissing,
And the mould sang in the bleached valleys under the rose.

Oh, when she was sad, she cast herself down into such a pure depth,
Even a father could not find her:
Scraping her cheek against straw;
Stirring the clearest water.

My sparrow, you are not here,
Waiting like a fern, making a spiney shadow.
The sides of wet stones cannot console me,
Nor the moss, wound with the last light.

If only I could nudge you from this sleep,
My maimed darling, my skittery pigeon.
Over this damp grave I speak the words of my love:
I, with no rights in this matter,
Neither father nor lover.

RICHARD WILBUR

JOHN CHRYSOSTOM

He who had gone a beast
Down on his knees and hands
Remembering lust and murder
Felt now a gust of grace,
Lifted his burnished face
From the psalter of the sands
And found his thoughts in order
And cleared his throat at last.

What they heard was a voice
That spoke what they could learn

RICHARD WILBUR (1921-   ), born in New York City, went to Amherst College, took part in the Italian campaign in World War II, and then received an M.A. from Harvard. He has taught at Harvard, Wellesley, and Wesleyan. In 1957 he won the Pulitzer Prize for poetry.

From any gelded priest,
Yet rang like a great choir,
He having taught hell's fire
A singing way to burn,
And borrowed of some dumb beast
The wildness to rejoice.

LOUIS SIMPSON

THE SAINTS ARE FEASTING IN HEAVEN

You saints, whose virtue was to bleed,
To lose an arm, an eye, a head,
Here is the harvest of that seed;
The feast of Paradise is spread.

Martyr, pick up your broken skull
And boldly take your place to dine.
Eat, eat, and yet be never full!
These delicacies are divine.

To give you music with your meat
The damned are burned and flayed with whips.
These are the proud who used to eat
The world, and wash their fingertips.

As with the Church, your naked spouse,
You lie through the unending night,
The sinners' knocks, locked from the house,
Renew the edge of your delight.

You saints, whose virtue was to bleed,
To be thrust back, rejected, cursed
By Pride and Luxury and Greed,
The last of all, shall be the first.

LOUIS SIMPSON (1923-   ) was born in Jamaica and educated at Columbia University, where he now teaches. He has been an editor and the moderator of a television series interviewing modern poets.

JAMES WRIGHT

AN OFFERING FOR MR. BLUEHART

That was a place, when I was young,
Where two or three good friends and I
Tested the fruit against the tongue
Or threw the withered windfalls by.
The sparrows, angry in the sky,
Denounced us from a broken bough.
They limp along the wind and die.
The apples all are eaten now.

Behind the orchard, past one hill
The lean satanic owner lay
And threatened us with murder till
We stole his riches all away.
He caught us in the act one day
And damned us to the laughing bone,
And fired his gun across the gray
Autumn where now his life is done.

Sorry for him, or any man
Who lost his labored wealth to thieves,
Today I mourn him, as I can,
By leaving in their golden leaves
Some luscious apples overhead.
Now may my abstinence restore
Peace to the orchard and the dead.
We shall not nag them any more.

JAMES WRIGHT (1927-   ) won the Yale Series of Younger Poets Award in 1957 with his first volume. His second, *St. Judas,* was published in 1959. He teaches at the University of Minnesota.

VII

THE TWENTIETH CENTURY

REGIONALISM

THE writer's identification with the region of his closest associations has produced in America a rich body of literature. The dominant emotion in this kind of writing is one of loyalty—loyalty to traditions of the past, customs of the present, and hopes for the future. Sometimes this loyalty takes the form of criticism, a lesson instilled through the corrective rod. More often it is seen in the love—fierce or gentle—that men reserve for the land and their own kind of people who work or populate that land.

New England and the South have provided the settings for more twentieth-century regional poetry than all other parts of the country combined. This is not to say that other regions have not been given lavish attention in other forms of literature; they have. But several of the best poets of our century have come either from the Northeast or the South and have chosen to pay tribute to these places.

Perhaps the earliest regional poetry by a major writer of the modern period is that of E. A. Robinson. He created a fictional village called Tilbury Town, which can be associated with Gardiner, Maine, a rural community of about 4500 people where Robinson spent most of the first twenty-seven years of his life. In several different volumes, he peopled his poems with fictional re-creations of village types, altered from the original models to meet the demands of his themes. Some of his poems, like *The Sheaves,* dealt only with the land.

Two episodes in the development of Robert Frost, another poet identi-fied with New England, carry some irony. The first is that the poet him-self was born in San Francisco; the second is that his first volume of verse, dedicated to New England under the title of *North of Boston,* had to find publication in England. Frost's birth on the West Coast, however, was only an accident of his father's travels. The Frost family had been New Englanders before the poet's parents went west, and when the poet's father died in California, his widow took her son back to Massachusetts. Frost does not celebrate the people of his region so much as Robinson does. As often as not, it is some element of nature, some custom, some way of life, that he writes about, as in *Stopping by Woods on a Snowy Evening, Mending Wall,* and *After Apple-Picking.* Yet we learn much about the regional character through such individuals as the neighbor of *Mending Wall.*

In the South, regional writing has been more organized. There it was the development of a group of men, working together and attempting to reëstablish certain patterns of existence from the past which they felt to have permanent value. The men, known variously as the Agrarians, the Fugitives, and the Nashville group, did not confine their activities to poetry but hoped that their plans for a new South would embrace political, economic, social, and cultural activities in all the arts as well. They gathered around John Crowe Ransom at Vanderbilt University, where several of them were his students. Those who became important in the poetry of their region were Ransom himself, Allen Tate, and Robert Penn Warren. Most of Ransom's poetry carries the unmistakable stamp of Southern accents, customs, and mores; his failure to publish verse after 1939 coincides with his removal to the North about that time. Tate's poetry has a base in broader interests, and much that he has written since the early years has little enough to do with the South; but his *Ode to the Confederate Dead* is perhaps the single most ambitious and powerful poem to come out of the movement. Warren's interests have been primarily in history and folklore.

Other poets have written pieces that can be called regional, and many should perhaps find places in this section of the anthology. Robinson Jeffers has described movingly the bleak stretches of rock-strewn beach in California, and Edgar Lee Masters has given us portraits and landscapes from the Midwest. Among the younger poets, perhaps Robert Lowell has identified himself most closely with a region and with his ancestors. Related to both James Russell and Amy Lowell, he exhibits a strong sense of family and home that has found expression in poetic studies of his relatives and their native city of Boston. His recent poem, *For the Union Dead*, shows an even closer identification with New England and its past than has been apparent in his earlier poems.

In England, A. E. Housman re-created his native Shropshire, and Thomas Hardy devoted himself to the West Country of Dorset and Somerset, which he called Wessex. More recently, Dylan Thomas drew repeatedly on people and places in his native Wales.

FOR FURTHER READING:

Barnard, Elsworth. *Edwin Arlington Robinson*. New York, 1952.
Bradbury, John M. *The Fugitives: A Critical Account*. Chapel Hill, N. C., 1958.
Lynen, John F. *The Pastoral Art of Robert Frost*. New Haven, 1960.
Nitchie, George W. *Human Values in the Poetry of Robert Frost*. Durham, N. C., 1960.
Sergeant, Elizabeth S. *Robert Frost: The Trial by Existence*. New York, 1960.

E. A. ROBINSON

LUKE HAVERGAL

Go to the western gate, Luke Havergal,
There where the vines cling crimson on the wall,
And in the twilight wait for what will come.
The leaves will whisper there of her, and some,
Like flying words, will strike you as they fall;
But go, and if you listen she will call.
Go to the western gate, Luke Havergal—
Luke Havergal.

No, there is not a dawn in eastern skies
To rift the fiery night that's in your eyes;
But there, where western glooms are gathering,
The dark will end the dark, if anything:
God slays himself with every leaf that flies,
And hell is more than half of paradise.
No, there is not a dawn in eastern skies—
In eastern skies.

Out of a grave I come to tell you this,
Out of a grave I come to quench the kiss
That flames upon your forehead with a glow
That blinds you to the way that you must go.
Yes, there is yet one way to where she is,
Bitter, but one that faith may never miss.
Out of a grave I come to tell you this—
To tell you this.

There is the western gate, Luke Havergal,
There are the crimson leaves upon the wall.
Go, for the winds are tearing them away,—
Nor think to riddle the dead words they say,
Nor any more to feel them as they fall;
But go, and if you trust her she will call.
There is the western gate, Luke Havergal—
Luke Havergal.

E. A. ROBINSON (1869-1935) was born in Head Tide, Maine, and studied at Harvard, leaving without a degree in 1893. For a time he lived in New York and worked in the city subway system. Learning of the poet's plight, President Theodore Roosevelt appointed him to the New York customs house in 1905. Robinson's voluminous production of verse won him the Pulitzer Prize for poetry three times.

FOR A DEAD LADY

No more with overflowing light
Shall fill the eyes that now are faded,
Nor shall another's fringe with night
Their woman-hidden world as they did.
No more shall quiver down the days
The flowing wonder of her ways,
Whereof no language may requite
The shifting and the many-shaded.

The grace, divine, definitive,
Clings only as a faint forestalling;
The laugh that love could not forgive
Is hushed, and answers to no calling;
The forehead and the little ears
Have gone where Saturn keeps the years;
The breast where roses could not live
Has done with rising and with falling.

The beauty, shattered by the laws
That have creation in their keeping,
No longer trembles at applause,
Or over children that are sleeping;
And we who delve in beauty's lore
Know all that we have known before
Of what inexorable cause
Makes Time so vicious in his reaping.

EROS TURANNOS

She fears him, and will always ask
    What fated her to choose him;
She meets in his engaging mask
    All reasons to refuse him;
But what she meets and what she fears
Are less than are the downward years,
Drawn slowly to the foamless weirs
    Of age, were she to lose him.

Between a blurred sagacity
    That once had power to sound him,

And Love, that will not let him be
   The Judas that she found him,
Her pride assuages her almost,
   As if it were alone the cost.
He sees that he will not be lost,
   And waits and looks around him.

A sense of ocean and old trees
   Envelops and allures him;
Tradition, touching all he sees,
   Beguiles and reassures him;
And all her doubts of what he says
Are dimmed with what she knows of days—
Till even prejudice delays
   And fades, and she secures him.

The falling leaf inaugurates
   The reign of her confusion;
The pounding wave reverberates
   The dirge of her illusion;
And home, where passion lived and died,
Becomes a place where she can hide,
While all the town and harbor-side
   Vibrate with her seclusion.

We tell you, tapping on our brows,
   The story as it should be,
As if the story of a house
   Were told, or ever could be;
We'll have no kindly veil between
Her visions and those we have seen,—
As if we guessed what hers have been,
   Or what they are or would be.

Meanwhile we do no harm; for they
   That with a god have striven,
Not hearing much of what we say,
   Take what the god has given;
Though like waves breaking it may be,
Or like a changed familiar tree,
Or like a stairway to the sea
   Where down the blind are driven.

THE SHEAVES

Where long the shadows of the wind had rolled,
Green wheat was yielding to the change assigned;
And as by some vast magic undivined
The world was turning slowly into gold.
Like nothing that was ever bought or sold
It waited there, the body and the mind;
And with a mighty meaning of a kind
That tells the more the more it is not told.

So in a land where all days are not fair,
Fair days went on till on another day
A thousand golden sheaves were lying there,
Shining and still, but not for long to stay—
As if a thousand girls with golden hair
Might rise from where they slept and go away.

ROBERT FROST

STOPPING BY WOODS ON A SNOWY EVENING

Whose woods these are I think I know.
His house is in the village though;
He will not see me stopping here
To watch his woods fill up with snow.

My little horse must think it queer
To stop without a farmhouse near
Between the woods and frozen lake
The darkest evening of the year.

He gives his harness bells a shake
To ask if there is some mistake.
The only other sound's the sweep
Of easy wind and downy flake.

ROBERT FROST (1874-   ), though born in San Francisco, has spent his life from childhood on in New England. He attended both Dartmouth and Harvard without taking a degree at either place. For a time he was a farmer, but since establishing his reputation as a poet in 1913-1914, he has been an educator, resident, or visiting lecturer at colleges all over the United States, including some twenty years as professor of English at Amherst. Generally acknowledged to be America's greatest living poet, he has won the Pulitzer Prize four times.

The woods are lovely, dark and deep.
But I have promises to keep,
And miles to go before I sleep,
And miles to go before I sleep.

MENDING WALL

Something there is that doesn't love a wall,
That sends the frozen-ground-swell under it,
And spills the upper boulders in the sun;
And makes gaps even two can pass abreast.
The work of hunters is another thing:
I have come after them and made repair
Where they have left not one stone on a stone,
But they would have the rabbit out of hiding,
To please the yelping dogs. The gaps I mean,
No one has seen them made or heard them made,
But at spring mending-time we find them there.
I let my neighbour know beyond the hill;
And on a day we meet to walk the line
And set the wall between us once again.
We keep the wall between us as we go.
To each the boulders that have fallen to each.
And some are loaves and some so nearly balls
We have to use a spell to make them balance:
"Stay where you are until our backs are turned!"
We wear our fingers rough with handling them.
Oh, just another kind of out-door game,
One on a side. It comes to little more:
There where it is we do not need the wall:
He is all pine and I am apple-orchard.
My apple trees will never get across
And eat the cones under his pines, I tell him.
He only says, "Good fences make good neighbours."
Spring is the mischief in me, and I wonder
If I could put a notion in his head:
"*Why* do they make good neighbours? Isn't it
Where there are cows? But here there are no cows.
Before I built a wall I'd ask to know
What I was walling in or walling out,
And to whom I was like to give offence.
Something there is that doesn't love a wall,
That wants it down." I could say "Elves" to him,

But it's not elves exactly, and I'd rather
He said it for himself. I see him there
Bringing a stone grasped firmly by the top
In each hand, like an old-stone savage armed.
He moves in darkness as it seems to me,
Not of woods only and the shade of trees.
He will not go behind his father's saying,
And he likes having thought of it so well
He says again, "Good fences make good neighbours."

THE ROAD NOT TAKEN

Two roads diverged in a yellow wood,
And sorry I could not travel both
And be one traveler, long I stood
And looked down one as far as I could
To where it bent in the undergrowth;

Then took the other, as just as fair,
And having perhaps the better claim,
Because it was grassy and wanted wear;
Though as for that the passing there
Had worn them really about the same,

And both that morning equally lay
In leaves no step had trodden black.
Oh, I kept the first for another day!
Yet knowing how way leads on to way,
I doubted if I should ever come back.

I shall be telling this with a sigh
Somewhere ages and ages hence:
Two roads diverged in a wood, and I—
I took the one less traveled by,
And that has made all the difference.

AFTER APPLE-PICKING

My long two-pointed ladder's sticking through a tree
Toward heaven still,
And there's a barrel that I didn't fill
Beside it, and there may be two or three
Apples I didn't pick upon some bough.

But I am done with apple-picking now.
Essence of winter sleep is on the night
The scent of apples: I am drowsing off.
I cannot rub the strangeness from my sight
I got from looking through a pane of glass
I skimmed this morning from the drinking trough
And held against the world of hoary grass.
It melted, and I let it fall and break.
But I was well
Upon my way to sleep before it fell,
And I could tell
What form my dreaming was about to take.
Magnified apples appear and disappear,
Stem end and blossom end,
And every fleck of russet showing clear.
My instep arch not only keeps the ache,
It keeps the pressure of a ladder-round.
I feel the ladder sway as the boughs bend.
And I keep hearing from the cellar bin
The rumbling sound
Of load on load of apples coming in.
For I have had too much
Of apple-picking: I am overtired
Of the great harvest I myself desired.
There were ten thousand thousand fruit to touch,
Cherish in hand, lift down, and not let fall.
For all
That struck the earth,
No matter if not bruised or spiked with stubble,
Went surely to the cider-apple heap
As of no worth.
One can see what will trouble
This sleep of mine, whatever sleep it is.
Were he not gone,
The woodchuck could say whether it's like his
Long sleep, as I describe its coming on,
Or just some human sleep.

A CONSIDERABLE SPECK (MICROSCOPIC)

A speck that would have been beneath my sight
On any but a paper sheet so white
Set off across what I had written there,

And I had idly poised my pen in air
To stop it with a period of ink,
When something strange about it made me think
This was no dust speck by my breathing blown,
But unmistakably a living mite
With inclinations it could call its own.
It paused as with suspicion of my pen,
And then came racing wildly on again
To where my manuscript was not yet dry,
Then paused again and either drank or smelt—
With horror, for again it turned to fly.
Plainly with an intelligence I dealt.
It seemed too tiny to have room for feet,
Yet must have had a set of them complete
To express how much it didn't want to die.
It ran with terror and with cunning crept.
It faltered! I could see it hesitate—
Then in the middle of the open sheet
Cower down in desperation to accept
Whatever I accorded it of fate.
I have none of the tenderer-than-thou
Political collectivistic love
With which the modern world is being swept—
But this poor microscopic item now!
Since it was nothing I knew evil of
I let it lie there till I hope it slept.
I have a mind myself, and recognize
Mind where I meet with it in any guise.
No one can know how glad I am to find
On any sheet the least display of mind.

JOHN CROWE RANSOM

LADY LOST

This morning, there flew up the lane
A timid lady-bird to our bird-bath

JOHN CROWE RANSOM (1888-   ), born in Pulaski, Tennessee, took a B.A. at Vanderbilt and from 1909 to 1912 was a Rhodes Scholar at Christ Church, Oxford. He joined the faculty of Vanderbilt upon his return and taught there until 1937, when he became professor of poetry at Kenyon College. There he founded the *Kenyon Review*.

And eyed her image dolefully as death;
This afternoon, knocked on our windowpane
To be let in from the rain.

And when I caught her eye
She looked aside, but at the clapping thunder
And sight of the whole earth blazing up like tinder
Looked in on us again most miserably,
Indeed as if she would cry.

So I will go out into the park and say,
"Who has lost a delicate brown-eyed lady
In the West End Section? Or has anybody
Injured some fine woman in some dark way,
Last night or yesterday?

"Let the owner come and claim possession,
No questions will be asked. But stroke her gently
With loving words, and she will evidently
Resume her full soft-haired white-breasted fashion,
And her right home and her right passion."

PIAZZA PIECE

—I am a gentleman in a dustcoat trying
To make you hear. Your ears are soft and small
And listen to an old man not at all;
They want the young men's whispering and sighing.
But see the roses on your trellis dying
And hear the spectral singing of the moon—
For I must have my lovely lady soon.
I am a gentleman in a dustcoat trying.

—I am a lady young in beauty waiting
Until my truelove comes, and then we kiss.
But what gray man among the vines is this
Whose words are dry and faint as in a dream?
Back from my trellis, sir, before I scream!
I am a lady young in beauty waiting.

PIAZZA PIECE The regionalism of John Crowe Ransom, like that of
any writer who transcends his own time and place, does not diminish the

universal aspects of his poetry. Ransom's espousal of the aristocratic values of the Old South appears chiefly in his gallantry, his graciousness, his soft accents, his decorum. The poet behind the mask of whatever character he makes do his talking—in *Piazza Piece*, the gentleman in the dustcoat—reflects the image of Southern gentility. Observe the tone in *Lady Lost, For a Dead Lady,* and *The Equilibrists* as well as that in *Piazza Piece.* Ransom's characters are men of impeccable honor, of perfect rectitude, of gallant chivalry; his ladies are of decent reticence, of charming purposelessness, of coquettish speech.

Although *piazza* is a term for veranda in other regions of the United States, it is generally associated with Southern houses. The speaker of the octave (the poem is a sonnet) is very courteous. He functions as two persons: he is a courtly old man, and he is Death. The word *dustcoat* is appropriate to both these personae. The poem was written in the 1920's, when the "duster," or ankle-length driving coat, was already an anachronism. A man dressed in such a garment would at once be marked as belonging to an older generation. The dustcoat gives to the figure, as a representative of death or as Death itself, a spectral appearance linked with the image of the moon ("spectral singing") in line 6. There is also in *dustcoat* a reminder of the mortality of the body, which came from dust and to dust will return.

As a wooer who has come up on the porch to speak soft words into the lady's ear, he is the rejected suitor whom the lady believes too old for her; he is also Death, to whom no one willingly listens. The withered roses of line 5 are a pivotal symbol, working both forward and backward. They represent the beauty, the youth, the vigor, the very life itself of the lady, and because they are dying, we understand that she also is dying: "For I must have my lovely lady soon." But they are also the real roses that die upon the trellis because the figure of Death himself approaches and, in coming near, withers them as he withers everything he touches.

Even Death, in the hands of Ransom, must observe courtesy. He is not like Hamlet's "fell sergeant" who is "strict in his arrest"; but rather he is a "gentleman" trying patiently to make the woman understand that she must go with him, although gentlemen must not hurry ladies. In his role as aged wooer, his patience involves both courtesy and the certain knowledge ("I must have my lovely lady soon") that she must accept the inevitability of her growing old and thus accept an older lover.

In back of the courtship which the octave describes is the imminence of marriage or at least of union. In a poem about two human beings, the inevitable success of the persevering man is pleasant to the reader, romantic and assuring; but in a poem in which only one of the lovers is human and the other is Death, the inescapable marriage is morbid, ironic, and terrifying.

Against the octave's realistic picture of the aging of the lady and her approaching death, the illusions of the sestet, with the lady's vain and pathetic belief in her youth and beauty, increase the irony of the poem. We realize, as she does not, that her "truelove" is destined to be Death and that the "kiss" of line 10 will be unwelcome. The use of *kiss* revitalizes the old cliché about the "kiss of death" because it presents along with the words a grisly image. The spectral aspect of the old man is not completely lost upon the lady, for she sees him as "gray" and hears his voice as "dry." But greater irony is developed through her believing that with girlish virtue, with lines learned from her mother perhaps, tinged with control, showing her breeding as an aristocratic lady of the South ("Back from my trellis, sir, before I scream!"), she can frighten off Death.

In *Piazza Piece* Ransom introduces interesting variation into the usual sonnet structure. The rhyme scheme is based on the Italian form, but because the poet uses the enveloping device of repeating the first line in the eighth and the ninth line in the fourteenth, certain alterations must be made. Instead of the standard Italian octave of *abba, abba,* Ransom uses a rhyme scheme of *abba, acca.* In the sestet the enveloping structure almost demands the *deeffd* rhyme in place of some more common Italian combination such as *cde, cde* or *cde, dec,* or *cde, ede.*

The key to the rhyme scheme is the phrase "spectral singing" in line 6. The *a* rhyme of the octave, the only one to appear four times, owing to Ransom's departure from the traditional scheme, is feminine rhyme (see glossary) based upon a *y-ing* sound. When read in a dramatic manner, the words *trying, sighing, dying,* and *trying* capture something of the "spectral singing" or ghostly accents of Death, who has come to call upon the lady. The very *-ing* syllable of the rhyme echoes the *-ing* of *singing* as well as of *whispering* in line 4. Words like *whispering* and *sighing* are, in fact, onomatopoeic words (see glossary) and suggest Death's sibilants and hushed tones.

In the sestet, the *-ing* recurs in *waiting,* another feminine ending. In this way the *-ing* syllable—certainly a singing sound—dominates the entire poem, appearing in six line-endings as well as in two internal positions.

THE EQUILIBRISTS

Full of her long white arms and milky skin
He had a thousand times remembered sin.
Alone in the press of people traveled he,
Minding her jacinth and myrrh and ivory.

Mouth he remembered: the quaint orifice
From which came heat that flamed upon the kiss,

Till cold words came down spiral from the head,
Gray doves from the officious tower illsped.

Body: it was a white field ready for love.
On her body's field, with the gaunt tower above,
The lilies grew, beseeching him to take,
If he would pluck and wear them, bruise and break.

Eyes talking: Never mind the cruel words,
Embrace my flowers, but not embrace the swords.
But what they said, the doves came straightway flying
And unsaid: Honor, Honor, they came crying.

Importunate her doves. Too pure, too wise,
Clambering on his shoulder, saying, Arise,
Leave me now, and never let us meet,
Eternal distance now command thy feet.

Predicament indeed, which thus discovers
Honor among thieves, Honor between lovers.
O such a little word is Honor, they feel!
But the gray word is between them cold as steel.

At length I saw these lovers fully were come
Into their torture of equilibrium;
Dreadfully had forsworn each other, and yet
They were bound each to each, and they did not forget

And rigid as two painful stars, and twirled
About the clustered night their prison world,
They burned with fierce love always to come near,
But Honor beat them back and kept them clear.

Ah, the strict lovers, they are ruined now!
I cried in anger. But with puddled brow
Devising for those gibbeted and brave
Came I descanting: Man, what would you have?

For spin your period out, and draw your breath,
A kinder saeculum begins with Death.
Would you ascend to Heaven and bodiless dwell?
Or take your bodies honorless to Hell?

In Heaven you have heard no marriage is,
No white flesh tinder to your lecheries,
Your male and female tissue sweetly shaped
Sublimed away, and furious blood escaped.

Great lovers lie in Hell, the stubborn ones
Infatuate of the flesh upon the bones;
Stuprate, they rend each other when they kiss,
The pieces kiss again, no end to this.

But still I watched them spinning, orbited nice.
Their flames were not more radiant than their ice.
I dug in the quiet earth and wrought the tomb
And made these lines to memorize their doom:—

Epitaph

Equilibrists lie here; stranger, tread light;
Close, but untouching in each other's sight;
Mouldered the lips and ashy the tall skull,
Let them lie perilous and beautiful.

HERE LIES A LADY

Here lies a lady of beauty and high degree.
Of chills and fever she died, of fever and chills,
The delight of her husband, her aunts, an infant of three,
And of medicos marveling sweetly on her ills.

For either she burned, and her confident eyes would blaze,
And her fingers fly in a manner to puzzle their heads—
What was she making? Why, nothing; she sat in a maze
Of old scraps of laces, snipped into curious shreds—

Or this would pass, and the light of her fire decline
Till she lay discouraged and cold as a thin stalk white and blown,
And would not open her eyes, to kisses, to wine;
The sixth of these states was her last; the cold settled down.

Sweet ladies, long may ye bloom, and toughly I hope ye may thole,
But was she not lucky? In flowers and lace and mourning,
In love and great honor we bade God rest her soul
After six little spaces of chill, and six of burning.

ALLEN TATE

ODE TO THE CONFEDERATE DEAD

Row after row with strict impunity
The headstones yield their names to the element,
The wind whirrs without recollection;
In the riven troughs the splayed leaves
Pile up, of nature the casual sacrament
To the seasonal eternity of death;
Then driven by the fierce scrutiny
Of heaven to their election in the vast breath,
They sought the rumor of mortality.

Autumn is desolation in the plot
Of a thousand acres where these memories grow
From the inexhaustible bodies that are not
Dead, but feed the grass row after rich row.
Think of the autumns that have come and gone!—
Ambitious November with the humors of the year,
With a particular zeal for every slab,
Staining the uncomfortable angels that rot
On the slabs, a wing chipped here, an arm there:
The brute curiosity of an angel's stare
Turns you, like them, to stone,
Transforms the heaving air
Till plunged to a heavier world below
You shift your sea-space blindly
Heaving, turning like the blind crab.

   Dazed by the wind, only the wind
   The leaves flying, plunge

You know who have waited by the wall
The twilight certainty of an animal,
Those midnight restitutions of the blood
You know—the immitigable pines, the smoky frieze
Of the sky, the sudden call: you know the rage,
The cold pool left by the mounting flood,
Of muted Zeno and Parmenides.
You who have waited for the angry resolution
Of those desires that should be yours tomorrow,

You know the unimportant shrift of death
And praise the vision
And praise the arrogant circumstance
Of those who fall
Rank upon rank, hurried beyond decision—
Here by the sagging gate, stopped by the wall.

Seeing, seeing only the leaves
Flying, plunge and expire

Turn your eyes to the immoderate past,
Turn to the inscrutable infantry rising
Demons out of the earth—they will not last.
Stonewall, Stonewall, and the sunken fields of hemp,
Shiloh, Antietam, Malvern Hill, Bull Run.
Lost in that orient of the thick and fast
You will curse the setting sun.

Cursing only the leaves crying
Like an old man in a storm

You hear the shout, the crazy hemlocks point
With troubled fingers to the silence which
Smothers you, a mummy, in time.
                              The hound bitch
Toothless and dying, in a musty cellar
Hears the wind only.

                    Now that the salt of their blood
Stiffens the saltier oblivion of the sea,
Seals the malignant purity of the flood,
What shall we who count our days and bow
Our heads with a commemorial woe
In the ribboned coats of grim felicity,
What shall we say of the bones, unclean,
Whose verdurous anonymity will grow?
The ragged arms, the ragged heads and eyes
Lost in these acres of the insane green?
The gray lean spiders come, they come and go;
In a tangle of willows without light
The singular screech-owl's tight
Invisible lyric seeds the mind
With the furious murmur of their chivalry.

We shall say only the leaves
Flying, plunge and expire

We shall say only the leaves whispering
In the improbable mist of nightfall
That flies on multiple wing:
Night is the beginning and the end
And in between the ends of distraction
Waits mute speculation, the patient curse
That stones the eyes, or like the jaguar leaps
For his own image in a jungle pool, his victim.

What shall we say who have knowledge
Carried to the heart? Shall we take the act
To the grave? Shall we, more hopeful, set up the grave
In the house? The ravenous grave?

                                              Leave now
The shut gate and the decomposing wall:
The gentle serpent, green in the mulberry bush,
Riots with his tongue through the hush—
Sentinel of the grave who counts us all!

ROBERT PENN WARREN

THE SNAKE

Daylong, light, gold, leans on the land.
You stoke the tractor. You *gee* and *haw*.
You feed the thresher's gap-toothed maw.
Then on a load-top, high, you stand
And see your shadow, black as law,

Stretch far now on the gold stubble.
By now breath's short. Sweat stings the eyes.
Blue denim is sweat-black at the thighs.
If you make a joke, you waste your trouble.
In that silence the shout rings with surprise.

ROBERT PENN WARREN (1905-   ) was born in Kentucky and educated at Vanderbilt University and the University of California. His novel of Louisiana politics, *All the King's Men*, won the Pulitzer Prize in 1947. He teaches at Yale University.

When you wreck a shock, the spot below
Is damp and green with a vernal gloom.
Field mouse or rabbit flees its doom,
And you scarcely notice how they go.
But a black snake rears big in his ruined room.

Defiant, tall in that blast of day,
Now eye for eye, he swaps his stare.
His outrage glitters on the air.
Men shout, ring around. He can't get away.
Yes, they are men, and a stone is there.

Against the wounded evening matched,
Snagged high on a pitchfork tine, he will make
Slow arabesque till the bullbats wake.
An old man, standing stooped, detached,
Spits once, says, "Hell, just another snake."

ROBERT LOWELL

FOR THE UNION DEAD

Relinquunt omnia servare rem publicam.

The old South Boston Aquarium stands
in a Sahara of snow now. Its broken windows are boarded.
The bronze weathervane cod has lost its scales.
The airy tanks are dry.

Once my nose crawled like a snail on the glass;
my hand tingled
to burst the bubbles,
drifting from the noses of the cowed, compliant fish.

My hand draws back. I often sigh still
for the dark downward and vegetating kingdom
of the fish and reptile. One morning last March;
I pressed against the new barbed and galvanized

ROBERT LOWELL (1917-   ), the great-grandnephew of James Russell Lowell and a distant cousin of Amy Lowell, was born in Boston and went to Harvard University and Kenyon College. He was a winner of the Pulitzer Prize for poetry in 1947.

fence on the Boston Common. Behind their cage;
yellow dinosaur steam shovels were grunting
as they cropped up tons of mush and grass
to gouge their underworld garage.

Parking lots luxuriate like civic
sand piles in the heart of Boston.
A girdle of orange, Puritan-pumpkin-colored girders
braces the tingling Statehouse, shaking

over the excavations, as it faces Colonel Shaw
and his bell-cheeked Negro infantry
on St. Gaudens' shaking Civil War relief,
propped by a plank splint against the garage's earthquake.

Two months after marching through Boston,
half the regiment was dead;
at the dedication,
William James could almost hear the bronze Negroes breathe.

The monument sticks like a fishbone
in the city's throat.
Its colonel is as lean
as a compass needle.

He has an angry wrenlike vigilance,
a greyhound's gentle tautness;
he seems to wince at pleasure
and suffocate for privacy.

He is out of bounds. He rejoices in man's lovely,
peculiar power to choose life and die—
when he leads his black soldiers to death,
he cannot bend his back.

On a thousand small-town New England greens,
the old white churches hold their air
of sparse, sincere rebellion; frayed flags
quilt the graveyards of the Grand Army of the Republic.

The stone statues of the abstract Union Soldier
grow slimmer and younger each year—
wasp-waisted, they doze over muskets,
and muse through their sideburns.

Shaw's father wanted no monument
except the ditch,
where his son's body was thrown
and lost with his "niggers."

The ditch is nearer.
There are no statues for the last war here;
on Boylston Street, a commercial photograph
showed Hiroshima boiling

over a Mosler Safe, "the Rock of Ages,"
that survived the blast. Space is nearer.
When I crouch to my television set,
the drained faces of Negro school children rise like balloons.

Colonel Shaw
is riding on his bubble,
he waits
for the blessed break.

The Aquarium is gone. Everywhere,
giant finned cars nose forward like fish;
a savage servility
slides by on grease.

GLOSSARY

Here are listed critical and technical terms pertinent to the study of poetry. Page numbers refer to discussions within the text.

A

ACCENT, the stress given to a syllable in English verse. A regular pattern of accented and unaccented syllables establishes meter. Some modern prosodists distinguish degrees of stress and use such terms as primary, secondary, and even tertiary accent. (7-8)

ALEXANDRINE, strictly speaking, a line of twelve syllables (six iambic feet), although in English usage, through substitution of either anapests (q.v.) or dactyls (q.v.), it may have more than twelve syllables. The final line of a Spenserian stanza (q.v.) is always an Alexandrine. (126)

ALLEGORY, a form of narrative in which abstractions are given concrete representation. Allegory differs from symbolism (q.v.), which need not have a narrative continuity. (398-399)

ALLITERATION, the repetition of initial consonant sounds within a line of poetry, as in Hopkins' "The Windhover," p. 429. (19-20)

ALLITERATIVE VERSE, poetry based upon alliteration rather than accent, such as the poetry of the Anglo-Saxon period and that of the fourteenth century now referred to as the "alliterative revival." (24)

AMBIGUITY, multiplicity of meaning in a word or group of words. Although unconscious ambiguity is damaging to clarity and precision, ambiguity may be used deliberately by a poet to achieve richness and allusiveness. (422)

ANAPEST, a three-syllable foot in which two unstressed syllables are followed by a stressed one. (7)

ANAPHORA, a rhetorical figure in which two or more consecutive lines of a poem begin with the same word or words. (19)

ANTITHESIS, a figure of speech in which one segment of a sentence is set against another to which it is strongly opposed in idea. (204-206)

APOSTROPHE, direct address to a person, place, or thing usually absent.

ARCHAISM, the deliberate use of language no longer in current usage. (12)

ARCHETYPE, literally, the original pattern or image from which other images or impressions are derived. In poetry it may refer to a conventional, widely recognized symbol for some fundamental concept. (14)

ASSONANCE, partial rhyme in which only the vowel sounds correspond, as in Wilfred Owen's "Arms and the Boy," pp. 448-449. (10)

B

BALLAD, a kind of poetry, usually short, narrative, and dramatic, which employs various stanzaic forms (*see* Ballad Stanza), sharp and colorful imagery, repetition, refrain, and ellipsis (105-117). The *folk ballad* (234) is anonymous, composed to be sung, and has its origins in oral tradition. When it is written down, a choice must usually be made from among many different oral versions. The *literary ballad* (234) is an imitation of the folk ballad, usually by a poet whose identity is known.

BALLAD STANZA, consists traditionally (although there are variations) of four lines, the first and third being iambic tetrameter and the second and fourth iambic trimeter, rhyming *abcb*, as in "The Wife of Usher's Well," pp. 116-117. (105)

BLANK VERSE, unrhymed iambic pentameter not confined to stanzaic forms but developed through verse paragraphs (q.v.). (10)

BURDEN. *See* Refrain.

C

CACOPHONY, discordant sound, harshness, and roughness, deliberately used for certain poetic effects.

CADENCE, the rhythmic flow of verse, involving both meter and rhythm.

CAESURA, a break in the rhythmical flow of a line of verse, coming usually from a sense pause, although also created by means of punctuation. Usually the caesura occurs near the middle of a line. (9)

CANTO, a main division or section used in long poems, as in Dante's *Divine Comedy*, Spenser's *Faerie Queene*, or Byron's *Don Juan*.

CANZONE, a complex metrical form of Provençal origin, widely used in Italian poetry and imitated by Swinburne and other English writers. (327)

CARPE DIEM, a Latin phrase meaning literally "seize the day" and thus "enjoy the present." The expression gives name to a widespread literary convention prevalent in English poetry from the fourteenth century to the present. (125)

CHANSONS COURTOIS. *See* Courtly Love Poetry.

CLOSED COUPLET. *See* Couplet.

CONCEIT, an extended metaphor or comparison. In the hands of the Metaphysical poets it was frequently elaborated to an extreme degree, as in Donne's "A Valediction of Weeping," p. 167. (151)

CONNOTATION, as distinguished from denotation (q.v.), refers to the verbal meanings which are secondary, implied, or understood through association— all that which is suggested rather than specifically denoted. (11)

CONSONANCE, partial rhyme in which only the consonants correspond. (9-10)

COUPLET, any two successive lines of verse which rhyme (10). *Closed couplet* (123), two rhyming lines of regular verse that are logically and grammatically complete; *Heroic couplet* (123), two consecutive rhyming lines in iambic pentameter, closed and with a minor pause at the end of the first line.

COURTLY LOVE POETRY, medieval poetry following the conventions of an elaborate code in which the beloved lady is looked upon as a creature who is unattainable yet worthy of extremes of devotion and sacrifice, to be heaped with praise and defended as the nonpareil of all beauty. (26)

D

DACTYL, a three-syllable foot in which one stressed syllable is followed by two unstressed syllables. (7)

DECASYLLABIC, a perfect line of exactly ten syllables permitting no extra-metrical substitutions, found more frequently in French than in English poetry. (126)

DENOTATION, as opposed to connotation (q.v.), is the exact literal meaning of a word, independent of its associations or implications. (11)

DENSITY, richness of language, employing multiple facets of meaning, often including ambiguity (q.v.). (297)

DICTION. *See* Poetic Diction.

DIDACTIC POETRY, verse which aims primarily to teach. Poetry limited to this aim generally does not attain the imaginative and lyrical reaches of other poetic forms. It is possible, however, to find some elements of didacticism in most of the world's poetry. (193-209)

DIMETER, a line of verse consisting of two feet. (8)

DOUBLE ENTENDRE, a term borrowed from the French, meaning literally "double meaning." It may apply to a single word, a phrase, or a situation. (122)

DOUBLE RHYME, a rhyme in which the stressed syllables of the rhyming words are followed by identical unstressed syllables, as in *fleeing* and *seeing*.

DRAMATIC MONOLOGUE, a poem in which everything is conveyed through the words of a single speaker, who reveals background circumstances and conflicts and provides insight into his own character, as well as that of others, through his conversation with a silent listener. (331-347)

DRAMATIC TONE. *See* Tone.

E

ECLOGUE, literally, a short poem, although the term has come to be applied exclusively to pastoral poetry (q.v.).

ELEGIAC, a technical term from classical prosody. Elegiac verse consists of two lines, the first a dactyllic hexameter, the second some variation of pentameter. (173) *See* Elegy.

ELEGY, originally any poem written in elegiac verses dealing with a solemn, but not necessarily mournful, subject. The term has come to be applied, however, solely to mournful, melancholy, or plaintive poems, especially dirges or funeral laments for the dead. (173-185)

ELLIPSIS, deliberate omission of elements in a sentence or of connectives between stanzas or within a stanza, very common in the folk ballad.

END-STOPPED LINE, a line of verse which comes to logical and grammatical completion. (234) *See* Enjambment.

ENGLISH SONNET. *See* Sonnet.

ENJAMBMENT, the device of carrying the sense and grammatical construction from one line of verse to the next without a break. (123) *See* End-stopped Line.

ENVELOPING STRUCTURE, the use of similar structural components to open and close any segment of poetry—a line, stanza, verse paragraph, or entire poem—as in Greene's "The Shepherd's Wife's Song," pp. 84-85. (401)

ENVOI, a poetic postscript.

EPIGRAM, a short, succinct, witty saying. The poetic epigram, written in verse form, is often satirical. (125)

EPITAPH, a brief verse, suitable for inscription on a tombstone or monument, such as William Browne of Tavistock's "On the Countess Dowager of Pembroke," p. 192. Frequently an epitaph forms the envoi (q.v.) of a funeral elegy, as in Gray's "Elegy Written in a Country Churchyard," p. 253. In Renaissance and later practice, epitaphs were often pinned upon hearses.

EXAGGERATION. See Hyperbole.

F

FEMININE RHYME, a rhyme in which the accented syllables are followed by unaccented syllables. (10)

FOLK BALLAD. See Ballad.

FOLK MOTIF, a theme or narrative situation constantly recurring in folklore. (113)

FOOT, the basic metrical unit; in English verse it is composed of two or three syllables in one of several basic variations of stressed and unstressed sounds. (7) See Iamb, Trochee, Anapest, Dactyl, Spondee, Pyrrhus.

FORM, a general term, loosely analogous to structure, used to designate the pattern or organization of the elements of a poem. In different contexts it refers to meter, stanza, paragraph, or total poem (7-11). Organic form (11) is poetic form which grows out of its subject matter or other internal considerations. The poet who surrenders his work to organic form almost always rejects the sonnet, couplet, quatrain, or other traditional stanzaic groupings.

FORMAL VERSE SATIRE. See Satire.

FOURTEENER, a single line of seven iambic feet, the name coming from the total of fourteen syllables. (105)

FREE VERSE, poetry characterized by irregular line length and metrical pattern, being governed by rhythmical units larger than the poetic foot. It should not be confused with blank verse (q.v.), which has uniform meter and consistent line length and is unrhymed. Free verse may use rhyme or other poetic devices. (422-423)

FUGITIVES, a group of writers of the 1920's associated with John Crowe Ransom at Vanderbilt University, also known as *Southern Agrarians* or the *Nashville Group*. (469-470)

H

HALF-RHYME, imperfect rhyme involving disparate vowel sounds. (10)

HEPTAMETER, a line of verse consisting of seven feet.

HEROIC COUPLET. See Couplet.

HEXAMETER, a line of verse consisting of six feet. (8)

HYPERBOLE, or EXAGGERATION, the heightening of claims or effect through overstatement. (18)

I

IAMB, or IAMBUS, a two-syllable foot in which one unstressed syllable is followed by a stressed one, the most common poetic foot in English. (7)

IDENTICAL RHYME, rhyme in which the entire rhyme word or rhyme syllable is identical with its mate, as *time* and *time* or *define* and *refine*. (10)

IMAGERY, the use of language to arouse sensory responses or to represent sensory experiences. Usually, but not necessarily, it is the visual sense to which the appeal of imagery is directed. Imagery is an ingredient of all metaphorical language. (13-14)

INCREMENTAL REFRAIN. *See* Refrain.

INCREMENTAL REPETITION. *See* Repetition.

INTERLOCKING RHYME, a device used to bind one stanza to another by carrying over the rhyme of the first stanza into the second. (10-11) *See* Terza Rima.

INTERNAL RHYME, rhyme which appears within a line, not at the end. (10)

IRONY involves a statement, image, symbol, or metaphor which seems on the surface to say the opposite of its real meaning. Irony may also be achieved by a literal statement that is ambiguous but directly contradicts the known attitude of the writer; such a statement is to be understood as a satirical pose. (16-17)

ITALIAN SONNET. *See* Sonnet.

L

LITERAL STATEMENT, the denotation of all the words involved in a poem, the story of a narrative poem. The term is used in contradistinction to the allegorical or symbolic meaning which may lie beneath the literal.

LITERARY BALLAD. *See* Ballad.

LYRIC, originally a poem to be sung. The term *lyric* now refers to any poem expressive of personal thought and feeling. Lyrics are usually short poems, although the term may be used adjectivally and applied to passages in longer works that are not basically lyrical.

M

MASCULINE RHYME, the most common of all types of rhyme, obtained when the final syllables of a word or line correspond. (10)

MASQUE, an elaborate court entertainment, highly developed in the seventeenth century. (120)

MEDIEVALISM, the cultivation of interest in the Middle Ages.

METAPHOR, a figure of speech in which one image, capable of comparison with another, is substituted directly or by implication for that other image. (15-16)

METAPHYSICAL POETRY, a historical term, suggested first by Dryden and then used with a complete definition and illustrations by Samuel Johnson. It refers to a school of poets and poetry in which comparisons, contrasts, resemblances, and dissimilarities were pushed to the extremities of imagination. The poetry is highly intellectual and philosophical, crowded with baroque imagery, and dependent frequently on turns of wit or ingenuity. (151-172)

METER, the regularly recurring pattern of stressed and unstressed syllables in a line of verse. (7-9)

METONYMY, a figure of speech in which one object is referred to by the name of a closely related object. (16)

MOCK-HEROIC POEM, one in which a trivial subject is treated with the grandeur of an epic poem for purposes of ridicule; Pope's *Rape of the Lock* is probably the best example in English. (190)

MODE, a term used in poetry to signify basic poetic types, such as the pastoral, lyric, epic, and dramatic modes.

MONOMETER, a line of verse consisting of one foot.

MYTHOLOGY, traditional or legendary stories. In poetry, myth is created frequently out of materials that do not come from the past. William Blake and Hart Crane, for instance, developed modern myths, Blake's outside of time and space, and Crane's conforming to twentieth-century mechanistic experience. The creation of new myths by poets is called mythopoesis. (423-424)

N

NARRATIVE POETRY, poetry which tells a story. (371)

NASHVILLE GROUP. *See* Fugitives.

NEOCLASSICISM, a return, chiefly by writers of the seventeenth and eighteenth centuries, to the critical principles of classical Rome, with emphasis upon clarity, simplicity, formality, and restraint. The most important verse form used in English Neoclassicism was the heroic couplet. (188-189)

NEOPLATONISM, revival of the philosophy of Plato, widely current in the Renaissance and adopted by some Romantic poets. (260)

NEW CRITICISM, a term applied very imprecisely to a large group of contemporary American critics interested in close textual analysis. (21)

NOBLE SAVAGE. *See* Primitivism.

O

OCTAVE, an eight-line stanza. Usually the term refers to the first division of the Italian sonnet, with the rhyme scheme *abbaabba*. *See* Sonnet.

ODE, a lyric poem of high seriousness and elaborate form. Three main types are recognized in English verse: the Pindaric (q.v.), which imitates the complex form of the Greek poet Pindar; the Horatian, the most regular of the three types; and the Cowleyan, thought by Abraham Cowley to be an irregular form of the Pindaric but not Pindaric at all. (210)

ONOMATOPOEIA, poetic language which imitates the sound of what is described. Sometimes such words are coined, as Poe's *tintinabulation;* sometimes they are words already in existence, such as *roar, sough, whisper,* etc. (20)

OTTAVA RIMA, an eight-line iambic pentameter stanza, rhyming *ababacc.*

OVERSTATEMENT. *See* Hyperbole.

P

PANTHEISM, a belief in the presence of God in all created things. (235)

PARADOX, a statement which seems self-contradictory but which can be demonstrated to hold truth. (122)

PARAPHRASE, the use of other words to express the meanings of a text or passage of verse. (21)

PASTORAL POETRY, poetry dealing with simple country life, usually involving shepherds and their pastimes but also including other aspects of rustic life. The pastoral tradition embraces both true rural life and a sophisticated, artificial interpretation of it. (79-91)

PENTAMETER, one line of verse containing five feet. (8)

PERFECTIBILITY, a belief in the possibility of continuous improvement in the nature of mankind, common in the late eighteenth and the nineteenth centuries. (232)

PERSONIFICATION, the representation of an abstract idea or inanimate object as though it were a person.

PETRARCHAN SONNET. *See* Sonnet.

PETRARCHISM, an elaborate set of conventions employed in Renaissance love poetry; these include a wide variety of attitudes, comparisons, praises, and hyperboles to illustrate the courtly and chivalric admiration of a man for a woman. The lady is seen always as an unparalleled beauty who disdains her lover; he is consistently pictured as a worshiping servant, doomed to the anguish of a hopeless love. (44)

PINDARIC ODE, an English imitation of the odes of the Greek poet Pindar, consisting of repeated three-stanza groupings. Each grouping contains a strophe and antistrophe, identical in form, and an epode, differing from the other two. (125)

POETIC DICTION, the way in which language is used in poetry, involving word choice and syntax. Tastes in poetic diction have varied in different periods. (11-12)

POETIC SYNTAX, the order and pattern of words used in poetry. Like poetic diction (q.v.), syntax in poetry has varied in different literary periods. (11-12)

POULTER'S MEASURE, a verse form named and defined in 1575 by George Gascoigne, who called it "the commonest sort of verse which we use nowadays." It consists of alternating six- and seven-foot lines. (105)

PRIMITIVISM, a belief in the inherent nobility of uncivilized man, tending to glorify the "noble savage." (237)

PROSODY, theory and principles of metrical practice and versification. (7)

PYRRHUS, a two-syllable foot in which both syllables are unstressed. (7)

Q

QUALITATIVE METER, the system of metrics, such as the English, which designates major and minor syllables according to their stress or accent. (126)

QUANTITATIVE METER, the system of metrics, such as the Greek and Latin, which designates major and minor syllables according to their length or quantity. In the English Renaissance some attempts were made, chiefly by Thomas Campion, to write quantitative verse in English, but they were rarely successful. (125)

QUATRAIN, any four-line stanza. (10)

R

REFRAIN, or BURDEN, one or more regularly repeated lines or parts of lines at the end of a stanza or group of stanzas (20-21). *Incremental refrain* (35), the addition of an element to the refrain each time it is repeated.

REPETITION, the re-use in a single poem of identical words, phrases, lines, or even stanzas, usually at regularly spaced intervals (20-21). *Incremental repetition* (21), repetition which advances action, statement, or narrative through slight alteration in successive appearances.

RHETORIC, technically, the science or art of all literary use of language, including figures of speech. When used in reference to poetry, rhetoric denotes the elaborate and ornate syntax, repetition, and metaphoric resources of language. (12-16)

RHYME, agreement of final sounds in two or more words. Such words terminate the lines in rhyming verse. The many kinds include feminine, half, internal, masculine, sight, and slant rhyme, all of which are treated separately. (9)

RHYME ROYAL, a stanzaic form named for the Scottish king James I, although Chaucer had used it earlier. It is a seven-line iambic pentameter stanza, rhyming *ababbcc*. (42)

RHYTHM, the cadence created chiefly by the pattern of stress and fall but affected also by syntax, breath pauses, punctuation, pitch, emotion, pace, and other elements. The term is usually reserved for units of language larger than the poetic foot. (8-9)

RUN-ON LINE. *See* Enjambment.

S

SATIRE, a work which exposes vice or folly to scorn and laughter. Although a weapon of attack, satire often seeks to reform rather than to destroy. (122-123)

SCANSION, the metrical analysis of verse. (7)

SESTET, any six-line stanza. Most frequently the term refers to the last six lines of the Italian sonnet. *See* Sonnet.

SESTINA, a poem of six stanzas, each stanza consisting of six lines, with an additional three-line envoi (q.v.). Only two rhymes are used throughout the poem; although never recurring in the same order, the same words are rhymed in each stanza. (327)

SHAKESPEARIAN SONNET. *See* Sonnet.

SIGHT RHYME, a correspondence between syllables or words based upon appearance rather than sound, i.e., *slough, rough.*

SIMILE, a directly stated comparison, using such words as *as, like,* or *than.* (15)

SLANT RHYME, a correspondence in sound, not close enough to be true rhyme, such as *lane/ lean, face/ nice.* (9)

SONNET, a fourteen-line iambic pentameter poem, employing various rhyme schemes (47-49). The *Italian* or *Petrarchan* sonnet (47-48) is divided into two major thought divisions of eight (octave) and six (sestet) lines respectively, the octave rhyming always *abbaabba* and the sestet employing any rhyme combination which does not conclude with a rhymed couplet, although in English usage this rule is sometimes violated. The *English* or *Shakespearian* sonnet (47-48) is divided into three quatrains and one couplet, rhyming *abab cdcd efef gg.* The *Spenserian* sonnet (49), one of many variations of the sonnet form, uses interlocking rhyme: *abab bcbc cdcd ee.*

SOUND, a general term used to describe all tonal devices of language. Most uses of rhetoric involve sound, as well as the resources of melody, harmony, and meter. (19-21)

SOUTHERN AGRARIANS. *See* Fugitives.

SPENSERIAN SONNET. *See* Sonnet.

SPENSERIAN STANZA, a nine-line stanza created by Edmund Spenser for use in the *Faerie Queene* and often imitated, notably by Keats in "The Eve of St. Agnes," pp. 326-336. It consists of eight lines of iambic pentameter, followed by an Alexandrine (q.v.), rhyming *ababbcbcc.* (49)

SPONDEE, a two-syllable foot in which both syllables are stressed. (7)

SPREZZATURA, an attitude of careless disdain for one's own work, cultivated by Renaissance poets. (43)

SPRUNG RHYTHM, a type of extra-syllabic meter developed by Gerard Manley Hopkins. (407-408)

STANZA, any formal arrangement of lines into regular patterns which are repeated within a poem. (10)

STRESS. *See* Accent.

STRUCTURE. *See* Form.

STYLE, the distinctive character or mode of writing, frequently dependent upon the literary age, the literary form or genre, and the personality of the writer. (12)

SYMBOLISM, the use of symbols or signs, words or images which stand for something other than what they specifically denote. Symbols may be either conventional or private. Conventional symbols, which embody universal suggestions of meaning, can usually be understood by the reader with little difficulty. Private symbols, which are not universally recognized and suggest meaning only from the context in which they are used, often cannot be fully comprehended without some interpretative assistance from the poet. Symbols may be complex or simple, suggesting multiple meanings or a single association (14-16). *French Symbolism* (422), a nineteenth-century poetic movement which had wide influence upon the course of English poetry.

SYNECDOCHE, a figure of speech in which a part of something is used to signify the whole; the term refers also to the use of a special instance to signify the general principle. (16)

T

TENSION, a precise and difficult term, coined for the critical vocabulary by Allen Tate, who defines it as "derived from lopping the prefixes off the logical terms *extension* and *intension*. . . . The meaning of poetry is its *tension,* the full organized body of all the extension and intension we can find in it. The remotest figurative significance that we can derive does not invalidate the extensions of the literal statement." (100)

TERCET, a three-line stanza. (10)

TERMINAL RHYME, rhyme occurring at the end of a stanza. (35)

TERZA RIMA, an Italian verse form most notably used by Dante in the *Divine Comedy.* It consists of interlocking tercets in iambic pentameter, rhyming *aba bcb cdc ded,* etc., and concluding *yzyz.* Shelley used this form in "Ode to the West Wind," pp. 299-301. (11)

TETRAMETER, one line of verse consisting of four feet. (8)

TONE, a reflection of the poet's attitude toward his subject. Tone may be conveyed through many devices, including formalism, colloquialism, precision, looseness, seriousness, sarcasm, richness, and simplicity (16-19). *Dramatic tone* (18-19) is achieved through the use of such tools of the drama as dialogue, concrete presentation, swift action, setting, and character.

TRIMETER, one line of verse consisting of three feet. (8)

TRIPLE RHYME, rhyme in which the stressed syllables of the rhyming words are followed by two identical unstressed syllables, as in *splattering/ smattering.* The term is also used to refer to three successive lines of verse which all end with the same sound. (10)

TROCHEE, a two-syllable foot in which the first is stressed and the second unstressed. (7)

TROUBADOURS, minstrels of southern France who developed lyric poetry. (26)

U

UNDERSTATEMENT, a device by which the poet leaves much unsaid, the opposite of overstatement or hyperbole (q.v.). Its effectiveness often depends upon the reader's realization that the emotion implied is too great for complete expression. (17)

V

VERISIMILITUDE, the appearance of truth. (204)

VERSE, either poetry in general or one line of a poem.

VERSE PARAGRAPH, a formal arrangement of lines of poetry based on thought groupings rather than upon arbitrary stanzaic division. The term is used primarily with blank verse (q.v.) and free verse (q.v.) but may apply to forms of narrative poetry such as Dante's terza rima (q.v.) or Chaucer's narrative couplets. (337)

VOCABULARY OF POETRY. *See* Poetic Diction.

W

WIT has had different meanings during different periods in literary history. To the Metaphysical poets it meant the ability to perceive startling relationships; in the eighteenth century Pope defined wit as "What oft was thought, but ne'er so well expressed." In modern usage wit refers to cleverness, frequently in sarcastic, ironic, sardonic, or comic terms.

GENERAL INDEX

The titles of poems included in this anthology and key page references are printed in **boldface** type. First lines are indexed except when they duplicate titles.